Tyrrhenian
Sea

Aeolian Islands
Lipari

Northeastern Sicily
Pages 162–195

Milazzo
Messina

Capo
d'Orlando

Cefalù

Randazzo
Taormina

NORTHEASTERN
SICILY

Nicosia

Paternò
Acireale

Enna
Caltanissetta
Catania

N

Canicattì

Plazza
Armerina

Lentini
Augusta

Caltagirone

SOUTHERN
SICILY
Syracuse

cata
Gela

Ragusa
Vittoria
Noto
Modica

Mediterranean
Sea

| 0 kilometres | 25 |
| 0 miles | 25 |

SICILY

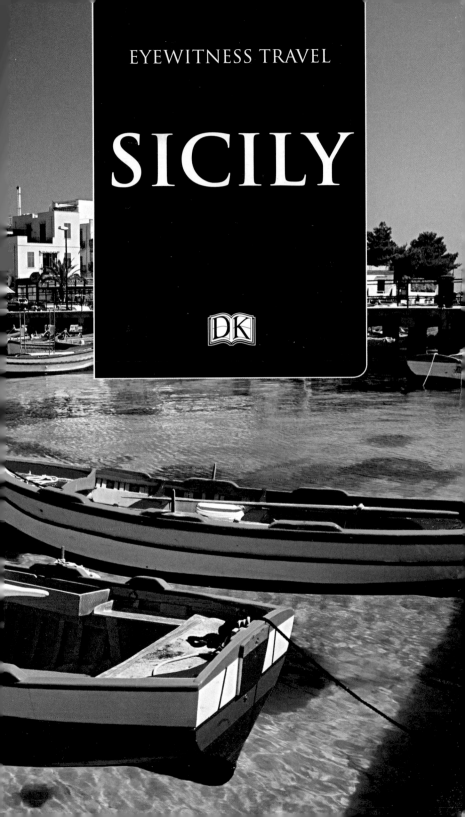

EYEWITNESS TRAVEL

SICILY

LONDON, NEW YORK,
MELBOURNE, MUNICH AND DELHI
www.dk.com

Produced by Fabio Ratti Editoria Libraria E Multimediale, Milan, Italy

Project Editor Giovanni Francesio
Editor Elena Marzorati
Secretary Emanuela Damiani
Designers Studio Matra–Silvia Tomasone, Lucia Tirabassi
Maps Oriana Bianchetti

Dorling Kindersley Ltd
Project Editor Fiona Wild
DTP Designers Maite Lantaron, Lee Redmond
Production Marie Ingledew, David Proffit
Managing Editors Fay Franklin, Louise Bostock Lang
Managing Art Editor Annette Jacobs
Editorial Director Vivien Crump
Art Director Gillian Allan
Publisher Douglas Amrine

Contributors Fabrizio Ardito, Cristina Gambaro
Additional tourist information by Marco Scapagnini

Illustrators Giorgia Boli, Silvana Ghioni, Alberto Ipsilanti, Nadia Viganò

English Translation Richard Pierce

Printed In Malaysia

First American Edition, 2000
15 16 17 18 10 9 8 7 6 5 4 3 2 1

Published in the United States by DK Publishing,
375 Hudson Street, New York, New York 10014

Reprinted with revisions 2003, 2005, 2007, 2009, 2011, 2013, 2015

Copyright © 2000, 2015 Dorling Kindersley Limited, London
A Penguin Random House Company

Published in Great Britain by Dorling Kindersley Ltd.

A catalog record for this book is available from the Library of Congress.

ISSN 1542-1554
ISBN 978-1-46542-664-2

Floors are referred to throughout in accordance with
European usage; ie the "first floor" is the floor above ground level.

MIX
Paper from
responsible sources
FSC™ C018179

Front cover main image: The medieval estate of Tonnara di Scopello, Castellammare del Golfo

◀ Colorful boats in the harbor at Mondello, on the outskirts of Palermo

Contents

**How to Use
this Guide 6**

Female head sculpted in the
5th century BC (see pp34–5)

Introducing Sicily

Palermo
Area by Area

Backcloth, Museo Internazionale delle
Marionette in Palermo (see pp54–5)

Castellammare del Golfo *(see p100)*, one of many fishing towns and villages on the Sicilian coast

Ancient theatre mask,
Museo Archeologico Eoliano *(see p194)*

Travellers' Needs

A cheese vendor at Catania's
open-air market *(see pp218–19)*

Survival Guide

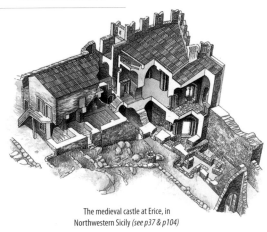

The medieval castle at Erice, in
Northwestern Sicily *(see p37 & p104)*

HOW TO USE THIS GUIDE

This guide will help you to get the most out of your visit to Sicily. It provides detailed practical information and expert recommendations. *Introducing Sicily* maps the island and sets Sicily in its historic, artistic, geographical and cultural context. *Palermo Area by Area* and the four regional sections describe the most important sights, with maps, floor plans, photographs and detailed illustrations. Restaurant and hotel recommendations are described in *Travellers' Needs* and the *Survival Guide* has tips on everything from transport to hiring a surfboard.

Palermo Area by Area

The historic centre of the city has been divided into two areas, East and West, each with its own chapter. *Further Afield* covers peripheral sights. All sights are numbered and plotted on the *Area Map*. The detailed information for each sight is easy to locate as it follows the numerical order on the map.

Sights at a Glance lists the chapter's sights by category: Churches and Cathedrals, Historic Buildings, Museums, Streets and Squares, Parks and Gardens.

All pages relating to Palermo have red thumb tabs.

A locator map shows where you are in relation to other areas of the city centre.

1 **Area map** For easy reference, all the major sights are numbered and located on this map.

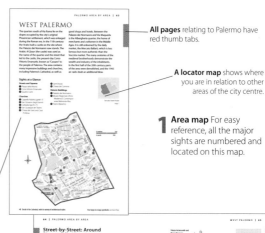

2 **Street-by-Street Map** This gives a bird's-eye view of the key areas in each chapter.

A suggested route for a walk is shown in red.

Stars indicate the sights that no visitor should miss.

3 **Detailed Information** The sights in Palermo are described individually. Addresses, telephone numbers, opening hours and admission charges are also provided. Map references refer to the *Street Finder* on pp82–3.

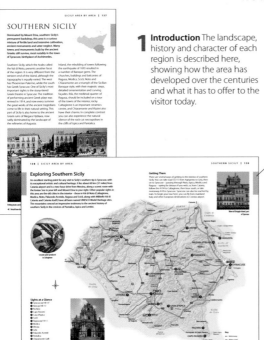

1 Introduction The landscape, history and character of each region is described here, showing how the area has developed over the centuries and what it has to offer to the visitor today.

Sicily Area by Area

Apart from Palermo, Sicily has been divided into four regions, each with a separate chapter. The most interesting towns, villages and sights to visit are numbered on a *Regional Map*.

Each area can be identified by its own colour coding.

2 Regional Map This shows the road network and gives an illustrated overview of the whole region. All the interesting places to visit are numbered and there are also useful tips on getting to, and around, the region by car and by public transport.

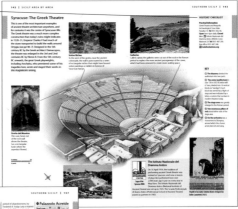

For all top sights, a Visitors' Checklist provides the practical information you will need to plan your visit.

3 Sicily's top sights These are given two or more full pages. Historic buildings are dissected to reveal their interiors. The most interesting towns or city centres are shown in a bird's-eye view, with sights picked out and described.

4 Places of Interest All the important towns and other places to visit are described individually. They are listed in order, following the numbering on the *Regional Map*. Within each town or city, there is detailed information on important buildings and other sights. The *Road Map* references refer to the inside back cover.

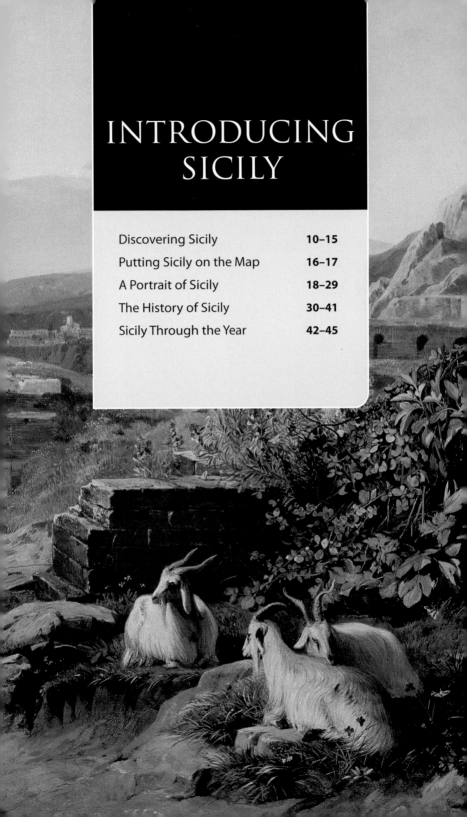

INTRODUCING SICILY

DISCOVERING SICILY

The itineraries on the pages that follow have been designed to help you make the most of this extraordinarily varied island. First come two-day tours of the region's most popular cities, Palermo and Syracuse, and a three-day trip around Sicily's most famous landmark, Mount Etna; each can be followed individually or linked together to form a longer tour. These are followed by seven-day tours of two of Sicily's most fascinating areas, both featured – for very different reasons – on UNESCO's World Heritage list. The first covers the Val di Noto,

where the flamboyant Baroque historic centres of towns like Noto, Ragusa and Modica testify to the brilliance of the architects who created them after a devastating eruption of Etna. This tour also takes in the splendid Roman mosaics of Piazza Armerina and the magnificently sited Greek temples of Agrigento. The second is a tour of a far more remote Sicily, the Aeolian Islands, with the focus on natural beauty. This details how to see the very best each of the seven islands how to offer on land, sea and – for those who like to snorkel – underwater.

The Duomo in Noto
Completely rebuilt after the earthquake of 1693, Noto comprises one of the most consistent groupings of magnificent Baroque architecture, crafted in mellow sandstone that seems to glow in the sun.

Key

— A Week in the Aeolian Islands
— A Week in Val di Noto and Agrigento
— Three Days around Mount Etna

Palermo

Torto

SICILY

Platani

Agrigento

Porto
Empedocle

Salso

Mediterranean
Sea

A Week in Val di Noto and Agrigento

- Marvel at the exuberant work of Baroque stonemasons in Noto.
- Indulge yourself in Sicily's ice-cream capital.
- Tread in the footsteps of the fictional Inspector Montalbano in pretty Scicli.
- Sample the chocolate of Modica – made to an ancient Aztec recipe.
- Shop for traditional ceramics, and see some of the finest mosaics of ancient Rome.
- Bask in the glory of the ancient Greeks at Agrigento's magnificent Valley of the Temples.

Mount Etna
A cable car ride over the lava slopes of Etna brings you thrillingly close to one of nature's most savage and primordial landscapes.

Lingua, Aeolian Islands

The site of the former salt mines that gave the island of Salina its name, Lingua is now a quiet little fishing port of pastel-coloured houses, a handful of restaurants and one famous granita bar.

A Week in the Aeolian Islands

- Wallow in a sulphurous warm mud bath on Vulcano.
- Eat the best granitas in Italy in the fishing hamlet of Lingua, on Salina.
- Watch the sun set from the village where nostalgic *Il Postino* was filmed.
- Laze away the day at Filucido's stylish Lido.
- Get away from it all with the 92 inhabitants of Alicudi, walking peaceful mule tracks and swimming from rocks.
- Climb Stromboli at sunset to witness the spectacle of Europe's most active volcano in action.

Tyrrhenian Sea

0 kilometres	25
0 miles	25

Three Days Around Mount Etna

- Explore the picturesque streets of Taormina, lined with perfect places for coffee and luscious pastries.
- Marvel at the bizarre basalt rock formations of the Alcantara ravine, and cool off with some wild swimming.
- Buy local produce to grill on barbecues at one of Etna's many picnic areas.
- Take winding drives around the mountain slopes, stopping at pretty hill towns.
- Taste the powerful wines from the vines that grow on Etna's lava-rich soil.
- Confront the mighty mountain itself with an unforgettable ascent.

Two Days in Palermo

An exuberant melting pot of East and West, once home to the wealthiest court in medieval Europe, Palermo's treasures include opulent Arab-Norman mosaics, Arabic cupolas, vibrant street markets and Sicily's finest collection of medieval and Renaissance art.

- **Arriving** From Punta Raisi airport, buses (Prestia e Comandè) run into the city centre every 30 minutes, taking 45 minutes, stopping outside Politeama theatre, Stazione Marittima and Stazione Centrale.

- **Getting around** Nerves of steel are required to drive in Palermo; fortunately, all the major attractions are within walking distance of each other. Delay renting a car until you're ready to move on from the capital; there are also excellent long-distance bus services to Sicily's other main towns and resorts.

Day One

Morning Begin with the formidable **Palazzo dei Normanni** *(p68)*, home under the Hohenstaufens to the most splendid court in medieval Europe, with the magnificent jewel-box-like **Cappella Palatina** *(pp66–7)* glinting with magnificent mosaics at its heart. Walk down to **San Giovanni degli Eremiti** *(p68)*, its five Arab domes witness to its past life as a mosque, then zigzag through the narrow streets of the Albergheria quarter to see the exotic majolica-tiled dome of the **Chiesa del Carmine** *(p73)* and the mighty Baroque façade of the **Chiesa del Gesù** *(p72)*, which appeared in the film version of one of Sicily's greatest novels, Giuseppe di Lampedusa's The Leopard *(Il Gattopardo)*. Explore the ebullient Ballarò street market nearby, sampling traditional hot *panelle* (chickpea fritters) and a freshly baked *cannoli* (sweet pastry) for lunch.

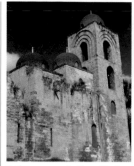

The former mosque, San Giovanni degli Eremiti, famed for its five domes

Afternoon Head up to **Quattro Canti** *(p69)*, a monumental – and heavily trafficked – crossroads, to Piazza Bellini, home to red-domed Arab-Norman **San Cataldo** *(p59)* and the Benedictine convent of **La Martorana** *(p58)*, with a unique mosaic portrait of King Roger II. Cast an eye over the controversial statuary of **Fontana Pretoria** *(p58)*, dubbed the "fountain of shame" when it was built for its over-abundance of sybaritic nudes. Then head to Palermo's Cathedral *(pp70–71)* where, after visiting its wonderful interior, you can take a tour of the roofs, which are open late at night in the summer.

Day Two

Morning Start your day at Piazza Verdi to take a look at the mighty **Teatro Massimo** *(p73)*, the largest opera house in Italy; half-hour tours of the lavish interior start at 9:30am. Or, if you prefer, begin at the fine

collections of the **Museo Archeologico Regionale A. Salinas** *(p60)*; don't miss the Pietra di Palermo. Walk down Via Roma, browsing the shop windows, then cut through the **Vucciria market** *(p60)* and up Corso Vittorio Emanuele to **Piazza Marina** *(p54)*, where Palermitani gather to play cards under immense liana-hung ficus trees. If there's time before lunch, discover the art of Sicilian puppetry nearby at the **Museo Internazionale delle Marionette** *(p54)*, or visit **Palazzo Mirto** *(p55)* for a chance to see inside an 18th-century aristocratic palace with its original furnishings.

Afternoon After lunch at Piazza Marina, begin the afternoon visiting **Palazzo Abatellis** *(pp56–7)* and its artistic treasures. Move on to pretty Arab-Norman **La Magione** *(p59)*, with its evocative cloisters, and roofless Gothic **Santa Maria dello Spasimo** *(p59)*, often a venue for concerts and exhibitions. Back on Via Alloro, the chic **Galleria d'Arte Moderna Sant'Anna** *(p59)* displays 19th- and 20th-century Sicilian art and has a lovely café – or, one of Palermo's best restaurants (Osteria dei Vespri, *p211*) is right across the street.

To extend your trip...
Take a third day to relax on the beach at **Mondello** *(p76)*, or explore the fabulous, mosaic-filled Cathedral of **Monreale** *(p80–81)*.

One of the façades of the Quattro Canti, Palermo's most fashionable square

Two Days in Syracuse

Explore the Baroque delights of the diminutive island of Ortygia, then cross to mainland Syracuse to see the superb relics of the city's days of Greek glory.

- **Arriving** The train and long-distance bus stations are both very central. There's a spacious car park just over the bridge into Ortygia.

- **Getting around** Ortygia is small enough to walk around; you might treat yourself to a taxi at the end of a day at the Neapolis.

Day One
Morning Explore Ortygia's **Piazza Duomo** (p146); see the temple of Minerva embedded in the Cathedral and the lavish Baroque façade of **Palazzo Beneventano del Bosco**. Head underground to the **Artemision** – the remains of an Ionic temple below Via Minerva.

Afternoon Stroll through the picturesque Jewish quarter to Piazza Archimede, to see the models of the inventions of Archimedes at the **Arkimedeion** (p141). From here you can walk down to the beach at the end of Via Roma, or spend the rest of the afternoon shopping on Corso Matteotti and Via Cavour.

Day Two
Morning Dive into Ortygia's morning market to buy a picnic from its stalls, bakeries and delis, then head for the **Neapolis Archaeological Zone** (pp140–43) to explore its fabulous temples, grottoes and tombs; don't miss the spooky caves of the Latomie.

Afternoon After picnicking, perhaps on the steps of the Greek Theatre, head over to the superb **Museo Archeologico Regionale** (pp144–5). Here you'll see magnificent statues, tomb art, jewellery and coins, and even just the simple artifacts of everyday living that will bring Syracuse's rich history to life.

The impressive Neapolis Archaeological Zone, Syracusa

Three Days Around Mount Etna

A tour that begins on the Ionian coast in lovely Taormina, and builds up to a breathtaking climax at Europe's highest and most active volcano.

- **Arriving** Taormina lies midway along the coastal highway between Catania, with its airport, and Messina, for ferry services from mainland Italy.

- **Getting around** You'll need a car to explore this area; be prepared for steep and winding roads.

Day One
Spend the morning exploring **Taormina** (p180–84) – don't miss the magnificent view of Etna from the stunning Greek Theatre. Then, take the SS185 to Motta Camastra, passing through the most dramatic stretch of the **Alcantara ravine** (p185), then on to Francavilla di Sicilia, where a path leads down from the church to a series of waterfalls and pools where you can swim in summer. Stay in the lovely hill town of **Castiglione della Sicilia** (p185).

Day Two
Buy provisions, including meat and charcoal, as there are designated picnic areas with barbecues on the mountain. Drive to **Linguaglossa** (p179), and take the circular road around Etna's north slopes, to see extraordinary lava fields and views that stretch to Calabria on

a clear day. You can stay on the mountain at the **Rifugio Ragabó** (p205), or head back towards Castiglione. Wine lovers should go via Passopisciaro on SS120, where there are some of the only vineyards in Europe to have survived the phylloxera epidemic of the late 19th century; you may have time to enjoy a winery tour and tasting.

Day Three
Drive via the pretty town of **Zafferano Etnea** (p173) – pausing to pick up some of its superb chestnut or citrus blossom honey – to **Rifugio Sapienza** (p177) on Etna's south side, departure point for the cable car that climbs to a height of 2,500m (8,000 ft). You can add on a jeep trip continuing upwards to see the craters – as long as there are no eruptions in process! Either stay at the Rifugio – perhaps joining a thrilling evening trek – or down in the pleasant town of Nicolosi.

Tourists bathing river near the mouth of the Alcantara ravine

A Week in Val di Noto and Agrigento

- **Arrive** A new airport at Comiso serves this region, with Ryanair international services and plenty of connections via Rome and Milan.
- **Transport** Hiring a car at the airport will give you maximum freedom for this free-ranging itinerary.

Day 1 Noto

Start your trip exploring **Noto** *(pp148–51)*, a marvellous Baroque town of apricot-gold limestone. Admire the exuberant architecture of the **Cathedral**, **Palazzo Ducezio** and **Palazzo Nicolaci Villadorata** *(pp150–51)* as you sample ice creams famous throughout Italy. Noto was completely rebuilt after being devastated by the 1693 earthquake, and the ruins of the old city, **Noto Antica**, lie about 8 km (5 miles) above Noto on a mountaintop; wonderfully atmospheric, they are perfect for an afternoon or early evening stroll. Stay in Noto.

Day 3

Drive to **Capo Passero** *(p152)*, the southernmost tip of Sicily, where the Ionian Sea meets the Sicilian Channel – with dramatic consequences in stormy weather – and visit the evocatively restored *tonnara* (tuna fishery) of **Marzamemi** *(p152)*. Drive on to the beach resort of Sampieri and Baroque

Scicli *(p153)*, where many scenes from the TV series *Inspector Montalbano*, based on the books by Andrea Camilleri, were filmed. Scicli has some great B&Bs *(p204)* and an outstanding, if pricy, restaurant, Satra *(p215)*.

Day 4

Explore Scicli, an appealingly slow-paced town with lots of mellow Baroque buildings spilling along three river valleys dominated by soaring limestone cliffs. Then visit **Modica** *(p156)* – famous for the manufacture of chocolate according to an ancient Aztec recipe. Wander along the main street for chocolate sampling, then climb the 250-step staircase to the spectacular Baroque church of San Giorgio. Spend the night at Modica.

Day 5

On to **Ragusa** *(pp154–5)* and a day wandering its lovely old quarter, Ibla. Its mellow tangle of limestone pavements squeeze past the grand façades of limestone palaces, churches and town houses. The main piazza is dominated by the **Duomo**, a lovely three-tiered Baroque wedding cake of a cathedral. Ragusa is an excellent town for dinner and lodgings.

Day 6

Drive via the rarely visited towns of **Chiaramonte Gulfi** *(p157)* and **Vizzini** *(p157)*, with lovely churches and interesting, if rustic, Baroque cores, to **Caltagirone** *(pp158–9)*, renowned for its

A sunset illuminating the beautiful village of Ragusa

ceramics. See the town's famous, vividly coloured ceramic-tiled staircase, then browse the workshops to watch potters and painters practising their craft. Stay in Caltagirone.

Day 7

Move on to **Piazza Armerina** *(p133)* to spend the morning discovering the astonishing mosaics of the **Villa del Casale** *(pp134–5)*. If you've got the energy after lunch, pop over to the museum at nearby **Aidone** to see the exquisite *Goddess of Morgantina*, a treasured statue recently returned to Sicily after being looted and sold. Stay in Piazza Armerina.

Day 7

Drive to **Agrigento** *(pp118–19)* to finish your tour with an amazing high, the incomparable ancient Greek ruins of the **Valley of the Temples** *(pp120–21)* and its associated Museo Archeologico. This will easily occupy the whole day, though Montalbano fans might also want to take a tour of Agrigento town and Porto Empedocle, where the original books were set. Stay in Agrigento. From here, it's about a two-hour drive along SS115 to Comiso airport.

To extend your trip...

Spend an extra couple of days in Agrigento and fit in other excursions – to the birthplace (and resting place) of Luigi Pirandello, or the weird landscape of the Vulcanetti di Macalube. There are great beaches, too.

Temple Concordia, one of the Greek ruins located in the Valley of the Temples in Agrigento

For practical information on travelling around Italy, see pp 242–243

A Week in the Aeolian Islands

- **Arrive** Year-round, hydrofoils (and much slower car ferries) leave several times daily from Milazzo, and once daily from Messina. In summer both services are more frequent, and there is one daily hydrofoil connection with Palermo.

- **Transport** Island-hopping is by hydrofoil.

Wallow in a sulphurous warm mud bath on Vulcano

Day One

Arriving from Milazzo, start your trip on smouldering, sulphurous **Vulcano** (p194), the closest Aeolian Island to the mainland. It has been rather carelessly developed, but it is, however, worth the trip to climb the volcano (and walk through billowing clouds of sulphur). Bring a picnic to eat on your descent, and leave time to relax afterwards, wallowing in mud baths and swimming above natural springs around **Porto di Levante**. Catch the last hydrofoil to **Lipari** (p194) in time for an *aperitivo* and dinner. Sleep in Lipari.

Day Two

Wander the bustling main town of Lipari, with its flower-hung alleys and the pretty pleasure harbour of **Marina Corta**, then climb to the old castle to see the superb and imaginatively presented collection of the Archeological Museum. If it is not too hot, take a bus to the Cave Caolina and walk to the thermal baths of **San Calogero**. In hot weather, head for one of the beaches – the white pumice beach at **Porticello** is the most unusual, scattered with hunks of obsidian (black volcanic glass) after storms. Take a late afternoon hydrofoil to **Salina** (p194). Sleep in Santa Marina or Malfa.

Day Three

Twin-peaked Salina is the greenest and most diverse of the islands. Take a bus or walk (30 min from Santa Marina) to the hamlet of **Lingua**, to have lunch and one of **Alfredo's** famous granitas (p217) in the seaside piazza, and visit the tiny ethnographic and prehistoric museums overlooking the salt lake. Take a bus to **Pollara**, a remote hamlet clustered within a collapsed volcanic caldera, where the Italian cult classic *Il Postino* was filmed. Either stay, watch the sun set and have dinner, or, if there is still plenty of light, take another bus to the inland village of Valdichiesa and walk down a paved mule track to the tiny second port of **Rinella**, with a sandy beach and plenty of little places to eat and drink. Sleep in Salina.

Day Four

Catch the first morning hydrofoil to **Filicudi** (p195), taking the minibus taxi that greets arrivals to the picturesque village of **Pecorini Mare**. Spend a lazy day at the stylish Lido, or

The tranquil village of Salina Malfa, a good option for accommodation

take a boat tour right around the island. Dinner and sleep in Pecorini Mare.

Day Five

Make a day trip by hydrofoil – or an organized boat excursion – to the remote island of **Alicudi** (p195) to walk the mule tracks, and swim from rocks. In low season bring a picnic as there is no restaurant. Spend a second night on Filicudi – or take an evening hydrofoil, if there is one, to Salina or Lipari – one step closer to tomorrow's destination, Stromboli.

Day Six

Island-hop to **Stromboli** (p195) and spend the morning strolling around exquisite Stromboli town – a whitewashed labyrinth with cascades of bougainvillea and plumbago – or laze on one of the black sand beaches. Have lunch in town, then make the ascent of the volcano in time to arrive at the summit at sunset. Dinner and sleep in Stromboli.

Day Seven

Hydrofoil to **Panarea** (p195). Explore the chic little town, then wander along smartly paved mule tracks to Zimmari beach (with a good lunch bar open in summer), the prehistoric village of **Capo Milazzese** and the gorgeous bay of **Cala Junco**. Hikers can make a full circuit of this small island from here. Otherwise, take it easy on the beach. Sleep in Panarea, then take a morning hydrofoil back to Milazzo.

Putting Sicily on the Map

Sicily is the largest region in Italy (25,708 sq km/ 9,923 sq miles) and the fourth most populous, with almost five million inhabitants. The terrain is mostly hilly – the plains and plateaus make up only 14 per cent of the total land area. The most interesting features of the mountain zones are the volcanoes, especially Mount Etna, which is the largest active volcano in Europe. The longest river is the Salso, which is 144 km (89 miles) long. Besides Sicily itself, the Region of Sicily includes other smaller islands: the Aeolian Islands, Ustica, the Egadi Islands, Pantelleria and the Pelagie Islands. Palermo is the Sicilian regional capital, and with its population of more than 650,000 is the fifth largest city in Italy after Rome, Milan, Naples and Turin.

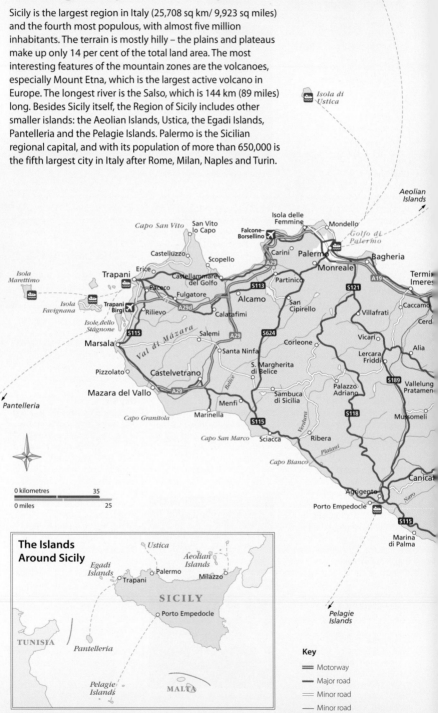

Civitavecchia, Napoli, Genoa, Cagliari

Isola di Ustica

Aeolian Islands

Capo San Vito
San Vito lo Capo
San Vito lo Capo
Isola delle Femmine
Mondello
Falcone–Borsellino
Golfo di Palermo
Castelluzzo
Scopello
Carini
Palermo
Bagheria
Erice
Castellammare del Golfo
Monreale
Termini Imeres
Isola Marettimo
Trapani
Paceco
Fulgatore
Partinico
A29
S113
Alcamo
San Cipirello
Villafrati
Caccamo
Isola Favignana
Trapani Birgi
Rilievo
Calatafimi
S121
A19
Cerd
Isole dello Stagnone
S115
Salemi
A29
S624
Corleone
Vicari
Alia
Marsala
Val di Mázara
Santa Ninfa
Lercara Friddi
Pizzolato
Castelvetrano
S. Margherita di Belice
Palazzo Adriano
S189
Vallelung Pratamen
Pantelleria
Mazara del Vallo
A29
Menfi
Sambuca di Sicilia
S118
Mussomeli
Capo Granitola
Marinella
S115
Capo San Marco
Sciacca
Ribera
Capo Bianco
Canicat
Agrigento
Porto Empedocle
S115
Marina di Palma

0 kilometres   35
0 miles   25

The Islands Around Sicily

Ustica
Egadi Islands
Aeolian Islands
Palermo
Trapani
Milazzo
SICILY
Porto Empedocle
TUNISIA
Pantelleria
Pelagie Islands
MALTA
Pelagie Islands

Key
■ Motorway
■ Major road
■ Minor road
■ Minor road

For additional map symbols *see back flap*

A PORTRAIT OF SICILY

Sicilian shores are washed by three different seas, and this is reflected in the ancient name for Sicily: "Trinacria", the three-cornered island. Each part of the island has its own history, its own character, creating a varied and complex whole. Yet over the centuries Sicily has acquired a sense of unity and identity.

Sicily's history can be traced back more than 3,000 years, during which time it has been dominated by many different peoples, from the Greeks to the Romans, Byzantines and Arabs, and from the Normans to the Spanish. Each succeeding culture left its mark on the island and may perhaps help to explain aspects of the modern Sicilian character. This diverse inheritance manifests itself in a curious combination of dignified reserve and exuberant hospitality.

The western side of the island, which is centred upon Palermo, is historically considered to be of Punic-Arab influence. The eastern side was once the centre of Magna Graecia, with its coastal towns of Messina, Catania and Syracuse. This difference may be discerned in the speech of local people: the "sing-song" dialect of Palermo as opposed to the

more clipped accent of Catania and Syracuse. Accent differences are still noticeable, though they have moderated to some degree over the centuries. There are east-west economic and social differences as well as linguistic ones.

However, the island's long, eventful and tortuous history has not been the only factor influencing its life and inhabitants. Few places have been so affected by their climate and topography: in Sicily the temperature is 30°C (86°F) for four months of the year, and when the sun disappears, destructive torrential rains can take its place. The Sicilian climate is one of extremes and can sometimes even be cruel; it has shaped the island's extraordinary landscape which, as the Sicilian novelist Tomasi di Lampedusa described it, includes the hell of Randazzo (the closest town to the craters

The rural landscape of the Sicilian interior, until recently characterized by its large estates

◀ Roman heritage on display: mosaic in the Villa del Casale in Piazza Armerina

Livestock raising, one of the mainstays of the economy in the Sicilian interior

of Mount Edna) and, just a few miles away, the paradise of Taormina. Then there are the splendid verdant coasts, with the arid interior a stone's throw away, marvellous towns overlooking the sea, and villages perched on hilltops surrounded by inhospitable, barren uplands. An aerial view of this unique island offers a spectacle that is at once both magnificent and awe-inspiring.

Economy and Society

The historic, geographic and climatic differences in Sicily have produced a complex and varied society. Yet Sicilians have a strong sense of identity and for

A watermelon seller in Palermo

centuries made their unique nature a point of honour (in a spirit of independence they used to call the rest of Italy "the continent"). Today this society is at a crossroads between tradition and modernity, much more so than other Mediterranean regions. Sicilian society is attempting to reconcile newer lifestyles and outlooks with deeply rooted age-old customs. One of the poorest regions in Italy, Sicily has had to strive for a more streamlined and profitable economy against the resistance of the ancient *latifundia* (feudal estate) system, just as the fervent civic and democratic spirit of the Sicilian people clashes with what remains of Mafia mentality and practice.

The criminal organization known to all as the Mafia is one of Sicily's most notorious creations. Sociologists and criminologists both in Italy and abroad have tried to define the phenomenon without success. Is it a criminal structure that is simply stronger and more efficiently organized than others, partly because of the massive emigration in the early 20th century, which took many

Villagers observing passers-by

An outdoor café on the island of Lampedusa

Sicilians to the other side of the Atlantic? Or is it an anti-government movement whose leaders have played on old Sicilian feelings of independence and diversity? Is the Mafia the tool of the remaining large estate owners, determined to retain power? Whatever the answer may be, eliminating the Mafia is one of Sicily's greatest challenges. After the early 1990s, which saw the deaths of several anti-Mafia figures, the tide now seems to be turning in favour of a new, "Mafia-free" Sicily, and many dons have been captured after years on the run. The fugitive operations of the "most-wanted" Mafia boss of all, Matteo Messina Denaro – in hiding since 1992 – were dealt a major blow with a massive crackdown in 2013, aimed at choking off his supply of illegal funds.

Art and Culture

For more than 3,000 years, Sicily has inspired the creation of artistic masterpieces, from the architecture of Magna Graecia and the great medieval cathedrals, to the paintings of Antonello da Messina and the music of Vincenzo Bellini, and from the birth of Italian literature under Frederick II to the poets and novelists of the 19th and 20th centuries. Sadly, this glorious artistic heritage is not always well cared for and appreciated, although attitudes are changing. Noto, near Syracuse, is a prime example of this. The town, one of the great achievements of Sicilian Baroque architecture, was subjected to neglect, leading to the collapse of the Cathedral dome in 1996. After repairs, UNESCO awarded the site World Heritage status in 2002, a prestigious honour that has made the inhabitants more aware of their surroundings. The creation of new nature reserves, renewed interest in preserving historic centres, and initiatives such as extended church opening hours have all followed.

But the arts and culture face severe competition for resources today, as Sicily is challenged by the arrival of vast numbers of refugees – some 4,000 in 2014 alone – fleeing war and poverty in Africa and the Middle East by sea. Yet another "foreign invasion", perhaps, but one that, despite the strain it has placed on the island's finances and infrastructure, has been received by many Sicilians with extraordinary sympathy and generosity.

Renato Guttuso, *View of Bagheria* (1951)

Sicily's Geology, Landscape and Wildlife

The typical Sicilian landscape consists of coast and sun-baked hills. The irregular and varied coastline is over 1,000 km (620 miles) long, or 1,500 km (931 miles) if the smaller islands are included. The island's geological makeup is also quite varied, with sulphur mines in the centre and volcanic activity in the east. Sicily's many volcanoes, in particular Mount Etna (the largest in Europe), have created a landscape that is unique in the Mediterranean.

Sicilian Fauna

Painted frog

Sicily has preserved a variety of habitats in its large nature reserves, the most famous of which is the Mount Etna National Park. These parks are home to a wide range of species, some of which are endangered, including wildcats, martens and porcupines. The birdlife includes the rare golden eagle.

Rugged Coasts and Stacks

Vanessa butterfly

The Sicilian coastline is steep and rugged, particularly along the Tyrrhenian sea and the northern stretch of the Ionian, where there are many peninsulas, river mouths, bays and rocky headlands. It is also characterized by stacks, steep-sided pillars of rock separated from the coastal cliffs by erosion.

The sawwort *Serratula cichoriacea* is a perennial found along Sicily's coastlines.

Sandy Coastlines

Flamingo

Around the Trapani area the Sicilian coast begins to slope down to the Mozia salt marshes, followed by uniform and sandy Mediterranean beaches. This type of coastline continues along the Ionian side of Sicily, where there are marshy areas populated by flamingoes. These birds can be seen nesting as far inland as the Plain of Catania.

The dwarf palm, called *scupazzu* in Sicilian dialect, is a typical western Mediterranean plant.

Astroides calycularis is an alga that thrives in shaded cliff areas.

The prickly pear is an example of an imported plant that was initially cultivated in gardens and then ended up crowding out the local flora.

All kinds of coleoptera, including this shiny-backed carabid beetle, can be found in Sicily. In the Mount Etna area alone, 354 different species have been identified.

The reptile family is represented by numerous species, ranging from various types of snake to smaller creatures such as this green lizard, which is well known for its shiny skin and sinuous body.

Foxes were at one time rare in Sicily, but in recent years they have been spotted near towns foraging for food among household refuse.

Martens love to roam in the woods around Mount Etna. Weasels and ferrets can also be found in Sicily.

The Interior

Green woodpecker

Sicily's hinterland has not always looked the way it does today. Maquis vegetation once carpeted areas that, except for a few stretches far from the towns, are arid steppes today. As a result, apart from grain, which has always been the island's staple, the flora is not native, originating in North Africa or the Italian mainland. Birds like the woodpecker can be seen.

Volcanic Areas

A falcon, an Etna raptor

Volcanic zones, particularly around Mount Etna, are very fertile and yield rich vegetation, from olive trees growing on mountain slopes to the pines, birch and beech that thrive at 2,000 m (6,560 ft). Higher up grows the milk vetch, forming spiky racemes. Above 3,000 m (9,840 ft) nothing grows. Raptors can often be seen circling.

Moss and lichens cover the walls of houses on the slopes of Mount Etna, which are built using volcanic sand.

Orchids come in a great number of varieties, but they are sadly becoming more and more rare. They can be seen in uncultivated areas or along screes.

The vegetation in the interior often looks like this: quite low-growing and with brightly coloured flowers.

Cerastium and Sicilian soapwort flourish on the Mediterranean uplands.

Architecture in Sicily

Three periods have shaped much of Sicily's architecture. The first was the time of Greek occupation, when monumental works (especially temples and theatres) were built. Aesthetically they were often equal to, and in some cases superior to, those in Greece itself. The medieval period witnessed the fusion of the Byzantine, Arab and Norman styles in such buildings as the Cathedral at Monreale near Palermo. Last came the flowering of Baroque architecture in the 17th–18th centuries. The style was so individual that it became known as Sicilian Baroque.

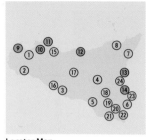

Locator Map

☐ Classical Architecture
■ Medieval Architecture
☐ Baroque Architecture

Styles of Classical Greek Temple

The earliest version of the Greek temple consisted of a rectangular chamber housing the statue of a god. Later, columns were added and the wooden elements were replaced by stone. There were three Greek architectural orders: the Doric, Ionic and Corinthian, in chronological order. They are easily distinguished by the column capitals. The temples built in Sicily displayed an experimental, innovative nature compared with those in Greece.

The Doric Temple The Doric temple stood on a three-stepped base. The columns had no base, were thicker in the middle and tapered upwards, and the capital was a rectangular slab. Other elements were the frieze with its alternating metopes and triglyphs, and the triangular pediment.

The Ionic Temple The differences between the Ionic and Doric styles lay in the number of columns and in the fact that Ionic columns rest on a base and their capitals have two volutes, giving the appearance of rams' horns.

The Corinthian Temple The Corinthian temple featured columns that were more slender than in the Ionic temple, and the elaborate capitals were decorated with stylized acanthus leaves.

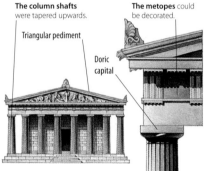

The column shafts were tapered upwards.

Triangular pediment

The metopes could be decorated.

Doric capital

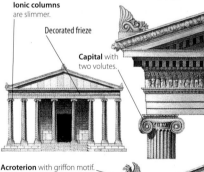

Ionic columns are slimmer.

Decorated frieze

Capital with two volutes.

Acroterion with griffon motif.

Corinthian capital, decorated with acanthus leaves.

Classical Architecture

① Segesta *p102*
② Selinunte *pp108–10*
③ Valle dei Templi (Agrigento) *pp120–21*
④ Morgantina *pp132–3*
⑤ Gela *p157*
⑥ Syracuse *pp140–47*
⑦ Taormina *pp180–84*
⑧ Tyndaris *p190*

Medieval Churches

The drawings illustrate two of the greatest achievements of medieval architecture in Sicily. The Cathedral of Monreale *(left)* is a masterpiece from the Norman period, with a splendid fusion of Byzantine, Arab and Norman figurative elements in the mosaics in the interior. A similar fusion of styles and cultures can be seen in the exterior architectural features. The Cathedral in Cefalù *(below)* also dates from the Norman period and, like Monreale, has beautiful mosaics. Its austere and stately quality is created by Romanesque elements such as the two lateral towers.

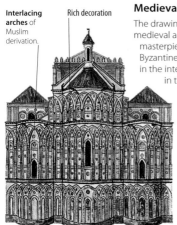

Interlacing arches of Muslim derivation.

Rich decoration

The windows, double and single lancet, make the towers look lighter.

Romanesque side towers

Interlacing arches

The Gothic portal is under a 15th-century narthex.

Medieval Architecture

Baroque Churches

After the 1693 earthquake the towns of eastern Sicily were almost totally rebuilt. Spanish-influenced Baroque was combined with Sicilian decorative and structural elements (convex church façades and impressive flights of steps), giving rise to an original, innovative style. Two great examples are shown here: the Cathedral in Syracuse *(left)* and the Basilica di San Giorgio in Ragusa *(below)*. The architects were GB Vaccarini (1702–1769), who also rebuilt Catania, and R Gagliardi (1698–1762).

Curved decorative elements

Decorative elements include statues.

The façade has a typically convex shape.

The columns protrude from the façade.

Jutting cornices define the sections of the façade, adding a rhythmic element.

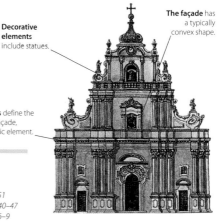

Baroque Architecture

Sicilian Literature and Art

In the history of Sicilian art and literature there have been periods of tremendous creativity and others when little of note was produced. In the field of literature, the 13th-century Sicilian School of lyric poetry, 19th-century *verismo* or realism and Luigi Pirandello's novels and plays scale the heights of Italian and European literary production. In the field of art, Sicily has produced such great artists as Antonello da Messina, one of the great figures in 15th-century rationalism and portraiture, and the modern painter Renato Guttuso.

Metope from Temple E in Selinunte: Artemis and Actaeon

Writers

Only fragments remain of Greek-Sicilian literary works. Unlike other artistic fields such as architecture, Siceliot (ancient Greek-Sicilian) literature is indistinguishable from the local production, as both were the expression of the same religious, cultural and civic milieu.

Apart from Pindar, who dedicated lyric poems to Syracuse and Agrigento, the names of two Siceliot poets have survived. Stesichorus, who lived in Catania in the 7th–6th centuries BC, "achieved great fame in all Hellas" according to Cicero, leaving a few fragments written in the Homeric style. Theocritus, a Syracusan who lived in the 4th–3rd centuries BC, created the genre of pastorals, short poems on bucolic or mythological subjects. Another important figure in the Greek context was the historian Diodorus Siculus (1st century BC).

The first known figure in medieval Sicilian literature is the Arab poet 'Ibn Hamdis, who was born in Syracuse in 1055 and was forced to leave the island while still young. He wrote moving verses filled with nostalgia for the land of his youth.

In the 13th century, the first school of lyric poetry in Italy developed at the court of Emperor Frederick II and his successor Manfred. It later became known as the Sicilian School. Among the key figures were Jacopo da Lentini, Pier della Vigna, Stefano Pronotaro, Rinaldo d'Aquino and Guido delle Colonne. Their love poetry took up the themes of Provençal lyric poetry but were written in vernacular Italian instead of Latin. Their psychological penetration and the stylistic and metric innovations led to the invention of the sonnet. After this period of splendour, Sicilian literature went into a decline, as did conditions generally in Sicily. This literary "drought" lasted throughout the Renaissance and Baroque periods, and the only author of note at this time is Antonio Veneziano (born in Monreale in 1543), a poet who wrote in the local dialect and left a collection of love poems.

The 18th century was another fallow period for literary production, and it was not until the mid-1800s that there was a rebirth of Sicilian literature. The writers Giovanni Verga and Federico De Roberto became the mainspring of the realistic novel, *verismo*. This style of writing was an extreme and, to a certain extent, more refined version of French naturalism, as embodied in the work of Emile Zola. Giovanni Verga was born in Catania in

Guidebook by Federico De Roberto

1840. After producing work in a late Romantic vein, in the 1870s he was drawn to French naturalism by creating his so-called "poetic of the defeated", in which he set out to depict the hardship of contemporary social reality. He began with short stories set in a rural context (the first was *Nedda*, 1873), which were followed by his masterpieces, the novels *I Malavoglia* (The House by the Medlar Tree, 1881) and *Mastro Don Gesualdo* (1889), which both depict the immutable Sicilian society of the time. The former – a truly innovative work from a stylistic and linguistic standpoint – is the story of a family of fishermen at Aci Trezza who, after a short-lived period of relative well-being, plunge into a life of poverty and suffering. *Mastro Don Gesualdo* narrates the rise on the social scale

Giovanni Verga, author of *I Malavoglia* (1881)

and existential drama of a workman (*mastro*) who, thanks to his marriage, becomes a "don". These two novels were part of Verga's planned *ciclo dei*

Renato Guttuso, *Boogie-woogie* (1953–4)

vinti (cycle of the defeated), which was to have consisted of five novels; but the author left the project unfinished.

In the same vein as Verga were two other Sicilian writers, Luigi Capuana (1839–1915) and, more importantly, Federico De Roberto (1861–1927), who wrote *I Viceré* (The Viceroys, 1894), about a 19th-century aristocratic family in Catania.

The literature of Sicily continued to be at the forefront in the 20th century. The first half was dominated by Luigi Pirandello (1867–1936), who won the Nobel Prize for Literature in 1934. In his novels (such as *The Late Mattia Pascal*, 1904), nearly 300 short stories, plays *(see p29)* and essays he combines wit with a lucid and sometimes ruthless vision of reality.

One of Pirandello's earliest plays

Among the many note-worthy post-war Sicilian writers are the "hermetic" poet Salvatore Quasimodo (1901–68), author of the collection of poems *Ed è subito sera* (And Suddenly it's Evening, 1942). He won the Nobel Prize in 1959. Giuseppe Tomasi di Lampedusa (1896–1957) wrote *Il Gattopardo* (The Leopard, 1958; *see p126*), a vivid portrait of feudal Sicily later made into a film, and Leonardo Sciascia (1921–89) wrote novels and essays painting a penetrating, lively portrait of post-war Sicily. Another great novelist, Gesualdo Bufalino (1920–1996), became famous with his first novel, *Diceria dell'untore* (The Plague-Spreader's Rumour).

Author Leonardo Sciascia

Artists

Until the Renaissance, Sicilian art was basically decorative. During the Greek period probably the best painting was produced in the 7th century BC, when Siceliot vase painters stopped imitating the mainland models and adopted a fresh, eclectic style that elaborated upon the original Greek red-figure ware motifs. The only known artist was Zeuxis, and this only through literature, not his works. The Roman period distinguished itself for some fine wall paintings, in which wax-derived colours were applied, fused into a layer and then fixed onto the wall with heat. The decorative arts in the Middle Ages in Sicily were dominated by mosaics. Among earlier fine works in this medium are the mosaics of the late Roman period at Piazza Armerina and those in the Cappella Palatina in Palermo and Cefalù Cathedral, which are a magnificent combination of Byzantine, Arab and Norman motifs and stylistic elements. Sicilian art reached a peak during the Renaissance, thanks to artists such as Giuffrè (15th century), Quartarano (1484–1501), the unknown creator of *Trionfo della morte* (The Triumph of Death), and to the genius of Antonello

da Messina (1430–79), one of the greatest Renaissance portraitists and exponents of figurative rationalism.

Although Sicily was a favourite subject of European landscape artists, from the 17th to the 19th centuries the island produced only one important painter, Pietro Novelli, known as "the man from Monreale" (1603–47). Later, Francesco Lojacono (1838–1915) was also known for his Sicilian landscapes.

In the 20th century, the painter Renato Guttuso (1912–87) took up his artistic heritage in a realistic vein. Painter and engraver Piero Guccione (1935–) is a key contemporary figure on the Sicilian art scene.

Antonello da Messina, *St Sebastian* (1476)

Cinema and Theatre in Sicily

Anyone who witnesses the colour of Carnival in Sicily, the bustle of the Vucciria market in Palermo or the sombre pageantry of Easter week processions will appreciate that Sicily is a theatrical place in its own right. The reasons perhaps lie in the turbulent history of the place. One thing is certain: the island has been a source of inspiration for both theatre and cinema, providing subjects from peasant life to the decadent aristocracy and the Mafia, and producing world-famous playwrights and award-winning films.

Burt Lancaster as the Prince of Salina in
Il Gattopardo (The Leopard; 1963)

Sicilian Cinema

The first Sicilian to forge a successful career in the seventh art was probably the playwright Nino Martoglio, who in 1914 directed *Sperduti nel Buio* (Lost in the Dark), a film set in Naples and edited with a highly original technique. Shortly afterwards, in 1919, Luigi Pirandello wrote two screenplays, *Pantera di Neve* (Snow Panther) and *La Rosa* (The Rose), followed by *Acciaio* (Steel) in 1933. The great playwright and the directors of the films experienced difficulties, however, and the results were not entirely successful. After World War II Sicilian cinema and films set in Sicily reached a peak. In 1948 Luchino Visconti produced *La Terra Trema*, a loose adaptation of Giovanni Verga's *I Malavoglia (see p173)*. The Milanese director returned to the island in 1963 to film *Il Gattopardo* (The Leopard),

based on the novel of the same name by Tomasi di Lampedusa *(see p126)* and starring Burt Lancaster, Alain Delon and Claudia Cardinale.

In the same period, the Palermitan director Vittorio De Seta, following some fascinating documentaries on Sicily, directed a feature film set in Sardinia, *Banditi a Orgosolo* (Bandits at Orgosolo, 1961), and Neapolitan director Francesco Rosi made *Salvatore Giuliano* (1961), the story of the famous Sicilian bandit, acclaimed as "the greatest film on southern Italy". That same year Pietro Germi shot another film in Sicily: *Divorzio all'Italiana*, (Divorce – Italian Style), with Marcello Mastroianni and Stefania Sandrelli. Roman director Elio Petri made another important film about the island in the 1960s: *A Ciascuno il Suo* (To Each His Own, 1967), an adaptation of Leonardo Sciascia's novel of the same name *(see p27)*. The 1970s and 1980s produced many films about the Mafia, while filmmaker Giuseppe Tornatore directed *Cinema Paradiso*, set in Palazzo

Adriano *(see p124)*, which won an Academy Award as the best foreign film of 1990. The TV series *Inspector Montalbano*, from the books by Andrea Camilleri, was also almost entirely shot in Ragusa.

Marlon Brando as Don Corleone in
The Godfather

Cinema and the Mafia

Since the end of World War II the Mafia has been a favourite subject for film. (However, there is a distinction between Italian-made and Hollywood films.) The most distinguished Mafia films made in Italy are Francesco Rosi's *Salvatore Giuliano*; *Il Giorno della Civetta* (Mafia, 1968), adapted from Leonardo Sciascia's novel *(see p27)* and directed by Damiano Damiani, who also made *Confessione di un Commissario di Polizia al Procuratore della Repubblica* (1971); and Elio Petri's *A Ciascuno il Suo* (To Each His Own, 1967). Last, the Mafia is also the subject of two films by Giuseppe Ferrara, *Il Sasso in Bocca* (1969) and more recently *Cento Giorni a Palermo* (100 Days in Palermo, 1983), the tragic story of the Carabiniere general Dalla Chiesa, who was killed by the Mafia.

Any number of Hollywood movies have been made about the Mafia, though they are almost always set in the US. The most famous is the Academy Award-winning *The Godfather* (1972), directed by Francis Ford Coppola and starring Marlon Brando and Al Pacino.

Neon sign of the Nuovo Cinema Paradiso in Giuseppe
Tornatore's award-winning film

The original script of *Il Berretto a Sonagli* by Pirandello (1917)

Sicilian Theatre

Sicilian theatre is most closely identified with Luigi Pirandello, but there is also a rich tradition of theatre in Sicilian dialect. This theatre form dates from the Middle Ages, but its greatest interpreters were active in the late 19th century. Popular actors included Giuseppe Rizzotto (*I Mafiusi de la Vicaria*, The Mafiosi of the Vicariate, 1863) and Giovanni Grasso, and in 1903 the publisher, playwright and, later, film director Nino Martoglio founded the Grande Compagnia Drammatica Siciliana. Luigi Pirandello also began his theatre career with comedies in dialect, such as *Il Berretto a Sonagli* (1917), but he gained international renown in the 1920s with his plays written in Italian. In 1921 he wrote *Six Characters in Search of an Author* and, the following year, *Henry IV*. In these plays, probably his greatest, Pirandello deals with the themes that made him world-famous: the relationship between illusion and reality, existential hypocrisy and the need to find a profound identity.

Sicilian playwright Nino Martoglio (1870–1921)

Classical Theatre in Sicily

Ancient theatre in Sicily can boast a great genius as its adoptive father, since Aeschylus (525–456 BC), who is regarded as the inventor of Greek tragedy, spent long periods on the island and died here. A number of his works were first produced in Syracuse *(see pp142–3)*. Sicily was therefore well acquainted with, and assimilated, the subject matter of Greek theatre: freedom versus destiny, the sense of divine power and human suffering, the anguish of the tragedies and the excoriating, bitter satire of the comedies. Classical theatre declined with the fall of the western Roman Empire, and it was not until the 20th century that the great tragedies were again performed in Sicily. In 1913, Count Mario Tommaso Gargallo and his fellow Syracusans, including archaeologist Paolo Orsi *(see pp144–5)* decided to champion the production of Aeschylus' *Agamemnon*. The premiere was held on 16 April 1914 and since then, with the exception of wartime, the Greek Theatre in Syracuse, one of the most beautiful in the world, has remained a venue for ancient theatre – thanks to the efforts of the Istituto Nazionale del Dramma Antico (National Institute of Ancient Drama, *see p143*). Many famous theatre personalities have participated in these productions over the years, including poets Salvatore Quasimodo *(see p27)* and Pier Paolo Pasolini *(see p143)* as translators, and the actors Giorgio Albertazzi and Vittorio Gassman.

Programme of the Istituto Nazionale del Dramma Antico, set up in 1925

THE HISTORY OF SICILY

The most striking aspect of Sicilian history is the enormous influence of all the different peoples who have colonized the island. Even the Sikanians, Elymians, Sicels and Ausonians, the first populations to leave traces of their cultures in Sicily, came from other parts of the Mediterranean. They were followed by the Carthaginians and then by the Greeks, under whom Sicily saw its first real period of great splendour. Greek domination ended in 212 BC with the siege of Syracuse, in which the great inventor Archimedes was killed. For the next six centuries, the island became the "bread-basket" of the Roman Empire, and during this period acquired a social system that was to be its distinguishing characteristic for centuries. After the fall of the Roman Empire and the barbarian invasions, Sicily was ruled by the Byzantines. The island was then conquered by the Arabs, under whom it became one of the most prosperous and tolerant lands in the Mediterranean. The next rulers were the Normans, who laid the foundations for the splendid court of Frederick II in Palermo. A long period of decadence coincided with the dwindling of the Middle Ages. The Angevins, Aragonese and Bourbons in turn took power in Sicily, but these dynasties exploited the island and treated it like a colony instead of improving life for the people there. Giuseppe Garibaldi's expedition in 1860 paved the way for the unification of Italy. Despite initial neglect by the central Italian government, Sicilians were finally given control of their own affairs. Yet many long-standing economic and social problems still need to be tackled and resolved; in particular, the continuing presence of the Mafia.

Sicily in a 1692 print showing its three provinces: Val di Demona, Val di Noto, Val di Mazara

◀ Pietro Novelli, *St Benedict Offering the Book of the Order*, San Castrense Monreale

The Conquerors of Sicily

Because of its strategic position in the middle of the Mediterranean, Sicily has always been fought over by leading powers. Its history is therefore one of successive waves of foreign domination: Greek tyrants, Roman proconsuls and barbarian chieftains, then the Byzantines, Arabs and Normans, the Hohenstaufen monarchs, the Angevin and Aragonese dynasties, the Spanish viceroys and finally the Bourbons, the last foreign rulers in Sicily before Italy was unified.

5th century BC Battles for supremacy in Sicily between the Greek and Punic colonies

Cleandros initiates the period of tyrannical rule in Gela

Hippocrates succeeds Cleandros and extends Gela's dominion

Agathocles, king of Syracuse (317–289 BC)

King Pyrrhus at Syracuse (280–275 BC)

Hieron II (265–215 BC)

Verres becomes the Roman governor in 73–71 BC and is notorious for his corrupt rule

Genseric, chief of the Vandals, conquers Sicily in AD 440

Justinian I, the Byzantine emperor, annexes Sicily in AD 535

600 BC	400	200	AD 1	200	400	600
Greeks		Romans			Barbarians and Byz	
600 BC	400	200	AD 1	200	400	600

Gelon conquers Syracuse in 490 BC

Theron, tyrant in Agrigento in 488 BC

Ducetius, last king of the Siculi, dies in 440 BC

The Peloponnesian War (431–404 BC) brings an attack on Syracuse by the Athenian army, who are later defeated

Timoleon restores democracy in Syracuse in 339 BC

The Romans conquer Sicily definitively in 212 BC

Dionysius the Younger succeeds his father in 368 BC

Dionysius the Elder becomes tyrant of Syracuse in 405 BC and rules for 38 years

Odoacer and the Ostrogoths conquer Sicily in AD 491. He is succeeded by **Theodoric**

Artists and Scientists

In at least two significant periods, artists and scientists played a leading role in the long and eventful history of Sicily. The outstanding figure was Archimedes, born in Syracuse in 287 BC and on intimate terms with the ruler Hieron II. Thanks to the ingenious machines of war he invented, the city was able to resist Roman siege for three years (215–212 BC). Another great moment in Sicilian history came when the court of Frederick II in Palermo became known for its artists, poets and architects in the 1200s. Palermo became a leading centre for intellectuals.

Archimedes, the great Syracusan scientist

Diocletian divides the Roman Empire in AD 285. Sicily remains part of the Western Empire

Charles I of Anjou, born in 1226, wrests the throne of Sicily from Manfred. He dies in 1285

Charles II succeeds his father Charles I but is forced to cede Sicily to Manfred's daughter and her husband, **Peter III of Aragón**, who occupied the island in 1282

Ferdinand II (1830–59) is the last Bourbon ruler in Sicily

Frederick II, emperor from 1216, is King of Sicily from 1197 to 1250, the year of his death. He moved his court to Palermo

James II of Aragón (1286–96)

The viceroys (above, Severino Filangieri) govern Sicily for the Spanish sovereigns until 1713

Tancred (1190–94)

Frederick II of Aragón (1296–1337)

Ferdinand (1759–1825) unifies the kingdoms of Naples and Sicily in 1816

William I (1154–66)

Peter II of Aragón (1337–41)

Roger I, the Norman lord, conquers Sicily in 1091 after a war lasting 30 years

Louis of Aragón (1341–55)

800	1000	1200	1400	1600	1800	
Arabs		Normans	Angevins and Aragonese		Bourbons	Savoy
800	1000	1200	1400	1600	1800	

Manfred, the natural son of Frederick II, rules Sicily until 1266

Duke John of Peñafiel is designated first viceroy of Sicily by his father, Ferdinand I of Aragón, in 1412. This system of rule is to last for three centuries

Roger II (1105–1154)

Vittorio Amedeo II of Savoy acquires Sicily in 1713 through the Peace of Utrecht, ceding it to the **Habsburgs of Austria** in 1718

Henry VI, emperor and son of Barbarossa, conquers Sicily in 1194. He dies in 1197

Vittorio Emanuele II of Savoy becomes the first king of a unified Italy. Sicily forms a part of the new kingdom, having voted for annexation following Garibaldi's conquest of the island in 1860

William II (1166–89)

Frederick III of Aragón (1355–77), dies, triggering a period of struggle and strife that brings about the end of the Kingdom of Sicily

The Arabs begin their invasion of Sicily in 827 and conquer the island in 902

Charles III of Spain acquires Sicily from Austria in 1735 and governs until 1759

Prehistoric and Ancient Sicily

When Greek colonists arrived in Sicily in the 8th century BC, in the east they found the Sicels – a Mediterranean population that had been there since 7000 BC – and the Phoenicians to the west. The former were soon assimilated, while the latter were ousted after the Battle of Himera (480 BC). This marked the beginning of Greek supremacy and the height of the Magna Graecia civilization, which ended in 212 BC with the Roman conquest of Syracuse. Roman Sicily saw the rise of large feudal estates and the imposition of taxes. Christianity began to spread in the 3rd–4th centuries AD.

Greek Colonization of the Mediterranean

The double oar on the stern was used as a rudder.

Voyage to Sicily

The ships the Greeks used for the dangerous trip to Sicily were called triremes. These galleys were about 35 m (115 ft) long, were faster and more agile than the Phoenician vessels and travelled about 100 km (62 miles) per day. They were manned by a crew of 200 and were equipped for transport and battle.

Stern

Myths and Gods

Magna Graecia adopted the religion of the mother country while adding local myths and legends. Mount Etna was seen as the home of Hephaestus, the god of fire, whom the Romans identified with Vulcan. Homer chose the island of Vulcano, in the Aeolians, as the workplace of this fiery god of blacksmiths. At Aci Trezza on the Ionian Sea coast, a group of stacks is known as "the islands of the Cyclops", since it was believed that they were the boulders Polyphemus hurled against Ulysses in the famous episode in Homer's *Odyssey*.

Zeus, the supreme Greek deity

Mother Goddess
This intense limestone statue, an archetype of femininity, dates from the middle of the 6th century BC and is in the Museo Archeologico of Syracuse *(see pp144–5)*.

	1500 BC Contacts between Aeolian and Cretan and Minoan cultures	**730–650 BC** Fourth period of Siculan civilization	**628 BC** Selinunte founded	**413 BC** Athenian invasion led by Nicias and Alcibiades a total failure
	1000–850 BC Second period of Siculan civilization	**733 BC** Dorians from Corinth found Syracuse		
1600 BC	**1300 BC**	**1000 BC**	**800 BC**	**600 BC** 400
1270–1000 BC First period of Siculan civilization	**850–730 BC** Third period of Siculan civilization		**729 BC** Katane (Catania) founded	**480 BC** Battle of Himera: Greeks defeat Carthaginians
	8th century BC Greeks colonize east, Phoenicians west. Panormos (Palermo) founded			

The goddess Athena

The Roman Villas
Roman dominion in Sicily brought about the spread of *latifundia* (large feudal estates) and landowners' villas such as the Villa del Casale *(see pp134–5)*, whose mosaics were preserved thanks to a flood that buried them for centuries.

Where to see Ancient Sicily

4th-century BC crater

Almost every Sicilian town of any size has an archaeological museum. The most interesting prehistoric ruins are to be found in the islands, particularly the Aeolians *(see pp192–5)*, while the few Punic remains are on display in the museums. The main Greek sites include Segesta *(see p102)*, Selinunte *(see pp108–11)*, Syracuse *(see pp140–47)*, the Valle dei Templi at Agrigento *(see pp120–21)* and Morgantina *(see pp132–3)*. One of the best preserved Roman sites is the ancient villa at Piazza Armerina *(see pp134–5)*.

A trireme drew only about 60 cm (24 in) per oar rowed.

The spur was used to destroy the oars on enemy vessels.

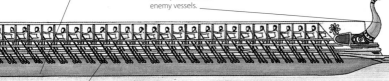

The third rank of oars (hence "trireme" or three oars), was on an external deck jutting out from the hull. Everything was carefully calculated so that the 170 oar movements were synchronized.

Prehistoric Village
Remains of settlements dating from the beginning of the first millennium BC lie all over Sicily. However, the first populations who left traces in Sicily (Sikanians, Elymians and Sicels) were not native people.

Aeschylus, the great Greek tragedian who was also active in Syracuse

AD 293 The emperor Diocletian makes Sicily *regio suburbicaria*, or directly dependent on Rome

AD 325 Christianization of the Syracuse area

AD 535 Sicily becomes part of Justinian's Eastern Roman Empire

200	AD 1	AD 200	AD 400	AD 600

212 BC Syracuse conquered by Romans. Sicily loses its autonomy

Female clay bust

AD 440 During the barbarian invasions of Italy the Vandals led by Genseric conquer Sicily

AD 600 Christianization of all of Sicily

AD 491 The Ostrogoths under Odoacer take Sicily from the Vandals

Medieval Sicily

The frequent Arab raids became in 827 a real campaign to conquer Sicily, which ended successfully in 902. Arab dominion coincided with the rebirth of the island after the decadence of the final years of Byzantine rule. In 1061 the Christian crusade began, the Normans conquering Sicily 30 years later. The Kingdom of Sicily was established in 1130 and reached its zenith with the splendour of Frederick II's court. In 1266 the Angevin dynasty took power, followed by the Aragonese, initiating a long period of decline in which powerful feudal landowners ruled the island.

The Arab Regions of Sicily
- Val Demone
- Val di Noto
- Val di Mazara

Tancred
The natural son of Roger III of Puglia, Tancred was appointed king of Sicily by the feudal barons in 1190. He was the last Norman to rule Sicily. When he died, the emperor Henry VI, son of Barbarossa and father of Federico II, ascended the throne.

Sicily under Arab Rule
During the century of Arab dominion Sicily was the richest and most tolerant land in the Mediterranean. The governing administration was reorganized and the arts and culture flourished to an exceptional degree, as can be seen in this decorated coffer.

The poor and ill are spared.

The dog leads the man in the night of death.

725 Worship of sacred images is prohibited. The possessions of the Sicilian church are confiscated by the patriarchate in Constantinople

831 Palermo becomes capital of the Arab emirate

902 Taormina surrenders, Arab conquest completed

1091 After 30 years warfare, Sicily is once again Christian land thanks to the Norman Roger

700   800   900   1000

827 Arab conquest of Sicily begins

1038–1043 Eastern Sicily is temporarily reconquered by Byzantium

The Virgin of Odigitria, Lentini

Coin with Arab inscriptions

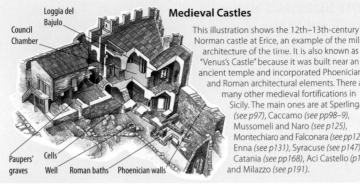

Medieval Castles

Loggia del Bajulo

Council Chamber

Paupers' graves

Cells

Well

Roman baths

Phoenician walls

This illustration shows the 12th–13th-century Norman castle at Erice, an example of the military architecture of the time. It is also known as "Venus's Castle" because it was built near an ancient temple and incorporated Phoenician and Roman architectural elements. There are many other medieval fortifications in Sicily. The main ones are at Sperlinga (see p97), Caccamo (see pp98–9), Mussomeli and Naro (see p125), Montechiaro and Falconara (see pp126–7), Enna (see p131), Syracuse (see p147), Catania (see pp168), Aci Castello (p172) and Milazzo (see p191).

Death strikes with bow and arrows, like a horseman of the Apocalypse.

A lady maintains her proud attitude.

Representation of the World

After the conquest of Sicily, the Normans and Hohenstaufens assimilated the culture of the Arabs, as can be seen in this representation of the world, executed in the Norman period by an Arab artist.

The Triumph of Death

This mid-15th-century fresco, painted and kept in Palermo (see pp56–7), drew inspiration from the Apocalypse: Death is a horseman armed with bow and arrows who kills the rich and spares the poor. These symbolic "triumphs" were common in medieval iconography.

Where to see Medieval Sicily

Besides the castles (see above), do not miss the Cappella Palatina in Palermo (see pp66–7), Monreale Cathedral (see pp80–81), and the towns of Cefalù (see pp92–5) and Erice (see pp104–5), including their cathedrals. Despite some rebuilding, the many villages that have preserved their Arab town planning layout are also interesting sites.

The rich and powerful are killed with arrows.

1194 Henry VI conquers Sicily and makes it part of his empire

The tiara of Constance of Aragón, Frederick II's wife

1282 The Sicilian Vespers revolt overthrows the Angevin rulers and Peter of Aragón becomes the new king

1415 Ferdinand I of Aragón sends his viceroy, John of Peñafiel, to Sicily

1100	1200	1300	1400

1130 Roger II is crowned King of Sicily. Palermo is the capital

1250 The death of the emperor Frederick II marks the end of Sicily's most glorious period

1265 Charles of Anjou crowned King of Sicily by the Pope

1302 The Peace of Caltabellotta sanctions the independence of the Kingdom of Sicily

1377 Under Maria of Aragón war breaks out among the feudal landowners, which leads to the union of the Kingdom of Sicily and the Kingdom of Aragón

From Spanish Rule to a Unified Italy

In the early 15th century Sicily became an Aragonese province ruled by a viceroy. The island's economic and cultural decadence continued, and received the final blow when the Jews were driven away from Spanish territories in 1492. A series of revolts was subdued with the help of the Pope's Holy Office. There was a slight recovery after the devastating earthquake of 1693, which destroyed eastern Sicily. After brief periods of Savoyard and Austrian dominion, in 1735 Sicily passed to the Bourbons, in constant battles with the land barons. In 1814 the island became a province of the Kingdom of Naples; popular unrest led to Garibaldi's 1860 expedition and union with the burgeoning Kingdom of Italy. The late 1800s were marked by banditry and poverty in the rural areas.

The States of Italy
- Kingdom of Two Sicilies
- Papal States
- Grand Duchy of Tuscany
- Habsburg Empire
- Kingdom of Sardinia
- Duchy of Modena
- Duchy of Parma-Piacenza
- Duchy of Lucca

The 1693 Earthquake
On the night of 9 January 1693, Mount Etna burst into life. Two days later, "the Earth was rent from its bowels", as the historian Di Blasi put it. The earthquake, seen above in a print of the time, levelled 23 towns, including Catania, Noto and Lentini.

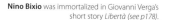
Nino Bixio was immortalized in Giovanni Verga's short story *Libertà (see p178).*

Many volunteers joined Garibaldi's 1,000 Red Shirts.

Giuseppe Garibaldi, a socialist, set off for Sicily despite Cavour's initial opposition.

1415 John, son of Ferdinand I of Aragón, is Sicily's first viceroy

1458 Alfonso V dies; Sicily is again under the rule of John, now King of Aragón

1571 The harbour in Messina houses the Christian fleet that later wins the Battle of Lepanto against the Ottomans

1649 Palermo revolt

1450 **1500** **1550** **1600**

1442 Alfonso V of Aragón unites the crowns of Sicily and Naples, thus founding the Kingdom of Two Sicilies

1535 Emperor Charles V visits Sicily

The Battle of Lepanto

The Revolt of Messina
This print depicts the 1848 insurrection at Messina. The city was bombarded by Ferdinand, afterwards known as "re Bomba", or "king Bomb".

The Sulphur Mines
After the unification of Italy, sulphur mining began in the Sicilian interior. Children were employed for their small size and agility.

The Baroque Period
This stucco work (c.1690) in an oratorio in Palermo *(see pp60–61)* by Giacomo Serpotta represents the *Battle of Lepanto* and is a marvellous example of the style that became known as "Sicilian Baroque".

Garibaldi Invades Sicily
On 11 May 1860, a thousand volunteers led by Giuseppe Garibaldi (1807–82) landed in Marsala to conquer the Kingdom of the Two Sicilies. They succeeded in this incredible feat, taking Palermo, then Messina and lastly Naples by storm.

Composers and Authors
In the 19th century, cultural life flourished in Sicily. The leading figures at this time were writer Giovanni Verga (1840–1922) and composer Vincenzo Bellini (1801–35), seen in this portrait.

The Sicilian Parliament

1674 Revolt in Messina

1759 Sicily taken over by the Kingdom of Naples

1812 The Sicilian Parliament sanctions an English-type constitution

1860 Garibaldi's Red Shirts invade in May. In October the people vote to merge with Kingdom of Italy

1650	1700	1750	1800	1850

1693 A disastrous earthquake destroys most of eastern Sicily

1735 The Spanish Bourbons become new rulers of Sicily

1713 With the Peace of Utrecht, Sicily is ceded first to Vittorio Amedeo II of Savoy and then (1720) to the Habsburgs

1820 First uprisings

1848 The entire island hit by revolts, especially Messina

Giovanni Verga

Modern Sicily

The 20th century began with the catastrophic 1908 earthquake in Messina. For the most part excluded from the process of modernization in Italy, Sicily was a living contradiction: its splendid cultural life as opposed to poverty, backwardness and the spread of the Mafia which, despite all attempts to curb its activities, had become a veritable state within a state. However, thanks to the perseverance and courage of public servants and growing public awareness of the problem, the Mafia seems to be less powerful than before.

1943 After heavy bombardment, the Allies land in Sicily on 10 July and take it in 38 days

1902 Heavy autumn rainfall triggers a tragic flood in southern Sicily, especially in Modica, in which 300 people lose their lives

1941 Syracusan novelist Elio Vittorini publishes *Conversation in Sicily*

1950 The bandit Giuliano is betrayed by his cousin Gaspare Pisciotta and killed

1937 Popular Catanian actor Angelo Musco dies

1908 The night of 28 December marks the greatest disaster in 20th-century Sicily: a quake totally destroys Messina and kills 100,000 people

1936 Luigi Pirandello dies in Rome

1900	1910	1920	1930	1940	1950	1960

1900	1910	1920	1930	1940	1950	1960

1945 The founder of the the Sicilian Separatist Movement, Finocchiaro, is arrested

1934 Pirandello wins Nobel Prize for Literature

1957 Rebellion in Ucciardone prison in Palermo

1947 Salvatore Giuliano's bandits shoot demonstrators: 11 dead, 56 wounded

1919 Don Luigi Sturzo, from Caltagirone, founds the Partito Popolare and becomes its leader. After World War II the party is renamed Democrazia Cristiana

1930 Mussolini sends prefect Cesare Mori to try to suppress the Mafia

1959 Poet Salvatore Quasimodo, born in Modica, wins Nobel Prize for Literature, the second Sicilian to do so in less than 20 years

1921 In Rome, Luigi Pirandello directs the première of his famous play *Six Characters in Search of an Author*

1923 Mount Etna eruption in June destroys towns of Catena and Cerro, barely missing Linguaglossa and Castiglione. The king and Mussolini inspect the damage

1980 A DC9 plane crashes near Ustica, with 81 victims. The cause of the accident has never been explained

1983 Thanks to a sophisticated system of controlled explosions, a lava flow from Mount Etna is deviated for the first time

1984 The former mayor of Palermo, Vito Ciancimino, is arrested

1966 A landslide at Agrigento, perhaps caused by illegal building construction, leaves 10,000 people homeless

1987 In a trial in Palermo hundreds of Mafiosi are condemned to a total of 2,600 years in prison. The verdict is based on the confessions of Tommaso Buscetta

1995 After years in hiding, top Mafia boss Totò Riina is arrested

2011 Celebrations are held all over Sicily for the 150th anniversary of Italian Unification

1968 A huge quake in the Belice Valley claims over 400 victims

2006 After 43 years on the run, Mafia godfather Bernardo Provenzano is arrested in Sicily

2014 Rescue operation Mare Nostrum brings 4,000 refugees from Africa and the Middle East to Sicily

1970	1980	1990	2000	2010	2020
1970	1980	1990	2000	2010	2020

1972 In May a plane crashes near Punta Raisi, the Palermo airport, and 115 people are killed. In December, Mafia boss Tommaso Buscetta is arrested; he is the first Mafioso to cooperate with Italian justice

2009 A mudslide caused by torrential rain leaves 24 dead and 35 missing near Messina

1971 Another eruption of Mount Etna. In Palermo, the Mafia kills Public Prosecutor Pietro Scaglione

2002 The ancient bronze Satiro Danzante is discovered by fishermen off the coast of Mazara del Vallo. Etna erupts again, completely destroying the cableway

1992 In July Paolo Borsellino, the magistrate who worked with Falcone, is assassinated in Palermo

1968 Clashes between farm labourers and police at Avola cause two deaths

1992 In May Judge Giovanni Falcone, for years a huge thorn in the side of the Mafia, is killed in an ambush near Capaci

SICILY THROUGH THE YEAR

Sicilians say that Sicily has the most beautiful sky in the world; certainly the island enjoys more than 2,000 hours of sunshine per year, more than any other part of Europe. The climate is generally mild, but it can get hot in high summer. In 1885 the temperature rose to 49.6° C (121.3° F), the highest ever recorded in Italy. However, winters can be cold, especially inland, and Mount Etna remains snow-capped into the spring. A land of ancient customs and deep-rooted beliefs, Sicily has preserved most of its traditional celebrations, almost all of them religious in nature.

Spring

Spring generally begins early in Sicily, although the weather can be quite unpredictable and patterns vary from year to year. In areas with orchards the air is filled with the scent of spring blossoms, and early flowers make this a particularly lovely time for visiting ancient sites. This is also the season with the greatest number of feast days, processions and festivals (sagre). Almost all these events are linked with the celebration of Easter.

Festa della Crocifissione (Feast of the Crucifixion) procession, Calatafimi

April
Sagra della Ricotta e del Formaggio (cheeses), Vizzini.
Sagra del Carciofo (artichokes), Cerda, Palermo.

The Sfilata dei Misteri, which takes place on Good Friday in Trapani

Easter Week
Celebrazione dei Misteri (all week), Enna. The Stations of the Cross commemorations and processions all week long.
Festa del Pane (bread) (all week), San Biagio dei Platani and Agrigento. Bread sculpture and decoration. **Settimana Santa** (Wed, Thu, Fri),

Caltanissetta. "Days of suffering and grief", with impressive processions. **Maundy Thursday Procession**, Marsala. A kilometre of masked figures.
Festa del SS Crocifisso (Fri), Calatafimi, Trapani. **Il Cristo Morto** (Fri), Partanna, Trapani. The Crucifixion is re-enacted.
Processione dei Misteri (Fri), Trapani. Floats with statues grouped in scenes from the Passion and hooded men commemorate Christ's sacrifice in the Procession of Mysteries, which lasts for 20 hours.
Ballo dei Diavoli (Sun), Prizzi, Palermo. Masked men perform the "devils' dance", which symbolizes the struggle between good and evil.

May
International Windsurfing Championship, Mondello and Palermo.
Classic Theatre, every year at Syracuse and Segesta.
Settimana delle Egadi, island of Favignana. The traditional mattanza tuna fishing method is celebrated.
L'Infiorata, Noto. The streets are filled with images and words created with flowers.

Sagra della Ricotta (24 May), The soft cheese used in many a Sicilian dish is celebrated at Mussomeli near Caltanissetta.

Summer

Sports, summer vacations, many important musical events, folk celebrations and food festivals characterize the long summer in Sicily.

The weather does, however, get extremely hot in certain

Christ's Crucifixion re-enacted at Partanna, Trapani

Average Daily Hours of Sunshine

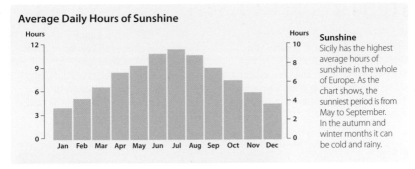

Sunshine
Sicily has the highest average hours of sunshine in the whole of Europe. As the chart shows, the sunniest period is from May to September. In the autumn and winter months it can be cold and rainy.

Taormina's stunning Greek amphitheatre, a venue for cultural events in summer

places on the island, particularly inland but occasionally even in coastal areas.

June
Torneo Internazionale di Tennis Challenger (early Jun), Caltanissetta. Brings together some of the best tennis talents from around the world at the Amadeo tennis club.
Sagra delle Fragole e dei Frutti di Bosco (strawberries and fruits of the forest), Maletto sull'Etna, Catania. This festival features a market display of fruits and berries, fruit products and tastings, as well as folklore, drama and musical events.
Taormina Arte (Jun–Sep). Cultural events at the Greek Theatre, with leading figures from the entertainment world.

July
Festa di Santa Rosalia (9–14 Jul), Palermo. Six days of festivities in honour of the city's patron saint, who, according to legend, saved Palermo from the terrible plague of 1624.
Festa di San Giuseppe (last week). Terrasini, Palermo.

St Joseph is honoured with a procession of fishing boats bearing the saint's statue. There is fried fish for everybody in the main square.
Festa di San Giacomo (24 & 25 July), Caltagirone. The town's long ceramic stairway is decorated with lighted candles representing assorted figures and scenes.
International Cinema, Music, Theatre and Dance Festival (Jul–Aug), Taormina. An important and popular international festival that forms part of the Taormina Arte series of events.

August
Sagra della Spiga (9–14 Aug), Gangi, Palermo. An entire week of parades and spectacles.
Festa dei Burgisi (9–14 Aug), Gangi, Palermo. Festival dedicated to the goddess Demeter, symbolising man's labour and the fruits of the earth. A parade of young people in traditional costume plays a central role.
Palio dei Normanni (12–14 Aug), Piazza Armerina. Historical re-enactment in period

costume of various tests of courage on horseback, in honour of the great Norman king, Roger I.
Processione della Vara and Cavalcata dei Giganti (15 Aug), Messina. Gigantic statues of the founders of Messina, Mata and Grifone, are paraded through the streets, followed by a float bearing a huge, elaborate triumphal cart and tableau called the "Vara".
Sagra della Mostarda (syruped and candied fruit), Regalbuto and Gagliano Castelferrato, Enna.
Sagra del Pane (bread) (last Sun in Aug), Monterosso Almo, Ragusa.
Sagra del Pomodoro (tomatoes), Villalba, Caltanissetta. A celebration dedicated to one of the island's most commonly and successfully grown products, the tomato.
Sagra del Grano (wheat), Raddusa, Caltanissetta.

The statues of Mata and Grifone at Messina

Average Monthly Rainfall

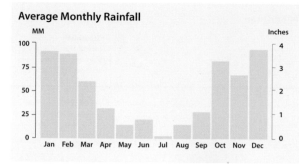

Rainfall
As the chart shows, in the six months from April to September there is very little rain. In autumn, by contrast, violent storms are common throughout the island, raising the average rainfall.

Autumn

This season begins late in Sicily, as September and often October continue sunny and warm. In autumn you can see many of the characteristic festivals celebrating local produce, such as grapes, and the theatre, classical music, opera and football (soccer) seasons all resume their annual cycle.

September
International Tennis Tournament, Palermo. The tournament takes place at the Country Time Club, 7 km (4 miles) from the city centre.
Sagra del Peperone (peppers), Sutera, Caltanissetta.
Sagra dell'Uva (grapes), Vallelunga, Caltanissetta; Roccazzo and Chiaramonte Gulfi, Ragusa.
Festa della Madonna della Luce *(7–8 Sep)*, Mistretta, Messina. The symbolic dance of two armed giants and the Madonna della Luce procession.
Festa di San Vincenzo Aragona, Agrigento. Masked revellers go

Statue for the Festa di San Vincenzo, at Aragona

in procession through the town.
Madonna della Rocca *(2nd weekend Sep)*, Taormina. Religious procession and a magnificent feast. The Madonna della Rocca statue is carried from the sanctuary to the town, where a feast takes place.
Bellini Festival, Catania. Organized by the city opera company.
Sagra dei Vini dell'Etna, Milo sull'Etna, Catania. Exhibition and sale of wines made from grapes

grown on the slopes of Etna.
Efebo d'Oro International Prize *(end Sep–early Oct)*, Agrigento. A prize is awarded to the best film adaptation of a novel.

October
Coppa degli Assi, Palermo. Grand Prix of horsemanship at the Parco della Favorita.
Sagra del Miele (honey) *(first Sun in Oct)*, Sortino, Syracuse.
Sagra delle Pesche (peaches), *(first weekend Oct)*, Leonforte, Enna. The luscious yellow peaches grown here have Italy's version of *appellation contrôlée* status.
Ottobrata, Zafferana Etnea, Catania. Every Sunday in October, in this village close to Mount Etna, the main square is filled with stalls selling produce and articles made by local craftsmen.

November
Festival di Musica Sacra, Monreale. Another great musical event, which takes

The procession at the Festa della Madonna della Luce

Average Monthly Temperature

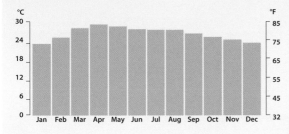

Temperature
From May to September the average temperature is rarely below 20° C (68° F), and, except for very unusual weather, it is seldom below 10° C (50° F) any other month. July and August may see peaks of more than 40° C (104° F).

place in Monreale's splendid medieval abbey.

Festival di Morgana *(Oct–Nov)*, Palermo. International marionette workshop of the Opera dei Pupi, held at the Museo Internazionale delle Marionette, with plays and exhibits.

Festa di San Martino *(Nov 11)*. In towns and at wineries, the saint's day is celebrated with festive sampling of the year's new wine.

Winter

Winter in Sicily is usually cool and often rainy, and may not be the ideal season to visit the interior and the larger towns. In February you might see one of the many Carnival festivities held throughout the island, which are famous for their originality

The Madonna del Soccorso, celebrated at Sciacca in February

and for the enthusiastic participation of the local people. There are also a limited number of events in January.

December

Convegno di Studi Pirandelliani *(early Dec)*, Agrigento. This workshop includes lectures and productions of Pirandello's plays.

Festa di Santa Lucia *(13 Dec)*, Syracuse. On the saint's feast day, her statue is taken out in a public procession and is then placed on public exhibition for eight days.

Christmas Season *(Dec)*. Churches across Sicily display nativity scenes, a custom believed to have been started by St Francis of Assisi.

The Festa del Mandorlo in Fiore, Valle dei Templi at Agrigento

January

Festa di San Sebastiano Acireale, Catania. On 20 Jan the saint's statue is taken from his church on a wooden float and borne in a procession in front of a huge crowd.

February

Festa della Madonna del Soccorso, Sciacca.

Festa del Mandorlo in Fiore (Festival of the Almond Tree in Bloom), Agrigento. The arrival of spring is celebrated in the Valley of Temples. At the same time there is the **Folklore Festival**, which for more than 50 years has featured folk music and dance from all over the world.

Festa di Sant'Agata *(3–5 Feb)*, Catania. The city is filled with "strangers" who invoke the saint's protection, while Catanians, dressed only in "sackcloth", bear her statue.

Carnival, Acireale. Allegorical floats, a colourful atmosphere and huge crowds.

Carnival, Sciacca. One of the most famous in Sicily.

Sagra della Salsiccia, del Dolce e della Trota (sausage, pastries and trout), Palazzolo Acreide, Syracuse.

The carnival at Acireale, considered one of the most colourful in Sicily

PALERMO AREA BY AREA

Palermo at a Glance

The capital of Sicily is built along the bay at the foot of Monte Pellegrino. Palermo owes its name to the sea: it was originally called *Panormos*, or "port", in Phoenician times. The town prospered under the Romans, but its golden age was under Arab domination, when it rivalled Cordoba and Cairo in beauty. Later, Palermo became the capital of the Norman kingdom. Today very little remains of the fabulous city of bygone times, but the Middle Eastern influence can still be seen in the architecture of the churches, the many alleys in the old town and the markets. The other age of splendour, which left a lasting mark on the city's civic and religious buildings, was the Baroque period (17th–18th centuries). Palermo suffered badly in the massive bombardments of 1943 and was then rebuilt chaotically, the result of political corruption and the Mafia. Recently things have taken a turn for the better.

The Palazzo dei Normanni, built on Punic foundations, has superb mosaic and fresco decoration. It became the royal palace under the Normans (see p68).

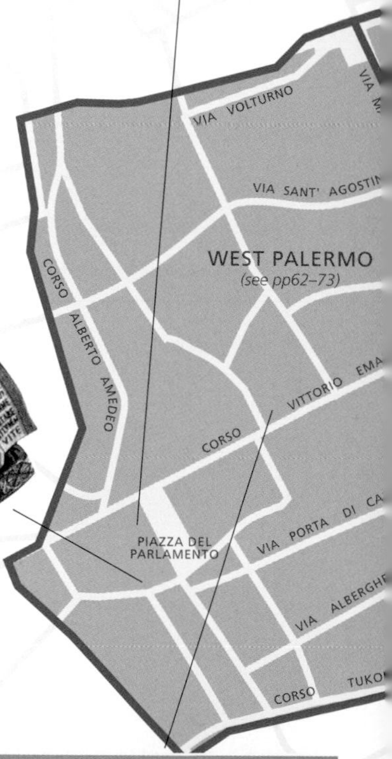

The Cappella Palatina, a masterpiece of Norman art, is covered with Byzantine-influenced mosaics representing scenes from the Bible (see pp66–7).

VIA VOLTURNO

VIA SANT' AGOSTI

CORSO ALBERTO AMEDEO

WEST PALERMO
(see pp62–73)

VITTORIO EMA

CORSO

VIA PORTA DI CA

PIAZZA DEL PARLAMENTO

VIA ALBERGHE

CORSO TUKO

Palermo's Cathedral was built in the Norman style in 1184 on the site of an ancient basilica, which had been transformed into a mosque by the Arabs. It has been rebuilt many times over the centuries (see pp70–71).

◄ Arabic influence in the architecture of the cloister, Monreale Cathedral

The Oratorio del Rosario di Santa Cita (or Santa Zita), with its stuccoes by Giacomo Serpotta, is a splendid example of Baroque ornamentation *(see pp60–61)*.

PALERMO

VIA CAVOUR

VIA ROMA

CORSO VITTORIO EMANUELE

VIA A. PATERNOSTRO

PIAZZA VERGOGNA

VIA ALLORO

FORO ITALICO

EAST PALERMO
(see pp50–61)

VIA ROMA

VIA MAQUEDA

VIA UNIVERSITA

VIA ABRAMO LINCOLN

0 metres   350
0 yards   350

San Domenico is one of Palermo's most interesting and typical Baroque churches. Note the lovely façade flanked by two bell towers and decorated with statues and columns *(see p61)*.

Palazzo Abatellis houses the Galleria Regionale di Sicilia, which has a rich collection of paintings and sculptures, including this marvellous bust of Eleonora of Aragon, Francesco Laurana's masterpiece *(see pp56–7)*.

EAST PALERMO

Between Via Maqueda and the sea lie the old Arab quarters of Palermo, with their maze of narrow streets and blind alleys. This area includes the Kalsa quarter (from the Arabic al-Halisah, or the Chosen), which was built by the Arabs in the first half of the 10th century as the seat of the Emirate, the government and the army. During the Norman era it became the sailors' and fishermen's quarter. It was badly damaged in World War II, and many parts are still being restored. Most of the Aragonese monuments, dating from the late Middle Ages and the Renaissance, are in the Kalsa. The focal point is Piazza Marina, for a long time the heart of city life and seat of the Aragonese court and the Inquisition courtroom. Via Maqueda opens onto Piazza Pretoria, the civic heart of Palermo, with Palazzo delle Aquile, Santa Caterina and San Giuseppe dei Teatini. West of Corso Vittorio Emanuele is Castellammare, with the Vucciria market and the Loggia quarter near the port, where Catalan, Pisan and Genoese communities once lived.

Sights at a Glance

Museums and Galleries
❷ Palazzo Abatellis pp56–7
❹ Museo Internazionale delle Marionette
⓬ Galleria d'Arte Moderna Sant'Anna
⓯ Museo Archeologico Regionale A. Salinas

Historic Buildings
❺ Palazzo Mirto

Streets and Squares
❶ Piazza Marina

Churches
❸ La Gancia
❻ San Francesco d'Assisi
❾ Santa Caterina d'Alessandria
❿ La Martorana
⓫ San Cataldo
⓭ La Magione
⓮ Santa Maria dello Spasimo

Markets
⓰ Mercato della Vucciria

Monuments
❼ Fontana Pretoria
❽ Palazzo delle Aquile

⓱ Oratorio del Rosario di Santa Cita
⓲ San Domenico
⓳ Oratorio del Rosario di San Domenico

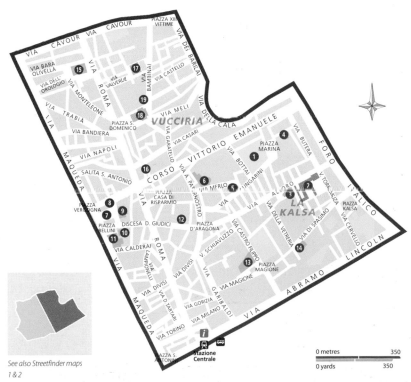

See also Streetfinder maps 1 & 2

0 metres 350
0 yards 350

◀ Nativity scene in 12th-century gilded mosaic, church of La Martorana

For keys to map symbols see back flap

Street-by-Street: Around Piazza Marina

The main square in Old Palermo lies at the edge of the Kalsa quarter. From the Middle Ages onwards it was used for knights' tournaments, theatre performances, markets and public executions. On the occasion of royal weddings, such as the marriage of Charles II and Marie Louise in 1679, impressive shows were put on in specially built wooden theatres. The square's irregular four sides are flanked by such monuments as Palazzo Steri-Chiaramonte, Palazzo del Castillo, Palazzo della Zecca, San Giovanni dei Napoletani, Palazzo della Gran Guardia, Santa Maria della Catena, Palazzo Galletti and Palazzo Villafiorita. In the middle is the Giardino Garibaldi, shaded by enormous fig trees.

Locator Map
See Street Finder map 2

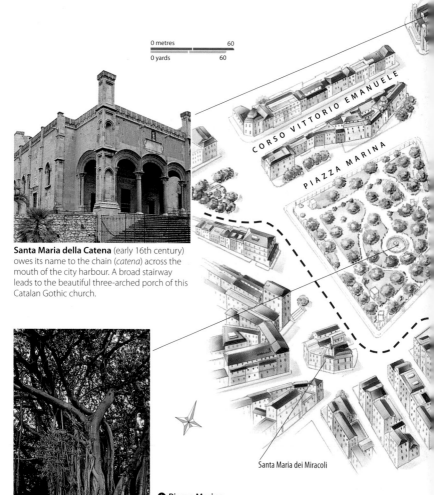

Santa Maria della Catena (early 16th century) owes its name to the chain (*catena*) across the mouth of the city harbour. A broad stairway leads to the beautiful three-arched porch of this Catalan Gothic church.

Santa Maria dei Miracoli

❶ Piazza Marina
This is one of the largest squares in Palermo. Once part of the harbour, but long since silted up and reclaimed, its central garden is home to massive *Ficus magnolioides* trees, with strange, exposed roots.

Key
— Suggested route

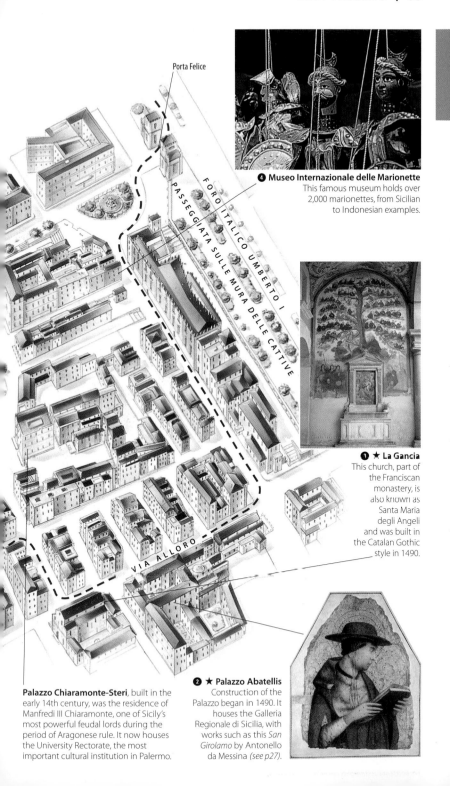

Porta Felice

FORO ITALICO UMBERTO I

PASSEGGIATA SULLE MURA DELLE CATTIVE

VIA ALLORO

❹ Museo Internazionale delle Marionette
This famous museum holds over 2,000 marionettes, from Sicilian to Indonesian examples.

❸ ★ La Gancia
This church, part of the Franciscan monastery, is also known as Santa Maria degli Angeli and was built in the Catalan Gothic style in 1490.

❷ ★ Palazzo Abatellis
Construction of the Palazzo began in 1490. It houses the Galleria Regionale di Sicilia, with works such as this *San Girolamo* by Antonello da Messina *(see p27)*.

Palazzo Chiaramonte-Steri, built in the early 14th century, was the residence of Manfredi III Chiaramonte, one of Sicily's most powerful feudal lords during the period of Aragonese rule. It now houses the University Rectorate, the most important cultural institution in Palermo.

The Giardino Garibaldi, in the middle of Piazza Marina

❶ Piazza Marina

Map 2 E3

One of the largest in Palermo, Piazza Marina lies on what was once the southern side of the natural harbour. In the middle of Piazza Marina is the **Giardino Garibaldi**, designed in 1863 by GB Basile and planted with *Ficus magnolioides*, a species of fig tree, which are now enormous. The garden is surrounded by a cast-iron fence decorated with bows and arrows, rabbits and birds. Inside are a fountain and busts of Risorgimento figures, including Benedetto De Lisi's monument to the Italian leader Garibaldi.

The most important building in Piazza Marina is **Palazzo Chiaramonte Steri**, built in 1307 by Manfredi III Chiaramonte, a member of one of Sicily's most powerful families. In the Middle Ages the Chiaramonte family controlled most of the island. The name "Steri" comes from *Hosterium*, or fortified building, as most patrician mansions were just that during the turbulent period of Hohenstaufen rule. Built in the Gothic style with Arab and Norman influences, the palazzo has an austere façade. The portal is decorated with a double arched lintel of ashlars and a series of double and triple Gothic lancet windows with multicoloured inlay.

When the new Aragonese rulers arrived in 1392, Andrea Chiaramonte was beheaded right in front of Palazzo Steri. It became the palace of the Aragonese kings and then of the viceroys. In the 17th century it housed the Inquisition courtroom, or Holy Office, where suspected heretics were interrogated and often tortured. Later, the palazzo became the city court of law and today it is the administrative headquarters of the University Rectorate. The courtyard is open to the public and tours of the palazzo are available.

Across the square is the Renaissance **Santa Maria dei Miracoli** (1547). On the corner of Via Vittorio Emanuele is the Baroque **Fontana del Garraffo**, a fountain with three shell-shaped basins supported by dolphins' heads. At the northeastern corner is the church of **San Giovanni dei Napoletani** (1526–1617), with a trapezoidal portico.

❷ Palazzo Abatellis

See pp56–7.

The Gothic portal of La Gancia, with bas-relief on the arch

❸ La Gancia

Via Alloro 27. **Map** 2 E3.
Tel 338-451 20 11 or 338-722 87 75.
Open 9:30am–1:30pm Mon–Sat.
Closed Sun & hols.

This church was built in 1485 and dedicated to Santa Maria degli Angeli. The façade is decorated with two Spanish-Gothic portals. The aisleless nave in the interior has 16 side chapels, a multicoloured marble floor and a wooden patterned ceiling. In the Baroque period, stucco decoration was added by the sculptor Giacomo Serpotta. The choir, in a separate room near the church's entrance, has a late-16th-century organ. The panels dating from 1697 show Franciscan saints painted by Antonio Grano.

Palermitan marionette from the theatre of Francesco Sclafani

❹ Museo Internazionale delle Marionette

Piazzetta A. Pasqualino 5. **Map** 2 E3.
Tel 091-328 060. **Open** Jun–Aug: 9am–1pm, 2:30–6:30pm Mon–Sat; Sep–May: 9am–1pm, 2:30–6:30pm Mon–Sat, 10am–1pm Sun. **Closed** one week mid-Aug. Show times vary; see website for updates. 🖼
W museomarionettepalermo.it

This museum boasts one of the world's main collections of puppets, marionettes and shadow puppets. In the first room are the great schools of marionettes, from the Catania style to those of Liège, Naples

Stage backdrop in the Museo delle Marionette depicting knights errant

6 San Francesco d'Assisi

Piazza San Francesco d'Assisi. **Map** 2 D3. **Tel** 091-616 28 19. **Open** 9am–5pm Mon–Fri, 9–11am Sat

This church has retained its medieval aspect despite the numerous alterations it has undergone. Built in the early 13th century together with the Franciscan monastery, it was destroyed by Frederick II soon afterwards when he was excommunicated by the Pope. In 1255, work on the new church began, reaching completion only in 1277. The 15th and particularly the 16th centuries witnessed additions and alterations; for example, the wooden roof was replaced and the presbytery was enlarged.

After the bombardments suffered in 1943 the church was restored to its original state. The austere façade has a large rose window and Gothic portal, while the interior boasts many noteworthy works of art, including sculptures by Giacomo Serpotta and Antonello Gagini. The side chapels house funerary stelae and sarcophagi.

The fourth chapel in the left-hand aisle is the Cappella Mastrantonio, with one of the first Renaissance works in Sicily, the portal by Francesco Laurana. Behind the high altar is a wooden choir built in 1520, as well as 17th-century paintings of the *Resurrection, Ascension* and *Mission*.

and Brussels. The second room has a collection of figures belonging to puppeteers from Palermo, Castellammare del Golfo, Alcamo and Partinico. Among the stage scenery here is *Charlemagne's Council* and *Alcina's Garden*. The international section includes Chinese shadow theatre puppets, Thai *hun krabok*, Vietnamese, Burmese and Rajasthan marionettes, and Javanese *wayang* figures, as well as animated figures from Oceania and Africa. The theatre of puppeteer Gaspare Canino di Alcamo has backcloths showing the feats of Orlando; most productions of the Opera dei Pupi (puppet opera) featured the exploits of Charlemagne's knights errant.

The museum also organizes the Festival di Morgana *(see p45),* which features puppet operas from around the world, all performed in Italian.

5 Palazzo Mirto

Via Merlo 2. **Map** 2 D3. **Tel** 091-616 75 41. **Open** 9am–6pm Tue–Sat, 9am–1pm Sun & hols. **Closed** Mon

This is a splendid example of a centuries-old nobleman's mansion that has miraculously preserved its original furnishings. Palazzo Mirto was built in the 18th century on top of pre-existing 15th- and 16th-century architectural structures. The palazzo passed from the aristocratic De Spuches family to the equally noble Filangeri, who lived here until 1980, when the last heir donated it to the Region of Sicily. An 18th-century portal with the coat of arms of the Filangeri family leads to the courtyard, where a majestic marble stairway takes you to the piano nobile. Here there is a series of elegantly furnished drawing rooms. The first of these is the Sala degli Arazzi (Tapestry Hall), with mythological scenes painted by Giuseppe Velasco in 1804, then there is the "Chinese" room, and lastly the so-called Baldachin Salon with late 18th-century allegorical frescoes. The furniture and other furnishings date from the 18th and 19th centuries. Some rooms overlook a courtyard garden dominated by a theatrical Rococo fountain flanked by two aviaries.

Coat of arms of Palazzo Mirto

The drawing rooms in Palazzo Mirto, still with their original furniture

❷ Palazzo Abatellis

This Catalan Gothic building, which now houses the 19 rooms of the Galleria Regionale della Sicilia, has an austere air. The elegant doorway leads to the large courtyard, which has a portico on the right side and a stairway to the upper floors. On the ground floor is one of its most famous works, the *Triumph of Death* fresco (painted by an unknown artist, and located in the former chapel) as well as a fine collection of statues by Antonello Gagini and Francesco Laurana. The first floor has noteworthy late medieval crucifixes including one by Pietro Ruzzolone (16th century), and paintings by Antonello da Messina. The most interesting work by a foreign artist is the *Malvagna Triptych* by Jan Gossaert (known as Mabuse).

★ Annunciation
This is perhaps the best-known work by the great Antonello da Messina (1430–79). It is a masterful and exquisite example of 15th-century figurative rationalism and the artist's fusion of Northern and Italian painting.

★ The Triumph of Death
Among the sculptures in this room is a fine medieval fresco by an unknown artist, portraying Death in the guise of a knight shooting his bow *(see pp36–7)*.

The **"Laurana Room"** houses the great sculptor's famous Bust of Eleonora of Aragon *(see p49)*.

Ground floor

Main entrance

Virgin and Child
This sculpture group, attributed to Domenico Gagini (c.1420–1492), comes from the Basilica di San Francesco d'Assisi in Palermo *(see p55)*. Note the delicate treatment of the Virgin's features.

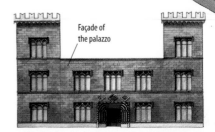

Façade of the palazzo

The Malvagna Triptych
This work by the Flemish artist Mabuse (1478–1532) portrays the Virgin and Child among angels and saints.

VISITORS' CHECKLIST

Practical Information
Via Alloro 4. **Map** 2 E3. **Tel** 091-623 00 11. **Open** 9am–6:30pm Tue–Fri, 9am–1pm Sat, Sun & hols. **Closed** Mon. 🎟 combined tickets with Palazzo Mirto available. 🎧 for tours in English see website. 🌐 regione.sicilia.it/beniculturali/palazzoabatellis/english/home.htm

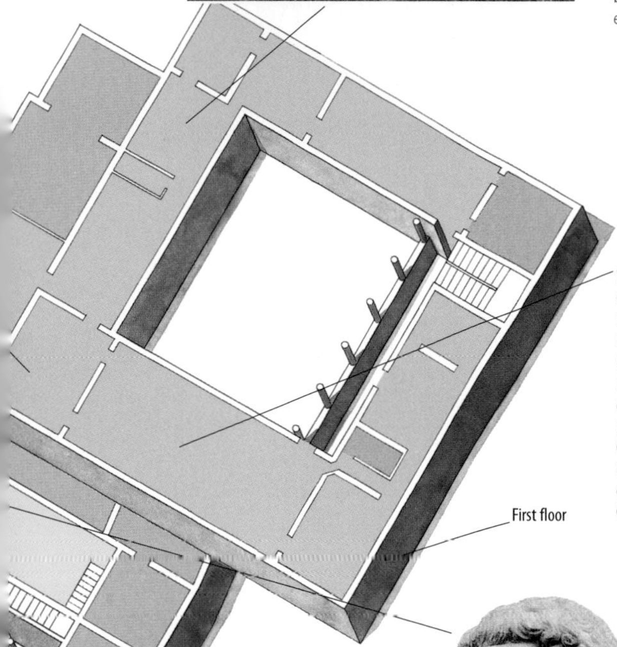

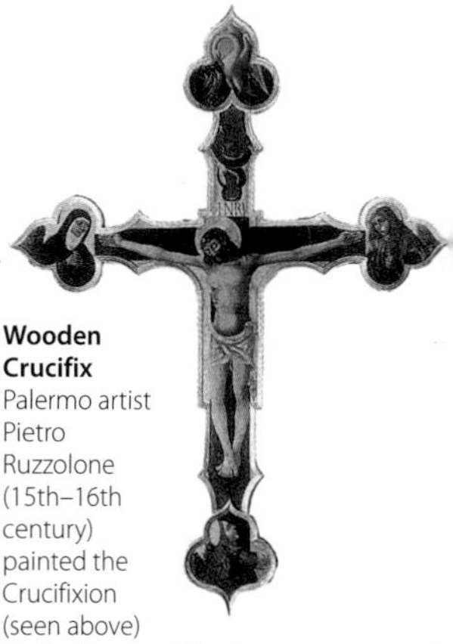

Wooden Crucifix
Palermo artist Pietro Ruzzolone (15th–16th century) painted the Crucifixion (seen above) on the front and the risen Christ on the reverse.

First floor

Portrait of a Youth
This work is attributed to Antonello Gagini (1478–1536), son of Domenico, and was once part of a statue of San Vito in the Palermo church of the same name. The facial features reveal the influence of Frescesco Laurana.

Ticket office

History of the Palazzo

Palazzo Abatellis was designed in 1490–95 by Matteo Carnalivari for Francesco Abatellis, the city's harbour-master and magistrate, who wanted to live in a luxurious mansion as befitted his social status. He died without leaving an heir, and his mansion was taken over by the Benedictine order and then by the Region of Sicily. It was damaged in the 1943 bombings and then restored by architect Carlo Scarpa.

The loggia

Key to Floorplan

- 🟦 12th-century carvings
- 🟦 14th–15th-century sculptures 14th–16th-century majolicas
- 🟦 5th–16th-century sculptures and paintings
- 🟦 13th–16th-century paintings
- 🟦 non-exhibition space

The Fontana Pretoria, once called "the fountain of shame" because of its statues of nude figures

❼ Fontana Pretoria

Piazza Pretoria. **Map** 1 C3.

Located in the middle of Palermo, this fountain is on a slightly higher level than Via Maqueda. It was designed in 1552–5 by Tuscan sculptor Francesco Camilliani for the garden of a Florentine villa and was later installed in Piazza Pretoria. The concentric basins are arranged on three levels, with statues of mythological creatures, monsters, tritons, sirens and the four rivers of Palermo (Oreto, Papireto, Gabriele, Maredolce). Due to the nude statues it was known as "the fountain of shame".

A statue on the Fontana Pretoria

❽ Palazzo delle Aquile

Piazza Pretoria. **Map** 1 C3. **Tel** 091-740 11 11. **Open** 9am–1:30pm, 3–7pm Mon–Fri, 9am–1pm Sat.

Its proper name is Palazzo Senatorio, or Palazzo del Municipio, but it is commonly called "delle Aquile" because of the four eagles (aquile)

decorating the exterior and the portal. Now the town hall, it is Palermo's major civic monument, although its original 16th-century structure was radically altered by 19th-century restoration. However, a statue of Santa Rosalia by Carlo Aprile (1661) still occupies a niche on the top of the façade. At the entrance, a grand staircase with a coffered ceiling takes you to the first floor and various public rooms: the Sala delle Lapidi, Sala dei Gonfaloni and Sala Rossa, which is also known as the Mayor's Hall.

❾ Santa Caterina d'Alessandria

Piazza Bellini. **Map** 1 C3.
Closed for restoration scheduled; to be completed in 2016.

The church of the Dominican monastery of Santa Caterina is a splendid example of Sicilian Baroque art, despite the fact that both buildings originated in the 14th century.

The main features of the late Renaissance façade (the present church was built in 1580–96) are its double stairway and the statue of St Catherine (Caterina) in the middle of the portal. The large cupola was built in the mid-18th century. The interior has marble inlay, sculpture pieces, stuccoes and frescoes. In the chapel to the right of the transept is a fine statue of Santa Caterina, sculpted by Antonello Gagini in 1534.

❿ La Martorana

Piazza Bellini 3. **Map** 1 C4. **Tel** 345 828 82 31. **Open** 9:30am–1pm, 3:30–5:30pm Mon–Sat, 9am–1pm Sun & hols.

Santa Maria dell'Ammiraglio is called La Martorana in memory of Eloisa della Martorana, who founded the nearby Bene-dictine convent. Eloisa used to decorate the church with handmade marzipan fruit; as a result, Frutta di Martorana is now one of Palermo's most famed delicacies. Built in 1143 on a Greek cross plan, this church was partly altered and enlarged in the Baroque period, and combines Norman features and decor with later

The portal on the Baroque façade of La Martorana

styles. You enter by the bell tower, whose dome was destroyed in the 1726 earthquake. The Baroque interior is decorated with stuccoes and enamel. The bay vaulting has frescoes and the original church was decorated with 12th-century mosaics. The cupola shows *Christ Pantocrator Surrounded by Angels*; on the tambour are *The Prophets* and *The Four Evangelists*, and on the walls are an *Annunciation, The Nativity* and *The Presentation at the Temple*. The most intriguing mosaic is of Roger II being crowned; it is the only known portrait of the king.

⓫ San Cataldo

Piazza Bellini 3. **Map** 1 C4. **Tel** 091-348 728. **Open** 9:30am–12:30pm, 3:30–5:30pm Mon–Sat, 9:30am–1:30pm Sun & hols.

San Cataldo was the chapel of a palazzo built by Maio of Bari, William I's admiral, in the 12th century. It has kept the linear Arab-Norman style, with three red domes raised above the wall, the windows with pointed arches and the battlement decoration. Inscriptions with quotations from the Koran can still be seen. The interior has no decoration except for the mosaic-patterned floor. In the middle of the nave is a series of Arab arches supported by ancient columns.

⓬ Galleria d'arte Moderna Sant'Anna

Via Sant'Anna 21, Palermo. **Map** 2 D3. **Tel** 091-843 16 05. **Open** 9:30am–6:30pm Tue–Sun.

Housed in the restored 15th-century convent of Sant'Anna, this gallery features a range of works from the past 150 years. Many of the Italian and international artists on display have featured prominently in the Venice Biennale.

⓭ La Magione

Via Magione 44. **Map** 2 D4. **Tel** 091-617 05 96. **Open** summer: 9am–7pm daily; winter: 9am–7pm Mon–Sat, 9am–1pm Sun. Cloister & Chapels: **Open** 9:30am–6:30pm Mon–Sat, 9:30am–12:30pm Sun & hols.

Founded by Matteo d'Aiello in the mid-1100s, this church was frequently rebuilt and was then damaged in the bombings of 1943. Careful restoration has revived its original Norman features. A Baroque portico, with marble columns and statues, affords access to a garden. The façade has three doorways with double arched lintels and convex rustication, a series of blind arches and windows. Pointed arches run along the length of the nave.

The roofless interior of Santa Maria dello Spasimo

⓮ Santa Maria dello Spasimo

Via dello Spasimo. **Map** 2 E4. **Tel** 091-616 14 86. **Open** 9:30am–5:30pm daily.

Santa Maria dello Spasimo lies in the heart of the Kalsa quarter. It was founded in 1506 by the monks of Santa Maria di Monte Oliveto and was dedicated to the Virgin Mary grieving before Christ on the Cross, subject of a painting by Raphael in 1516, which is now in the Prado Museum in Madrid. Santa Maria was the last example of Spanish Gothic architecture in the city. The cells and courtyards of the monastery were built around the church and in 1536 the complex, at that time outside the city walls, was incorporated into a rampart, so that it now looks like a watchtower.

The church was bought by the city and became, in turn, a theatre, warehouse, hospice and hospital, while all the time falling into a state of neglect. In 1995, the Spasimo area was redeveloped and transformed into a cultural centre for exhibitions and concerts. Performances are held inside the church, part of which no longer has a roof.

San Cataldo, with its characteristic Arab architectural elements

One of the rooms in the Museo Archeologico Regionale

⑮ Museo Archeologico Regionale A. Salinas

Piazza Olivella 24. **Map** 1 C2. **Tel** 091-611 68 05/6/7. **Open** 9am–1:15pm, 3–6:15pm Mon–Fri, 9am–1:15pm Sat, Sun & hols. 🖼

The Archaeological Museum is housed in a 17th-century monastery and holds treasures from excavations across the island. The entrance leads to a small cloister with a fountain bearing a statue of Triton. The former cells contain finds such as the large Phoenician sarcophagi in the shape of human beings (6th–5th centuries BC) and the *Pietra di Palermo*, a slab with a hieroglyphic inscription from 2900 BC. On the first floor there is a display of Punic inscriptions and objects, as well as terracotta and bronze sculpture, including a fine 3rd-century BC ram's head. On the second floor is the Sala dei Mosaici, with mosaics and frescoes from digs at Palermo, Solunto and Marsala. The large cloister houses Roman statues, slabs and tombstones. At the end of the cloister are three rooms with the marvellous pieces taken from the temples at Selinunte; these include a lovely leonine head from the Temple of Victory and the valuable metopes from other temples.

Those from Temple C represent *Helios's Chariot, Perseus Helped by Athena while Killing the Gorgon* and *Heracles Punishing the Cercopes*; the metopes from Temple E are *Heracles Fighting the Amazons, Hera and Zeus on Mount Ida, Actaeon Attacked by Dogs in the Presence of Artemis (see p26)* and *Athena Slaying the Giant Enceladus*.

Roman head, Museo Archeologico

⑯ Mercato della Vucciria

Piazza Caracciolo and adjacent streets. **Map** 1 C3.

This is Palermo's most famous market, immortalized by Renato Guttuso in his painting *La Vucciria (see p218)*. There are two theories as to the origin of the market's name. Some say it is a corruption of the French *boucherie*, or butcher, while others suggest the name means "the place of loud voices", from when vendors called out their wares. Today, this outdoor marketplace trades not only in vegetables, dried fruit and preserves, but also in other foods such as cheese, fish and meat, amid a tumult of colours, sounds and smells reminiscent of the souks in North Africa. The Vucciria is especially impressive in the morning, when the fishmongers set up shop. There are stalls that serve sea urchin or will do skewered giblets for you on the spot. Another speciality is boiled spleen and liver fried in lard, also used for making *ca' meusa* bread, the locals' favourite snack. To get to the market, from Piazza San Domenico take Via Maccheronai, once the colourful pasta-producing area, where freshly made pasta was hung out to dry.

⑰ Oratorio del Rosario di Santa Cita

Via Valverde 3. **Map** 1 C2. **Tel** 091-332 779. **Open** Apr–Oct: 9am–6pm Mon–Fri, 9am–3pm Sat; Nov–Mar: 9am–3pm Mon–Sat. 🖼

Founded in 1590 by the Society of the Rosary, this was one of the city's richest oratories. A marble staircase opens onto a cloister and then goes up to an upper loggia decorated with marble busts, and to the vestibule, with portraits of the Superiors of the Society. The Oratory is an example of

The Mercato della Vucciria, Palermo's colourful open-air market

The Baroque façade of San Domenico

transept is adorned with lateral vo025tes and bronze friezes, while the 18th-century high altar is made of marble and decorated with semi-precious stones.

⑲ Oratorio del Rosario di San Domenico

Via dei Bambinai. **Map** 1 C2. **Tel** 091-332 779. **Open** Apr–Oct: 9am–6pm Mon–Fri, 9am–3pm Sat; Nov–Mar: 9am–3pm Mon–Sat.

Behind San Lorenzo, in the Vucciria market area, is the Oratory of San Domenico, founded at the end of the 16th century by the Society of the Holy Rosary. Two Society members were painter Pietro Novelli and sculptor Giacomo Serpotta, who left the marks of their genius on this elegant monument.

The black and white majolica floors fit in well with the tumult of figures of great ladies, knights and playful putti. These form a kind of frame for the statues of Christian virtues by Giacomo Serpotta and the paintings representing the mysteries of the Rosary. The latter were executed by Pietro Novelli and Flemish artists, while the altarpiece, *Madonna of the Rosary with St Dominic and the Patronesses of Palermo*, was painted by Van Dyck in 1628. In the middle of the vault is Novelli's *Coronation of the Virgin*.

Giacomo Serpotta's best work *(see p39)*, a lavish display of Baroque decoration, its fusion of putti volutes, statues, floral elements and festoons creating an amazing theatrical atmosphere. The *Battle of Lepanto* sculpture group *(see p39)* is spectacular. On the sides of the tribune are statues of Esther and Judith, while the altarpiece is Carlo Maratta's *Madonna of the Rosary* (1695). Along the walls are seats with mother-of-pearl inlay; the floor is made of red, white and black marble.

⑱ San Domenico

Piazza San Domenico. **Map** 1 C3. **Tel** 338-722 87 75/451 20 11. **Open** 9:30am–12:30pm Tue–Sat.

This basilica, which belongs to the Dominican monastery, has been rebuilt many times over the past six centuries. The most drastic alteration was in 1640, when Andrea Cirincione tore

down part of the cloister to enlarge the church. In 1724, when Piazza San Domenico was remodelled, the façade was rebuilt and is now animated by the fusion of curves on the one hand, and jutting columns and statues, niches and twin bell towers on the other. The interior has a typical Latin cross plan with two aisles and a deep semicircular dome. The total lack of decoration serves to heighten the elegance of the archi-tecture. In contrast, the chapels, used since the 19th century as the burial place for the city's most illustrious personages, are quite richly decorated. The third chapel is the tomb of the Oneto di Sperlinga family and has multicoloured marble funerary monuments, a statue of St Joseph by Antonello Gagini, and stucco- and putti-decorated walls. The altar in the

Detail of stucco-work, Santa Cita

Van Dyck's fine canvas stands behind the Oratorio del Rosario di San Domenico's altar

WEST PALERMO

The quarters south of Via Roma lie on the slopes occupied by the city's original Phoenician settlement, which was enlarged during the Roman era. In the 11th century the Arabs built a castle on the site where the Palazzo dei Normanni now stands. The Arabic *Al Qasar* (the castle) was used as the name of the quarter and the street that led to the castle, the present-day Corso Vittorio Emanuele, known as "Cassaro" to the people of Palermo. The area contains many impressive buildings and churches, including Palermo's Cathedral, as well as

good shops and hotels. Between the Palazzo dei Normanni and Via Maqueda is the Albergheria quarter, the home of merchants and craftsmen in the Middle Ages. It is still enlivened by the daily market, the Mercato Ballarò, which is less famous but more authentic than the Vucciria market. The many oratories of the medieval brotherhoods demonstrate the wealth and industry of the inhabitants. In the first half of the 20th century parts of the area were demolished, and the 1943 air raids dealt an additional blow.

Sights at a Glance

Streets and Squares
1 Piazza della Vittoria
6 Corso Vittorio Emanuele
8 Quattro Canti

Churches
3 Cappella Palatina (pp66–7)
4 San Giovanni degli Eremiti
5 Cathedral (pp70–71)
9 San Giuseppe dei Teatini
10 Chiesa del Gesù and Casa Professa

11 Sant'Orsola
12 Chiesa del Carmine

Historic Buildings
2 Palazzo dei Normanni
7 Museo Regionale d'Arte Moderna E Contemporanea Belmonte-Riso
13 Teatro Massimo

See also Street Finder map 1

| 0 metres | 350 |
| 0 yards | 350 |

Street-by-Street: Around Piazza della Vittoria

Piazza della Vittoria, opposite the Palazzo dei Normanni, is one of the city's major squares. Since the time of the Roman *castrum superius* (military camp), the Arab Al Qasar and the Norman Palace, this area has been the military, political and administrative heart of Sicily, and religious prestige was added in the 12th century when the Cathedral was built nearby. In the 17th and 18th centuries the square was the venue for public festivities. It became a public garden in the early 1900s, surrounded by important monuments such as Porta Nuova, Palazzo Sclafani and Palazzo Arcivescovile.

The monument to Philip V, in the middle of Piazza della Vittoria, was built of marble in 1662.

The former hospital of San Giacomo

Porta Nuova was built in 1569 to commemorate Charles V's arrival in Palermo in 1535.

CORSO VITTO

PIAZZA DEL PARLAMENTO

❷ Palazzo dei Normanni
This has always been the palace of the city's rulers. Traces of the original Arab-Norman architecture can still be seen on the exterior.

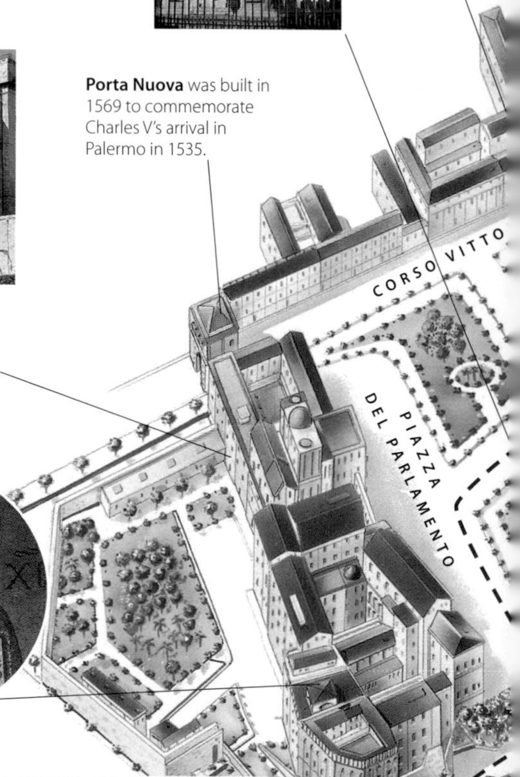

❸ ★ Cappella Palatina
Founded in 1130 by the Norman king Roger II, the chapel boasts an extraordinary cycle of mosaics.

❹ ★ San Giovanni degli Eremiti
This church, surrounded by a luxuriant garden, is one of the most important monuments in Palermo, partly because of its unique Arab-Norman architecture.

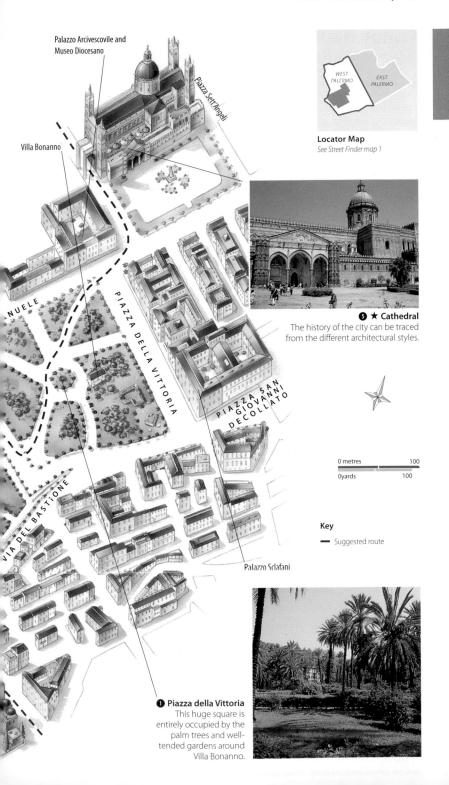

Palazzo Arcivescovile and
Museo Diocesano

Piazza Sett'Angeli

Villa Bonanno

NUELE

PIAZZA DELLA VITTORIA

PIAZZA SAN
GIOVANNI
DECOLLATO

VIA DEL BASTIONE

Palazzo Sclafani

Locator Map
See Street Finder map 1

WEST
PALERMO

EAST
PALERMO

5 ★ Cathedral
The history of the city can be traced
from the different architectural styles.

| 0 metres | 100 |
| 0 yards | 100 |

Key
— Suggested route

1 Piazza della Vittoria
This huge square is
entirely occupied by the
palm trees and well-
tended gardens around
Villa Bonanno.

❸ Cappella Palatina

Founded in 1132 by Roger II *(see pp32–3)*, the Cappella Palatina with its splendid mosaics is a jewel of Arab-Norman art. The basilica has two side aisles and three apses with granite columns dividing the nave. The walls are decorated with biblical scenes. On the cupola and the bowl of the central apse is the image of *Christ Pantocrator surrounded by angels*, while the niches house the *Four Evangelists*. Old Testament kings and prophets are on the arches, *Christ blessing the faithful* dominates the middle apse, and the transept walls bear scenes from the Gospel. Other important features are the wooden ceiling, a masterpiece of Muslim art, and the marble pulpit and candelabrum. The overall harmony of the design, and the perfection of the details, make this a unique monument.

★ The Central Apse
In the middle is the Christ Pantocrator; below him the Virgin Mary and the saints.

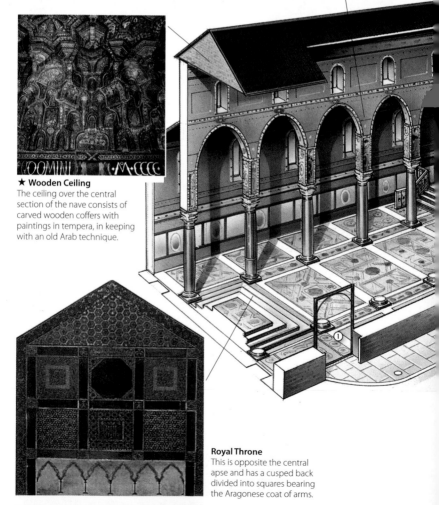

★ Wooden Ceiling
The ceiling over the central section of the nave consists of carved wooden coffers with paintings in tempera, in keeping with an old Arab technique.

Royal Throne
This is opposite the central apse and has a cusped back divided into squares bearing the Aragonese coat of arms.

★ Christ Pantocrator

In the middle of the cupola is this glory of mosaic decoration, the figure of Christ Pantocrator, surrounded by angels and archangels dressed in Norman warrior garb.

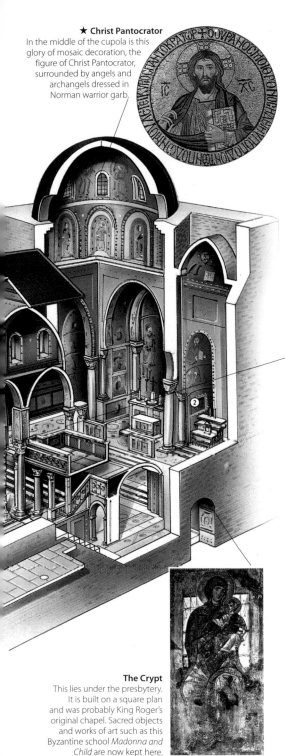

VISITORS' CHECKLIST

Practical Information
Piazza Indipendenza. **Map** 1 A5.
Tel 091-626 28 33. **Open**
8:15am–5pm Mon–Sat,
8:15am–12:15pm Sun & hols.
w federicosecondo.org

Candelabrum

Made entirely of white marble, this beautiful candelabrum is the oldest Romanesque work of art in Sicily. Four lions devouring animals decorate the base, while there are interlaced floral and human motifs along the shaft. On the top are three slender figures supporting the disc that held the Easter candle.

The Crypt

This lies under the presbytery. It is built on a square plan and was probably King Roger's original chapel. Sacred objects and works of art such as this Byzantine school *Madonna and Child* are now kept here.

KEY

① **The entrance** is a 19th-century portal with a two-winged wooden door.

② **The side apse** is decorated with images of St Paul and the Virgin Mary.

Piazza della Vittoria, with Palazzo dei Normanni in the background

❶ Piazza della Vittoria

This square is completely occupied by the **Villa Bonanno** garden. In the middle is the **Teatro Marmoreo** fountain, built in honour of Philip V, with statues of the continents partly under this ruler's dominion (Europe, America, Asia and Africa). Archaeological digs have unearthed Roman villas and mosaics; the finds are in the Museo Archeologico Regionale *(see p60)* and the Sala dell'Orfeo pavilion. Among the palazzi and churches facing the square are the Baroque **Cappella della Soledad**, with multicoloured marble and stucco decoration, and the former hospital of **San Giacomo** (now the Bonsignore barracks), with the lovely Norman **Santa Maria Maddalena** in the interior.

❷ Palazzo dei Normanni

Piazza Indipendenza. **Map** 1 A5. **Tel** 091-626 28 33. **Open** 8:15am–5pm Mon, Fri & Sat; 8:15am–12:15pm Sun & hols. 🖼 🖳 **federicosecondo.org**

The Arabs built this palace over the ruins of a Punic fortress in the 11th century. The following century it was enlarged and became the royal palace of the Norman king Roger II, with Arab architects and craftsmen building towers and pavilions for the king and his retinue. Not much is left from the Norman age,

partly because the palace was abandoned when Frederick II left his Palermo court. The Spanish viceroys preferred to use the more modern Palazzo Steri. The present-day appearance of the palace, now the seat of the Sicilian Regional Assembly, dates back to alterations made in the 16th and 17th centuries. The entrance is in Piazza Indipendenza. A short walk uphill is the Maqueda courtyard, built in 1600 with three rows of arcades and a large staircase leading to the first floor and the Cappella Palatina *(see pp66–7)*, one of the few parts remaining from the Norman period. The royal apartments, which now house the Sicilian Parliament, are on

the second floor and can only be visited accompanied by a guard. The most interesting room is the Sala di Re Ruggero, the walls and arches of which are covered with 12th-century mosaics with animal and plant motifs in a naturalistic vein that probably reveals a Persian influence: there are centaurs, leopards, lions, deer and peacocks. The vault has geometric motifs and medallions with owls, deer, centaurs and lions. The tour ends with the Chinese Room, frescoed by Giovanni and Salvatore Patricolo, and the Sala Gialla, with tempera decoration on the vaults.

❸ Cappella Palatina

See pp66–7.

❹ San Giovanni degli Eremiti

Via dei Benedettini 18. **Map** 1 A5. **Tel** 091-651 50 19. **Open** 9am–6:30pm Mon–Sat, 9am–1pm Sun & hols. 🖼

Built in 1132 for Roger II *(see pp32–3)* over the foundation of a Benedictine monastery that had been constructed in 581, San Giovanni degli Eremiti displays a clearly Oriental influence. It was built by Arab-Norman craftsmen and labourers, and their work is

King Roger's Hall in Palazzo dei Normanni, showing the mosaics

The five typically Arab domes on San Giovanni degli Eremiti

at its most striking in the red domes and cubic forms. The delightful garden of citrus trees, pomegranate, roses and jasmine leads to the ruins of the monastery, a small cloister with twin columns and pointed arches.

The cross-plan interior has an aisle-less nave ending in the presbytery with three apses. The right-hand apse is covered by one of the red domes, while above the left-hand one is a fine bell tower with pointed windows and a smaller red dome on top.

❺ Cathedral

See pp70–71.

❻ Corso Vittorio Emanuele

This is the main street in the heart of Palermo, which lies on the Phoenician road that connected the ancient city and the seaside. The locals call it "Cassaro", from the Arab *Al Qasar*, or castle, to which the road led. In the Middle Ages it was the most important artery in the city, but in the 1500s it became an elegant street. In that period the street was extended to the sea, and two city gates were built: **Porta Felice** to the north and **Porta Nuova** to the south, next to Palazzo dei Normanni. It was called Via Toledo during the Spanish period. The stretch

between Porta Nuova and the Quattro Canti boasts several patrician mansions. On the western side is the former hospital of San Giacomo, now the Bonsignore barracks; the Baroque **Collegio Massimo dei Gesuiti**, the present Regional Library; **Palazzo Geraci**, a Baroque residence rebuilt in the Rococo style; the **Palazzo Belmonte-Riso**, which houses the Contemporary Art Museum; and the 18th-century **Palazzo Tarallo della Miraglia**, restored as the Hotel Centrale. On the eastern side are **San Salvatore**, a lavishly decorated Baroque church and **San Giuseppe dei Teatini**. Just beyond Vicolo Castelbuono is **Piazza Bologni**, which has several Baroque buildings, among them the Palazzo Alliata di Villafranca.

❼ Museo Regionale d'Arte Moderna e Contemporanea Belmonte-Riso

Corsa Vittorio Emanuele 365. **Tel** 091-320 532. **Open** 10am–7:30pm Tue, Wed, Sun; 10am–midnight Thu–Sat.

In a restored palazzo right in front of the Piazza Bologni, the Contemporary Art Gallery was conceived as a multi-functional centre, with a bookshop, café and multimedia room on the premises. The palazzo itself was built in 1784 by Venanzio Marvuglia, who was one of the most prolific architects of the time. The collection has been laid out so that the whole building can be admired; works are placed both inside and outside the museum, taking visitors through old courtyards and hidden corners. Works by artists such as Pietro Consagra, Allesandro Bazan and Carla Accardi are part of the permanent collection.

❽ Quattro Canti

Piazza Vigliena. **Map** 1 C3.

The intersection of Corso Vittorio Emanuele and Via Maqueda is Palermo's most fashionable square. Quattro Canti dates from 1600, when the new town plan was put into effect and the city was divided into four parts, called *Mandamenti*: the northeastern *Kalsa* section, the southeastern one of Albergheria, Capo to the southwest and Castellammare or Loggia in the southeast. The piazza is rounded, shaped by the concave façades of the four corner buildings (hence the name) with superimposed architectural orders – Doric, Corinthian and Ionic. Each façade is decorated with a fountain and statues of the *Mandamenti* patron saints, of the seasons and of the Spanish kings.

One of the façades of the Quattro Canti

❺ Cathedral

Dedicated to Our Lady of the Assumption, the Cathedral stands on the site of an Early Christian basilica, later a mosque. It was built in 1179–85 but, because of frequent rebuilding and alterations, very little of the original structure remains. In the late 1700s the nave was widened and the central cupola was added. The original Norman structure can be seen under the small cupolas with majolica tiles, with the typical arched crenellation decoration on the wall tops. The exteriors of the apses have maintained their original character with interlaced arches and small columns. As a result of the mixture of styles, the right-hand side forms a kind of "carved history" of the city. Opposite the façade, on the other side of the street, is the medieval campanile. The tiara of Constance of Aragón *(see p3 and p37)* is kept here.

Cupolas with Majolica Tiles
The small cupolas were built in 1781 over the side chapels, the addition of which drastically changed the Cathedral's original plan.

KEY

① **The portal** was built in the 1400s and is decorated with a two-winged wooden door with a mosaic of the Virgin Mary above.

② **The cupola**, in Baroque style, was added in the late 1700s to a design by Ferdinando Fuga.

③ **The arched crenellation motif** characteristic of Norman architecture runs along the right side of the Cathedral.

④ **The exterior of the apses**, decorated with interlaced arches, is the best preserved part of the original design.

★ Catalan Gothic Portico
The work of Antonio Gambara (1430), the portico has three pointed arches and a Gothic tympanum with Biblical scenes and the city coat of arms in bas-relief.

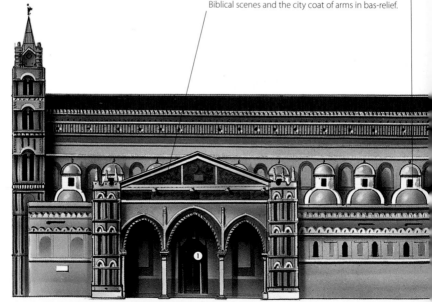

The Interior of the Cathedral

Alterations carried out in the 18th century gave the interior a Neo-Classical look. Of the many chapels, the most important are the first two on the right-hand side of the nave with the Imperial tombs, and the chapel of Santa Rosalia, where the saint's remains are in a silver coffer on the altar.

The Cappella di Santa Rosalia, patron saint of Palermo

Middle section of the nave, with statues by Antonello Gagini

VISITORS' CHECKLIST

Practical Information
Corso Vittorio Emanuele. **Map** 1 B4. **Tel** 091-334 373. **Open** Mar–Oct: 9am–5:30pm Mon–Sat; Nov–Feb: 9:30am–1pm Mon–Sat. Sun: open only between services. 🕐 7:30am, 6pm Mon–Sat; 8:45am, 9:45am, 11am, 6pm Sun & hols. 🌐 to visit tomb area, crypt and roofs. **W** cattedrale.palermo.it

Transport
🚌 104.

★ **Towers with Gothic Double Lancet Windows**
The slender Gothic turrets with their lancet windows were added to the 12th-century Norman clock tower in the 14th–15th centuries.

Arab Inscription
Various parts of the former mosque were retained in the Cathedral, such as this passage from the Koran inscribed on the left-hand column of the southern portico.

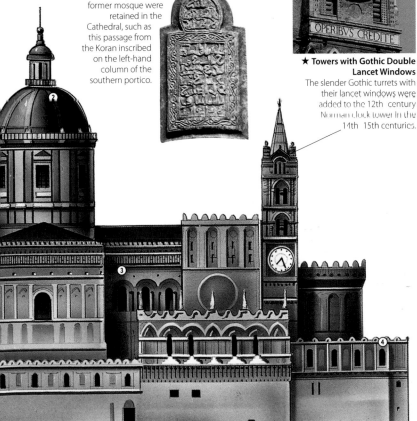

The lavishly decorated Baroque interior of the Chiesa del Gesù

❾ San Giuseppe dei Teatini

Piazza Pretoria. **Map** 1 C4. **Tel** 091-331 239. **Open** mid-Jul–mid-Sep: 7:30–11am, 6–8pm Mon–Sat, 9am–noon, 6:15–8pm Sun; mid-Sep–mid-Jul: 7:30am–noon, 5:30–8pm Mon–Sat, 8:30am–1pm, 6–8pm Sun.

The Theatine congregation spared no expense in the construction of this church (1612–45). Despite the fact that the façade was finished in 1844 in Neo-Classical style, the church exudes a Baroque spirit, beginning with the cupola covered with majolica tiles. The two-aisle nave is flanked by huge columns, the ceiling is frescoed and the walls are covered with polychrome marble decoration. On either side of the entrance are two marble stoups held up by angels. The chapels are richly decorated with stucco and frescoes, and the high altar is made of semi-precious stones.

❿ Chiesa del Gesù and Casa Professa

Piazza Casa Professa. **Map** 1 C4. **Tel** 091-580 655, 338-451 20 11/722 87 75. **Open** 9:30am–1:30pm, 4–7pm Mon–Sat; 9am–12:30pm & 5–6:30pm Sun & hols.

This church perhaps represents the peak of Baroque art in Palermo. The late 16th-century façade was one of the sets for the film *Il Gattopardo (The Leopard; see p28).* Work on the decoration began in 1597 and was interrupted permanently when the Jesuits were expelled in 1860. The interior is entirely covered with marble inlay – walls, columns and floor – in a profusion of forms and colours, blending in well with the fine stuccoes of Giacomo Serpotta *(see p39),* the imitation bas-relief columns and the various decorative motifs. The pulpit in the middle of the nave was the work of the Genoese School (1646). To the right of the church is the western section of the Casa Professa, with a 1685 portal and an 18th-century cloister affording access to the City Library.

⓫ Sant'Orsola

Via Maqueda. **Map** 1 C4. **Tel** 091-616 23 21. **Open** 8:30–11am. Oratory visits by request only.

Sant'Orsola was built in the early 17th century by the Society of St Ursula, known as "Dei Negri" because of the dark habits the members wore during processions. The late Renaissance façade is decorated with figures of souls in Purgatory and angels. Three skulls lie on the architrave. The aisle-less interior is an example of a light-filled Baroque church, with deep semicircular chapels linked by galleries. The vault over the nave is decorated with the fresco *The Glory of St Ursula* and two medallions depicting Faith and Charity. The painting *The Martyrdom of St Ursula* by Pietro Novelli *(see p27)* is in the second chapel on the right, while frescoes of scenes of the saint's life are on the vault. Another work by Novelli, *Madonna with the Salvator Mundi,* is in the sacristy. From the sacristy there is access to the Oratorio di Sant'Orsola, decorated with 17th-century paintings and stucco sculpture.

The 18th-century cloister of the Casa Professa

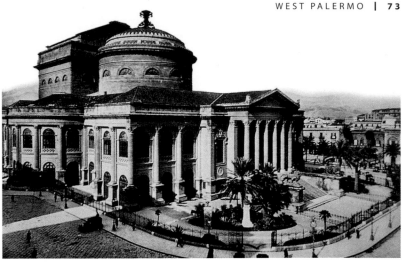

An old commemorative postcard of the Teatro Massimo, Palermo's opera house

⑫ Chiesa del Carmine

Via Giovanni Grasso 13a. **Map** 1 C5. **Tel** 091-651 20 18. **Open** 8:30–11:30am Mon–Sat.

This church, seat of the Carmelite friars, dates from the 1600s. It lies on a much higher level than the nearby Mercato del Ballarò and is topped by a cupola covered with multicoloured majolica tiles supported by four Atlantes. The interior is dominated by an altar resting on pairs of spiral columns decorated with stuccoes by Giuseppe and Giacomo Serpotta (1683) of scenes from the life of Mary. The painting by Pietro Novelli *(see p27)*, *The Vision of Sant'Andrea Corsini*, is also worth a look.

⑬ Teatro Massimo

Piazza Giuseppe Verdi. **Map** 1 B2. **Tel** 091-605 35 21. **Open** for tours: 9:30am–5:30pm Tue–Sun (not during rehearsals). 🚇 🛒 **teatromassimo.it**

The Teatro Massimo is one of the symbols of Palermo's rebirth. Designed in 1864 by Italian architect Giovanni Battista Filippo Basile, it was finished in 1897. In order to make room for it, the city walls of Porta Maqueda, the Aragonese quarter, San Giuliano convent and church, and the Chiesa delle Stimmate di San Francesco and its monastery were all demolished.

Dedicated to King Victor Emanuel II, its 7,700 sq m (9,200 sq yd) makes this not only the biggest opera house in Italy, but also one of the largest in Europe. The exterior is superbly designed in Neo-Classical style and features elements from the Greek temples at Selinunte and Agrigento.

The theatre now boasts five rows of boxes, a lavishly decorated gallery and a ceiling frescoed by Ettore Maria Bergler and Rocco Lentini. The entrance, with its Corinthian columns, is also monumental in style.

Groups of ten or more can attend the interesting Cocktail Tour, which is a special guided tour of the theatre that includes having a cocktail in the Royal Box. Alternatively, the Backstage Tour offers behind-the-scenes access to the sets of the Massimo. Both tours require at least a week's advance booking.

The cupola with polychrome majolica tiles, Chiesa del Carmine

The Albergheria Quarter

The Albergheria is one of the poorest and most run-down quarters in the old town, but it is also one of the most intriguing. The highlight is the Mercato di Ballarò, one of the best markets in the city, a vivid combination of colours, smells and lively atmosphere. Here you can taste and purchase typical Sicilian produce. Locals buy vegetables, meat, fish and also many household items. However, a visit to the market is not complete without tasting the delicious *panelle* (pancakes made using chickpea flour), served in a bread roll with some excellent seasoning.

Detail of a mural in the Albergheria quarter

FURTHER AFIELD

The destruction of the 16th-century defensive ramparts took place in the late 1700s, but it was only after the Unification of Italy that Palermo expanded westwards past the city walls, which involved making new roads and demolishing old quarters. The heart of town shifted to Piazzas Verdi and Castelnuovo, where the Massimo and Politeama theatres were built. This expansion also meant the disappearance of most of the lovely Arab-Norman gardens and parks the rulers had used for hunting and entertainment. Only a few, such as Castello della Zisa, have remained. At this time, "Greater Palermo" was created – an area that now includes Mondello and Monreale Cathedral.

Sights at a Glance

Galleries and Museums
4 Museo Etnografico Pitrè

Historic Buildings
3 Casina Cinese
5 Teatro Politeama Garibaldi
7 Castello della Zisa

8 La Cuba
13 Ponte dell'Ammiraglio

Churches
6 Catacombe dei Cappuccini
11 Santo Spirito
12 San Giovanni dei Lebbrosi
14 Monreale Cathedral pp80–81

Parks and Gardens
2 Parco della Favorita
9 Villa Giulia
10 Orto Botanico

Beaches
1 Mondello

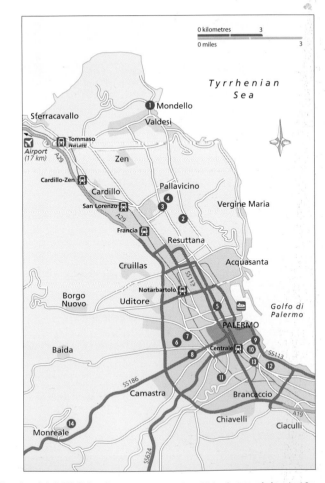

Key
- Historic centre
- Urban area
- Motorway (Highway)
- Major road
- Minor road
- Railway line

◀ Frescoed pavilion in the Pompeian style in the Villa Giulia gardens

For additional map symbols *see back flap*

The lively fishing harbour at Mondello, filled with boats

❶ Mondello

10 km (6 miles) north of Palermo.

A favourite with Palermitans, Mondello beach lies a short distance from the centre of the town, between the rocky promontories of Monte Pellegrino and Monte Gallo. Mondello was once a small village of tuna fishermen, centred around a 15th-century square tower, but in the last 100 years it has become a residential area immersed in greenery. Mondello's golden age was at the turn of the 19th century, when a kind of garden-city was founded and well-to-do Palermitans had lovely Art Nouveau villas built here. The Kursaal bathhouse, built on piles in the sea a few yards from the beach, also dates from this period. Designed by Rudolph Stualket in the Art Nouveau style, it is decorated with mythological figures and sea monsters. Mondello is a popular town, perhaps even more so on summer evenings, when the city dwellers come to escape from the heat and dine in one of the many fish and seafood restaurants lining the road in the old fishing quarter.

❷ Parco della Favorita

Viale Ercole, Viale Diana.

This public park, unfortunately in a state of neglect, extends for almost 3 km (2 miles) behind Monte Pellegrino. It was originally a hunting reserve, but King Ferdinand I *(see p33)* turned it into a garden in 1799, when he fled to Palermo with his retinue after being forced into exile from Naples by Napoleon's troops. The park has two large roads. Viale Diana, which goes to Mondello, is intersected by Viale d'Ercole, at the end of which is a marble fountain with a statue of Hercules, a copy of the famous *Farnese Hercules* that the king had wanted for himself in his court at Naples.

Most of the park is occupied by sports facilities (tennis courts, pools, a stadium and racetrack). On the edge of the park there are many villas built in the 18th century as summer residences for the Sicilian nobility. The most interesting are the Villa Sofia, now a hospital; Villa Castelnuovo, an agricultural institute; and Villa Niscemi, mentioned in di Lampedusa's novel *The Leopard (see p27)*, now the venue for cultural activities.

The extravagant façade of the Casina Cinese

❸ Casina Cinese

Viale Duca degli Abruzzi, Parco della Favorita. **Tel** 091-707 14 08.
Open 9am–5pm Tue–Sat, 9am–1pm Sun & public hols.

At the edge of the Parco della Favorita, the former hunting grounds of the Bourbons, is the "little Chinese palace", the summer residence of Ferdinand I and his wife Maria Carolina during their period of exile in Sicily. It was designed by Venanzio Marvuglia in 1799 and,

Sanctuary of Santa Rosalia on Monte Pellegrino

Period print of Santa Rosalia's float

On Monte Pellegrino, which dominates the city, is the Sanctuary dedicated to Santa Rosalia, the patron saint of Palermo. The daughter of the Duke of Sinibaldo, Rosalia decided to lead the life of a hermit in a cave. Five centuries after her death in 1166, the discovery of her remains coincided exactly with the end of the plague that had struck the city. Since then the saint has been venerated twice a year: on 11–15 July a triumphal float with her remains is taken in a procession through the city, and on 4 September the same procession goes to the Sanctuary. This was built in 1625; it consists of a convent and the saint's cave, filled with ex-voto offerings.

it seems, the king himself had a hand in the palace's Oriental architecture, which was much in vogue at the time. Ferdinand I entertained such illustrious guests as Horatio Nelson and his wife, Lady Hamilton, here.

The Casina Cinese was the first example of eclectic architecture in Palermo, a combination of Chinese decorative motifs and Gothic, Egyptian and Arab elements. Overall it is an extravagant work, exemplified by details such as the repetition of bells in the shape of a pagoda on the fence, the cornices and the roof. The interior is equally flamboyant: Neo-Classical stuccoes and paintings are combined with 18th-century chinoiserie, scenes of Chinese life and Pompeian painting. The building is undergoing an extensive renovation to bring it back to its original splendour.

❹ Museo Etnografico Pitré

Viale Duca degli Abruzzi. **Tel** 091-616 01 24. **Open** 9:30am–6pm Tue–Sun.

The Ethnographic Museum, next to the Casina Cinese, has a collection of about 4,000 exhibits, documenting Sicilian life, traditions and folk art. The museum was

Aerial view of the Neo-Classical Politeama

founded in honour of the Palermian ethnographer Giuseppe Pitré, who wrote the first bilingual Italian-Sicilian dictionary; the library houses over 26,000 volumes. Rooms feature local embroidery and weaving, along with sections on traditional costumes and rugs. A great many display cases contain ceramics and glassware, as well as a fine collection of oil lamps. A further section displays traditional Sicilian carts, late 19th-century glass painting, and carts and floats dedicated to Santa Rosalia. The Sala del Teatrino dell'Opera dei Pupi has on display a number of rod

puppets, which are traditional characters in Sicilian puppet opera, as well as playbills decorated with scenes taken from the puppeteers' works. The Sala dei Presepi features more than 300 nativity scenes, some by the 18th-century artist Giocanni Matera.

❺ Teatro Politeama Garibaldi

Piazza Ruggero Settimo. **Map** 1 B1. **Tel** 091-607 25 11 (box office 091-607 25 32).

This historic theatre is in the heart of modern-day Palermo, at the corner of Via Ruggero Settimo and tree-lined Viale della Libertà, the city's "outdoor living room". Giuseppe Damiani Almeyda designed the Neo-Classical building in 1867–74. The theatre's semi-circular shape resembles a horseshoe, while the columns in the two tiers of colonnades are in the Doric and Ionian orders. The exterior is frescoed in Pompeii red and gold, in tune with the Neo-Classical movement at the time. The façade is a triumphal arch whose attic level is decorated with sculpture crowned by a chariot. While the Teatro Massimo was closed, the Politeama was the centre of the city's cultural life. It still plays host to some operatic and theatrical performances (Oct–Jun).

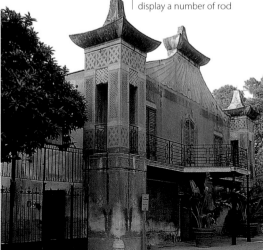
Entrance to the Museo Pitré, devoted to Sicilian folk art and customs

❻ Catacombe dei Cappuccini

Via Cappuccini. **Tel** 091-652 41 56 or 329-415 04 62. **Open** 9am–12:30pm, 3–5:30pm. **Closed** Oct–Mar: Sun pm.

The catacombs of the Capuchins contain the bodies – some mummified, others skeletons – of the prelates and well-to-do citizens of Palermo. They are divided according to sex, profession and social standing, wearing their best clothes, some of which are moth-eaten. Visitors can see the cells where the corpses were put to dry. At the end of the stairway is the body of the first friar "buried" here, Fra' Silvestro da Gubbio, who died in 1599. In 1881, interment in the catacombs ceased, but on display in the Cappella dell' Addolorata is the body of a little girl who died in 1920 and was so skilfully embalmed that she seems asleep. In the outdoor cemetery behind the catacombs is the tomb of Giuseppe di Lampedusa.

❼ Castello della Zisa

Piazza Zisa 1. **Tel** 091-652 02 69. **Open** 9am–7pm Mon–Sat, 9am–1:30pm Sun & hols. Museo d'Arte Islamica: **Open** same as the Castello della Zisa.

This remarkable palace, built in 1165–7, once overlooked a pond and was surrounded by a large park with many streams and fish ponds. Sadly, the Zisa Castle now stands in the middle of an ugly fringe area of Palermo. After years of neglect, the castle has now been restored and once again merits the name given to it by the Arabs – *aziz*, or splendid. The handsome exterior gives the impression of a rectangular fortress; the blind arcades,

which once enclosed small double lancet windows, lend it elegance. Two square towers stand on the short sides of the castle. On the ground floor is the Sala della Fontana (Fountain Hall), one of the rooms with a cross plan and exedrae (semicircular recess) on three sides. The cross vault above is connected to the side recesses by means of a series of *muqarnas* (small stalactite vaults typical of Arab architecture). Along the walls is a fine mosaic frieze. Water gushing from the fountain runs along a gutter from the wall to the pavement and then pours into two square fish ponds. The air vents channelled the warm air towards the Sala della Fontana, where it then became cooler. The second floor of the palace is home to the Museo d'Arte Islamia.

Embalmed body in the crypt

❽ La Cuba

Corso Calatafimi 100. **Tel** 091-590 299. **Open** 9am–6:30pm Mon–Sat, 8am–1pm Sun & hols.

William II ordered this magnificent Fatimite-style Norman palace to be built in 1180. It too stood in a large park, the Genoardo,

surrounded by an artificial pond, and served as a pavilion in which to spend the hot afternoons. This palace was so famous that Boccaccio used it as the setting for one of the tales in the *Decameron* (Day 5, no 6).

The rectangular construction acquires rhythm and movement from the pointed blind arcading. The interior ran around an atrium that may have been open to the air. The recesses under the small towers originally would have housed fountains.

❾ Villa Giulia

Via Abramo Lincoln.

Despite its name, the Villa Giulia is not a house but an impressive Italianate garden designed in 1778 outside the city walls by Nicolò Palma and then enlarged in 1866. It was named after Giulia Avalos Guevara, wife of the viceroy, and was the city's first public park. Its square plan is divided by roads decorated with statues, such as the marble image of the "Genius of Palermo" and the statues representing *Glory Vanquishing Envy* and *Abundance Driving Out Famine*. The roads converge centrally in an area with four Pompeian-style niches by Giuseppe Damiani Almeyda decorated with frescoes in great need of restoration.

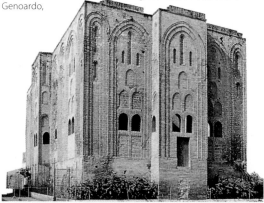

The distinctive Fatimite architecture of La Cuba, used by Boccaccio as the setting for one of the tales in the *Decameron*

San Giovanni dei Lebbrosi, built in the Arab-Norman style

❿ Orto Botanico

Via Abramo Lincoln 2B. **Map** 2 E4.
Tel 091-2389 12 36. **Open** Mar & Oct:
9am–5pm; Apr & Sep: 9am–6pm;
May–Aug: 9am–7pm; Nov–Feb:
9am–4pm. 🚲 🅆 **ortobotanico.
unipa.it**

Laid out in 1785, this garden has
attained international fame
thanks to the wealth and range
of its plant species: palm trees,
bamboo, dracaenas, various
cacti, euphorbias, spiny kapok
trees with bottle-shaped trunks,
pineapples and huge tropical
plants. One of the marvels is a
150-year-old *Ficus magnolioides*
fig tree with aerial roots. The
Neo-Classical Gymnasium (now
a museum), library and herbaria
are by the entrance, a pond
with waterlilies and papyrus is
in the centre, and glasshouses
line both sides.

⓫ Santo Spirito

Via Santo Spirito, Cimitero di
Sant'Orsola. **Tel** 091-422 691.
Open 8am–noon daily.

Lying inside the Sant'Orsola
Cemetery, this Norman
church was founded by
Archbishop Gualtiero Offamilio
in 1178. It is also known as
the "Chiesa dei Vespri" because,
on 31 March 1282, at the hour
of Vespers, a Sicilian uprising
against the Angevin rulers
(see p37) began right in front
of the church.
    Simple and elegant, like all
Norman churches, Santo
Spirito has black volcanic
stone inlay on its right side
and on the apse. The two-aisle
nave with three apses is bare
but full of atmosphere. The
wooden ceiling has floral
ornamentation and there is a
fine wooden crucifix over the
high altar.

⓬ San Giovanni dei Lebbrosi

Via Cappello 38. **Tel** 091-475 024. **Open**
9:30–11am, 4–7pm Mon–Sat (am only
Tue); 7:30am–12:30pm Sun & hols.

One of the oldest Norman
churches in Sicily lies in the
middle of a luxuriant garden
of palms. San Giovanni dei
Lebbrosi was founded in 1071
by Roger I and, in 1119, a
lepers' hospital was built next
to it, hence its name. It was
most probably constructed by
Arab craftsmen and workers, as
can be seen in the pointed
arches crowned by arched
lintels (also visible in San
Giovanni degli Eremiti, *see
pp68–9*; and San Cataldo, *see
p59*). The façade has a small
porch with a bell tower above.
Inside the church there are
three apses and a ceiling with
trusses. Digs to the right of the
church have unearthed
remains of the Saracen Yahia
fortress, which once defended
southeastern Palermo.

⓭ Ponte dell'Ammiraglio

Via dei Mille.

The Admiral's Bridge used
to span the Oreto river before
the latter was diverted. It is
made of large cambered
blocks of limestone resting
on 12 pointed arches, five of
them no more than small
openings in the imposts.
This beautiful and amazingly
well-preserved bridge was
built in 1113 by George of
Antioch, Roger II's High
Admiral (the *ammiraglio* of the
name), but is now a rather
incongruous sight, isolated
without a river.

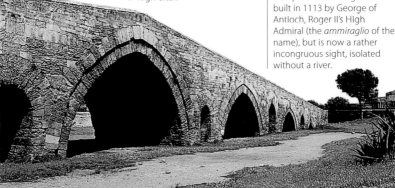

The impressive pointed arches of the 12th-century Ponte dell'Ammiraglio

⓮ Monreale Cathedral

Dominating the Conca d'Oro, the Cathedral of Monreale is the pinnacle of achievement of Arab-Norman art. It was founded in 1172 by William II and a Benedictine monastery was built next to it. The cathedral is famous for its remarkable interior with the magnificent gold mosaics representing episodes from the Old Testament. The cloister *(see pp46–7)* has pointed Arab arches with geometric motifs, and scenes from the Bible are sculpted on the capitals of the 228 white marble twin columns.

★ **Christ Pantocrator**
The church, with a Latin cross plan, is dominated by the 12th–13th-century mosaic of Christ in the middle apse.

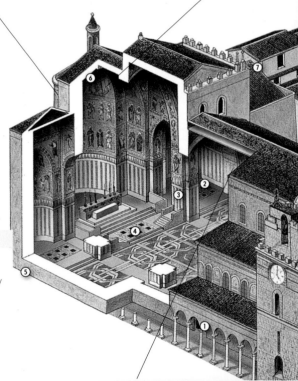

Exterior of the Apse
With its interlaced lava and tufa arches and its multicoloured motifs, the exterior of the apse is the apogee of Norman decoration.

KEY

① **The bronze door by Barisano da Trani** (1179), on the northern side, is under the porch designed by Gian Domenico and Fazio Gagini (1547–69).

② **The royal tomb** of William II, sculpted in white marble, is next to the tomb of William I in a corner of the transept.

③ **Roman columns** separate the sections of the nave.

④ **Choir pavement**

⑤ **Entrance to the Cappella del Crocifisso and the Treasury**

⑥ **Gilded wood ceiling**

⑦ **Cappella di San Placido**

⑧ **A wing of the original monastery** lies over the southern portico.

⑨ **Arab-inspired fountain**

⑩ **The 18th-century portico** is flanked by two bell towers.

★ **The Mosaic Cycle**
The stupendous 12th–13th-century mosaics occupy the entire nave and the aisles, the choir and the transepts. They illustrate scenes from the New and Old Testaments.

★ Cloister
This masterpiece of Norman art has 228 small double columns with varied decoration culminating in the highly elaborate capitals supporting the arches of Arab inspiration.

VISITORS' CHECKLIST

Practical Information
Cathedral: Piazza Duomo. **Tel** 091-640 44 13. **Open** 8.30am–12.30pm, 2:30–5pm Mon–Sat, 8–10am, 2:30–5pm Sun & public hols. 🔲 call 327 351 0886. to tour roof, north transept, treasury. Cloister: Piazza Guglielmo il Buono. **Tel** 091-640 44 03. **Open** 9am–1:30pm, 2–6:30pm Tue–Sat; 9am–1pm Sun, Mon & public hols.

Transport
🚌 AMAT 389 or AST from Piazza Indipendenza

Columns
The cloister columns were made by skilled craftsmen from throughout southern Italy. This carved detail shows Adam and Eve.

Bronze Door on the Portal
This lovely door by Bonanno da Pisa (1185) has 42 elaborately framed biblical scenes and other images. The lion and griffon were Norman symbols.

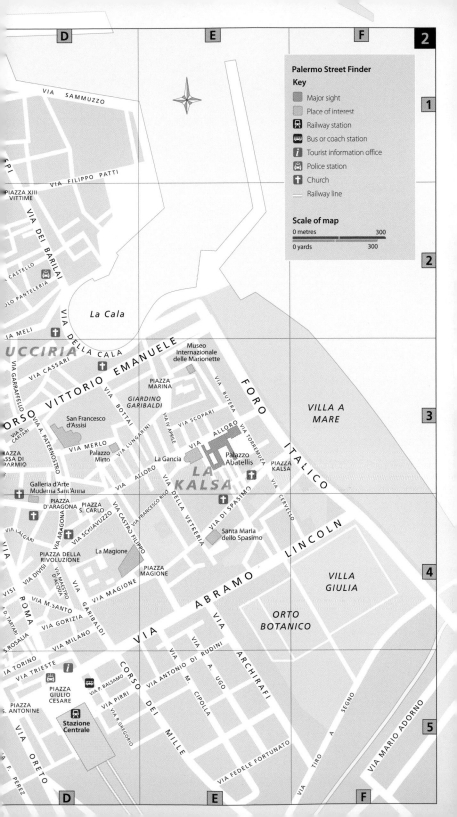

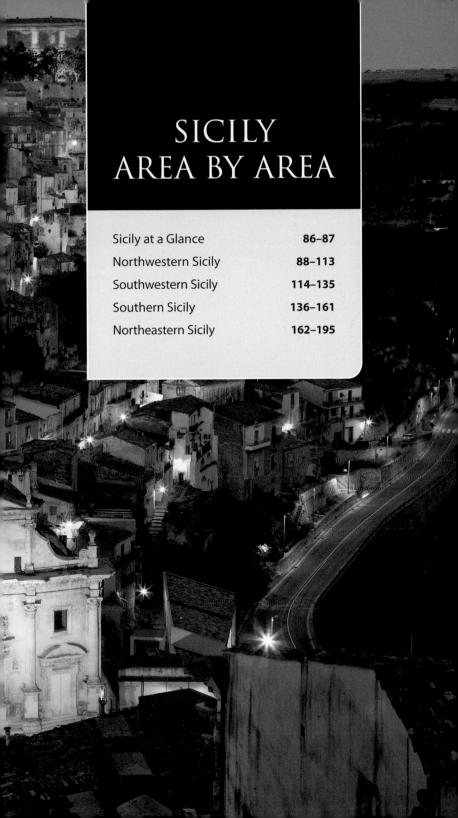

SICILY
AREA BY AREA

Sicily at a Glance

There are few places in the Mediterranean that can equal Sicily's striking landscapes and colourful history. There are noticeable differences between the eastern part of the island, culturally of Greek origin, and the Phoenician and Arab western side. However, Sicily is not simply an east and a west side – every village and town has its own unique story. Within a few kilometres of each other you may find splendidly luxuriant coastline and arid, sun-parched hills, just as you can pick out different layers of civilization side by side or overlapping one another. It is not that unusual to see Greek, Arab, Norman and Baroque influences in the same site, sometimes even in the same building.

The Chiesa Madre in Erice (see pp104–5), built in the 14th century, is a good example of Arab-Norman religious architecture.

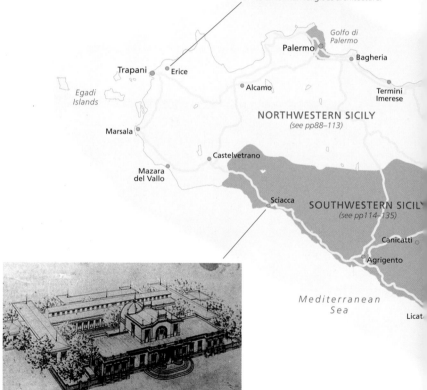

Golfo di Palermo

Palermo

Bagheria

Trapani • Erice

Egadi Islands

Alcamo

Termini Imerese

NORTHWESTERN SICILY
(see pp88–113)

Marsala

Castelvetrano

Mazara del Vallo

Sciacca

SOUTHWESTERN SICILY
(see pp114–135)

Canicatti

Agrigento

Mediterranean Sea

Licat

The Sciacca thermae (see pp122–3) date back to the distant past. The oldest bathhouse in Sicily, it is said to be the work of the mythical architect Daedalus.

0 kilometres   20
0 miles   20

◀ The town of Ragusa in Southern Sicily, illuminated as dusk falls

The 12th-century Cathedral at Cefalù *(see pp92 & 94)* dominates Piazza Duomo.

Catania Cathedral *(see p167)* was rebuilt in the Baroque style after the 1693 earthquake had destroyed the entire city.

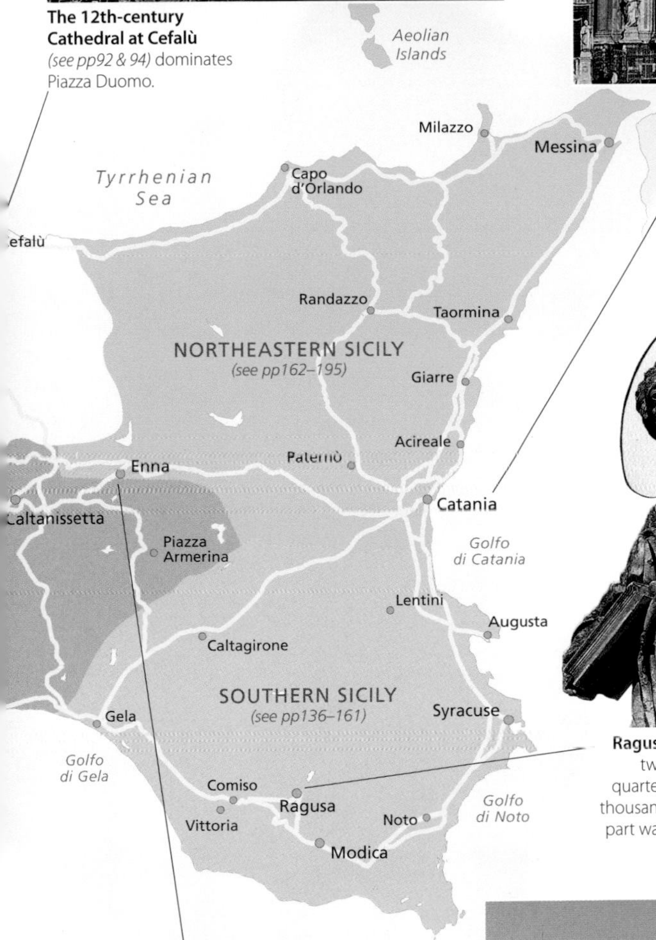

Aeolian Islands

Milazzo

Messina

Tyrrhenian Sea

Capo d'Orlando

Cefalù

Randazzo

Taormina

NORTHEASTERN SICILY *(see pp162–195)*

Giarre

Enna

Paternò

Acireale

Caltanissetta

Catania

Piazza Armerina

Golfo di Catania

Lentini

Augusta

Caltagirone

SOUTHERN SICILY *(see pp136–161)*

Syracuse

Gela

Golfo di Gela

Comiso

Ragusa

Noto

Golfo di Noto

Vittoria

Modica

Ragusa *(see pp154–5)* consists of two cities in one: the ancient quarter of Ibla dates back several thousand years, while the Baroque part was built in the 18th century.

The Castello di Lombardia at Enna *(see p131)* is one of the most important medieval fortifications in Sicily.

NORTHWESTERN SICILY

Over the centuries, this area of Sicily has been particularly exposed to influences from different colonizing civilizations. The Phoenicians settled in Mozia and founded harbour towns at Palermo and Solunto. They were followed by the Greeks and then the Arabs, who began their conquest of the island at Marsala.

These cultures are still very much alive in the names of the towns and sights, in the architecture, and in the layout of the towns from Marsala to Mazara del Vallo. But unfortunately, northwestern Sicily is also one of the areas most affected by the scourges of uncontrolled property development and lack of care for the environment. Prime examples of this are the huge area of unattractive houses between Palermo and Castellammare, which has disfigured what was one of the most fascinating coastlines in Sicily, and the squalidly reconstructed inhabited areas in the Valle del Belice, destroyed by the 1968 earthquake. However, there are other towns pursuing a policy of preserving and reassessing their history. Erice is one of these; its medieval architecture and town plan have been preserved, and many of the churches have been converted into art and culture centres, instead of being left in a state of neglect. The same holds true for Cefalù, Nicosia, Sperlinga and the two Petralias. There is also a good deal of unspoiled scenery apart from the nature reserves. The areas around Trapani and Belice are fascinating, as are the rugged valleys in the interior, characterized by villages perched on the top of steep cliffs with breathtaking views. Other beautiful sights include the Egadi Islands and Ustica.

The Palazzina Pepoli at Erice, converted into a villa in the 19th century

◀ Sunbathing and swimming in a sheltered cove, Riserva dello Zingaro

Exploring Northwestern Sicily

With the magnificent ruins of Segesta, Selinunte, Solunto and Mozia, this area is full of archaeological fascination. The splendid medieval towns of Cefalù and Erice are also worth a visit in themselves. In the interior there are villages where time seems to have stood still, especially in the Madonie mountains. For those who prefer natural history, there are the crystal-clear waters of Ustica and the Egadi Islands, the Riserva Naturale Marina and the Riserva Naturale dello Zingaro between Scopello and San Vito Lo Capo.

27 USTICA

A windmill and outbuilding in the salt marshes near Trapani

San Vito lo Capo

Terrasini

Castelluzzo — **15** RISERVA DELLO ZINGARO

Scopello — Partinico

19 ERICE

TRAPANI **20** — **14** CASTELLAMMARE DEL GOLFO

Paceco — Fulgatore — **13** ALCAMO

Isola di Levanzo
Isola Marettimo — Marettimo — Levanzo

Isola Marettimo — **26** — Isola Favignana — Favignana

EGADI ISLANDS — Rilievo — SEGESTA **16** Calatafimi — Cipirel

Camporeale

Isole dello Stagnone — **22** MOZIA

Tabaccaro — SALEMI **18** — GIBELLINA

MARSALA **21** — **17** Gibellina Vecchia

Santa Ninfa

Poggioreale

Pizzolato — Partanna — **188**

Delia — Partanna

MAZARA DEL VALLO **25** — **24** CASTELVETRANO — S. Margher di Belice

Campobello di Mazara — Menfi

Capo Granitola — **23**

SELINUNTE

Agrigento ▸

One of Caccamo Cathedral's statues

Key

— Motorway
— Major road
— Secondary road
— Minor road
— Main railway
— Minor railway

0 kilometres   20
0 miles   10

For hotels and restaurants see pp202–205 and pp210–217

Sights at a Glance

Getting Around

Northwestern Sicily has a very good road network. Toll-free *autostrada* (motorway) A29 links Palermo with Mazara del Vallo, while a connecting road goes to Trapani. Travelling eastwards, A20 now goes to Messina, and a toll is charged. The main roads along the coast and in the Valle del Belice are good, while those leading to the villages at the foot of the mountains are winding and slow and, in the winter, may be covered with snow or ice. There are frequent trains between Messina and Palermo, less frequently to Trapani, Marsala and Mazara. The bus network connects the main towns and smaller and more remote villages.

The theatre at Segesta, on the top of Monte Barbaro, set in an extraordinary landscape. As with all Greek theatres, the scenery formed part of the stage set

For keys to map symbols *see back flap*

❶ Street-by-Street: Cefalù

Founded on a steep promontory halfway between Palermo and Capo d'Orlando, Cefalù has retained its medieval appearance around the Norman cathedral, which was built by Roger II in the 12th century. The narrow streets of the town centre are lined with buildings featuring elaborate architectural decoration. There are also numerous churches, reflecting the town's status as a leading bishopric. The fishermen's quarter, with its old houses clustered along the seafront, is very appealing, as is the long beach with fine sand, considered to be one of the most beautiful stretches on the northern coast.

★ Cathedral
Oversized compared with the rest of the town, this masterpiece of Norman art contains magnificent mosaics in the presbytery.

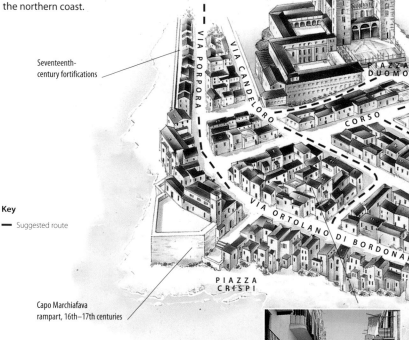

Seventeenth-century fortifications

Key
━ Suggested route

Capo Marchiafava rampart, 16th–17th centuries

| 0 metres | 40 |
| 0 yards | 40 |

Streets of Cefalù
The layout of the town is basically a grid plan crossed horizontally by Corso Ruggero and Via Vittorio Emanuele and intersected by alleys of medieval origin.

Chiesa del Purgatorio

Most of Cefalù's many churches date from the 17th century. The Chiesa del Purgatorio (1668), on Corso Ruggero, has a richly decorated Baroque doorway at the top of a double stairway.

★ **Museo Mandralisca**
This museum was founded by Enrico Piraino, the Baron of Mandralisca, and has a wide range of precious works of art, such as this 4th-century BC tragic mask.

RUGGERO
VIA
VIA MANDRALISCA
VIA GIOENI
XXV NOVEMBRE
IA PORTO SALVO
ETERANI
EMANUELE
VIA VITTORIO

Medieval Fountain
This recently restored medieval stone fountain was used for washing clothes until a few years ago.

Porta Pescara
This striking city gate overlooking the sea is a Gothic arch. It is the only one remaining of the four that originally pierced the city wall, affording access to Cefalù.

Exploring Cefalù

Cefalù is recorded for the first time in 396 BC, in an account by Diodorus Siculus, but the town is more famous for its medieval monuments. Piazza Garibaldi (where you have to leave the car) is a good starting point for a walk around the town. Follow Corso Ruggero to reach the open space of Piazza Duomo, home to one of Sicily's most splendid cathedrals.

The medieval façade of the Cathedral of Cefalù

🏛 Piazza Duomo

This lively square, dominated by the sheer mass of the **Cathedral** and the steep **Rocca**, is the heart of Cefalù. It is surrounded by buildings constructed in different styles. On the southern side are the **Oratorio del Santissimo Sacramento; Palazzo Maria**, which was most probably Roger II's *Domus Regiae* (palace; *see p33*), decorated with an ogee portal and a Gothic window; and **Palazzo Piraino**, with its late 16th-century ashlar door. To the north, the square is bordered by the **Seminario** and the **Palazzo Vescovile**, while to the west is the **Palazzo del Municipio** (Town Hall), which incorporates the former **Santa Caterina monastery**.

🏛 Cathedral

Piazza Duomo. **Tel** 0921-922 021. **Open** for opening and service times check website. 🏛 (cloister). 🌐 **cattedrale dicefalu.com**

Cefalù Cathedral is one of Sicily's major Norman monuments. Building began in 1131 under Roger II. When he died work continued in fits and starts. The façade has two rows of blind arcades set over the three-arch outer narthex and is flanked by two massive bell towers with single and double lancet windows. On the right-hand side you can see the interlaced arch motifs of the three side apses. The nave is divided by arches supported by marble columns. The wooden ceiling, with its painted beams, shows an obvious Islamic

Statue of a bishop, Cefalù Cathedral

influence, while the presbytery is covered with splendid mosaics. On high in the apse is the figure of *Christ Pantocrator with the Virgin Mary, Archangels and the Apostles*; on the choir walls are saints and prophets, while cherubs and seraphim decorate the vault. A door on the northern aisle leads to the entrance of the lovely cloister, which has been extensively restored.

🚌 Corso Ruggero

This avenue goes all the way across the old town, starting from **Piazza Garibaldi**, where the **Porta di Terra** city gate once stood. A few steps on your left is **Palazzo Osterio Magno**, said to have been the residence of Roger II, and built in the 13th and 14th centuries. Almost opposite, a modern building houses the remains of the ancient Roman road. Visits can be made from 9am to 4:30pm. Continuing to the right, you will come to **Piazzetta Spinola**, with **Santo Stefano** (or Delle Anime Purganti), its Baroque façade complemented by an elegant double staircase.

🏛 Museo Mandralisca

Via Mandralisca 13. **Tel** 0921-421 547. **Open** 9am–7pm daily (to 11pm Aug). 🏛 🌐 **fondazionemandralisca.it**

This museum was founded by Enrico Piraino, the Baron of Mandralisca, in the 19th century and includes fine archaeological, shell and coin collections. It also houses an art gallery and a library with over 9,000 historic and scientific works, including incunabulae, 16th-century books and nautical charts.

Among the most important paintings are the *Portrait of an unknown Man* by Antonello da Messina, *View of Cefalù* by Francesco Bevilacqua, *Christ on Judgment Day* by Johannes De Matta (mid-1500s), and a series of icons on the second floor.

Medieval fishermen's dwellings lining the seafront

Antonello da Messina, *Portrait of an Unknown Man* (1465)

Archaeological jewels include a late Hellenistic mosaic and a 4th-century BC krater with a figure of a tuna fish cutter. A curiosity exhibit is the collection of patience (solitaire) playing cards made out of precious materials.

🏛 Via Vittorio Emanuele

This street runs along the seafront, separated by a row of medieval houses facing the bay. Under one of these is the famous **Lavatoio**, the stone fountain known as *U' Ciumi*, or river, which was mentioned by the medieval writer Boccaccio and was used for washing clothes until a few years ago. A stairway leads to the basin where water gushes from holes on three walls. The lovely **Porta Marina** is the only remaining city gate of the four that once afforded

access to the town. It leads to the colourful fishermen's quarter, where scenes were shot for the film *Cinema Paradiso (see p124)*.

🏛 La Rocca

From Piazza Garibaldi a path halfway up the hill offers a fine view of the old town and the sea and leads to the ruins of the fortifications (most probably Byzantine) and the prehistoric sanctuary known as the **Tempio di Diana**, a 5th–4th century BC megalithic construction with a cistern dating from the 9th century AD. On the top of the Rocca are the ruins of a 12th–13th-century castle.

Environs

On the slopes of Pizzo Sant' Angelo is the **Santuario di Gibilmanna**, a sanctuary built in the 17th and 18th centuries and the most popular pilgrimage site in Sicily. The former convent stables house the **Museo dell' Ordine**, the museum of the Capuchin friars, with paintings, sculpture and vestments. The most interesting pieces are creche figures, enamelled reliquaries, a 16th-century alabaster rosary, and a white marble Pietà by the local sculptor Jacopo Lo Duca, a pupil of Michelangelo.

A 16th-century statuette, Santuario di Gibilmanna

❷ Castel di Tusa

Road map D2. 🔼 3,900. 🚆 892 021. 🅸 0921-330 405.

This beautiful swimming resort is dominated by the ruins of a 14th-century castle. The characteristic alleys with old stone houses and villas converge in the central square, which is paved with stone. To get to the little port you must go under the railway arches. The banks of the nearby Tusa river have been turned into an outdoor gallery with works by contemporary artists, including sculptor Pietro Consagra. Only a few miles away are the **Ruins of Halaesa Arconidea**.

🏛 Ruins of Halaesa Arconidea

3 km (2 miles) on the road to Tusa. **Tel** 0921-334 531. **Open** summer: 9am–7:30pm; winter: 9am–4:30pm.

On a hill covered with olive trees and asphodels are the ruins of the city of Halaesa Arconidea, a Greek colony founded in 403 BC, which prospered until it was sacked by the Roman praetor Verres. Excavations have started and you can see the Agora, remains of cyclopean walls and a Hellenistic temple. Near the archaeological site is the **Monastery of Santa Maria della Balate**.

Ruins of the Hellenistic temple at Halaesa, amid olive trees and asphodels

❸ Santo Stefano di Camastra

Road map D2. 🔼 4,500. **FS**
Messina–Palermo. ℹ️ Town hall
(0921-331 127/110). 🎭 Easter Week.

This town facing the Tyrrhenian Sea is one of the leading Sicilian centres for the production of ceramics. All the local craftsmen have their wares on display: vases, jugs, cornices and tiles with period designs, and there is a ceramics museum in the **Palazzo Trabia**. In the centre of town stands the **Chiesa Madre**, or San Nicolò, with a Renaissance doorway and late 18th-century stucco decoration in the interior.

❹ Nicosia

Road map D3. 🔼 14,000. 🚌 129 km (80 miles) from Catania, 44 km (27 miles) from Enna. ℹ️ Town hall, Piazza Garibaldi (0935-672 111). 🎭 Easter Week, O'Scontro (Easter), Macaroni Festival (May), Palio (2nd week Aug), Nicosia da Vivere Festival (Jul–Sep).

Sprawled over four hills, Nicosia is dominated by the ruins of an Arab-Norman castle. Originally a Byzantine settlement, the town was repopulated in the Norman era by Lombard and Piedmontese colonists, who have left traces of their local dialects. The many churches and patrician mansions are a sign of the town's former splendour. Narrow streets and alleys run up the hills, often providing spectacular panoramic views. **Piazza Garibaldi** is the heart of Nicosia,

The Villa Comunale, Santo Stefano di Camastra, with a tiled altar

with the Gothic **San Nicolò Cathedral** and old buildings, including the current Town Hall. The **Salita Salomone** steps lead to Romanesque **San Salvatore**. There is a fine view of the old town from the porch. The church has a series of sundials which, according to tradition, were once used as the town's "clocks". **Via Salomone**, lined with aristocratic palazzi, leads up to **Santa Maria Maggiore**, just under the castle rock. The doorway is decorated with pagan statues of Jove, Venus and Ceres. In the interior is Charles V's throne, in memory of the emperor's visit here in 1535, a gilded marble altarpiece

Detail of the ceiling of Nicosia's Cathedral

by Antonello Gagini and a crucifix known as *Father of Mercy*. From here you can go up to the **Castle**, with its Norman drawbridge and the remains of the keep. At the foot of the castle is the Norman **Basilica of San Michele**, with its austere apses and majestic 15th-century bell towers.

⛪ Cathedral

Piazza Garibaldi 38. **Open** Call 0935-646 792 for hours.

The cathedral is dedicated to the town's patron saint, San Nicolò. It was founded in the 14th century and partially rebuilt in the 19th century. What remains of the original structure are the 14th-century façade, with porticoes running along the left-hand side, and the bell tower with three sections, each distinguished by a different style, from Arab to Romanesque. The rebuilt interior has a crucifix attributed to Fra Umile de Petralia and a font by Antonello Gagini, while the choir was carved out of solid walnut by local artists. The vault, frescoed in the 19th century, conceals a fine Norman truss ceiling decorated in brilliant colours with scenes from the lives of the saints, hunting scenes, images of wild animals, a number of human heads, stylized flowers and geometric decorative motifs.

Nicosia, perched on a hill and once crucial to the area's defensive network

Panoramic view from the Norman castle at Sperlinga (c.1100)

❺ Sperlinga

Road map D3. 👤 900. 🚌 47 km (29 miles) from Enna. 🎫 0935-643 372/643 221. 🎭 Sagra del Tortone (16 Aug).

Sperlinga seems to have been pushed against a spectacular rock face, its parallel streets on different levels connected by steps. In the eastern section, right up against the sandstone cliff, numerous troglodytic cave dwellings have been carved out. Until the mid-1960s many of them were inhabited but some of them are now an ethnographic museum. During Norman rule, inhabitants from Northern Italy and the south of France settled here, and for this reason residents today speak a strange dialect called Galloitalico.

🏛 Norman Castle

Via Castello. **Tel** 0935-643 025. **Open** Apr–Sep: 9am–1:30pm, 3–7pm; Oct–Mar: 9am–1pm, 2–6pm. Museum: **Open** as for the castle. 🐾 📷
🌐 castellodisperlinga.it

Sperlinga's castle was built by the Normans under Roger I around the year 1100 on the top of an impregnable rock face. It was later reinforced by Frederick II. It is linked with the Sicilian Vespers revolt (see pp36–7) in 1282, when it was the last refuge of the

Angevin rulers, who managed to resist attacks for a year. The events are commemorated by an inscription in the vestibule: *Quod Siculis placuit sola Sperlinga negavit* ("Sperlinga alone denied the Sicilians what they desired"). The numerous chambers in the castle make it a veritable stone labyrinth. After passing the remains of a drawbridge, a moat and the Sala del Principe (Prince's Hall), visitors will find stables, a forge, a prison, cereal silos, reservoirs to collect rainwater and the foundry (hewn entirely out of the rock). In the middle of the cliff is **San Domenico Chapel**, which was rebuilt on its own ruins. An impressive flight of stairs leads to the top of the rock, with magnificent views.

❻ Gangi

Road map D3. 👤 7,000. 🚌 51 km (32 miles) from Cefalù. 🎫 Piazzetta Zoppo di Gangi (0921-501 471). 🎭 Sagra della Spiga (2nd Sun Aug).

This town lies on the south-western slope of Monte Marone, facing the Nebrodi and Madonie mountains. The birthplace of painters Gaspare Vazano and Giuseppe Salerno has retained its medieval character, with winding streets and steps connecting the different levels. The towering **Chiesa Madre** has a 14th-century bell tower and a lovely *Last Judgment* by Salerno, inspired by Michelangelo's painting in the Sistine Chapel.

❼ Petralia Sottana

Road map D3. 👤 3,800. 🚌 98 km (61 miles) from Palermo. 🎫 Town hall, Corso Agliata (0921-684 311/ 641 811). 🎭 Ballo della Cordella, dance (1st Sun after 15 Aug); San Calogero procession (18 Jun); Festa dei Sapori Madoniti, artisan foods (last weekend Oct).

Perched on a rock 1,000 m (3,300 ft) up, and nestled at the foot of the tallest peaks in the Madonie mountains, Petralia Sottana is laid out around **Via Agliata**, which ends in **Piazza Umberto I**, opposite the **Chiesa Madre**. The late Gothic church, partially rebuilt in the 1600s, contains a fine wooden triptych, *The Virgin Mary and Child between Saints Peter and Paul*. An arch connects the bell tower with the **Santissima Trinità**, which has a marble altarpiece by Domenico Gagini.

Petralia Sottana, in the middle of the verdant Valle dell'Imera

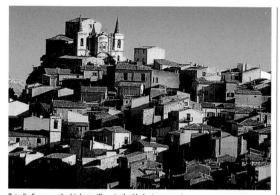

Petralia Soprana, the highest village in the Madonie mountains

❽ Petralia Soprana

Road map D3. 🔼 3,000. 🚌 104 km (65 miles) from Palermo. ℹ️ 0921-684-111. 🎪 Sagra del Salgemma, salt festival (Aug).

Situated on a plateau 1,147 m (3,760 ft) above sea level, where the panoramic view ranges from the Nebrodi hills to the volcanic cone of Mount Etna, Petralia Soprana is the highest village in the Madonie mountain. This town was an extremely important Greek and Phoenician city. Under Roman dominion ancient "Petra" was one of the largest wheat-producing *civitates* in the Empire. The city became Batraliah after the Arab conquest and a powerful defensive stronghold under the Normans. Later, the two Petralias (Soprana and Sottana) were taken over by noble families.

The village has preserved its medieval layout, with narrow paved streets, old stone houses, patrician residences and churches. The old **Chiesa Madre**, dedicated to saints Peter and Paul and rebuilt in the 14th century, stands in an attractive square with a 17th-century double-column colonnade designed by the Serpotta brothers. In the interior is the first crucifix by Fra' Umile Pintorno (1580– 1639), who also painted many other crucifixes throughout the island. **Santa Maria di Loreto** was built in the 18th century over the remains of a castle; it has a cross plan and the façade is flanked by two decorated bell towers.

❾ Polizzi Generosa

Road map D3. 🔼 3,700. 🚌 93 km (58 miles) from Palermo. ℹ️ Pro Loco, Via Garibaldi 13 (329-337 75 66). 🎪 Sagra delle Nocciole, hazelnut festival (1st Sun after 15 Aug).

On the western slopes of the Madonie mountains, this village grew up around an ancient fortress rebuilt by the Normans. Among its many churches is the **Chiesa Madre**, with a fine 16th-century *Madonna and Child* altarpiece by an unknown Flemish artist and a relief by Domenico Gagini (1482). A small museum shows the natural history of the area.

Environs

From Polizzi, ascend to Piano Battaglia, part of the nature reserve, with footpaths in summer and ski runs in winter.

❿ Caccamo

Road map C2. 🔼 8,500. 🚌 48 km (30 miles) from Palermo. ℹ️ Town hall, Piazza Duomo (091-810 32 07). 🚌 Sat.

Caccamo lies under the castellated walls of its **Norman castle**, in a lovely setting of softly rolling hills only 10 km (6 miles) from the Palermo-Catania motorway. The town is laid out on different levels, with well-maintained roads that open onto pretty squares. The most appealing of these is **Piazza Duomo**, with the **Chiesa Matrice** dedicated to San Giorgio, flanked by statues and two symmetrically arranged Baroque buildings: the **Oratorio della Compagnia del Sacramento** and the **Chiesa delle Anime Sante del Purgatorio**. The former was built by the Normans but was enlarged in the 17th century. Its richly decorated interior has a font by Gagini and a font workshop. The latter includes catacombs

Coat of arms of a noble family of Caccamo

where a large number of townspeople were buried until the mid-19th century. Not far away are the **Annunziata**, with twin bell towers, **San Marco** and **San Benedetto alla Badia**. The last is perhaps the loveliest of the three, with its Baroque stucco and majolica decoration, and a colourful floor depicting a ship sailing on the high seas, guarded by angels.

Interior of the impregnable Norman castle at Caccamo

The Gymnasium at Solunto, with its Doric columns intact

🏠 Norman Castle

Open 8:30am–12:30pm, 3–7pm Tue–Fri; 9:15am–12:30pm, 3:30–6:30pm Sat, Sun & hols. **Tel** 091-814 92 52. 🗂

This formidable Norman castle is truly impregnable. It was built on the top of a steep rock overlooking the valley and is protected by a series of walls. The first entranceway on the lower floor leads to a broad stairway flanked by castellated walls; this leads to the second entrance, where the guard-house once stood.

After crossing a drawbridge, you will find another door that leads to the inner courtyard. Through this you can reach the famous Sala della Congiura (Conspiracy Hall), so named because it was here in 1160 that the Norman barons hatched a plot against William I. The panoramic views from the large western terrace are breathtaking.

⓫ Solunto

Road map C2. 🚉 Santa Flavia–Solunto–Porticello. **Open** 9am–7am Tue–Fri (last entrance 6:30pm); 9:30am–1:30pm Sat, Sun & hols (last entrance 1pm). 🏛 Museum: **Tel** 338-784 51 40.

The ruins of the city of Solunto lie on the slopes of Monte Catalfano in a stupendous site with a beautiful panoramic view of the sea. Solunto was one of the first Phoenician colonies in Sicily and was mentioned, along with Palermo and Mozia, by the Greek historian Thucydides. In 254 BC it was conquered by the Romans. By the 2nd century AD the city had been largely abandoned, and it was later almost destroyed by the Saracens. At the entrance there is a museum displaying a site plan and finds from the various digs, which began in 1826 and are still under way.

Solunto follows a traditional layout. The path leading to the site takes you to Via dell'Agorà, with a fired-brick pavement and gutters for drainage. This street makes a right angle with the side stairs, which mark off the blocks of buildings (insulae). Six Doric columns and part of the roof of one of these, the Gymnasium, are still standing. Other insulae have mosaic floors and plastered or even painted walls. At the eastern end is the Agora, with workshops, cisterns to collect rainwater and a theatre with the stage area facing the sea.

Panoramic view of Solunto

The Villas in Bagheria

In the 18th century, Bagheria was the summer residence of Palermo's nobility, who built luxurious villas surrounded by orange groves as retreats from the torrid heat of the capital. Prince Ettore Branciforti built the first, Villa Barbera, in 1657, followed by other aristocrats such as the Valguarnera and Gravina families. The most famous is the Villa Palagonia (091-932 088; www.villapalagonia.it), restored in 2006 and decorated with hundreds of statues of monsters and mythological figures. Visitors can see the Salone degli Specchi (Hall of Mirrors), where balls were held, and the frescoed Room of the Labours of Hercules. The villas eventually proved too costly to keep and were either abandoned or put to other uses. When the gardens were destroyed to make room for ugly housing units, the villas lost most of their fascination.

Façade of Villa Palagonia, the most famous villa in Bagheria

"Monster" at the Villa Palagonia

Traditional Piana degli Albanesi costumes

⓬ Piana degli Albanesi

Road map B2. ⚊ 6,200.
🛈 Pro Loco, Via Kastrota 207 (091-857 45 04). ⚊ Sagra del Cannolo.
🆆 **pianalbanesi.it**

During the expansion of the Ottoman Empire in the Balkans, many groups of Albanians (*Albanesi*) fled to Italy. At the end of the 15th century, John II allowed an Albanian community to settle in this area, which originally took the name of Piana dei Greci because the inhabitants belonged to the Greek Orthodox Church. The place was renamed Piana degli Albanesi in 1941. The town is famous for its colourful religious festivities, such as those during Epiphany and Easter, which are still celebrated according to the Orthodox calendar. The celebrations in honour of the patron saint Santa Maria Odigitria are followed by traditional folk festivities.

Piazza Vittorio Emanuele, in the heart of town, is home to the Byzantine church of **Santa Maria Odigitria**, which has a beautiful iconostasis in the interior. Opposite the parish church is the oldest church in Piana degli Albanesi, **San Giorgio**, which was altered in the mid-1700s. Along the avenue named after Giorgio Kastriota Skanderbeg, one of Albania's national heroes, is the cathedral, **San Demetrio**. As is customary in Orthodox churches, the apses are closed off by the iconostasis. On the vault is a fresco by P Novelli representing the Apostles, Christ and the four Orthodox patriarchs. Near the town is a large artificial **lake** that was created by a dam built in the 1920s.

⓭ Alcamo

Road map B2. ⚊ 46,000. ⚊
Palermo–Trapani line. 🛈 Town hall, Piazza Ciullo (0924-223 01).

During the Arab period the fortress of Manzil Alqamah was built as part of this area's defensive network. The town of Alcamo developed later, and between the 13th and 14th centuries centred around the Chiesa Madre and the castle, which has been restored. Population growth over the decades has led to the expansion of the town and the demolition of parts of the old city walls. In Piazza Ciullo is **Sant'Oliva**, built in 1724 over an earlier church, while the nearby **Chiesa del Rosario** boasts late 15th-century frescoes. Facing Piazza della Repubblica is **Santa Maria del Gesù**, with the so-called Greek Madonna altarpiece (1516), showing the Madonna with the Counts of Modica. But the most important church here is the **Chiesa Madre**, founded in 1332. Its Baroque façade, overlooking Piazza IV Novembre, has a 14th-century bell tower with double lancet windows, and many paintings and sculptures can be seen in the chapels.

⓮ Castellammare del Golfo

Road map B2. ⚊ 15,000. ⚊
Palermo–Trapani. 🛈 Pro Loco, Corso B. Mattarella 24, (0924-35175).
🆆 **prolococastellammare.it**

This town was the Greek port for Segesta and Erice, and then an Arab fortress. It became an important trading and tuna-fishing centre in the Middle Ages. In the heart of the town, on an isthmus, is the Norman-Swabian **Castle**, and the old picturesque streets of the medieval quarter known as *castri di la terra*. On Via Garibaldi is the **Chiesa Madre**, frequently rebuilt in the 1700s and 1800s.

Castellammare del Golfo on the Tyrrhenian Sea, a leading port town in the Arab-Norman period

For hotels and restaurants see pp202–205 and pp210–217

ⓕ Riserva dello Zingaro

Twenty kilometres (12 miles) from Erice, along the coast going towards Palermo, is the Riserva dello Zingaro, a nature reserve of about 1,600 ha (3,950 acres) sloping down to the sea. It is a paradise for birds, especially for raptors such as Bonelli's eagles, peregrine falcons and kites, and even, on occasion, golden eagles.

San Vito Lo Capo

① *Monte Acci*
829 m/2,720 ft

Contrada Acci

Monte Passo del Lupo
868 m/2,847 ft

⑥

Contrada Uzzo **Ficarella**

②

Pizzo Aquila
759 m/2,490 ft

Contrada Sughero

③

Monte Speziale
913 m/2,994 ft

Contrada Pianello

Pizzo del Corvo
415 m/1,360 ft

⑥ Portella Mandra Nuova
A typical village 700 m (2,296 ft) above sea level.

Pizzo Passo del Lupo
610 m/2,000 ft

④

Contrada Scardina

Scopello ⑤

Key
■ Negotiable road
═ Path

Monte Scardina
680 m/2,230 ft

Tips for Walkers
Tour length: C2
Tour length: there are four marked footpaths. The shortest one (6 km/4 miles) goes from Scopello to Tonarella dell'Uzzo, taking about 2 hrs 20 mins. The longest is 19 km (12 miles) and takes about 9 hrs. The reserve can also be explored on horseback.
Ⓦ riservazingaro.it

① San Vito lo Capo
North of the reserve is this impressive promontory plunging into the sea.

② Grotta dell'Uzzo
Human skeletons over 12,000 years old have been found in this grotto.

③ Grotta del Sughero
Animals such as foxes, rabbits and porcupines live in these caves.

④ Contrada Capreria
Punta di Capreria, one of the loveliest parts of the reserve, lies in this area.

⑤ Baglio di Scopello
Scopello is a farming hamlet that grew up around an 18th-century fort.

0 kilometres   2
0 miles   1

For additional keys to symbols *see back flap*

⑯ Segesta

According to legend, the ancient capital of the Elymians was founded on the rolling green hills of the Castellammare del Golfo area by exiles from Troy. Segesta was constantly at war with Selinunte and was frequently attacked. Yet the majestic Doric temple has miraculously survived sacking and the ravages of time, and stands in splendid and solemn isolation on the hill facing Monte Barbaro. The city of Segesta was built above the temple on the top of the mountain. Here lie the ruins of some buildings and the well-preserved 3rd-century BC theatre, where ancient Greek plays are performed every other summer.

The Temple
Built in the 5th century BC, the temple is still well preserved; 36 Doric columns support the pediments and entablatures.

0 metres	350
0 yards	350

Panorama
Ancient Segesta and the beautiful setting create an atmospheric scene.

Ruins of the city

Monte Barbaro
(431 m/1,414 ft)

Interior of the Temple
The lack of architectural elements in the interior has led scholars to believe that the construction was interrupted by the war with Selinunte.

The Theatre
Segesta's theatre is a semicircle with a diameter of 63 m (207 ft) hewn out of the top of Monte Barbaro. A curious feature is that the stage area faces north, probably to allow a view of the hills and sea.

⓱ Gibellina

Road map B3. ⚠ 5,000. 🚌 89 km (55 miles) from Trapani. ℹ Town hall, Piazza XV Gennaio (0924-67877). 🎭 Oresteia (classical theatre, biennial, summer). 🌐 **fondazioneorestiadi.it**

In 1968 a terrible earthquake destroyed all the towns in the Valle del Belice and the vicinity, including Gibellina. The new town was rebuilt, after years of bureaucratic delay, in the Salinella zone about 20 km (12 miles) from the original village. Over 40 years after the event, the new Gibellina already seems old and rather sad. However, it is worth visiting because, thanks to the cooperation of contemporary architects and artists, the area has been enriched with many works of art, including a huge sculpture, *Stella* (Star) by Pietro Consagra, the city gate and symbol of Gibellina Nuova. Other attractions are the **Torre Civica Carillon**, a tower in Piazza del Municipio, and the **Centro Culturale**, the cultural centre built over the remains of the 17th-century **Palazzo Di Lorenzo**. Lastly, be sure to visit the **Museo Antropologico-Etnologico**, with everyday objects and tools illustrating local folk customs, and, above all, the **Museo Civico d'Arte Contemporanea**. This museum contains works by artists such

The town of Salemi, dominated by its impressive medieval castle

as Fausto Pirandello, Renato Guttuso, Antonio Sanfilippo and Mario Schifano.

🏛 Museo Civico d'Arte Contemporanea
Via Segesta. **Tel** 0924-67428. **Open** 9am–1pm, 4–7pm Mon–Sat.

Environs
Eighteen kilometres (11 miles) from the new town are the ruins of old Gibellina. Here you will see a disturbing and gigantic work of land art by Alberto Burri, who covered the ruins with a layer of white cement. The cracks cutting through this white expanse, known as *Burri's Crevice*, follow the course of the old streets, creating a labyrinth.

The Star of Gibellina, by Pietro Consagra

⓲ Salemi

Road map B3. ⚠ 12,500. 🚌 95 km (59 miles) from Palermo. ℹ Town hall, Piazza Dittatura 1 (0924-991 111). 🛍 Sat. 🎭 San Giuseppe (Mar).

This agricultural town in the Valle del Delia dates from ancient times (it was probably the Halicyae mentioned by Diodorus Siculus). Despite the 1968 earthquake, the Arab town plan has remained, with a jumble of narrow streets at the foot of the three towers of the **Castle**. Here, on 14 May 1860, Garibaldi proclaimed himself ruler of Sicily in the name of King Vittorio Emanuele II *(see pp38–9)*. The castle was built in the 12th century by Frederick II and rebuilt in 1210.

In the old town, interesting sights are **Sant'Agostino** with its large cloister and the 17th-century **Collegio dei Gesuiti**, which houses the **Chiesa dei Gesuiti**, the **Oratorio del Ritiro** and the town's museums, in particular the **Museo Civico d'Arte Sacra**.

🏛 Museo Civico d'Arte Sacra
Collegio dei Gesuiti. **Tel** 0924-982 376. **Open** 10am–12:30pm, 4–6:30pm Tue–Sat.

This museum of religious art has sculptures by Domenico Laurana and Antonello Gagini *(see p55)*, 17th-century paintings and wooden Baroque sculpture. The Risorgimento section features objects comme-morating Garibaldi's feats.

The landscape art work *Burri's Crevice*, covering part of the ruins of old Gibellina

⑲ Erice

The splendid town of Erice, perched on top of Monte San Giuliano, has very ancient origins, as is shown by the cult of the goddess of fertility, Venus Erycina. Laid out on a triangular plan, the town has preserved its medieval character, with fine city walls, beautifully paved streets, stone houses with decorated doorways, small squares and open spaces with numerous churches – including the medieval Chiesa Madre – many of which have recently become venues for scientific and cultural activities.

🏛 Cyclopean walls

These extend for 700 m (2,296 ft) on the northern side of the town, from Porta Spada to Porta Trapani.

The lower part of the wall, with its megalithic blocks of stone, dates back to the Phoenician period; the letters *beth, ain, phe* of the Phoenician alphabet are carved in it. The upper part and the gates were built by the Normans. The **Porta Spada** gate owes its name to the massacre of the local Angevin rulers during the Sicilian Vespers (*spada* means sword) (*see pp36–7*). Nearby are **Sant'Antonio Abate** and **Sant'Orsola**. The latter houses the 18th-century "Mysteries", sculptures borne in procession on Good Friday.

🏛 Castello di Venere

Via Conte Pepoli. **Tel** 3666-712 832. **Open** Apr–Oct: 10am–6pm daily (to 8pm summer); Nov–Mar: 10am–4pm Sat & hols, weekdays by appt. 🅿
W fondazioneericearte.org/castellodivenere.php

This Norman castle was built on an isolated rock over the ruins of the **Temple of Venus Erycina**. Entrance is gained via a tower, the only remaining original part of the castle, with Ghibelline castellation. It was used as a prison and watchtower. Above the entrance, with its pointed arch, is a plaque with the coat of arms of the

Spanish Habsburgs, surmounted by a 14th-century double lancet window. Inside are a sacred well and the ruins of the Temple of Venus Erycina, a Phoenician house and a Roman bath. The castle is the starting point of a system of fortifications including the **Torri del Balio**, formerly the headquarters of the Norman governor. Further down, on a ledge over the Pineta dei Runzi pine forest, is the **Torretta Pepoli** (*see p89*), built as a hunting lodge in 1872–80 and one of the symbols of Erice. In front of the castle are the 19th-century public gardens, **Giardini del Balio**, which link this zone with the eastern side of Erice.

The Norman castle, built on the site dedicated to Venus Erycina in ancient times

Erice Town Centre

① Chiesa Matrice
② Cyclopean walls
③ Polo Museale A. Cordici
④ Corso Vittorio Emanuele
⑤ Via General Salerno
⑥ San Pietro
⑦ San Giovanni Battista
⑧ Castello di Venere

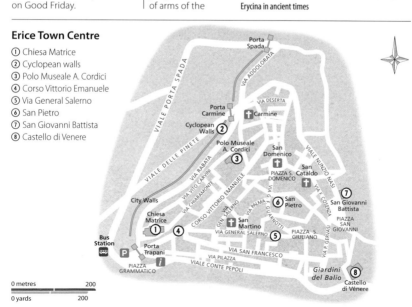

0 metres 200
0 yards 200

For keys to map symbols *see back flap*

The austere exterior of the Chiesa Madre in Erice

⛪ Chiesa Matrice
Piazza Matrice. **Tel** 0923-869 123.
Open Mar: 10am–4pm; Apr–Jun: Oct: 10am–6pm; Jul & Sep: 10am–7pm; Aug: 10am–8pm; Nov–Feb: 10am–12:30pm. 🅰

This church was built in 1314 and is dedicated to Our Lady of the Assumption. The austere façade has a portico with pointed arches surmounted by a beautiful rose window, it faces the detached campanile with double lancet windows, which was built as a lookout tower. The interior was drastically restored in 1865, and little remains of its original look.

Plaque commemorating the Sicilian scientist Ettore Majorana

🚌 Corso Vittorio Emanuele
The corso (main street) in Erice begins at **Porta Trapani**, one of the three gates through the massive city walls, and goes uphill. The street is lined with Baroque patrician houses and tempting pastry shops selling local specialities.

To the left is **San Salvatore**, which once had a monastery annexe and boasts a 15th-century portal. At the end of the corso, formerly called Via Regia, is **Piazza Umberto I**, redesigned in the 19th century, and the **Palazzo del Municipio** (town hall),

which houses the **Polo Museale A. Cordici**.

🏛 Polo Museale A. Cordici
Via V. Carvini. **Tel** 3465-773 550. **Open** Apr–Oct: 10am–6pm daily (to 8pm summer); Nov–Mar: 10am–4pm Sat & hols; weekdays by appt.
Ⓦ fondazioneericearte.org/museocordici.php

This museum features finds from the necropolis, coins, terracotta items and a small head of Venus. Some rooms also exhibit vestments and old paintings and sculpture such as the *Annunciation*, a marble group by the artist Antonello Gagini.

⛪ San Pietro
Via Filippo Guarnotti.
Founded in the 14th century in the middle of Erice, this church was rebuilt in 1745, and a fine Baroque portal added. The nearby convent is now one of the bases for the **Polo Museale A. Cordici**. This centre, founded in the early 1960s to honour the brilliant Sicilian scientist Ettore Majorana who disappeared in mysterious circumstances before World War II, runs courses and conferences on subjects from medicine to mathematical logic. The centre makes use of abandoned buildings such as the former convents of San Domenico, San Francesco and San Rocco.

🚌 Via General Salerno
This street, with its noble palazzi, connects **Corso Vittorio Emanuele** with the castle area. Immediately to the left is **San Martino**, a Norman church with a Baroque portal and interior, where there is a fine 17th-century wooden choir. The sacristy takes you to the **Oratorio dei Confrati del Purgatorio**, built in Rococo style, with a carved altar decorated with gilded stucco.

Further along the street is **San Giuliano**, which looks over a square made more spectacular by the pink colour façades of the

VISITORS' CHECKLIST

Practical Information
Road map A2. 🔼 25,000.
ℹ Viale Conte A. Pepoli 11 (348 691 2335). 🗓 Mon. 🎭 Misteri (Good Fri), Estate Ericina (Jul–Sep).

Transport
🚌 16 km (9 miles) from Trapani. Cable way Erice–Trapani (0923-869 720/569 306).

One example of the lovely paved streets in Erice

buildings on the square. The church was begun in 1080 by Roger I but was radically altered in the 1600s. It was closed when the vault caved in on the central section of the nave; now restored, the church is used as a cultural and artistic centre.

⛪ San Giovanni Battista
Piazzale San Giovanni. **Tel** 0923-869 123. **Open** only for events.
This white-domed church is the largest and probably the oldest in Erice, despite the many alterations that have changed its appearance. The last refurbishing phase took place in the 1600s, when the nave was totally rebuilt.

The church is now used only as an auditorium, but interesting works of art remain. These include the statue of St John the Baptist by Antonio Gagini, who came from a family of sculptors and whose work is the first example of Renaissance art in Sicily. The 14th-century frescoes come from the deconsecrated church of Santa Maria Maddalena.

Boats anchored at the port of Trapani

⑳ Trapani

Road map A2. 🚊 70,000.
✈ Vincenzo Florio a Birgi (0923-842
502). 🚆 892021. 🚌 0923-871 922.
ℹ Town hall, phone enquiries only
(0923-877 048/49). 🛍 Thu. 🎭
Processione dei Misteri (Good Friday).

The town was built on a
narrow, curved promontory
(hence the name, which
derives from the Greek word
drepanon, or sickle) that juts
out into the sea opposite the
Egadi Islands. In ancient times
Trapani was the port town
for Erice *(see pp104–5)*. It
flourished under the Carthaginians and languished under
the Vandals, Byzantines and
Saracens. The economy has
always been linked to the sea
and reached its peak in the
1600s and 1700s with
shipyards and tuna fishing. The
town now extends beyond the
promontory to the foot of
Monte San Giuliano and the
edge of the salt marshes.

🏛 Museo Pepoli
Via Conte Agostino Pepoli 200.
Tel 0923-553 269. **Open** 9am–1:30pm
Mon–Sat, 9am–12:30pm Sun & hols.
🎟 (free first week of the month).

This museum was opened in
1906 in the former Carmelite
monastery, thanks to Count
Agostino Pepoli, who donated
his private collection. A broad
polychrome marble staircase
leads to the first floor, which has
archaeological finds, 12th–18th
century Sicilian painting,
jewellery and ceramics. The art
produced in Trapani is interesting:
wooden 16th-century angels, an
18th-century coral and alabaster
nativity scene, jewellery, clocks
with painted dials, tapestries with
coral and majolica from Santa
Maria delle Grazie.

🏙 Via Garibaldi
This is the street that leads to the
old town. It begins in **Piazza
Vittorio Veneto**, the heart of the
town, with **Palazzo d'Ali**, now the
Town Hall.

The street is lined with
18th- century patrician
residences such as **Palazzo
Riccio di Morana** and **Palazzo
Fardella Fontana**. Almost directly
opposite the 1621 Baroque
façade of **Santa Maria d'Itria**
are the steps leading to **San
Domenico**, built in the 14th
century and restructured in the
18th. Inside the church is the
sarcophagus of Manfred, natural
son of Frederick II *(see p33)*.

🏙 Corso Vittorio Emanuele
This is the main street in the old
town, lined with late Baroque
buildings and **San Lorenzo
Cathedral**, which has a fine
portico. The main features of the
interior are the painted ceiling,
stucco decoration and, in the
right-hand altar, a *Crucifixion*
attributed to Van Dyck.

🏛 Santuario di Maria
Santissima Annunziata
Via Conte Agostino Pepoli. **Tel** 0923-
539 184. **Open** winter: 7am–noon,
4–7pm including hols; summer:
7am–noon, 4–8pm (7am–1pm,
4–8pm hols). 🌐 **madonnadi
trapani.org**

Known as the Madonna di
Trapani, this church was built by
the Carmelite fathers in 1224.
The portal and part of the rose
window are the only original
elements remaining, as the rest
of the church is Baroque, thanks
to restoration effected in 1714.
Inside are the Cappella dei
Pescatori, the Cappella dei
Marinai, and the Cappella
della Madonna di Trapani

Windmills, used for draining water from
the basins

The Salt Marshes

The Stagno and Trapani salt
marshes were exploited in
antiquity and reached the height
of their importance in the
19th century, when salt was
exported as far away as Norway.
The long periods of sunshine
(five or six months a year) and the
impermeable nature of the land made these marshes very
productive, although activity has declined in the last 20 years. At one
time, windmills supplied energy for the Archimedes screws used to
take water from basin to basin; some of them have now been
restored. At Nubia the Museo delle Saline (Salt Marsh Museum; www.
museodelsale.it) is now open, and the Stagnone area is a fully
fledged nature reserve. The seawater will be protected from
pollution, and the age-old tradition of salt extraction will survive.

A workman at the Stagnone salt marsh

Bell tower of the Santuario dell'Annunziata in Trapani

with the *Madonna and Child* by Nino Pisano, one of the most important Gothic sculptures in Sicily.

Chiesa del Purgatorio

Via San Francesco d'Assisi. **Tel** 0923-23261 (Curia Vescovile). **Open** 10am–noon Tue, 10am–noon & 5–7pm Fri (10am–noon, 4–7pm daily in Lent; 9am–midnight Jul & Aug).

This church is well known because it houses unusual 18th-century wooden statues with precious silver decoration representing the Stations of the Cross *(Misteri)*. At 2pm on Good Friday, they are carried in a 24-hour procession, a ritual dating from the 1700s.

Museo di Preistoria

Torre di Ligny. **Tel** 0923-547 275. **Open** summer: 10am–12:30pm, 5–7:30pm.

At the tip of the peninsula, the **Torre di Ligny** (1671) affords a fine view of the city and its port. The tower is now used as an archaeological museum, with objects from the Punic Wars and from the shipwrecks that occurred on the ancient trade routes on display are amphoras used to carry wine, dates and garum – a prized fish sauce.

Museo del Sale

Via delle Saline, Contrada Nubia, Paceco. **Tel** 0923-867 061. **Open** 9:30am–7pm daily. WWF Reserve: **Tel** 0923-867 700.

From Trapani to Marsala the coast is lined with salt marshes. The area is now a WWF nature reserve, a unique habitat for migratory birds. The landscape, with its salt marshes and windmills (three of which can be visited), is striking. A museum illustrates the practice of salt extraction.

㉑ Marsala

Road map A3. 83,000. 124 km (77 miles) from Marsala and 31 km (19 miles) from Trapani. 0923-714 097. Tue. Maundy Thursday procession.

Sicily's largest wine-producing centre was founded by the colonists from Mozia who survived the destruction of the island by Dionysius of Syracuse in 397 BC. It then became a major Carthaginian city, but in the first Punic War it was conquered by the Romans, who made it their main Mediterranean naval base. The city plan is basically Roman, other quarters being added by the Arabs, who conquered the city in 830 and made it a flourishing trade centre.

Piazza della Repubblica, bounded by **Palazzo Senatorio** and the **Cathedral**, dedicated to St Thomas of Canterbury, is the heart of the town. The Cathedral was founded by the Normans and completed in the 1950s. It boasts sculptures by the Gaginis and their school. Behind the apse is the **Museo degli Arazzi Fiamminghi**, with eight 16th-century Flemish tapestries depicting Titus's war against the Hebrews. They were donated by Philip II of Spain to the Archbishop of Messina and later taken to Marsala Cathedral.

Museo degli Arazzi Fiamminghi

Chiesa Madre, Via G Garaffa 57. **Tel** 0923-711 327. **Open** 9am–1pm, 4–6pm. **Closed** Mon.

Museo Archeologico Regionale Baglio Anselmi

Lungomare Boéo. **Tel** 0923-952 535. **Open** 9am–7pm Tue–Sat, 9am–1pm Mon, 3–7:30pm Sun & hols.

This archaeological museum features prehistoric and ancient finds from local digs, including the mosaics from the Roman ruins at Capo Boeo and a 3rd-century BC Punic shipwreck.

㉒ Mozia

Road map A2–3. from Trapani and Marsala (dawn to sunset). STR Trapani (0923-565 412/872 652). Museum: **Tel** 0923-712 598. **Open** Apr–Oct: 9:30am–6:30pm; Nov–Mar: 9am–3pm. **fondazionewhitaker.it**

The Phoenician city of Mozia was built on the island of San Pantaleo, just off Sicily. The ancient site is linked with Joseph Whitaker, the son of an English wine merchant who made his fortune from Marsala wine. He became owner of the island in the early 1900s, began archaeological digs in 1913, and founded a museum that houses the "young man from Mozia" statues. Along with those in Carthage, the dry docks here are the most ancient in the Mediterranean.

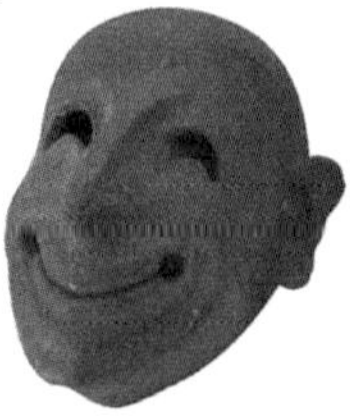

Punic head, Mozia museum

Ruins of the northern gate of the city of Mozia, destroyed in 397 BC

㉓ Selinunte

The ruins of Selinunte, overlooking the sea, are among the most striking archaeological sites in the Mediterranean and a supreme example of the fusion of Phoenician and Greek culture. Founded in the 7th century BC by colonists from Megara Hyblaea, Selinunte soon became a powerful city with flourishing trade and artistic activity. A rival to Segesta and Mozia, Selinunte was destroyed by Carthage in 409 BC and largely forgotten. Excavations (still under way in the oldest parts of the ruins) have brought to light eight temples with colossal Doric columns, as well as a fortification system.

★ **Temple C** (580–550 BC)
Decorated with metopes now kept in Palermo, this was the largest and oldest temple on the Acropolis, possibly dedicated to Heracles or Apollo.

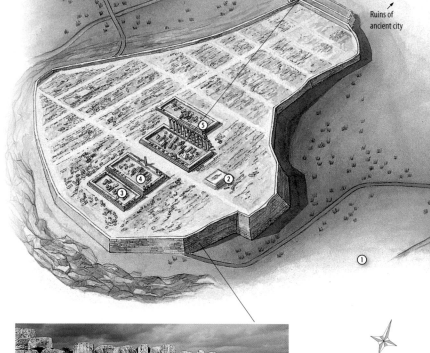

Sanctuary of Malophoros

Ruins of ancient city

★ **Acropolis**
This was the hub of public life. It centred around two main streets that divided it into four quarters protected by a wall 1,260 m (4,132 ft) long.

★ **Temple E** (490–480 BC)
This temple, located at the top of an eight-stepped base (crepidoma), was partly rebuilt in the 1960s. It was probably sacred to Hera and is considered one of the finest examples of Doric architecture in Sicily.

KEY

① Car park

② **Temple B (c.250 BC)** was probably the only one built in the Hellenistic age.

③ **Temple O (480–470 BC)**

④ **Temple A (480–470 BC)** is thought to have been dedicated to Leto.

⑤ **Temple D (570–550 BC)** was possibly dedicated to Aphrodite.

⑥ **The harbour area** lay at the junction of the Cotone river and the road connecting the Acropolis to the eastern hill.

⑦ **Temple F (560–530 BC)** may have been dedicated to Athena and is the most ancient temple on the eastern hill. Sadly it is totally in ruins.

⑧ **Eastern hill**

⑨ **Entrance and car park**

| 0 metres | 150 |
| 0 yards | 150 |

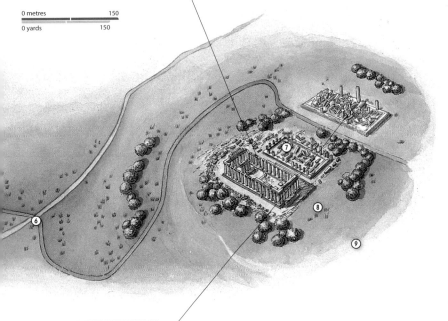

Temple G (540–480 BC)
This temple is also completely in ruins but is still an important monument because, at 6,120 sq m (65,850 sq ft), it was one of the largest temples in antiquity. It reached a height of 30 m (98 ft) when complete.

VISITORS' CHECKLIST

Practical Information
Road map B3. 🛈 0924-46277 or 46251. **Open** 9am–6pm (to 4pm in winter). 🅰

Transport
✈ Palermo Punta Raisi (Falcone Borsellino) and Trapani Birgi (V. Florio). 🚉 Castelvetrano (892021). 🚌 Castelvetrano.

Exploring Selinunte

You will need at least two hours to visit the archaeological site of Selinunte. The excavated area is divided into four zones, starting off from the east: the eastern hill with its group of temples; the Acropolis; the ancient city; and the Sanctuary of Malophoros. Besides Selinunte's great cultural interest, the surrounding landscape is very beautiful, and there are lovely views of the sea.

The metopes of Temple C are now in Palermo's archeological museum *(see p60)*

Acropolis

This lies on a bluff right over the sea, between the Modione river to the west and the Gorgo Cottone river to the east. Their mouths once formed the city harbour, now silted up. The Acropolis was surrounded by colossal stone walls 3 m (10 ft) high, with two gates, the larger one on the northern side. This area contained the public buildings and temples, all facing east. From the southern end, the first places are the sparse ruins of **Temples O and A**, close together and much alike. There were originally six columns along the short sides and 14 on the

Hellenistic vases, Museo Archeologico, Palermo (see p60)

longer ones. Further on you come to the small **Temple B**, which was thought to have been brightly coloured.

Temple C is the most ancient on the Acropolis. It may have been dedicated to Apollo and had six columns on the short sides and 17 on the long ones. The pediment was decorated with superb metopes, three of which are now in the Museo Archeologico in Palermo *(see p60)*. In 1925–6, 14 columns on the northern side and on part of the architrave were reconstructed. The sight of these among the other blocks of

massive columns placed here and there around the ancient sacred precinct is quite impressive.

Temple D is also reduced to a state of fragmentary ruins. The Acropolis area was divided by two main perpendicular streets, which can be reached by means of stone steps.

The eastern hill

The sacred precinct has remains of three temples set parallel to one another at the entrance to the archaeological zone. In ancient times it was surrounded by an enclosure. The partially reconstructed **Temple E** was built in the pure Doric style. An inscription on a votive stele found in 1865 suggests it was dedicated to Hera (Juno). Its 68 columns still support part of the trabeation.

An eight-step stairway leads to **Temple F**, possibly dedicated to either Athena or Dionysus, the smallest and most badly damaged of the three. It was built in the archaic style, surrounded by 36 columns which were more than 9 m (29 ft) high. The vestibule had a second row of columns, and the lower part of the peristyle was enclosed by a wall.

The bronze ephebus, Selinunte

Temple E, one of the best examples of Doric architecture in Sicily

The Collegio dei Gesuiti at Mazara del Vallo, home to the Museo Civico

The dimensions of **Temple G** must have exceeded 110 by 50 m (350 by 150 ft). It was begun in the 6th century BC and took another 100 years to complete. It was considered the city's main religious building. Today it is only a huge mass of stones, in the middle of which stands a column, which was restored in 1832. It was probably dedicated to Zeus, but its construction was never completed.

🏛 The Ancient City
Set on the Collina di Manuzza hill north of the Acropolis, the ancient city only became the subject of archaeological excavations late in the 20th century. After the destruction of Selinunte in 409 BC, this ancient part was used as a necropolis by those inhabitants who remained.

🏛 Malophoros Sanctuary
Situated west of the Modione river, about a kilometre (half a mile) away from the Acropolis, the Malophoros Sanctuary is extremely old and perhaps was founded even before the city itself.
   The main building in this sanctuary is enclosed by walls and was dedicated to a female divinity, Malophoros (meaning "bearer of pomegranate"), the goddess of fertility, many statuettes of whom have been found in the vicinity. According to experts, the sanctuary was a stopping point on the long, impressive funeral processions making their way to the Manicalunga necropolis.

㉔ Castelvetrano

Road map B3. 🏘 31,000. 🚌 73 km (45 miles) from Trapani, 110 km (68 miles) from Palermo. *i* Town hall, Piazza Aragona E Tagliavia (0924-902 004). 🚍 Tue. 🎭 Funzione dell'Aurora (Easter).

The centre consists of three linked squares. The main one is **Piazza Garibaldi**, where the mainly 16th-century **Chiesa Madre** has an interesting medieval portal. Inside are stuccoes by Ferraro and Serpotta, and a *Madonna* by the Gagini School. By the church are the **Municipio** (Town Hall), the **Campanile** and the Mannerist **Fontana della Ninfa**. Nearby is the **Chiesa del Purgatorio**, built in 1624–64, its façade filled with statues, and the Neo-Doric **Teatro Selinus** (1873).

Environs
At **Delia**, 3.5 km (2 miles) from town, is Santa Trinità, a church built in the Norman period.

㉕ Mazara del Vallo

Road map A3. 🏘 51,000. 🚌 50 km (31 miles) from Trapani, 124 km (77 miles) from Palermo. *i* Via XX Settembre (0923-944 610). 🚍 Wed. 🎭 Festino di San Vito (Aug).

Facing the Canale di Sicilia, at the mouth of the Mazarò river, the town, a colony of Selinunte, was destroyed in 409 BC by the Carthaginians, passed to the Romans and then became a prosperous city under the Arabs, who made it the capital of one of the three "valleys" into which they split Sicily (*see p36*). In 1073 Mazara was conquered by Roger I; he convened the first Norman Parliament of Sicily here.
   In **Piazza Mokarta** remains of the castle can be seen. Behind this is the **Cathedral**, of medieval origin but rebuilt in 1694. It houses the *Transfiguration*, a sculpture group by Antonello Gagini. The left side of the Cathedral closes off Piazza della Repubblica, with the façade of the **Seminario dei Chierici** and the **Palazzo Vescovile**. On Lungomare Mazzini you will see the **Collegio dei Gesuiti**, seat of the **Museo Civico**, and can enter the old Arab town.

🏛 Museo del Satiro Danzante
Piazza Plebiscito. **Tel** 0923-933 917. **Open** 9am–6:30pm daily. 🎨
There are several interesting artifacts on display here, but the highlight is the statue of a dancing satyr, which is a rare example of a Greek bronze.

Mazara del Vallo, one of the most important fishing harbours in Italy

㉖ Egadi Islands

Road map A2. 🏔 4,300. 🚢 from Trapani (Siremar: 0923-249 68). 🛈 Favignana town hall (0923-925 443/565 412); STR Trapani (0923-806 800). 🔲 **isoleegadi.it**

The Egadi islands of Favignana (the largest of the three), Levanzo and Marettimo were connected to mainland Sicily 600,000 years ago. As the sea level gradually rose over the years, the links were submerged, slowly changing the islands into an archipelago in the centre of the Mediterranean. These charming islands are now popular as places for vacations and swimming as they are easily reached from Trapani.

A stretch of the Favignana coastline

Favignana

This island has two distinct parts. The eastern side is flat, with pastureland and farmland, while the other half is craggy and barren. In the middle is the small town of **Favignana**, which was rebuilt in the 1600s over its original medieval layout. Sights worth visiting are the **Chiesa Matrice** (dedicated to the Immaculate Conception), the buildings constructed during the height of the tuna fishing industry and the 19th-century **Palazzo Florio**, which is now the Town Hall.

There are different coves to visit, from the beautiful **Cala Stornello** to the **Previto Islet**, from **Cala Rotonda** to **Cala Grande**, and from **Punta Ferro** to **Punta Faraglione**, where prehistoric caves with Paleolithic finds can be seen. The perimeter of the eastern part starts from **Punta San Nicola** and arrives at **Cala Rossa**, where there are

heaps of tufa from the island quarries. From **Cala Rossa** to **Bue Marino** and from **Cala Azzurra** to **Punta Lunga**, the coast is characterized by fine tuff sand beaches and crystalline waters.

Levanzo

The smallest of the Egadi Islands has a wilder aspect than Favignana: the tall, rocky coastline is dominated by a cultivated plateau. There is only one small village, **Cala Dogana**, and the landscape is barren and desolate, interrupted here and there by the green maquis vegetation. A series of footpaths crosses the island and provides very pleasant walks to the beautiful **Cala Tramontana** bay.

Northwest of Cala Dogana is the **Grotta del Genovese**, which can be reached on foot in about two hours or by boat. The grotto has a series of carved

Palaeolithic and Neolithic drawings of human figures, animals and idols, some in a rather naturalistic style, others rendered more schematically.

Marettimo

The rugged, mountainous and varied landscape of Marettimo, the first island in the group to break off from the mainland, is very striking. The paths crossing the island – there are no roads or hotels here – will introduce you to a world of limestone pinnacles and caves leading up to Monte Falcone (686 m/ 2,250 ft). The island has many rare plant species that grow only here – caused by the long isolation of Marettimo – as well as some introduced moufflon and boar. The **Punta Troia fort** housed a Bourbon penal colony where the Risorgimento hero Guglielmo Pepe was held for three years. Not far from the tiny village of Marettimo there are some ancient Roman buildings and, in the vicinity, a small Byzantine church.

The little harbour at Cala Dogana, the only village on Levanzo

The Grotta Azzurra, a major attraction on boat tours around Ustica

㉗ Ustica

Road map B1. 🏔 1,300. ⛴ from Palermo (Siremar: 091-749 33 15; Ustica Lines: 092-387 38 13). ✈ Palermo Punta Raisi 091-591 663. ℹ STR Palermo (091-639 80 28/11); Town hall (091-844 81 24); Guardia Costiera (0923-844 96 52). 🌐 ampustica.it

Ustica is the result of ancient volcanic eruptions: its name derives from the word *ustum* (burned) and the land is made up of sharp black volcanic rock, which gives it its unique appearance. The emerged part of the gigantic submerged volcano, about 49 km (30 miles) from the Sicilian coast, is only 8.6 sq km (3.32 sq miles), but its extremely fertile lava terrain is ideal for the cultivation of capers and lentils. The steep and rocky coasts and the seascape that surrounds the island make it an ideal spot for underwater sports. Because of the importance of the sea beds, the first **Marine Reserve** in Italy was established here on 12 November 1986; it is run by the local authorities. The park is divided into three sections, and the degree of protection ranges from total (from Caletta to Cala Sidoti) to partial. Guided tours are organized by the Marine Reserve itself, and in July the island plays host to a series of international skin- and scuba-diving programmes. A particularly interesting underwater excursion is the one that starts off at **Punta Gavazzi**, with what could be described as an archaeological

diving tour of the ancient Roman amphorae, old anchors, and traces of the passage of sailors since the beginning of human history in this part of the sea.

The village of **Ustica** is dominated by the **Capo Falconara** promontory, where the Bourbon rulers built a little fort offering a splendid view as far as the Sicilian coast. Ustica was founded in the mid-1700s and is still inhabited. Local life revolves around Piazza Umberto I, where there is a whitewashed parish church. Age-old human presence on the island is visible in a number of interesting sites, such as the

prehistoric village of **Faraglioni** and the Phoenician tombs at **Falconara**, which were used at different times by the Greeks, the Romans and the Byzantines.

The main feature of a boat tour of the island is the great number of underwater caves in the rocky coastline: the **Grotta Azzurra**, whose large caverns are preceded by an imposing natural arch, the **Grotta delle Colonne**, with a cliff of the same name, and the **Grotta Blasi, Grotta dell'Oro** and **Grotta delle Barche** (where fishermen used to moor their boats during storms), are only a few of the many caves to be seen.

Underwater exploration around the island of Ustica

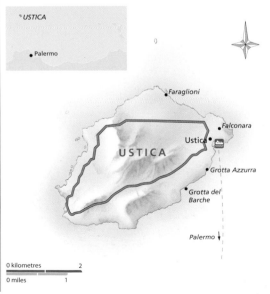

For keys to map symbols *see back flap*

SOUTHWESTERN SICILY

This corner of Sicily is only a stone's throw from North Africa. The landscape is varied, much of it hilly or mountainous, with rugged cliffs along parts of the coast and arid, barren plateaus inland. The Greeks built classically beautiful temples at Agrigento, and the Romans left an extensive villa at Piazza Armerina, saved for posterity by being buried under mud for centuries.

Along the coast, steep craggy cliffs alternate with flatter stretches of sand. This southern shore was a favourite landing place for travellers plying the Mediterranean, with their ships putting in at places like Agrigento, Eraclea and Sciacca.

Agrigento became an important Greek centre, and an entire valley of temples still remains as evidence of their skills. Some are still in good condition 2,000 years later. The mud-preserved Roman mosaics at the Villa del Casale at Piazza Armerina are in marvellous condition and provide an excellent picture of Roman life.

The land rises away from the sea to become soft, rolling hills and then, quite abruptly, rugged mountains. Rivers may emerge for only a few weeks each year.

Around the towns of Enna and Caltanissetta lies the stony heart of the island, exploited for its sulphur mines and quarries for centuries. Inland, Southwestern Sicily is a totally different world from the coast. Towns like Enna seem to perch precariously on hilltops. Many of the people of these rather isolated places have retained a deep-seated religious faith, which is expressed in the colourful processions held during Easter Week *(see p130)*. The flatter land and slopes nearer to the sea were once the domain of ancient feudal estates with their olive and orange groves, vividly described in Giuseppe di Lampedusa's novel *The Leopard*. This, perhaps the most truly "Sicilian" part of Sicily, was also the birthplace of the great Italian writer Pirandello.

A boar being captured in one of the fine hunting scene mosaics in the Villa del Casale, at Piazza Armerina

◄ The beautifully preserved columns of the Temple of Hera in the Valley of the Temples at Agrigento

Exploring Southwestern Sicily

A good starting point for a visit to this region of Sicily is Agrigento, as it is within easy reach of the eastern coast, with the towns of Palma di Montechiaro and Licata, and the western coast, moving towards the ancient site of Eraclea Minoa and the thermal spas at Sciacca. Major communications routes travel into the interior towards Caltanissetta and Enna on the one hand and, westwards, into the hinterland towards Palermo. From the port at Agrigento there is a regular boat service to the islands of Lampedusa and Linosa.

Bust of Persephone found at Aidone, near Enna

Getting Around

You can visit the sights of Agrigento by public transport if you choose to, but if you want to see the interior you will need a car. The main roads in this area are the SS189 Agrigento–Palermo, the SS640 to Caltanissetta (from Caltanissetta to Enna it becomes the SS117b and returns to the coast via Piazza Armerina and Gela) and lastly the SS115, which runs along the entire southwestern coastline of Sicily.

The ruins of the Hellenistic city of Morgantina

0 kilometres 20
0 miles 10

↑ *Palermo*

A19

Resuttano

Alimena

Nicosia ↑

117

121

Salso

Lago di Nicoletti

Leonforte

Calascibetta

Santa Caterina Villarmosa

121

Villarosa

ENNA ⑳

Catania →

A19

Sabucina

Pergusa

192

Valguarnera Caropepe

San Cataldo

⑲ **CALTANISSETTA**

Raddusa

122

640

Pietraperzia

117

⑪ **MORGANTINA**

Aidone

PIAZZA ARMERINA ⑫

626

Barrafranca

Delia

190

Sommatino

Mazzarino

San Cono

Gela

Ferro

Campobello Licata

Riesi

San Michele di Ganzaria

Ravanusa

Salso

417

117

Butera

Niscemi

626

⑭ ⑮

CASTELLO DI FALCONARA

Golfo di Gela

Gela

115

Maroglio

← *Ragusa*

Sights at a Glance

❶ *Agrigento pp118–21*
❷ Siculiana
❸ Eraclea Minoa
❹ Sciacca
❺ Caltabellotta
❻ Palazzo Adriano
❼ Prizzi
❽ Cammarata
❾ Mussomeli
❿ Racalmuto
⓫ Naro
⓬ Canicattì
⓭ Palma di Montechiaro
⓮ Licata
⓯ Castello di Falconara
⓳ Caltanissetta
⓴ Enna
㉑ *Morgantina p132*
㉒ *Piazza Armerina pp133–5*

Islands

⓰ Pantelleria
⓱ Lampedusa
⓲ Linosa

For additional keys to symbols *see back flap*

Key

▭ Motorway
▭ Major road
▬ Secondary road
─ Minor road
─ Minor railway
△ Summit

❶ Agrigento

There are two main sights in Agrigento: the magnificent remains of the Greek colony in the Valle dei Templi *(see pp120–21)* and the rocky hill where the medieval town was built. The town of Akragas was founded by the Greeks, then conquered by the Romans in 210 BC, who gave it the name of Agrigentum. During a period of barbarian invasions the town moved from the valley to the rock. It was then ruled by the Byzantines and for some time by the Arabs, whose dominion came to an end with the Normans in 1087.

Façade of Agrigento Cathedral (11th century)

Cathedral and Museo Diocesano

Piazza Don Minzoni. Museo Diocesano: **Tel** 0922-490 040. **Open** daily. Ⓦ museodiocesanoag.it

Agrigento's Cathedral was founded in the 12th century and subsequently enlarged and altered, as can be seen in some of the exterior details. For example, the bell tower has a series of Catalan-Gothic single lancet windows, while others are in the original style.

Inside is the Cappella di San Gerlando, named after the bishop who founded the church, with a Gothic portal. The ceiling features painted and coffered sections dating from the 16th and 17th centuries. An acoustic phenomenon known as the *portavoce* takes place in the chapel: those who stand under the apse can clearly hear the whispering of people at the other end of the nave, 80 m (262 ft) away.

The **Museum** has some Roman sarcophagi and a series of frescoes taken from the Cathedral walls in 1951.

🎭 Teatro Pirandello

Piazza Pirandello. **Tel** 0922-590 360/590 220.
Ⓦ teatroluigipirandello.it

Founded in 1870 and originally called Teatro Regina Margherita, the Teatro Pirandello was renamed after the Agrigento-born playwright *(see p26 & p29)*. Part of the Town Hall, it was designed by Dionisio Sciascia, and the decoration was executed by Palermo architect Giovanni Basile.

🏛 Museo Civico Santo Spirito

Via Santo Spirito 8. **Tel** 0922-590 371/401 450. **Closed** Sat & hols. Collegio dei Filippini: Via Atenea 270. **Open** Sun & public hols.

This museum, which is located next to the old Convento Suore Benedettine, houses medieval sculptures and an ethno-anthropological section. The nearby **Collegio dei Filippini** contains paintings from the 14th–20th centuries.

🏠 San Lorenzo

Piazza del Purgatorio. **Open** daily.
Little remains of this church (also known as Chiesa del Purgatorio), which was rebuilt in the Baroque style in the 1600s. The two-stage façade has an interesting portal flanked by

Agrigento

① Cathedral and Museo Diocesano
② Teatro Pirandello
③ Museo Civico Santo Spirito
④ San Lorenzo
⑤ Convento di Santo Spirito
⑥ Piazza Vittorio Emanuele
⑦ Museo Archeologico Regionale
⑧ *Valle dei Templi (see pp120–21)*

For hotels and restaurants see pp202–205 and pp210–217

two large spiral columns and a large bell tower. Both interior and exterior have a series of allegorical statues representing the Christian Virtues, executed in the early 1700s by Giuseppe and Giacomo Serpotta, and a *Madonna of the Pomegranate* attributed to Antonello Gagini.

Near the church, under a stone lion, is the Ipogeo del Purgatorio (Hypogeum of

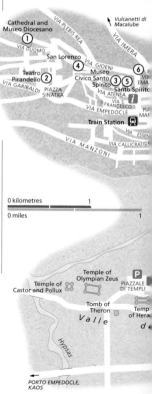

The arched coupled windows in the Convento di Santo Spirito (1295)

Purgatory), a network of underground conduits built in the 5th century BC by Greek architects to supply water to the various quarters of the city.

🏛 Convento di Santo Spirito

Salita Santo Spirito. **Open** daily.
This abbey complex is of ancient origin. The church and adjacent Cistercian monastery were founded in the 13th century by the Countess Prefoglio of the powerful Chiaramonte family. They were altered several times, particularly the façade, which, however, still maintains a Gothic portal and rose window. For many centuries the church was the most important in the Agrigento area and was known as the Badia Grande. In the 18th century the nave was decorated with lavish stuccowork that mirrors the shapes of the church; the motif is also developed in sculpted panels.

Next to the church is the monastery, now city property, where the cloister is well worth a visit. The impressive chapterhouse is lined with Gothic arcades.

🏛 Piazza Vittorio Emanuele

This large, lively, traffic-filled square connects the old town of Agrigento with the newer part, which developed during the 19th century. The two areas, Girgenti to the west and Rupe Atenea to the east, were once separated by a valley that was filled in during the late 19th century, blocking what was traditionally known as "Empedocles' opening", through which the north wind passed, cooling the valley below.

Environs

Towards the sea is the parish of Kaos, near Villaseta, worth visiting to see the **Birthplace of Luigi Pirandello**, the house of the great dramatist and novelist and Nobel Prize for Literature winner; it is now a museum (see pp26 & 29). The urn containing Pirandello's ashes can be found in a crack in a rock next to an old fallen pine, facing the sea.

Nearby, **Porto Empedocle** was once an important outlet for the mining activity in the interior. In the old harbour is the Bastione di Carlo V (Rampart of Charles V), while there is a constant bustle of fishing boats around the more industrialized area.

Heading north from Agrigento and turning off SS189 at the Comitini crossroads, 2 kilometres (1 mile) of dirt road to the south takes you to a place famous for a curious geological phenomenon: little volcano-shaped cones known as the **Vulcanetti di Macalube** emit methane gas bubbles and brackish mud in a lunar landscape made sterile by this pseudo-volcanic activity.

🏛 Museo Archeologico Regionale

Contrada San Nicola. **Tel** 0922-401 565. **Open** 9am–7:30pm Tue–Sat, 9am–1:30pm Mon, Sun & hols.
Part of the Convento di San Nicola and located in a panoramic spot that affords beautiful views over the Valley of the Temples (see pp120–21), this interesting archaeological museum shows material recovered from excavations around Agrigento. Among the items on display are a remarkable Attic vase, the Crater of Dionysus, and the marble statue of a young athlete known as the Ephebus of Agrigento.

🏛 Birthplace of Pirandello

Contrada Kaos, SS 115. **Tel** 0922-511 826. **Open** 9am–1pm, 2:30–7pm daily.

The eerie landscape of the Vulcanetti di Macalube

For keys to map symbols see back flap

Map labels

VIA CICERONE
VIA MINEHUH
VIA GIOVANNI XXIII
VIALE DELLA VITTORIA
VIA F CRISPI
A U LA MALFA
ARC A
VIA DEMETRA
San Biagio
Museo Archeologico Regionale 7
an Nicola
Hellenistic Roman Quarter
VIA DEL TEMPLI
Temple of Concord
ACRA
Temple of Hera
SS 115
Templi
Temple of Asclepius

Valle dei Templi

Agrigento was founded in 581 BC by colonists from Gela, who named the town Akragas. Yet only a century later the population had grown to 200,000, and the Greek poet Pindar described it as "the fairest city inhabited by mortals". It was ruled briefly by the Carthaginians. The Valley of the Temples is the site of the main temples (dedicated to Olympian Zeus, Heracles, Concord and Hera), minor shrines (Sanctuary of the Chthonic Divinities) and the Archaeological Museum.

★ **Museo Archeologico**
The Archaeological Museum was opened to the public in 1967. The 13 rooms display objects ranging from prehistoric times to the early Christian period, including pieces from the Classical era.

Temple of Hephaistos
(5th century BC)

Temple of Olympian Zeus (5th century BC)
Only fragmentary ruins remain of this temple, except for this Telamon, now on display in the Museo Archeologico.

⑤

④

③ ②

①

0 metres   200
0 yards   200

Entrance

Temple of Castor and Pollux (5th century BC)
The four surviving columns, a symbol of the Valley of the Temples, were restored in the 19th century.

Temple of Heracles (6th century BC)
These eight columns, put back in place in 1924, belonged to the oldest temple dedicated to the hero worshipped by both the Greeks and the Romans (as Hercules). The archaic Doric structure has an elongated rectangle plan.

Early Christian Catacombs

The Valle dei Templi is famous for its splendid monuments of the Magna Graecia civilization, but it also has early Christian ruins. The Ipogei of Villa Igea (also known as the Grotta di Frangipane), between the Temple of Heracles and the Temple of Concord, were cut out of the rock to house the bodies of the first Christians here. A series of niches, closed off by stone slabs, alternated with chapels that still bear traces of wall paintings.

The niches, hewn along the floors and walls

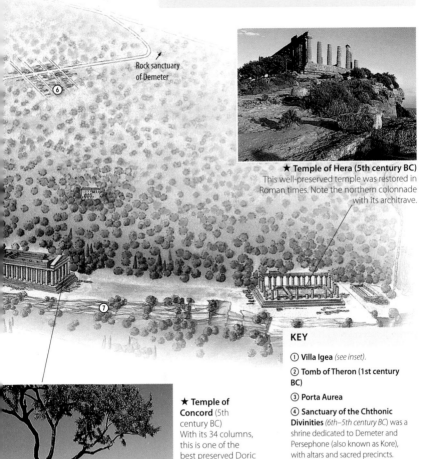

Rock sanctuary of Demeter

★ **Temple of Hera (5th century BC)**
This well-preserved temple was restored in Roman times. Note the northern colonnade with its architrave.

★ **Temple of Concord** (5th century BC)
With its 34 columns, this is one of the best preserved Doric temples in the world, partly thanks to alterations made in the 4th century AD, when it became a Christian basilica. It was restored to its original Classical form in 1748.

KEY

① **Villa Igea** *(see inset)*.

② **Tomb of Theron (1st century BC)**

③ **Porta Aurea**

④ **Sanctuary of the Chthonic Divinities** *(6th–5th century BC)* was a shrine dedicated to Demeter and Persephone (also known as Kore), with altars and sacred precincts.

⑤ **Giardino della Kolymbetra** is considered the most beautiful garden in Italy

⑥ **The Hellenistic-Roman quarter** is all that remains of the large post-Classical age settlement.

⑦ **Line of fortifications**

❷ Siculiana

Road map C4. 🏘 4,600. 🚋 from Palermo and Trapani to Castelvetrano, then 🚌 *i* Town hall, Piazza Basile 23 (0922-818 011).

The present-day town of Siculiana was built on the site of an Arab fort destroyed by the Normans in the late 11th century. The new lords – the Chiaramonte family from Agrigento – rebuilt the fortress in the 1300s and it was altered several times afterwards. Despite all the changes, Siculiana has retained some Arab features.

In central Piazza Umberto I is the Baroque **Chiesa Madre**, dedicated to San Leonardo Abate, dominating the square at the top of a flight of steps. In the old centre, divided into large blocks, you can glimpse entrances to courtyards and alleys, which were once part of the covered Arab town.

Siculiana, built on a hill during Arab rule

The archaeological site at Eraclea Minoa, close to the rocky shore

❸ Eraclea Minoa

Road map B4. Digs: Cattolica Eraclea. **Tel** 0922-846 005. **Open** Summer: 9am–7pm; winter: 9am–1 hr before sunset. 🎭

This settlement was founded during the Mycenaean age and then developed by Spartan colonists who arrived in the 6th century BC and gave it its present name. After being fought over by Agrigento and Carthage, Eraclea became a Roman colony. Today it is a stone's throw from the craggy coast jutting out into the sea. Eraclea is a combination of a lovely setting and atmospheric ruins. The **theatre** is well preserved – excavations began in the 1950s – and hosts special performances of Greek theatre, although the overall impression is marred somewhat by the plastic used to protect it in bad weather. All around the theatre are the ruins of the ancient city with its defence system, as well as some necropolises.

❹ Sciacca

Road map B3. 🏘 41,000. 🚋 from Palermo and Trapani. *i* STR, Corso Vittorio Emanuele 84 (0925-21182 or 22744); AAR Terme di Sciacca, Via Agatocle 2 (0925-961 111). 🌐 **sciacca.it**

From a distance, Sciacca seems to be overwhelmed by Monte San Calogero, with its thermal waters and steam vapours, which have made the town famous over the centuries. Although the hot springs had been used since prehistoric times, Sciacca was founded as a mere military outpost for Selinunte during the interminable warfare with the city of Agrigento, and was called *Thermae Selinuntinae* (Selinunte baths) by the Romans. It developed rapidly under Arab rule (Sciacca derives from *as-saqah*) and many traces of their culture can be seen in the old Rabato and Giudecca-Cadda quarters, with their blind alleys and maze of roofed courtyards.

The Oranges of Ribera

Locally grown oranges, still harvested by hand in this area

Orange decoration for the festival

The principle home of orange-growing is the plain around Mount Etna, but oranges play an important role in the southwestern corner of Sicily, too. At Ribera, an agricultural town where the statesman Francesco Crispi was born, they grow a special type of navel orange that was brought to Sicily from America by emigrants returning home. These enormous and delicious oranges are celebrated in an annual orange festival during which the public gardens are filled with sculptures made of fruit. A short distance from Ribera, the impressive ruins of the Poggio Diana castle tower above the wooded gullies of the Verdura river.

The rusticated façade of the Catalan-Gothic Palazzo Steripinto, Sciacca

The town was further fortified by the Normans, who quickly recognized its strategic importance in controlling the trade routes. Much fought over in the years that followed, the town was fortified again and again, in particular against the assault of Charles I of Valois.

In the middle of town is **Palazzo Steripinto**, built in Catalan-Gothic style in 1501 with a rusticated façade. The church of **Santa Margherita** has a splendid Gothic portal; note the bas-relief sculpture in the lunette representing Santa Margherita, the Archangel Gabriel, Our Lady of the Assumption and saints Calogero and Maddalena. Do not miss the cloister of the former **Convent of San Francesco** and the unfinished Baroque façade of the **Chiesa del Carmine**, with its 14th-century rose window. In central Piazza Don Minzoni stands the **Cathedral**, dedicated to Santa Maria Maddalena. It was rebuilt in 1656, but retains three Norman apses.

However, the main attractions in Sciacca are **Monte San Calogero** and its thermal pools. From the large square at the summit, with the sanctuary dedicated to the evangelist San Calogero, who in the 5th century eliminated pagan rites in the mountain caves, the panorama is breathtaking. The summit is almost 400 m (1,312 ft) high, and on a clear day there is a commanding view from Capo Bianco to Capo

Lilibeo, with the limestone ridge of Caltabellotta in the background and Pantelleria island before you. The older spas are on the slopes of the mountain, while new ones have been built closer to the seaside.

Sciacca is also known for its ceramics, mentioned in antiquity by Diodorus Siculus. Local production thrived during the period of Arab rule, and another golden age came in the 16th century. The tradition is being maintained today by local craftsmen.

❺ Caltabellotta

Road map B3. 🔼 4,000. ℹ️ Town hall, Piazza Umberto I 7 (0925-951 013).

Visible from most of the hilly area of Sciacca, the rocky crest of Caltabellotta (950 m/3,116 ft) has been inhabited for millennia, as can be seen in the many ancient necropolises and hypogea. The site was fortified at different stages until the arrival of the Arabs, who gave the castle its definitive form, calling it *Kal'at–at–al ballut* (rock of the oak trees). The county capital, Caltabellotta witnessed the signing of peace between Charles I of Valois and Frederick II of Aragón in 1302 *(see pp32–3)*, who took over the whole of Sicily. Perched on the ridge above the houses of the Torrevecchia quarter are the ruins of the **Norman castle** and **San Salvatore**, while on the other side of the rock is the **Chiesa Madre**, now being restored, founded by Roger I to celebrate his victory over the Arabs. On the western slope, the **Hermitage of San Pellegrino**, which consists of a monastery and a chapel, dominates the town.

Sculpture at the Hermitage of San Pellegrino

The town of Caltabellotta at the foot of Monte Castello

The façade of San Nicolò, in the upper part of Palazzo Adriano

❻ Palazzo Adriano

Road map C3. 🔺 2,300. 🛈 Pro Loco, Piazza Umberto I (091-834 99 01/28).

Almost 700 m (2,296 ft) above sea level, on the ridge of Cozzo Braduscia, is Palazzo Adriano, founded in the mid-15th century by Albanian refugees who had fled from their Turkish conquerors. Central Piazza Umberto I boasts two important churches: the Greek Orthodox **Santa Maria Assunta**, built in the 16th century and then rebuilt (the interior has a lovely iconostasis and an icon of Our Lady of the Assumption); and **Santa Maria del Lume**, which is Catholic and was founded in the 18th century. In the middle of the square, bordered by **Palazzo Dara**, now the Town Hall, and **Palazzo Mancuso**, there is a lovely octagonal fountain sculpted in 1607. Further up the hill, in the oldest part of Palazzo Adriano, the red dome of the 15th-century **San Nicolò** overlooks the alleyways of this quarter, which were built around the castle that stood here before the town was founded.

❼ Prizzi

Road map C3. 🔺 5,200. 🛈 Town hall, Corso Umberto I 64 (091-834 46 11).

The slopes of wind-blown Mount Prizzi, overlooking the surrounding valleys, have been inhabited since ancient times. There was once a fortified Arab town here, but present-day Prizzi mostly reflects the influence of the Middle Ages. The maze of alleys winding up the slopes to the summit (960 m/3,150 ft) is crowned by the ruins of the medieval castle. Along the narrow streets you will see **San Rocco**, a large stretch of open space with **Santa Maria delle Grazie**, and the 18th-century **Chiesa Madre**, dedicated to St George and bearing a fine statue of the Archangel Michael.

❽ Cammarata

Road map C3. 🔺 6,500. 🚆 from Palermo & Agrigento. 🛈 Town hall, via Roma (0922-907 233).

The earliest historical records for this town date from the Norman period, when Roger I donated the fief to Lucia de Cammarata. The **Chiesa Madre**, San Nicolò di Bari, and the **Dominican monastery**, whose church was rebuilt in the 1930s, are all worth a visit. But the fascination of Cammarata lies in the overall layout: a labyrinth of alleys and steps – narrow or wide, depending on the natural slope of the rock – offering an unforgettable view of the valleys below this medieval hill town.

Cinema Paradiso

In 1990 the film *Cinema Paradiso*, by the Sicilian director Giuseppe Tornatore *(see p28)*, won an Oscar for the best foreign film. The film tells the story of the arrival of cinema (the "Nuovo Cinema Paradiso") in an isolated village in Sicily and the effect the big screen has on the main character, a young boy. *Cinema Paradiso* was filmed in the streets and squares of Palazzo Adriano and used many of the locals as extras, conferring fame on the village. The weeks the film unit and the inhabitants of Palazzo Adriano spent working together are commemorated on a majolica plaque on a corner of Piazza Umberto I.

The plaque commemorating the filming of *Cinema Paradiso*

The characteristic stone trough at Piazza Fontana, in Racalmuto

❾ Mussomeli

Road map C3. 🔺 11,000. ℹ️ 0934-961 111. Castello Manfredonico: **Tel** 0934-992 009 **Open** summer: 9:30am–noon, 3:30–6pm daily; winter: 9:30am–noon daily. **Closed** Mon. 🌐 **comunedimussomeli.it**

In the 14th century, Manfredi III Chiaramonte founded the town of Mussomeli and the large fortress that still towers over what has since become a large agricultural centre. The **castle**, called Manfredano or Chiaramontano in honour of its founder and built over the remains of a Hohenstaufen fortification, was altered in the 15th century by the Castellar family. It has a second walled enclosure in the interior as well as the Sala dei Baroni, with noteworthy portals. From the outer walls there are panoramic views of the valleys and hills of the interior of the island.

❿ Racalmuto

Road map C4. 🔺 9,000. 🚉 from Catania and Palermo (via Caltanissetta). ℹ️ Town Hall (0922-940 043).

The town of Racalmuto (the name derives from the Arab *rahalmut*, or destroyed hamlet) was founded by Federico Chiaramonte, head of the powerful Sicilian Chiaramonte family, over an existing fortification. For centuries the growth of the town went hand in hand with the development of various monastic orders (Carmelite, Franciscan, Minor and Augustines), but the place still bears traces of the typical Arab layout marked by courtyards and alleys. For centuries Racalmuto thrived on the mining of rock salt and sulphur. The town is also the birthplace of author Leonardo Sciascia *(see p27)*. Today it is a famous agricultural centre, especially known for its dessert grapes.

In the middle of town, in Piazza Umberto I, is the 17th-century **Chiesa Madre dell'Annunziata**, its interior decorated with lavish stucco, as well as **San Giuseppe** and the ruins of the 13th-century **Chiaramonte castle** (closed to the public). Steps lead to Piazza del Municipio, with the **Santa Chiara Convent**, now the Town Hall, and the **Teatro Regina Margherita**, founded in 1879 by Dionisio Sciascia. Further up the hill, at the far end of the steps, is the **Sanctuary of Santa Maria del Monte**, where an important annual festival is held on 11–14 July. Inside the sanctuary is a statue of the Virgin Mary from 1503. Other churches worth visiting are the Carmelite (with canvases by Pietro D'Asaro), the Itria and San Giuliano, which was once the chapel of the **Sant'Agostino Convent**. A short walk from the centre takes you to **Piazza Fontana**, with a stone drinking trough, and, further along, Piazza San Francesco, where there is the monastery complex of the Conventual friars, rebuilt in the 1600s.

⓫ Naro

Road map C4. 🔺 8,000. ℹ️ Pro Loco (0922-953 021/009).

Naro lies on a hill in the middle of a water-rich area. Its name derives from ancient Greek and Arab origins – the Greek word for river is *naron*, and *nahr* is the Arab translation of the same.

A "resplendent" royal city during the reign of Frederick II Hohenstaufen, it was fortified at different times. Besides the Baroque churches and the remains of monasteries, there are the ruins of the medieval **Chiaramonte castle**, which is always closed, 14th-century Santa Caterina and the 16th-century Chiesa Madre.

The Chiaramonte castle at Naro, built in the 14th century

The 15th-century Castello di Montechiaro, overlooking the sea

⑫ Canicattì

Road map C4. 35,000. Town hall (0922-734 111/734 508); Proloco Largo Aosta (328-677 13 61).

The large agricultural town of Canicattì owes its fame to the production of dessert grapes (a festival in celebration is held each autumn). Known to Arab geographers as *al-Qattà*, this town became a part of documented Sicilian history in the 14th century, when it was registered as the fief of the Palmieri family from Naro. The late 18th century marked a period of prosperity and growth under the Bonanno family, who commissioned numerous buildings and public works.

In the centre of town are the **Castello Bonanno** and the **Torre dell'Orologio**, both rebuilt from ruins in the 1930s. Economic prosperity is confirmed by the many churches – **San Diego**, rebuilt in the Baroque period with stucco decoration; the **Chiesa del Purgatorio**, with a statue of the Sacred Heart; the **Chiesa del Carmelo**, rebuilt in the early 20th century with funds donated by the local sulphur mine workers – and civic works such as the **Fountain of Neptune** and the **Teatro Sociale**. The **Chiesa Madre** is dedicated to San Pancrazio. It was rebuilt in the early 20th century. The current façade is the work of Francesco Basile and among its many interesting sculptures and paintings is the *Madonna delle Grazie*, sculpted in the 16th century in Byzantine style. Along the main street in the upper town there are three monasteries.

Baroque decoration on a building in Licata

⑬ Palma di Montechiaro

Road map C4. 24,000. Town hall (800-476 738).

Founded in 1637 by Carlo Tomasi, the Prince of Lampedusa, Palma owes its name to the palm tree on the coat of arms of the De Caro family, relatives of the Tomasi. The town was the property of the Tomasi di Lampedusa family up to the early 19th century, but the family name became really famous only after the publication of the novel *Il Gattopardo (The Leopard)* in 1958.

Palma was created with a town plan, partly the inspiration of the 17th-century astronomer Giovanni Battista Odierna, and loosely based on that of Jerusalem. The layout revolves around **Piazza Provenzani**, with the church of **Santissimo Rosario** and a Benedictine monastery. Further up is the monumental stairway leading to Piazza Santa Rosalia, with the **Chiesa Madre**, built in the late 1600s with an impressive two-stage façade flanked by twin bell towers. On Sundays and holidays this square is the hub of city life.

A walk through town reveals a number of interesting Baroque buildings. A few miles

Giuseppe Tomasi di Lampedusa (1896–1957)

Il Gattopardo (The Leopard)

Tomasi di Lampedusa's famous novel *(see p27)* was a great success when it was published posthumously in 1958, selling over 100,000 copies. It was later made into a highly acclaimed film by Luchino Visconti. The novel was published thanks to the efforts of novelist Giorgio Bassani, who met Tomasi di Lampedusa in 1954, three years before he died. Most of the novel is set in Palermo, but there are recognizable descriptions of the villages and landscape in this part of Sicily, with which the author had strong bonds.

The Teatro Sociale in Canicattì, completed in 1908

away, not far from the sea, are the evocative ruins of **Castello di Montechiaro**, founded, according to tradition, by Federico III Chiaramonte. Although it is now closed for restoration, it is worthwhile visiting the site of this 15th-century castle because of the wonderful views of the coastline from its walls.

⓮ Licata

Road map C4. ⚏ 39,000.
🚆 from Syracuse, Palermo & Catania, via Caltanissetta (0922-774 122).
ℹ Town hall (0922-868 111); Proloco (328-061 36 53/349-508 19 50).
🅦 **prolocolicata.it**

Licata is one of the chief market garden towns in southern Sicily. It was built in the Greek period and under Roman rule became the port for the shipment of local produce. Evidence of the town's former wealth can be seen in the many rock-hewn Byzantine churches. After the period of Arab rule, in 1234 Frederick II made it part of the public domain, building fortresses which over the centuries have disappeared (Castel Nuovo was destroyed by the Turks at the end of the 1561 siege). Licata again became a part of history on 10 July 1943, when Allied troops landed nearby and advanced northwards in their conquest of Italian territory.

The centre of town life is Piazza Progresso, where there is the Art Deco **Municipio** or Town Hall, designed in 1935 by Ernesto Basile, which houses some interesting artworks, including a statue of the *Madonna and Child* and a 15th-century triptych. Also worth visiting is the **Museo Archeologico**, which has exhibits of prehistoric artifacts from the Palaeolithic to the Bronze Age, archaic Greek and Hellenistic archaeological finds, and a series of medieval statues representing the Christian virtues. Along Corso Vittorio Emanuele, which leads towards the coast, there are some patrician mansions such as **Palazzo Frangipane**, which has an 18th-century façade decorated with reliefs. On the Corso you can also see the **Chiesa Matrice di**

Santa Maria la Nova, which, according to local legend, the Turks tried to burn down in 1553. Founded in the 1500s, it houses a 16th-century crucifix and a 17th-century Flemish Nativity scene. A lively area on the waterfront for eating and shopping is the new Marina di Cala del Sole. A popular mooring with visitors arriving by boat, the Marina is the centre of Licata's sailing scene, with bars, cafés, a mall and a multi-plex cinema, as well as useful tourist facilities.

🏛 **Museo Archeologico**
Via Dante, Badia di Licata. **Tel** 0922-772 602. **Open** 8am–8pm Mon–Sat, 8am–1pm Sun.

⓯ Castello di Falconara

Road map D4. **Open** by appt only.
Tel 091-329 082. 🅦 **castello difalconara.it**

Not far from Licata, on the road towards Gela, is the village of Falconara, famous most of all for the impressive castle towering above the sea from the top of a rocky bluff. The Castello di Falconara was built in the 15th century. It is usually closed, but you can make an appointment to view with the custodian.

Towards Licata is the Salso river, the second longest in Sicily. Its name derives from the many outcrops of rock salt that make its waters salty (*salso* means saline). The river flows through the Sommatino plateau and down a series of gullies before meandering across the coastal plains.

Castello di Falconara, constructed in the 15th century and set among greenery at the water's edge

⑯ Pantelleria

Road map A5. ⛰ 8,000. 🚢 ✈
ℹ Town hall (0923-695 035/036); Pro
Loco (334-390 93 60 or 338-810 56
44). 🅦 **comune.pantelleria.it**

Pantelleria, the largest island
off the Sicilian coastline, is
closer to the Tunisian coast
(Capo Mustafà is 70 km or
44 miles away) than to Capo
Granitola in Sicily (100 km,
62 miles). Despite its isolation,
Pantelleria was colonized by the
Phoenicians and then by the
Greeks. It was controlled by the
Arabs for almost 400 years (in
fact, its name derives from *Bent
el-Rhia*, "daughter of the wind")
and was then conquered and
fortified in 1123 by Roger I.
Since that time its history
has run in parallel to the
vicissitudes of Sicily.

The strong wind that blows
here all year round has forced
the inhabitants to protect their
plants and kitchen gardens with
enclosures and walls, and to
prune the olive trees so that
they grow almost horizontally,
close to the ground. Wind is also
responsible for a typical style of
building called *dammuso*, a
square, whitewashed peasant's
house with walls almost 2 m
(6 ft) thick and tiny windows in
order to provide the best
insulation. Water is scarce on
the island, so the roofs of these
homes are shaped to collect
rainwater. The coastal road is
53 km (33 miles) in length; it
starts at the town of Pantelleria
and goes past the **archaeological zone of Mursia** (with a

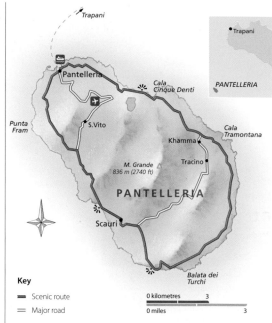

series of megalithic
structures called
sesi in local dialect)
and then up to
high ground. The
main sights here
are **Punta Fram,
Cala dell'Altura**
and **Punta Tre
Pietre**, where
another road takes
you to the little port
of **Scauri**. The coast is steep and
craggy with some inlets (like
the **Balata dei Turchi**, once
a favourite landing place for
Saracen pirates, or the lovely
Cala Rotonda) up to the **Punta**

Walled gardens on Pantelleria

Key
━ Scenic route
═ Major road

0 kilometres 3
0 miles 3

Tracino promontory – with a
striking rock formation in front
of it – which separates the
Tramontana and **Levante
inlets**. After the village of Gadir
and the lighthouse at Punta
Spasdillo the road descends to
the **Cala Cinque Denti** inlet or
the **Bagno dell'Acqua** hot
springs and then back to its
starting point. The town of
Pantelleria, at the foot of the
Barbacane Castle, was almost
destroyed by Allied bombings
in World War II. Life revolves
around **Piazza Cavour** and the
new **Chiesa Madre**, both facing
the sea. Renting a bicycle is a
very pleasant way of getting to
know the island and the local
way of life, as well as the
handicrafts, the famous
Moscato *passito* dessert wine
and the locally grown capers.

Arco dell'Elefante, one of the most beautiful spots in Pantelleria

Baia dei Conigli in Lampedusa, where the rare sea turtle still survives

⓱ Lampedusa

Road map B5. 🚠 (with Linosa) 6,000. 🚢 from Porto Empedocle (Ustica Lines: 0923-873 813). ✈ 0922-970 588. ℹ STR Agrigento (0922-20391). 🎉 22 Sep. Ⓦ **comune. lampedusaelinosa.ag.it**

The largest island in the Pelagie (the archipelago that includes Linosa and the small island of Lampione), Lampedusa is 200 km (124 miles) from Sicily and 150 km (93 miles) from Malta. The Greek name *Pelaghiè* reflects their chief characteristic – isolation in the middle of the sea. Inhabited for a little more than a century – from the time Ferdinand II of Bourbon sent a group of colonists and prisoners there – Lampedusa was soon deforested, which in turn brought about the almost total

degradation of the soil and any possibility of cultivating it. Human settlements have also led to a dramatic decrease in local fauna, and the Baia dei Conigli nature reserve was set up to create a safe refuge for sea turtles (*Caretta caretta*). The island's main beaches are **Cala Maluk, Cala Croce, Baia dei Conigli, Cala Galera** and **Cala Greca**, and diving is one of the many popular sports. Near the town of **Lampedusa** (almost completely destroyed in 1943) is the **Madonna di Lampedusa Sanctuary**, where on 22 September the Bourbon takeover is commemorated.

Entrance to a house in Linosa

⓲ Linosa

Road map B5. 🚠 (with Lampedusa) 6,000. 🚢 ℹ STR Agrigento (0922-20391); Consorzio Albergatori 35° Parallelo. Ⓦ **comune. lampedusaelinosa.ag.it.**

Ancient Aethusa, 40 km (25 miles) from Lampedusa, is a small volcanic island where life centres around the village of Linosa, with its brightly coloured houses. Thanks to the naturally fertile volcanic soil, agriculture thrives on the island. One of the best ways of exploring Linosa is by leaving the road behind and rambling around the craters and the fenced-in fields.

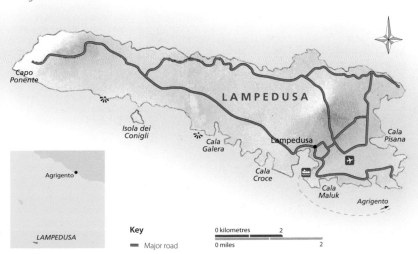

Key

━ Major road

0 kilometres 2

0 miles 2

⑲ Caltanissetta

Road map D3. 🚹 61,000. 🚆 from Catania & Palermo (095-532 719). 🛈 Proloco, Palazzo Moncada (0934-585 890/338-441 43 00). 🅆 caltanissettaturismo.it

One of the earliest traces of a settlement in this area is the **Abbazia di Santo Spirito**, a Norman abbey commissioned by Roger I and his wife Adelasia in the late 11th century and consecrated in 1153. It is still one of the most interesting sights in Caltanissetta and its immediate vicinity. In common with other hill towns in the interior, Caltanissetta was surrounded by medieval walls and then expanded towards the monasteries, built around the town from the 15th century on. The centre of a thriving mineral-rich area, it became prosperous after the Unification of Italy thanks to the **sulphur and rock salt mines**. It was during this period that the look of the town changed with the construction of buildings and public works.

In the heart of town, in Piazza Garibaldi, are the Baroque **San Sebastiano** and the **Cathedral** (dedicated to Santa Maria la Nova and San Michele). A brief

The Baroque façade of San Sebastiano, completed in the 1800s

walk down Corso Umberto I will take you to **Sant'Agata** – or Chiesa del Collegio – built in 1605 for the Jesuits of Caltanissetta, next to their seminary. The rich decoration inside includes a marble statue of *St Ignatius in Glory* on the left-hand transept altar, the altarpiece *San Francesco Saverio* in a side chapel and a canvas of the *Martyrdom of Sant'Agata*. Not far from the **Castello di Pietrarossa**, probably a former Arab fortress, is the **Museo Archeologico**, where the sections are given over to archaeology and modern art.

The **Museo Mineralogico, Paleontologico e della Zolfara**, established by the local Mineralogy School, S. Mottura, has a fine and extensive collection of minerals and fossils.

🏛 **Abbazia di Santo Spirito**
Tel 0934-566 596. **Open** 9am–noon, 4–7pm daily.

🏛 **Museo Archeologico**
Contrada Santo Spirito. **Tel** 0934-567 062. **Open** 9am–1pm, 3:30–7pm daily. **Closed** last Mon of month. 📷

🏛 **Museo Mineralogico**
Tel 0934-591 280. **Open** 9am–1pm Mon–Sat, by request Sun (call 349-710 25 25). 📷 📷 call 349-710 25 25.

Environs
About 5 km (3 miles) along the main road to Enna is the site of the ancient city of **Sabucina**, where you can see a prehistoric village and cave tombs dating from the 12th–10th centuries BC. The city became a Greek colony, but subsequently declined and was later abandoned.

The Abbazia di Santo Spirito, one of the major Norman churches in Sicily

Easter Week

In the interior of Sicily the celebrations of the *Misteri*, or statues of the Stations of the Cross, during Easter Week are of the greatest importance. At Enna they begin on Palm Sunday. For four days, the 15 city confraternities take part in processions through the streets to the Cathedral; on Good Friday a huge torchlit procession bears the statue of the Madonna of the Seven Griefs, the Reliquary of Christ's Thorn and the Dead Christ's Urn through the city; then on Easter Sunday the Resurrected Christ and the Virgin Mary statues meet in Piazza Duomo. At Caltanissetta, celebrations begin on Wednesday with the Procession of the Holy Sacrament, followed by the representatives of the 11 city confraternities. On Maundy Thursday the large statues of the Passion of Christ are taken through the city and on Good Friday the Passion of the Black Christ ends the celebrations.

Part of the colourful Easter Week celebrations

Sabucina
Tel 0934-566 982. **Open** by appointment only.

The Sulphur Mines
i Ente Parco Minerario Floristella, Grottacalda (0935-958 105).
w enteparcofloristella.it

For centuries the Floristella sulphur field was one of the most important sources of wealth in the Sicilian hinterland. Mining activity ceased in 1988 and the mines are closed to the public, but now work is under way to turn this yellow-stained land into a mining park. Extraction reached its height during the 19th century – when Palazzo Pennisi, the residence of the mine owners, was built.

❷⓪ Enna

Road map D3. 30,000. from Catania and Palermo (0935-500 91 10).
i STR Piazza Colajanni 6 (0935-500 875); Proloco (340-148 26 41).
w pro-loco-enna-proserpina.it

A mountain town – at 931 m (3,054 ft) the highest provincial capital in Italy – in antiquity Enna was first Greek, then Carthaginian and finally Roman. It remained a Byzantine stronghold even after the Arab conquest of Palermo, and was then conquered by general Al-Abbas Ibn Fadhl in 859 and was wrested from the Muslims only in 1087. From that time it was repeatedly fortified around the strongholds of Castello di

Enna Cathedral, built in the 15th century and rebuilt after a fire

The Castello di Lombardia, built over an Arab fortification

Lombardia and Castello Vecchio (present-day Torre di Federico). The defensive walls, no longer visible, were the basis of the town's plan, while all the principal sites of religious and civic power were constructed on what is now Via Roma.

Because of its altitude, Enna has a climate unique in the interior of Sicily and even in summer the temperature is pleasant. The town's exceptional position means splendid views. Going up Via Roma, you first come to Piazza Vittorio Emanuele, site of **San Francesco d'Assisi**, the only original part of which is the fine 15th-century bell tower. In Piazza Colajanni you will see the façade of **Palazzo Pollicarini**, which has many Catalan Gothic features on the side next to the stairway, as well as the former church of **Santa Chiara**.

In 1307 Eleonora, wife of Frederick II of Aragón, founded the **Cathedral** of Enna. The building was destroyed by fire in the mid-1400s and subsequently rebuilt. A fine 16th-century doorway – with a bas-relief depicting *St Martin and the Beggar* – leads to the Latin cross interior with two aisles. The Cathedral is richly decorated with an assortment of statues and paintings.

In the historic town centre is the **Museo Musical Art 3M**, which is the first multimedia museum to feature Sicilian art. The collection showcases important works of art by Sicilian painters, such as Antonello da Messina, Caravaggio and Filippo Paladini, through a virtual display. This exhibition is accompanied by music composed by Sebastian Occhino, a famous contemporary musician and composer from Enna.

Nearby, the **Museo Archeologico** has a fine display of prehistoric, Greek and Roman archaeological items found in the town, in the area around and near Lake Pergusa. But the pride and joy of Enna are its fortresses. The **Castello di Lombardia**, built by the Hohenstaufens and altered in the Aragónese era, is one of the grandest in Sicily. A tour here includes the three courtyards, the Torre Pisana and the Rocca di Cerere. In the public gardens is the octagonal **Torre di Federico II**, the only remaining part of the original defences.

Museo Musical Art 3M
Via Roma 533. **Tel** 338-502 33 61 or 339 200 24 63. **Open** 9am–1pm, 3–7pm daily. **Closed** Mon.

Museo Archeologico
Tel 0935-507 63 19. **Open** 9am–1 hr before sunset.

Castello di Lombardia
Tel 0935-500 875 (STR).
Open 8am–8pm.

Torre di Federico II
Open 8am–6pm Mon–Sat, 9am–1pm Sun & public hols.

㉑ Morgantina

Situated about 4 km (2 miles) from Aidone, the ancient city of Morgantina was founded by the Morgeti, a population from Latium who settled here around 1000 BC. The city was then occupied by Greek colonists. Its golden age, when it was a strategic trade centre between the north and south of Sicily, was in the Hellenistic and Roman periods. From the top of the hill visitors have a fine view of what remains of the theatre, the city streets and the agora. The coins of Morgantina and the Venus of Morgantina, which were looted and sold to US museums, have now been returned.

The Gymnasium
This was a large area for athletic exercises, with baths (above), dressing rooms and rooms with equipment for the athletes.

The Market
This lay in the middle of the upper agora. Above is the *tholos*, a round structure which had a number of different functions.

★ Theatre
Constructed at the end of the 4th century BC, the theatre at Morgantina was carved out of the slope of a hill and could seat about a thousand spectators.

★ Agora
Unusually, the agora, or forum, was divided into two parts, one above the other, linked by a trapezoidal, 14-step stairway.

Practical Information
Road map D4. STR, Via
Generale Muscarà 47a, Piazza
Armerina. **Tel** 0935-680 201.
Morgantina archaeological site:
Tel 0935-879 55. **Open** 8am–1 hr
before sunset.

Reconstruction of Morgantina

*This drawing shows the
city as it appeared around
300 BC. The reconstruction
is based on studies made
by archaeologists from
Princeton University in the
United States.*

0 metres   50
0 yards   50

KEY

① **Sanctuary of Demeter
and Persephone**

② **This area** was filled with
the workshops of craftsmen,
mostly ceramicists.

③ **Colonnade** *(stoa)*

④ **Residential quarter**

⑤ **Remains of paving** in the
eastern residential quarter
indicate where the paved street
led out of the city walls.

㉒ Piazza Armerina

Road map D4. 21,000. STR,
Via Generale Muscarà 47a. **Tel** 0935-
680 201. Palio dei Normanni
(13–14 Aug).

In the middle of an area
inhabited since the 8th century
BC, Piazza Armerina developed
in the Middle Ages, a period
marked by frequent clashes
between the local population
– strongly influenced by the
centuries of Arab domination
– and the Latin conquerors.
After the huge devastation
wrought in the 12th century
by battles between these two
factions, Piazza Armerina was
recreated around the Colle
Mira hill (in the middle of the
present-day Monte quarter)
and was populated by a
colony of Lombards from
Piacenza. A new, massive
defensive wall system was built
in the late 14th century, but the
city soon spread well beyond
this into the surrounding hills
and slopes.

In the heart of town is a large
Aragonese Castle, built by
King Martin I in the late 14th
century, whose massive towers
dominate the **Cathedral**.
Dedicated to Our Lady of the
Assumption, the Cathedral is
flanked by the campanile of
another church which had
been built on the same site in
the 14th century. Inside, look
out for the choir, built in 1627,
and a wooden crucifix painted
in the late 15th century. The
Cathedral also affords access to
the small **Museo Diocesano**,

The Cathedral at Piazza Armerina, with its
14th-century bell tower

which has vestments,
monstrances and reliquaries
on display. Elsewhere in the
town are many other interesting
attractions. **Piazza Garibaldi** is
the heart of town life, boasting
the Baroque **Palazzo del Senato**
and two palatial mansions
belonging to the barons of
Capodarso. The whole of the
historic centre deserves further
exploration on foot, through
charming medieval alleys,
steps and lanes.

Not far from the centre, at
the end of Via Tasso, is the **Chiesa
del Priorato di Sant'Andrea**,
founded in 1096 and then
acquired by the Knights of the
Order of the Holy Sepulchre.
This magnificent example of
Sicilian Romanesque architecture has a commanding
view over a valley. Do not miss
seeing the series of 12th- to
14th-century frescoes in the
interior (visits are allowed
only on Sundays, when mass
is celebrated).

View of Piazza Armerina, which developed around the Colle Mira hill

Piazza Armerina: Villa del Casale

This famous villa was part of a 3rd–4th century AD estate, and is one of the most fascinating attractions in archaeologically rich Sicily. The exceptionally beautiful mosaics that decorated every one of the rooms of the landowner's apartments have been preserved through the centuries, thanks to a flood that buried them in mud in the 12th century. The villa was discovered in the late 19th century. A logical sequence for a visit to the site is as follows: the thermae, the large peristyle, the long corridor with hunting scenes and, lastly, the owners' private apartments.

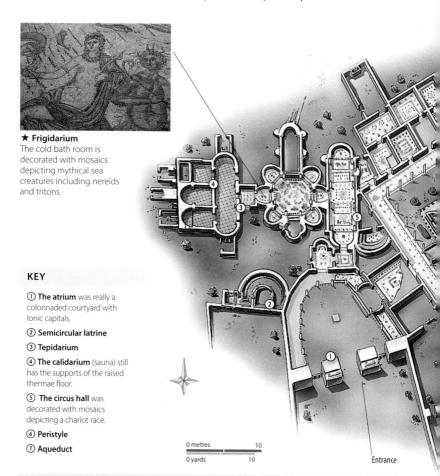

★ Frigidarium
The cold bath room is decorated with mosaics depicting mythical sea creatures including nereids and tritons.

KEY

① **The atrium** was really a colonnaded courtyard with Ionic capitals.

② **Semicircular latrine**

③ **Tepidarium**

④ **The calidarium** (sauna) still has the supports of the raised thermae floor.

⑤ **The circus hall** was decorated with mosaics depicting a chariot race.

⑥ **Peristyle**

⑦ **Aqueduct**

0 metres   10
0 yards   10

Entrance

The exterior of the Villa del Casale

The Discovery of the Villa

The first archaeological digs in the area were carried out at the end of the 19th century and were resumed in 1929 and 1935. But it was the 1950–60 excavations that resulted in the major discoveries, and these brought fame to the Villa del Casale. Perfectly preserved by a layer of mud caused by a flood many centuries ago, the mosaics are now being restored. Visitors today may come across expert archaeologists working on the tesserae of what have been called "the most exceptional Roman mosaics in the world".

★ Corridor with Hunting Scenes
This passageway contains splendid mosaics representing wild game hunting. Ferocious beasts such as boar and lions are being loaded onto ships after capture.

VISITORS' CHECKLIST

Practical Information
Road map D4. **Tel** 0935-687 667.
 STR, Piazza Armerina (0935-680 201). **Open** late Mar–late Oct: 9am–7pm (last entrance 6pm); late Oct–late Mar: 9am–5pm (last entrance 4pm).
Closed Mon.
W villaromanadelcasale.it

Northern Area
The vestibule in the private apartments of the villa has a large mosaic depicting Ulysses and Polyphemus.

★ The Myth of Arion
In the colonnaded semicircular atrium the mosaic shows Arion saved by a dolphin; surrounding him are female figures *(left)*, sea creatures and cupids.

★ Hall of the Female Gymnasts in Bikinis
The ten gymnasts seen in the mosaics in this hall are a rare and precious record of the Roman fashions of the time.

Triclinium
The mosaics in the dining room feature the Labours of Hercules and other mythological subjects.

SOUTHERN SICILY

Dominated by Mount Etna, southern Sicily's permanent backdrop, this area is a curious mixture of fertile land and intensive cultivation, ancient monuments and utter neglect. Many towns and monuments built by the ancient Greeks still survive, most notably in the town of Syracuse, birthplace of Archimedes.

Southern Sicily, which the Arabs called the Val di Noto, presents another facet of the region. It is very different from the western end of the island, although the topography is equally varied. The west has Phoenician Palermo, while the south has Greek Syracuse. One of Sicily's most important sights is the stony-tiered Greek theatre in Syracuse. The tradition of performing ancient Greek plays was revived in 1914, and now every summer the great works of the ancient tragedians come to life in their natural setting. This part of Sicily is also home to the ancient Greek ruins of Megara Hyblaea, now sadly dominated by the landscape of the refineries of Augusta.

Inland, the rebuilding of towns following the earthquake of 1693 resulted in a number of Baroque gems. The churches, buildings and balconies of Ragusa, Modica, Scicli, Noto and Chiaramonte are a triumph of the Sicilian Baroque style, with their majestic steps, detailed ornamentation and curving façades. Ibla, the medieval quarter of Ragusa, should be included on a tour of the towns of the interior; rocky Caltagirone is an important ceramics centre, and Chiaramonte and Vizzini also have their charms. In complete contrast you can also experience the natural silence of the rock-cut necropolises in the cliffs of Ispica and Pantalica.

Fishing boats anchored in Ortygia harbour in Syracuse

◀ Detail from the Baroque façade of the Duomo in Ortygia

Exploring Southern Sicily

An excellent starting point for any visit to Sicily's southern tip is Syracuse, with its exceptional artistic and cultural heritage. It lies about 60 km (37 miles) from Catania airport and is a two-hour drive from Messina, along a scenic route with the Ionian Sea to your left and Mount Etna to your right. Other popular sights in this area are the old cities in the interior – those in Val di Noto (Caltagirone, Modica, Noto, Palazzolo Acreide, Ragusa and Scicli, along with Militello Val di Catania and Catania itself) have all been named UNESCO World Heritage sites. The mountains conceal an impressive testimony to the ancient history of southern Sicily in the crevices of Pantalica, Ispica and Lentini.

Ceramic plate produced
in Caltagirone

The Baroque façade of the Basilica di
San Giorgio in Ragusa

Sights at a Glance

Getting There

There are several ways of getting to the interior of southern Sicily. You can take road SS115 from Agrigento to Gela, then on to Syracuse – passing through Noto, Ispica, Modica and Ragusa – opting for detours if you wish, or, from Catania, follow the A194 to Caltagirone, then bear south, or take motorway A18 to Syracuse. Syracuse can also be reached by train. To begin your tour here, you can fly from mainland Italy and other European destinations to Comiso airport.

View of Ortygia island, part of Syracuse

Gornalunga

Catania

Piana di Catania

Ramacca

417

194

Golfo di Catania

Palagonia

385

Agnone Bagni

Scordia

Capo Campolato

Militello

15 LENTINI

114

Mineo

Carlentini

Capo Santa Croce

Francofonte

193

17 AUGUSTA

194

MEGARA HYBLAEA **16**

Golfo di Augusta

codia ubea

Sortino

Melilli

Penisola Magnisi

12 VIZZINI

124

Buccheri

18 PANTALICA

Lago di Dirillo

194

Ferla

Anapo

124

Solarino

Castello Euriolo

Monterosso Almo

Buscemi

Floridia

SYRACUSE **1**

Giarratana

13

Ortygia

11 CHIARAMONTE GULFI

PALAZZOLO ACREIDE

Canicattini Bagni

194

115

Ognina

Lago di Rosalia

287

Cassibile

Cassibile

Casa Nobile

Noto Antica

A18

7 RAGUSA

NOTO **2**

Avola

Iatano

8

115

Calabernardo

MODICA

115

5 CAVA D'ISPICA

Golfo di Noto

Grande

Rosolini

Modica

6 SCICLI

Ispica

nalucata

Marzamemi

Sampieri

Pozzallo

PACHINO **3**

Punta Religione

Portopalo di Capo Passero

Isola Capo Passero

CAPO PASSERO **4**

Capo delle Correnti

Isola delle Correnti

Key

— Motorway

— Major road

— Secondary road

— Minor road

— Main railway

— Minor railway

0 kilometres — 10

0 miles — 10

For additional keys to symbols *see back flap*

● Syracuse

For 27 centuries the city of Syracuse – in modern Italian, Siracusa – has been of great economic and cultural importance. From the prehistoric populations to the Corinthians who founded the Greek city, to the introduction of Baroque architecture, the history of Syracuse is an open book, clearly visible in many streets and buildings. The Greek theatre survives in good condition, and you can still see the stone quarries, or Latomie, which provided stone for many of the ancient monuments, but also served as prisons.

Entrance to the Orecchio di Dioniso, in the Latomie area

🏛 The Neapolis Archaeological Zone
Viale Paradiso 14. **Tel** 0931-66206.
Open summer: 9am–6pm; winter: 9am–3pm. **Closed** Mon. 🖼

The Neapolis Archaeological Zone was established in 1955 with the aim of grouping the antiquities of Syracuse within one site, enabling visitors to make an uninterrupted tour of the city's most remote past. Not far from the ticket office for the park is medieval **San Nicolò dei Cordari**, built over a reservoir *(piscina)* cut out of the rock, which was used for cleaning the nearby Roman amphitheatre.

🏛 Greek Theatre
See pp142–3.

🏛 Latomie
A huge hollow separates the theatre area and the southern section of the site. This is the area of the Latomie – stone quarries – from which Syracuse architects extracted millions of cubic metres of stone for building. The enormous caves were also used as prisons for centuries. The Ear of Dionysius (**Orecchio di Dioniso**) is one of the most impressive quarries. According to legend, the extraordinary acoustics of this cave enabled

the local tyrant Dionysius to hear the whispers of his most dangerous prisoners and take due precautions. There are other huge adjacent caves, such as

Syracuse

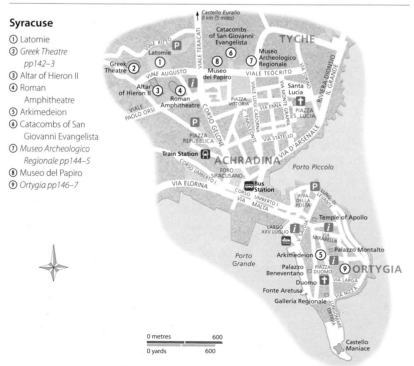

The large Grotta dei Cordari, the most interesting of the Latomie caves

VISITORS' CHECKLIST

Practical Information
Road map F4. 🅰 123,000.
🅸 STR (0931-464 255). 🎎 Santa
Lucia (13 Dec); Santa Lucia delle
Quaglie (first Sunday in May).
🆆 **siracusaturismo.net**

Transport
🆁🆂 from Messina, Naples,
Rome, Rome Piazza Stazione
(892021).🚌 Interbus (0931-146
27 11); AST (0931-66 710). 🚢

the **Grotta dei Cordari**, which until recently was used by local rope makers (*cordari*), and the **Latomia Intagliatella** and **Latomia Santa Venera**.

🏛 Altar of Hieron II and Roman Amphitheatre

These lie on the other side of the road that cuts the Neapolis area in two. Although only the foundations remain of the **Altar of Hieron II**, its impressive size (198 x 23 m/649 x 75 ft) is clear. Dedicated to Zeus, it was used for public sacrifices in which as many as 400 bulls were put to death at one time.

A huge public work undertaken in the early years of the empire, the **Roman Amphitheatre** (outer diameter, 140 x 119 m/459 x 390 ft) is only slightly smaller than the Arena in Verona. The walls in the interior were part of the underground

section, used to house the stage scenery. Beneath the tiers were corridors through which the gladiators and wild beasts entered the arena.

🏛 Museo Archeologico Regionale
See pp144–5.

🏛 Catacombs of San Giovanni Evangelista
Via San Giovanni alle Catacombe. **Tel** 0931-646 94. **Open** Apr–Oct: 9:30am–noon, 2:30–4:30pm; May–Jun: 9:30am–1pm, 2:30–5:30pm; Jul–Aug: 9:30am–1:30pm, 2:30-6pm.

This underground complex, dating to 360–315 BC, housed hundreds of *loculi*, or rooms, used to bury the followers of the new Christian religion in Roman times. The main gallery of the catacombs leads to a series of round chapels that still bear traces of frescoes.

🏛 Arkimedeion
Piazza Archimede 11. **Tel** 0931-61121 or 392-992 83 51. **Open** 9:30am–7pm daily. 🄯 🆆 **arkimedeion.it**

This interactive science museum is dedicated to the work of Archimedes, the great scientist of antiquity who lived in Syracuse in the 3rd century BC *(see p32)*. Perfect models of his machines and inventions, some of which visitors can interact with, are found here, while monitors with touchpads and videos explain the theory behind Archimedes' laws.

🏛 Museo del Papiro
Via Nizza 14. **Tel** 0931-22100. **Open** May–Sep 9am–7pm Tue–Sat, 9am–2pm Sun & hols; Oct: Apr 9am–2pm Tue–Sun. 🆆 **museodelpapiro.it**

This museum is devoted to the *Cyperus papyrus* plant. The largest European colony of the papyrus plant thrives on the banks of the Ciane river near Syracuse.

The stepped base of the Altar of Hieron II, giving an idea of the impressive size of the original sacrificial site

Syracuse: The Greek Theatre

This is one of the most important examples of ancient theatre architecture anywhere, and for centuries it was the centre of Syracusan life. The Greek theatre was a much more complex construction than today's ruins might indicate; in 1520–31, Emperor Charles V had much of the stone transported to build the walls around Ortygia *(see pp146–7)*. Designed in the 5th century BC by the Greek architect Damacopos, the theatre was enlarged in the 3rd and 2nd centuries BC by Hieron II. From the 5th century BC onwards, the great Greek playwrights, including Aeschylus, who premiered some of his tragedies here, wrote and staged their works in this magnificent setting.

Votive Niches
To the west of the grotto, near the ancient colonnade, the wall is punctuated by a series of rectangular niches that might have housed votive paintings or tablets in honour of Syracusan heroes.

Grotta del Museion
This cave, hewn out of the rock wall above the theatre, has a rectangular basin where the aqueduct flowed.

0 metres		10
0 yards		10

Classical Greek Theatre
Every year, the theatre hosts a summer programme of Classical theatre.

VISITORS' CHECKLIST

Practical Information
Greek Theatre and Neapolis
Archaeological Zone: Viale
Paradiso 14. **Tel** 0931-662 06.
Open 9am–6pm daily. **Closed**
Mon. 🏛 Istituto Nazionale del
Dramma Antico (INDA): Corso
Matteotti 29. **Tel** 0931-487 200.
Box office: 0931-487 248.
W indafondazione.org

Galleries
Called *criptae*, the galleries were cut out of the rock in the Roman period to replace the more ancient passageways of the *cavea*, which had been removed to create more seating space.

KEY

① **The diazoma** divided the auditorium into two parts.

② **The *cavea* (auditorium)** is over 138 m (453 ft) wide with 67 tiers, divided into 10 vertical blocks (or "wedges"). Each block was served by a flight of steps and was indicated by a letter, a custom that survives in modern theatres today.

③ **The stage area** was greatly enlarged in the Roman period.

④ **Two enormous pillars of rock** stood either side of the stage area.

⑤ **On the orchestra** was a monument to Dionysus, around which the chorus acted, danced and sang.

The Istituto Nazionale del Dramma Antico

Logo of the Syracuse INDA

On 16 April 1914, the tradition of performing ancient Greek theatre was revived at Syracuse, and now a season of plays first performed here over 2,500 years ago is put on every year in May/June. The Istituto Nazionale del Dramma Antico (National Institute of Ancient Drama) was set up in 1925. The Scuola Professionale di Teatro Antico (Professional School of Ancient Theatre) joined as partners in 1983.

Playbill of Aeschylus' *Libation Bearers* designed by Duilio Cambellotti (1921)

Syracuse: Museo Archeologico Regionale Paolo Orsi

Founded in 1967 (and opened to the public in 1988), in order to establish a proper home for the enormous quantity of material excavated from digs throughout southeastern Sicily, the Regional Archaeological Museum has over 18,000 pieces on display. The museum is named after the eminent archaeologist Paolo Orsi, head of the Antiquities Department of Sicily from 1888, who was instrumental in fostering interest in the island's past and was personally responsible for many important excavations and discoveries. The collections named after him have been reorganized since the museum moved from its Ortygia site. Two more sections have since been opened: Il Medagliere, a unique collection of coins and medals dating from the Greek period to the medieval era, and an area dedicated to the magnificent tomb of a Roman noblewoman that was discovered in the catacombs of San Giovanni in the northeast of Sicily.

Section B

★ Funerary Statue
This came from the digs at Megara Hyblaea and dates from 560–550 BC. The inscription on the right thigh shows it was dedicated to the physician Sambroditas.

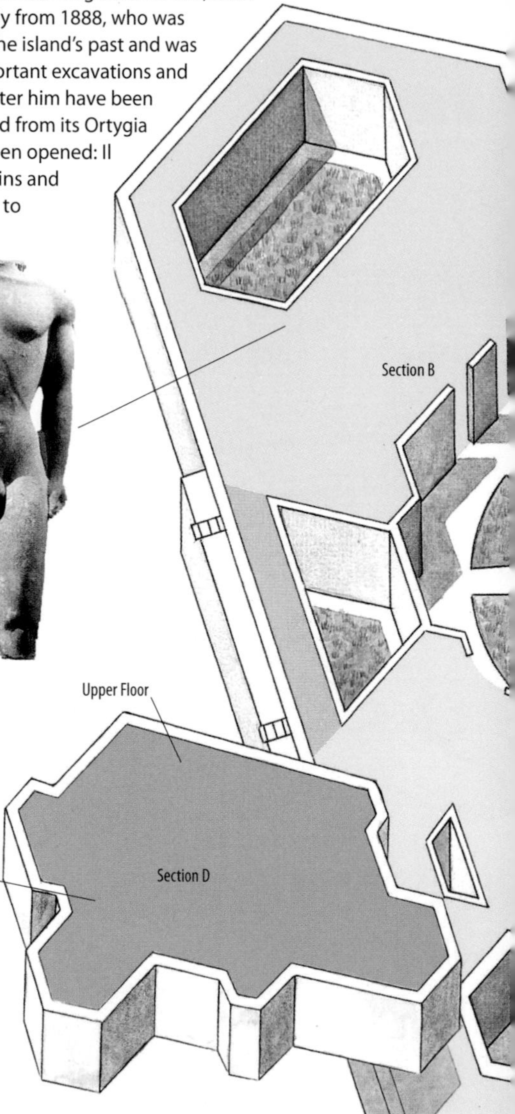

Upper Floor

Section D

★ Venus Anadyomene
Also known as the "Landolina Venus" from the name of its discoverer, this is a Roman copy of a Greek statue.

Key to Floorplan

☐ Prehistory and protohistory
☐ Greek colonies in eastern Sicily
▨ Subcolonies, Hellenized towns
▰ Sicilian culture and topography
☐ Sarcophagus of Adelfia

The Syracuse Bust
This clay bust dates from the 5th–4th centuries BC and is one of the many important objects found during the 20-year excavations carried out at Syracuse.

Lower Floor

Section C

Sarcophagus of Adelfia
This marble tomb sculpted with biblical scenes probably dates to the 4th century AD. The rondel in the centre shows the noblewoman Adelfia and her devoted husband Valerio.

Section F

yard

★ Enthroned Goddess
This marble and terracotta statue from Grammichele dates from the 6th century BC and probably represents the goddess Kore (Persephone).

ion A

Entrance to Basement

Main Entrance

Limestone Door Slabs
These come from tombs dating from the Sicilian Bronze Age.

Guide to the Museum

The museum is divided into several main sections. Section A features the geological history of Sicily and then the prehistoric, protohistoric and Siculan cultures. Section B is given over to the Greek colonies. Section C has material from the subcolonies founded by the Syracusans in 663–598 BC and from digs in the Hellenized towns in the interior. Section D emphasises the cultural impact of Syracuse since 4 BC, and section F contains the Sarcophagus of Adelfia.

Syracuse: Exploring Ortygia

The island of Ortygia has always been the focal point of Syracuse. A stronghold until the end of the 19th century, it separates the city's two harbours (connected by the dock canal). Ortygia (in Italian, Ortigia) is linked to the mainland by the Umbertino and Santa Lucia bridges. The town's long history is visible in many buildings, going back as far as the 6th-century BC Temple of Apollo.

Façade of Palazzo Beneventano del Bosco, opposite the Cathedral

🪸 Lungomare di Levante

This is the promenade that overlooks the **Porto Piccolo**, or little port, and is still the maritime heart of town. By going southwards along the promenade you reach **Spirito Santo**, with an 18th-century façade dramatically facing the sea. This church was the seat of the Holy Spirit Confraternity, hence its name.

🏛 Temple of Apollo

Largo XXV Luglio
A good part of Piazza Pancali, as you enter Ortygia, consists of the ruins of the Temple of Apollo, which were discovered in 1860 inside the old Spanish barracks. The temple, built in the early 6th century BC, is the oldest extant Doric temple in western Europe. It is of an imposing size – 58 x 24 m (190 x 79 ft). On the top step of the base, an inscription to Apollo provides proof that the building was dedicated to the god. Over the centuries the temple has served as a Byzantine church, a mosque, again a Christian church under the Normans, and a military stronghold.

🏛 Artemision

Piazza Minerva. **Tel** 333-162 67 95.
Open 9am–9pm daily. 🖼
🌐 artemisionsiracusa.com
Excavated beneath the Town Hall, in an area identified as the oldest part of the city, this very early Ionic temple to Artemis probably dates to the late 6th century BC. Entrance is through a striking modern pavilion.

🏛 Palazzo Beneventano del Bosco

🌐 beneventanodelbosco.it
Piazza Duomo is home to Palazzo Beneventano del Bosco, built in 1779 by architect Luciano Alì. The façade, with its doorway supporting a lovely balcony, is an impressive sight. The interior is also interesting; a broad staircase leads up to the private apartments filled with Venetian furniture, where Admiral Horatio Nelson and King Ferdinand III of Bourbon once stayed.

Decorative coat of arms on the Duomo façade

🏛 Duomo (Tempio di Minerva)

Piazza Duomo, 4. **Tel** 0931-646 94.
Open 7:30am–8pm. 🖼
In Piazza Duomo, next to the **Palazzo del Senato**, now the Town Hall, is the city's Cathedral, built in 1728–53. It was designed by Andrea Palma, and incorporates an ancient Temple of Minerva, which in turn had been built over the site of a 6th-century BC monument, which Gelon had dedicated to Athena. The intact ancient structures can be best seen by skirting the outer northern side of the church, where a series of columns from the temple are clearly visible. Initially a temple, and then a Christian church, the building became a Muslim

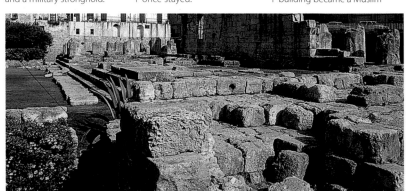

The ruins of the Temple of Apollo, in the heart of Ortygia

The Baroque façade of the Duomo, designed by Andrea Palma (1728–53)

mosque and finally a glorious example of Sicilian Baroque religious architecture. The Duomo contains a 13th-century font, Norman-era mosaics, and many fine paintings and sculptures. The sacristy has 16 wooden choir stalls carved in 1489.

📖 Galleria Regionale di Palazzo Bellomo

Via Capodieci, 14. **Tel** 0931-695 11 or 653 43. **Open** 9am–7pm Tue–Sat, 9am–1pm Sun. 🖼️

This museum, housed in the **Parisio** and **Bellomo** palazzi, has both interesting architecture (much of the original Hohenstaufen construction still stands) and artworks on display. The first rooms contain medieval and Renaissance sculpture. The courtyard, decorated with coats of arms, leads to the first floor, with the jewel of the collection, Antonello da Messina's *Annunciation* (1474, *see p27*). In the next room is a display of Christmas cribs. The exhibition ends with Arab and Sicilian ceramics and jewels.

📷 Fonte Aretusa

On Largo Aretusa, facing the **Porto Grande**, the waters of this spring still gush just as they did in Greek times. According to the myth made famous by Pindar and Virgil, Arethusa was a nymph transformed into a spring by the goddess Artemis.

🏛️ San Filippo Apostolo

In the heart of the Giudecca – the Jewish quarter of Syracuse – is **San Filippo Apostolo**, which was built over the old synagogue. In the crypt you can still see the basin of holy water in which the Jewish women purified themselves.

🏛️ Palazzo Margulensi-Montalto

Close to **Piazza Archimede**, with the 19th-century **Fountain of Artemis**, Palazzo Margulensi-Montalto is one of the most interesting medieval buildings in Syracuse. Built in 1397, this palazzo still features some original elements: the Gothic windows of the façade supported by spiral columns, the staircase and the arcade.

🏰 Castello Maniace

Tel 0931-464 420 **Open** 9:30am–1pm Tue–Sun. 🖼️

This castle is on the southern tip of Ortygia, where tradition says the temple of Hera and the villa of the Roman governor once stood. It was built by Frederick II in the 1200s and over the centuries had various functions: royal residence, fortress and even storehouse. The name derives from the Byzantine general Maniakes, who took the city from the Arabs.

Environs

On the hill overlooking the city is the main work of military architecture in the Greek world, the **Castello Eurialo**, built by Dionysius the Elder in 402 BC to protect Syracuse. Two rock-cut moats and a tower protected the fortress on the eastern side, a 15-m (49-ft) keep was built in the middle of the fortification, and the towers overlooked the sea.

🏰 Castello Eurialo

Frazione Belvedere, 8 km (5 miles) from Syracuse. **Tel** 0931-711 773/723. **Open** 9am–6pm daily (to 5pm in winter, to 7pm in summer); 8am–2pm Sun & hols.

The ruins of the extensive Castello Eurialo

❷ Street-by-Street: Noto

Throughout the 18th century, following the terrible earthquake of 1693, the ruined town of Noto became an enormous construction site run by prominent architects such as Rosario Gagliardi, Vincenzo Sinatra and Antonio Mazza. Today Noto's magnificent Baroque architecture is unique in Sicily, despite an unmistakable air of decay. However, substantial restoration work started after the town was named a UNESCO World Heritage site. Soon, Noto's Baroque buildings will be revealed in all their glory.

| 0 metres | 70 |
| 0 yards | 70 |

Palazzo Nicolaci

Montevergine church

Palazzo Astuto

VIA CAVOUR

VIA ROCCO PIRRI

VIA CORRADO NICOLACI

VIA A. DE BRESCIA

VIA SILVIO SPAVENT

VIA DUCEZIO

★ Cathedral
Dedicated to San Nicolò, the Cathedral looks down on three flights of steps. The cupola collapsed in 1996.

Palazzo Landolina (Sant'Alfano)

★ San Carlo al Corso
Formally called San Carlo Borromeo, this church contains paintings and frescoes attributed to Carasi.

Palazzo Ducezio
This building, now the Town Hall, stands opposite the Cathedral. The façade, with its lovely round arches, has been described as "a triumph of columns".

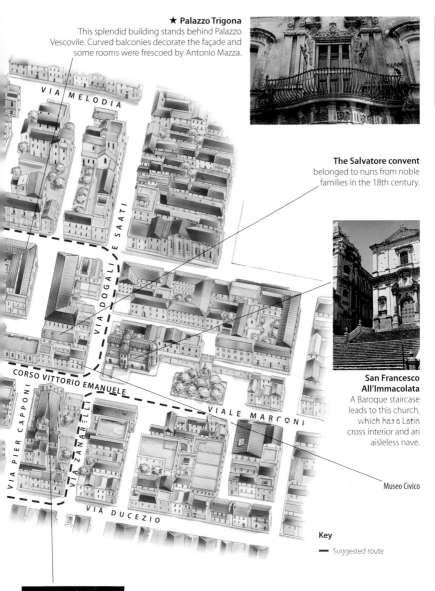

★ Palazzo Trigona
This splendid building stands behind Palazzo Vescovile. Curved balconies decorate the façade and some rooms were frescoed by Antonio Mazza.

The Salvatore convent belonged to nuns from noble families in the 18th century.

San Francesco All'Immacolata
A Baroque staircase leads to this church, which has a Latin cross interior and an aisleless nave.

Museo Civico

Key
— Suggested route

Santa Chiara
The church was designed by Rosario Gagliardi. It is built on an oval plan and is richly decorated. This 19th-century altarpiece of *San Benedetto and Santa Scolastica* is by the Palermo artist Lo Forte.

VISITORS' CHECKLIST

Practical Information
Road map E5. 23,000.
Piazza XVI Maggio (0931-573 779). (0931-835 201 or 835 005). Flower festival (3rd Sun May).
w infioratadinoto.it

Transport
Catania Fontanarossa (80 km/50 miles). **FS** from Syracuse (892021).

Exploring Noto

The heart of the town is the main avenue, the modern Viale Marconi, which becomes Corso Vittorio Emanuele at the monumental Porta Reale (or Ferdinandea) city gate, and passes through Piazza XXIV Maggio, Piazza Municipio (a good starting point for a visit) and Piazza XXX Ottobre. Steps lead to the upper town, with marvellous views of the landscape around.

The Cathedral prior to 1996

The Cathedral after the collapse of the cupola

⌂ Cathedral

In the winter of 1996, a loud rumble signalled the collapse of the Cathedral cupola, leaving a noticeable scar in the heart of Noto. It was a great loss to Sicilian Baroque art. The church was completed in 1776, and dedicated to San Nicolò. It stands at the end of a spectacular three-flight staircase designed by Paolo Labisi, the façade bearing twin bell towers and a bronze portal. The interior has a wealth of frescoes and other decoration, especially in the side chapels. The Cathedral has now been brought back to its former splendour following restoration.

▦ Palazzo Ducezio

Piazza Trigona.
Open 9:30am–1:30pm, 3–6pm daily.

This palazzo, which stands opposite the Cathedral, was built in 1746 by Vincenzo Sinatra. The façade is decorated with an impressive series of columns. In the interior, which now houses the Town Hall offices, there is a huge drawing room decorated in the French Louis XV style, with gold and stucco decorative elements and a fine fresco on the vault by Antonio Mazza.

▦ Museo Civico

Corso Vittorio Emanuele III, 34.
Tel 0931-836 462. **Open** 9am–1pm, 3:30–7:30pm Tue–Sun.

The Civic Museum (some rooms of which are closed for restoration) features ancient and medieval material from the old town, Noto Antica, and from many nearby places.

⌂ San Francesco All'Immacolata

Corso Vittorio Emanuele III, 142.
Open 8:30am–12:30pm, 4:30–6:30pm.

On the wide stretch of Piazza XXX Ottobre, a stairway leads to San Francesco, which was once part of a convent and is now a high school. The church, with stucco decoration, was built in the mid-18th century and has a wooden statue of the Virgin Mary (1564), which probably came from one of the churches in the old town, Noto Antica.

Statue on the Cathedral façade

▦ Palazzo Trigona

Closed to the public.

This palazzo is perhaps the most "classically" Baroque building in Noto. The façade with its curved balconies blends in with the adjacent religious and civic buildings, in line with the schemes of the architects who rebuilt Noto. The drawing rooms of the palazzo were frescoed by Antonio Mazza.

Baroque Architecture and Art in Noto

After the devastating earthquake of 1693, a programme of reconstruction was introduced throughout eastern Sicily in the early 18th century. The architects entrusted with this task elaborated upon the achievements of 17th-century Baroque architecture and adopted recurrent features that can still be seen in the streets of Noto. The façades of both churches and civic buildings became of fundamental importance in the hands of these men. Some of them, like Rosario Gagliardi, who designed the churches of Santa Chiara, Santissimo Crocefisso and San Domenico in Noto, were originally craftsmen themselves. Their skills can be seen in the great attention paid to decorative detail in façades and balconies. Rebuilding made the large monastery complexes – which together with the mansions of the landed gentry were the economic and social backbone of 18th- and 19th-century Noto – even more grandiose than before. In 2002 Noto and other Baroque towns were named World Heritage sites by UNESCO.

An 18th-century Baroque balcony on Palazzo Nicolaci in Noto

⬆ San Carlo

Along Corso Vittorio Emanuele, San Carlo (also called Chiesa del Collegio because of the attached former Jesuit monastery) has a slightly convex façade with three levels – Doric, Ionic and Corinthian. The impressive Latin cross plan interior is decorated with frescoes.

⬆ San Domenico

Looking over Piazza XXIV Maggio, the church of San Domenico is part of a group of buildings that includes the **Dominican Convent**, worth visiting because of its splendid entrance with a host of friezes. Like other buildings of this kind, the convent was abandoned after the elimination of all congregational orders, decreed by the Italian government in 1866. The lovely façade of the church, with its convex central part, was designed by the architect Rosario Gagliardi. The portal gives way to a rounded interior, which is crowned by five cupolas with fine stucco decoration.

The convex façade of San Domenico, designed by Gagliardi

⬛ Palazzo Nicolaci Villadorata

Open 10am–1pm, 3pm–1 hr before sunset. 🅿 ⬛ **palazzonicolaci.it**

On Via Nicolaci is Palazzo Nicolaci del Principe di Villadorata. The façade has six balconies supported by corbels which are decorated – in keeping with the pure Baroque style –

Palazzo Landolina, former residence of the Norman Sant'Alfano family

with complex wrought-iron work and grotesque and mythological figures: lions, sirens, griffons and cherubs. The interior has fresco decoration in the lavish rooms, the most striking of which is the Salone delle Feste (Hall of Festivities). The palazzo will soon house the **Biblioteca Comunale**, or City Library (currently on Via Cavour), founded in the mid-19th century, with many old volumes and the architects' original designs for Noto.

Detail of Baroque decoration

⬛ Palazzo Landolina

To the right of the Cathedral is the 19th-century **Palazzo Vescovile** (Bishop's Palace), while to the left is Palazzo Landolina, residence of the marquises of Sant'Alfano, an old and powerful family of the Norman aristocracy. Once past the elegant Baroque façade you enter a courtyard where two sphinxes flank the stairway leading to the main floor and frescoed rooms.

⬆ Chiesa del S.S. Crocefisso

Tel 0931-891 622.

In the heart of Noto Alta, at the end of a stairway that begins at Piazza Mazzini, is this church, built at the end of the street

that leads upwards from Piazza Municipio and the Cathedral. The façade – designed by Gagliardi but never finished – has a large Baroque door. The Latin cross plan interior boasts a magnificent Renaissance statue by Francesco Laurana, known as the *Madonna della Neve* (Madonna of the Snow, 1471) which miraculously survived the earthquake. At the end of the left-hand aisle is Cappella Landolina. The Romanesque statues of lions also come from the old town. The church is surrounded by palazzi, convents and churches. Among others, the façades of **Sant'Agata**, the **Badia della Santissima Annunziata** and **Santa Maria del Gesù** are well worth a longer look.

The unfinished façade of Chiesa del Crocefisso in Noto Alta

The road leading to Pachino, one of the most important agricultural towns in southern Sicily

❸ Pachino

Road map E5. 🚆 22,000. 🛈 Town Hall, weekdays only (0931-803 557).

The town of Pachino, founded in 1758 by the princes of Giardineli and populated by a few dozen families, has evolved into a large agricultural and wine-producing centre. Despite inroads made by modern architecture, there are still some traces of the original town plan: a series of courtyards and alleys reveals an Arab influence.

Pachino is also synonymous with a variety of small red tomato used for sauces and salads, which has become familiar throughout the country (it has even acquired DOC status). Besides the *pachini* tomatoes, the area – close to the sea and seaside resorts – is famous for the production of red wine.

Portopalo di Capo Passero, a fairly recent tourist attraction

❹ Capo Passero

Road map E5.

At the southern tip of Sicily, on the Capo Passero headland, lies the small town of **Portopalo di Capo Passero**, a centre for agricultural produce and fishing. Portopalo, together with the nearby town of **Marzamemi**, has become a popular summer tourist spot. Just off the coast is the small island of **Capo Passero**, which, because of its strategic position, has always been considered an excellent observation point. Proof is provided by the 17th-century watchtower, which replaced a series of military installations and fortifications, some of which were of ancient origin.

The southernmost point on the headland is **Capo delle Correnti**. Opposite the point a lighthouse stands on an island

Fishing boats on the beach at Capo Passero

called **Isola delle Correnti**. Near here – or more precisely, close to Portopalo – Allied troops landed on 10 July 1943 with the aim of establishing a bridgehead on Sicily.

North of Portopalo you can see a tuna fishery *(tonnara)* and a fish processing plant. In nearby Marzamemi the town also grew up around a tuna fishery and the residence of the noble Villadorata family, who are still the proprietors of the local *tonnara*.

The waters of the central Mediterranean are still populated by large schools of tuna fish which migrate annually. Enticed towards the *tonnara,* the fish become trapped in a complicated network of tuna fishing nets. Tuna caught using this traditional method is prized and considered highly superior to tuna caught out on the open sea, because the method of killing (which involves very rapid loss of blood) seems to enhance the flavour of the meat.

Byzantine fresco in the Grotto di San Nicola, in the Cava d'Ispica gorge

❺ Cava d'Ispica

Road map E5. Access from SS115 from Ispica to Modica, right-hand turn-off at Bettola del Capitano, follow the branch for 5.5 km (3.5 miles) as far as the Cavallo d'Ispica mill. FS Syracuse–Ispica (892 021). **Tel** 0932-771 667. **Open** Apr–Oct: 9am–7pm Mon–Sat, 9am–1pm Sun & hols; Nov–Mar: 9am–1:30pm Mon–Sat.

An ancient river carved the Cava d'Ispica out of the rock and the gorge has developed into an open-air monument. The sides of the canyon are perforated with the tombs of a necropolis, places of worship and cave dwellings where religious hermits went through mystical experiences. It was an Egyptian hermit, Sant'Ilarione, who initiated the monasticism in the canyon, which was used only as a burial site in antiquity.

Improved access has made it possible to visit the **Larderia Necropolis**, although since the establishment of a new enclosure, it is much more difficult to gain an overall idea of the complex of caves that have made Cava d'Ispica such a world-famous attraction for decades. While the Larderia Necropolis is an impressive network of catacombs (there is also a small museum), not far from the entrance you can visit – on request – the **Grotto di San Nicola**, a cave with a Byzantine fresco of the Madonna, or the small Byzantine church of **San Pancrazio**, in a claustrophobically narrow enclosure. Despite the difficult terrain, the unfenced part of the gorge is also well worth visiting. Every step of the way you will be well rewarded for the strenuous climb.

❻ Scicli

Road map E5. 🏛 25,200. FS from Syracuse (892 021). 🚌 from Noto. ℹ Town hall (800-221-678); Palazzo Spadaro (0932-839 608). 🎭 Festa delle Milizie: last Sun in Jun.
W comune.scicli.rg.it

The town lies at the point where the Modica river converges with the valleys of Bartolomeo and Santa Maria la Nova. Scicli, a UNESCO World Heritage site, once played a major role in controlling communications between the coast and the uplands. It was an Arab stronghold and then became a royal city under the Normans. It was totally rebuilt after the 1693 earthquake, and Baroque streets, façades and churches emerged from the devastated town.

For visitors arriving from Modica along the panoramic San Bartolomeo valley, the first stop is San Bartolomeo followed by the new town centre, built on the plain after the old hill town was abandoned. In the centre is the church of **Santa Maria la Nova**, rebuilt several times and now with Neo-Classical features; **Palazzo Beneventano** with its Baroque motifs, the former **Convent of the Carmelites** and the adjoining **Chiesa del Carmine**. The **Chiesa Madre** in Piazza Italia is worth visiting for its papier-mâché *Madonna dei Milici* and the Baroque street Via Mormino Penna. Higher up are the ruins of **San Matteo**, the old cathedral, at the foot of the ruined **castle** built by the Arabs. The town is often used as a film set; Marco Bellocchio's *Il regista dei matrimoni* had scenes shot here.

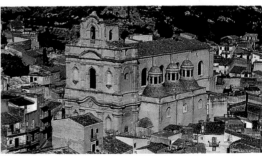

Santa Maria la Nova, at Scicli, rebuilt in the Neo-Classical style

❼ Ragusa

This ancient city was founded as Hybla Heraia when the Sicels moved into the interior to escape from the Greek colonists. Ragusa, a UNESCO World Heritage site, is divided into two communities: new Baroque Ragusa, built on the plateau after the 1693 earthquake, and quiet, atmospheric Ibla, which is linked to the modern city by a rocky crest. A visit to Ragusa therefore involves two stages.

The Duomo of Ibla in the heart of the old town

Exploring Ragusa

The new town was designed to suit the needs of the emerging 17th-century landed gentry as opposed to the old feudal nobles, who preferred to stay entrenched in old Ibla. It was laid out on an octagonal plan, the result of detailed planning following the earthquake of 1693.

The beauty of the landscape, the sandy beaches and the Baroque and Art Nouveau architecture makes the whole area seem like an open-air stage. The famous TV series *Il Commissario Montalbano (Inspector Montalbano)* showcases the sun-drenched province of Ragusa at its best.

devoted to the cultures that have dominated the province of Ragusa. The first section has prehistoric finds from Modica, Pantalica and Cava d'Ispica. The second one is given over to Kamarina, the Syracusan subcolony founded on the banks of the Ippari river on a coastal site not far from present-day Vittoria. Kamarina once enjoyed important trade links with ancient Ibla. Among the displays here are the statue of a warrior, the bronzes of Kamarina and Attic vases, all recovered during the excavations at Kamarina, organized and sponsored by the Syracuse Archaeological Office. The third section of the museum features

the Siculi cultures, followed by an exhibit of Hellenistic finds – especially from Scornavacche, a very important trade and caravan centre – including an interesting reconstruction of a potter's oven. The fifth section focuses on the Roman epoch, while the last one illustrates the growth of this area in the Byzantine age, with finds from the ancient port of Caucana.

🏛 Cathedral

Piazza San Giovanni. **Open** 8am–noon, 4–7pm daily.

Ragusa's splendid Cathedral was built between 1706 and 1760 in the middle of the new town. It replaced a smaller building that had been hastily erected after the earthquake of 1693.

The low and broad façade is an excellent example of Sicilian Baroque, with a lovely monumental portal and fine sculptures of St John the Baptist, to whom the cathedral is dedicated, the Virgin Mary and St John the Evangelist. There is also an impressive porticoed terrace and a massive cusped bell tower.

The ornate Baroque interior has a Latin cross plan with two side aisles and fine stucco decoration.

🏛 Museo Archeologico Ibleo

Via Natalelli. **Tel** 0932-622 963. **Open** 9am–1:30pm, 4–7:30pm daily.

The Archaeological Museum is divided into six sections and is

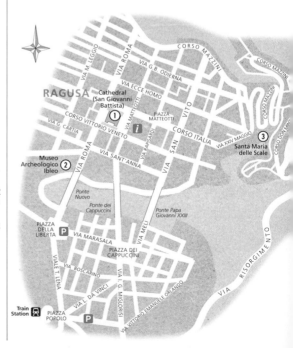

🏛 Santa Maria delle Scale

This church stands at the top of a flight of 340 steps connecting Ibla and Ragusa, hence the name, *scale* meaning stairs. Santa Maria delle Scale was built in the 14th century over a Norman convent and was rebuilt after the 1693 earthquake. The original Gothic doorway and external pulpit of the campanile are still intact.

Exploring Ibla

The hill of Ibla has probably been inhabited since the 3rd millennium BC and is rich in history. A UNESCO World Heritage site, its lovely old streets contain a number of fine architectural sights.

🏛 Duomo (San Giorgio)

The Cathedral stands at the top of a stairway that begins at **Piazza Duomo**, the real centre of Ibla. It was built over the foundations of San Nicolò, which was destroyed by the 1693 earthquake. The new church was designed by Rosario Gagliardi and built in 1738–75. The huge façade is immediately striking, with its three tiers of columns which, together with the

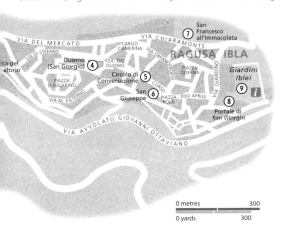

Statue of San Giuseppe

vertical lines of the monumental stairway leading to the church, accentuate the vertical thrust of the building. An impressive Neo-Classical cupola dominates the nave. Inside are paintings from different periods (including an 18th-century *Immaculate Conception* by Vito D'Anna) and 33 stained-glass windows.

🏛 Circolo di Conversazione

If you go down Corso XXV Aprile, you will see the Neo-Classical Circolo di Conversazione (Conversation Club), on your left. This private club has a plush Neo-Classical interior, steeped in the atmosphere of 19th-century Ibla.

🏛 San Giuseppe

Also along Corso XXV aprile, at Piazza Pola, is the Baroque San Giuseppe, which is in many ways similar to the Duomo, San Giorgio, its designer having been an apprentice to the architect Gagliardi. The oval-shaped interior has a large cupola decorated with Sebastiano Lo Monaco's fresco *Glory of St Benedict*. After leaving

The façade of San Giuseppe, with its Corinthian columns

this church, turn left on Via Orfanotrofio towards Piazza Chiaramonte, where you will find the beautiful church of **San Francesco all'Immacolata**, which was built over Palazzo Chiaramonte and incorporates the Gothic portal of the former nobleman's palace.

🏛 San Giuseppe

The splendid Catalan-Gothic **Portale di San Giorgio** of this church, for the most part destroyed by the 1693 earthquake, survives – its lunette has a bas-relief of St George killing the dragon and, above, the eagles from the House of Aragon coat of arms.

🌳 Giardino Ibleo

This delightful 19th-century public garden has a fine view of the area. It also contains a number of churches, such as San Giacomo and the Chiesa dei Cappuccini, with its interesting 15th-century altarpieces, including one by Pietro Novelli.

Ragusa and Ibla

① Cathedral (San Giovanni Battista)
② Museo Archeologico Ibleo
③ Santa Maria delle Scale
④ Duomo (San Giorgio)
⑤ Circolo di Conversazione
⑥ San Giuseppe
⑦ San Francesco all'Immacolata
⑧ Portale di San Giorgio
⑨ Giardino Ibleo

For keys to map symbols *see back flap*

The Duomo at Modica, a remarkable example of Sicilian Baroque

🏛 Modica

Road map E5. 🚇 52,500.
🚆 from Syracuse (0931-464 467).
🛈 Town hall, Corso Umberto I 141,
(0932-759 634).

Inhabited since the era of the Siculi culture, Modica (a UNESCO World Heritage site) rebelled against Roman rule in 212 BC and, thanks to its strategic position, became one of the most important towns in medieval and Renaissance Sicily. Peter I of Aragón made it capital of an area that roughly corresponds to the present-day province of Ragusa, and it was later ruled by the Chiaramonte and Cabrera families. Perched on the rocky spurs dominating the large "Y" formed by the confluence of the Janni Mauro and Pozzo Pruni rivers, Modica grew, occupying the valley where the rivers were filled in after a disastrous series of floods.

Modica Alta is built on the hill and is connected to the lower town, Modica Bassa, via flights of steps. Some of these are monumental, such as the 250-step flight built in the 19th century which descends from San Giorgio. Alleys and lanes evoke the walled town, which from 844 to 1091 was an important Arab city known as Mohac.

Sculpture on Corso Umberto I

🏛 Duomo (San Giorgio)
It is worthwhile making the effort to climb up the hill to see the Cathedral. It is dedicated to St George and was built by Count Alfonso Henríquez Cabrera on the site of a 13th-century church which had been destroyed by an earthquake. The magnificent façade (which, because of its similarity to several churches in Noto, is attributed to the architect Rosario Gagliardi) rises upwards elegantly with three ranks of columns. In the interior, there is a *polittico* by Bernardino Niger made of ten 16th-century wooden panels with scenes from the New Testament.

Corso Regina Margherita, the main street in Modica Alta, has many fine 19th-century palazzos.

🏛 Santa Maria di Betlem
By going up the road following one branch of the confluence of the valley rivers, now called Via Marchesa Tedeschi, you will come across the façade of Santa Maria di Betlem, a 16th-century church which was rebuilt after the 1693 earthquake. Inside the end of the right-hand aisle is the Cappella del Sacramento, a splendid example of late Gothic-Renaissance architecture. It was commissioned by the Cabrera family.

🏛 Corso Umberto I
The many interesting churches and buildings along the town's main street include the former **Monastero delle Benedettine** (a convent for Benedictine nuns now used as a courthouse), the 19th-century **Teatro Garibaldi**, the 18th-century **Palazzo Tedeschi**, **Santa Maria del Soccorso** and **Palazzo Manenti**, whose corbels are decorated with figures of all kinds.

🏛 San Pietro
Also on Corso Umberto I is a flight of Baroque monumental steps, flanked by statues of the Apostles, which leads to the entrance of **San Pietro**. This church was built after the 1693 earthquake on the site of a 14th-century church. The *Madonna dell'Ausilio*, a Gagini-school statue, stands in the second chapel in the right-hand aisle.

To the right of San Pietro is the 12th-century cave-church of **San Nicolò Inferiore** (St Nicholas). Discovered in the 20th century, it houses Byzantine wall paintings.

San Pietro stands at the top of a monumental Baroque staircase

🏛 Museo Civico Belgiorno
Corso Umberto I, 149. **Tel** 0932-759 642. **Open** Summer: 10am–1pm, 5–8pm Tue–Sun; winter: 9am–1pm, 3:30–7:30pm Tue–Sun.

Fossils and majolica tiles are featured in this museum, along-side Greek and Roman ceramics and artifacts recovered from graves in the Modica area, including the archaeological site of Cava d'Ispica. Highlights include a bronze statuette of Hercules, which is Hellenic in style and dates back to the 3rd century BC.

The ruins of the Greek walls at the Capo Soprano headland, Gela

❾ Vittoria

Road map D5. 🏛 54,300.
ℹ️ Pro Loco (0932-992 953).

Founded by Vittoria Colonna in 1603, this agricultural town lies on the plain between the Ippari and Dirillo rivers. In the central Piazza del Popolo are the **Teatro Comunale** (1877) and **Santa Maria delle Grazie**, a Baroque church built after the disastrous 1693 earthquake.

❿ Gela

Road map D4. 🏛 72,000. 🚆 from Syracuse (892 021). ℹ️ AAST (0931-462 711). Fortifications at Capo Soprano: **Tel** 0933-912 626.
Open 9am 1 hr before sunset. Museo Archeologico Comunale. **Tel** 0933-912 626. **Open** 9am–6pm. **Closed** Mon; winter: Sun & hols.
🎫 (combined with excavations.)
Acropolis excavations: **Open** 9am–1 hr before sunset. 🎫

According to Greek historian Thucydides, Gela was founded in 688 BC. In the 6th century BC its inhabitants founded Agrigento. Extending over two slopes – the present-day **Acropolis** and the **Capo Soprano** area – the town was revived, after a long period of abandonment, by Frederick II. Today Gela is marred by ugly buildings, industrial plants and a strong anti-Mafia military presence. However, there are the archaeological sites: a long stretch of Greek fortifications built by Timoleon at Capo Soprano and the sacred precinct and ancient Temple of Athena on the **Acropolis**, all good introductions to a visit to the **Museo Archeologico**.

⓫ Chiaramonte Gulfi

Road map E4. 🏛 8,000. 🌐 comune. chiaramonte-gulfi.gov.it

This town was founded in the 14th century by Manfredi Chiaramonte, the Count of Modica, on the steep slopes of a rise and then developed towards the valley. The **Chiesa del Salvatore** and **Matrice Santa Maria la Nova** are in the centre, while the **Madonna delle Grazie Sanctuary** is on the outskirts.

⓬ Vizzini

Road map E4. 🏛 7,000. ℹ️ Town hall (0933-968 211).

The fascination of Vizzini lies in the small streets and alleys of the old town, which has preserved its atmosphere and town plan – increasingly rare in Sicily because of modern urban growth. Also worth a look is the fine architecture of the **Chiesa Madre di San Gregorio** with its Gothic portal, taken from the destroyed Palazzo di Città.

⓭ Palazzolo Acreide

Road map E4. 🏛 9,000. ℹ️ Town hall (0931-871 260).

Originally named Akrai, this town, a UNESCO World Heritage site, has some important Baroque churches and buildings – the **Chiesa Madre di San Nicolò, Palazzo Zocco** and the 18th-century **Chiesa dell'Annunziata**. However, the most interesting sight is the peaceful plain with the **excavations of Akrai**.

A Baroque balcony in the centre of Palazzolo Acreide

🏛 Excavations at Akrai

2 km (1 mile) from the centre. **Tel** 0931-876 602. **Open** 9am–1 hr before sunset (Nov–Apr: 9–1pm, 3:30–5pm).

This area was inhabited in 664 BC, when the city was founded by the Syracusans. A small **theatre** stands by the entrance. The **acropolis** contains an **agora**, two **latomie** (the Intagliata and Intagliatella quarries, *see p140*), the ruins of the **Temple of Aphrodite** and the so-called **Santoni**, 12 rock-hewn statues representing the goddess Cybele.

The theatre at Palazzolo Acreide: the colony dates back to the early 7th century BC

⑭ Caltagirone

In the history of this city (a UNESCO World Heritage site), built between the Erei and Iblei hills, there is one element of continuity – ceramics production. Prehistoric pottery has been found on the hills around the Arab *Kalat al Giarin* ("castle of vases"). The local potters were world famous in the Middle Ages, and the tradition is maintained today.

San Giuliano, displaying some 20th-century architectural features

Exploring Caltagirone
It is pleasant to explore Caltagirone on foot, walking around the streets and squares, pausing at the local craftsmen's workshops. There is quite a difference in altitude between the lower part and the hill of Santa Maria del Monte, so plan your visit with this in mind.

🏛 Piazza Municipio
The former Piano della Loggia – now Piazza Municipio – is the heart of the city, where the main streets converge. In the piazza are the **Town Hall** and **Palazzo Senatorio**, formerly the city theatre, which is now home to the Galleria Sturzo.

⬆ Duomo di San Giuliano
The Cathedral is in Piazza Umberto I. The exterior of the church, dedicated to San Giuliano, has a long history: first it was Norman, then Baroque, and was rebuilt in the 20th century (the façade in 1909, the bell tower in 1954). In the interior is a 16th-century wooden crucifix. By going down Via Roma towards the **San Francesco bridge** you will come to an open space with the old Bourbon prison and the church of **Sant'Agata**.

🏛 Museo Civico
Via Roma. **Tel** 0933-31590. **Open** 9:30am–1:30pm, 4–7pm Tue & Fri–Sun.
This museum in the former 17th-century Bourbon prison has prehistoric, Greek and Roman material, sculptures and ceramics from the 1500s to the present.

⬆ San Francesco d'Assisi
The Ponte San Francesco, decorated with typical coloured tiles, leads to the church of San Francesco d'Assisi, which was founded in the 12th century and rebuilt in Baroque style after the 1693 earthquake.

🌳 Giardino Pubblico
The public gardens can be reached by going down Via Roma. The park was designed in the mid-1800s by Giovanni Battista Basile, and the long balustrade and the bandstand are richly decorated with coverings of ceramic tiles.

🏛 Museo Regionale della Ceramica
Viale Giardini Pubblici. **Tel** 0933-58418. **Open** 9am–6:30pm. 🚻
From the Belvedere del Teatrino, in Giardino della Villa, you can visit the Ceramics Museum. There are Bronze Age pots and Greek, Hellenistic and Roman kraters and figurines. The Middle Ages are represented by Arab vases and Sicilian pieces. The collection also has more recent pharmacy jars and glazed vases with religious figures.

⬆ Santa Maria del Monte Stairway
Once back in the centre of town, one of the most impressive sights is the

Ponte San Francesco in Caltagirone

Coloured majolica tiles, decorating every step of the Santa Maria del Monte staircase

Santa Maria del Monte
At the top of the stairway is the former Cathedral of Caltagirone, built in the mid-1500s and then rebuilt after the 1693 earthquake. A slender bell tower, designed by Natale Bonaiuto, was also added. A castle once stood at the top of the hill. Today, in an area that was once heavily fortified, can be found the **Sant'Agostino Convent** and **San Nicola**, both constructed in the 18th century.

monumental Santa Maria del Monte staircase, with its 142 steps decorated with majolica tiles. The flight of steps was built in 1606 to link the seat of religious power – the Cathedral – with that of civic power, the **Palazzo Senatorio**. During the feast days of San Giacomo (24 & 25 July) *(see p43)* the entire flight of stairs is illuminated with thousands of lamps, skilfully arranged to create interesting patterns of lighting effects.

The Centre of Caltagirone

① Piazza Municipio
② Duomo (San Giuliano)
③ Museo Civico
④ San Francesco d'Assisi
⑤ Giardino Pubblico
⑥ Museo Regionale della Ceramica
⑦ Santa Maria del Monte Stairway
⑧ Santa Maria del Monte (former Chiesa Matrice)

The Cathedral of Lentini, dedicated to Sant'Alfio, in Piazza Duomo

⑮ Lentini

Road map E4. 🚹 23,700. 🚉 from Catania, Syracuse & Messina (095-532 719). 🚹 APT Siracusa (0931-481 200 or 464 255); Pro Loco Lentini, Piazza Umberto 2 (095-901 433). Museo Archeologico: Via Museo 1 **Tel** 095-783 29 62. **Closed** for restoration; call ahead for up-to-date information. Digs at Leontinoi: **Open** 9am–1 hr before sunset, daily. 🎨 "Scesa e Cruci" (Good Friday); Festival of orange trees in bloom (1st week of May).

An ancient Siculan city originally named Xuthia, Lentini was conquered by the Chalcidians in 729 BC and fought against neighbouring Syracuse with the support of Athens. Defeated and then occupied by the Romans, the city went into a period of decline. In the Middle Ages it became an important agricultural centre. The local museum has finds from the ancient city, especially from the Siculan and Greek epochs. The digs at ancient Leontinoi, at the edge of town in the Colle Castellaccio area, can be reached via the ancient Porta Siracusana city gate. The various walls testify to the city's battle-worn history, and there are a number of ancient burial grounds inside the archaeological precinct.

⑯ Megara Hyblaea

Road map F4. 🚉 Augusta station. 🚹 0931-512 364. **Open** 9am–6pm daily (to 3pm in winter). 🎨

One of the first Greek colonies in Sicily was founded in 728 BC here at Megara. According to legend, the founders were the followers of Daedalus, who had escaped from Crete. Unfortunately, today the site is surrounded by the oil refineries of Augusta and in such a squalid environment it is difficult to visit the ruins of the ancient city and gain any sense of atmosphere. The Megara colonists who founded Megara Hyblaea were soon at war with Syracuse and Leontinoi, and a century later founded the city of Selinunte, in western Sicily *(see pp108–9)*. You should be able to see the ruins of the Hellenistic walls, the Agora quarter, and the remains of some temples, baths and colonnades. These excavations were led by the eminent archaeologist Paolo Orsi and the École Française of Rome. Information display boards will help you to get orientated.

Find from Megara Hyblaea, now in the Museo Archeologico in Syracuse

Ruined foundations in the ancient Greek colony of Megara Hyblaea, founded in the 8th century BC

The Porta Spagnola in Augusta (1681), the old city gate

⑰ Augusta

Road map F4. 🚉 34,000. 🚆 from Catania, Syracuse, Messina (0931-892 021). ℹ️ Augusta town hall (0931-980 111).

Augusta was founded on an island by Frederick II as a port protected by a castle. Under the Aragónese the city was constantly at war with Turkish and North African pirates. It was almost totally destroyed by the 1693 earthquake. In the early 1900s the city expanded and became a major petrochemical port, and this drastically changed the landscape. You enter the old town through the **Porta Spagnola** city gate, built by the viceroy Benavides in 1681, next to which are the ruins of the old walls. In the centre, the Baroque **Chiesa delle Anime Sante**, the **Chiesa Madre** (1769) and the **Museo delle Armi** (Arms Museum) are worth a look.

⑱ Pantalica

Road map E4 (19 km/12 miles from Ferla, 45 km/28 miles from Syracuse). **Open** 7am–7pm Sat & Sun (reservation).

Tombs, dwellings and temples line the walls of the limestone gorges at the confluence of the Bottiglieria and Anapo rivers. Pantalica was the heart of the ancient kingdom of Hybla which, in its heyday, used Syracuse as its port. The city was conquered by the Greeks when the coastal colonies became powerful in the 8th century BC, and Pantalica became important again during the early Middle Ages, when Arab invasions and constant wars led the locals to seek refuge in its inaccessible canyons. The cave dwellings and hermitages date from this period, as do the ruins of a settlement known as the "Byzantine village".

View of the steep gorges surrounding the necropolis of Pantalica

A Walk Through Pantalica

This archaeological site – the largest necropolis in Sicily – covers a large area, but the steep gorges mean there are few roads, and the only practical way of getting around is on foot. About 9 km (5 miles) from Ferla stands the Filiporto Necropolis, with more than 1,000 tombs cut out of the cliffs. Next is the North Necropolis; the last place to park is near the *Anaktoron*, the megalithic palace of the prince of ancient Hybla dating from the 12th century BC. The road ends 1 km (half a mile) further on. From this point, one path goes down to the Bottiglieria river, where steep walls are filled with rock-cut caves, and another takes you to the so-called "Byzantine village", the rock-hewn church of San Micidiario and the other necropolises in this area. It is not advisable to try to go to Pantalica from Sortino (the northern slope); it is an extremely long walk.

The North Necropolis at Pantalica

NORTHEASTERN SICILY

Thanks to the presence of Mount Etna, the Ionian coast of Sicily has often had to deal with violent volcanic eruptions. One of the most devastating was in 1669, when the molten lava even reached Catania and the sea. The lava flows have formed Etna's distinctive landscape, and flowers and festoons of black lava now adorn many of the churches and buildings in Catania and the surrounding towns.

In 734 BC the first colonists from Greece landed on this coast and founded Naxos, the first of a series of powerful colonies in Sicily that gave rise to a period of prosperity and cultural sophistication. However, volcanic eruptions and devastating earthquakes have destroyed almost all traces of the splendid Greek cities in this area, with the exception of the ancient theatre in Taormina, which was rebuilt in the Roman era. The panoramic position, mild climate and wealth of architectural beauty have made this coast a favourite with visitors. The first of these were people who undertook the Grand Tour in the 1700s and made their first stop at Messina, just as many modern travellers do. In summer, the Ionian coast is crowded because of the beauty of its beaches and sea. But it is also fascinating in the winter, when the top of Mount Etna is covered with snow and the citrus orchards are heavy with fruit, or in spring, when the air is filled with the scent of orange blossom and flower gardens in bloom. Another part of northeastern Sicily worth visiting is the archipelago of the unique Aeolian Islands, of volcanic origin.

The old harbour at Catania, still crowded with fishing boats

◀ Snow-capped Mount Etna, seen from the Greek Theatre in Taormina

Exploring Northeastern Sicily

The pearl of the Ionian coast is Taormina, famous for its stupendous panoramic views, but this area has many other fascinating sights too – from the fishing villages of Aci Trezza and Aci Castello to the Baroque splendour of Catania, as well as Mount Etna, the largest active volcano in Europe. You can go up to the edge of its awesome crater by jeep or on foot, or visit the villages on its black lava slopes with the quaint Ferrovia Circumetnea trains. Those who prefer the seaside can visit the beaches of the Aeolian Islands, which also offer unique scenery with volcanic soil and maquis vegetation.

The ravine of the Alcantara river near Taormina

Sights at a Glance

1. *Catania pp166–9*
2. Motta Sant'Anastasia
3. Paternò
4. Centuripe
5. Regalbuto
6. Agira
7. Adrano
8. Mascalucia
9. Aci Castello
10. Aci Trezza
11. Acireale
12. Zafferana Etnea
13. *Mount Etna pp174–7*
14. Bronte
15. Randazzo
16. Linguaglossa
17. Giarre
18. *Taormina pp180–84*
19. Giardini Naxos
20. Castiglione di Sicilia
21. *Messina pp186–9*
22. Tyndaris
23. Patti
24. Capo d'Orlando
25. Milazzo

Islands

26. *The Aeolian Islands pp192–4*

Key

- ━━━ Motorway
- ━━━ Major road
- ━━ Secondary road
- ── Minor road
- ⋯⋯ Main railway
- ── Minor railway
- △ Summit

The monastery of Santa Lucia at Adrano, on the slopes of Etna

For hotels and restaurants see pp202–205 and pp210–217

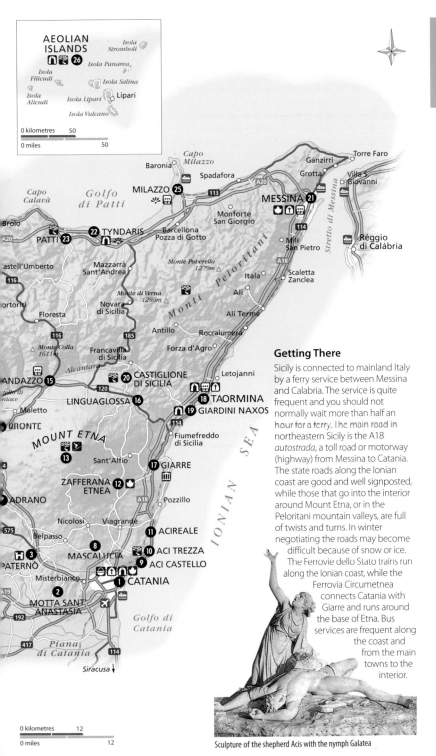

AEOLIAN ISLANDS 🏛 🌊 **26**

Isola Stromboli
Isola Panarea
Isola Filicudi
Isola Salina
Isola Alicudi
Isola Lipari **Lipari**
Isola Vulcano

0 kilometres 50

0 miles 50

Capo Calavà

Golfo di Patti

Capo Milazzo

Baronia

MILAZZO 🏛 **25**

Spadafora

Ganzirri

Grotta

Torre Faro

Villa S. Giovanni

A20

113

MESSINA 🏛 **21**

Stretto di Messina

Brolo

PATTI 🏛 **23**

TYNDARIS 🏛 **22**

astell'Umberto

A20

116

Mazzarrà Sant'Andrea

Monte Poverello 1279m

Barcellona Pozza di Gotto

Monforte San Giorgio

114

Mili San Pietro

Réggio di Calábria 🏛

ortorici

Floresta

Novara di Sicilia

Monte di Vernà 1286m

Italà

Monti Peloritani

A18

Scaletta Zanclea

Ali

116

Monte Colla 1611m

185

Francavilla di Sicilia

Antillo

Forza d'Agro

Alì

Alì Terme

Roccalumera

Alcántara

ANDAZZO 🏛 **15**

ller di iace

120

CASTIGLIONE DI SICILIA 🏛 **20**

Letojanni

🏛 **18** **TAORMINA**

🏛 **19** **GIARDINI NAXOS**

Maletto

LINGUAGLOSSA 🏛 **16**

BRONTE

MOUNT ETNA

114

Fiumefreddo di Sicilia

4

🏛 **13**

Sant'Alfio

🏛 **17** **GIARRE**

ZAFFERANA ETNEA 🏛 **12**

ADRANO

575

Nicolosi

A18

Pozzillo

Belpasso

Viagrande

🏛 **11** **ACIREALE**

🏛 **8**

🏛 **10** **ACI TREZZA**

🏛 **3**

MASCALUCIA

🏛 **9** **ACI CASTELLO**

PATERNO

Misterbianco

🏛 **1** **CATANIA**

19

🏛 **2**

MOTTA SANT' ANASTASIA

192

Piana di Catania

Golfo di Catania

417

114

Siracusa

IONIAN SEA

Getting There

Sicily is connected to mainland Italy by a ferry service between Messina and Calabria. The service is quite frequent and you should not normally wait more than half an hour for a ferry. The main road in northeastern Sicily is the A18 *autostrada*, a toll road or motorway (highway) from Messina to Catania. The state roads along the Ionian coast are good and well signposted, while those that go into the interior around Mount Etna, or in the Peloritani mountain valleys, are full of twists and turns. In winter negotiating the roads may become difficult because of snow or ice. The Ferrovie dello Stato trains run along the Ionian coast, while the Ferrovia Circumetnea connects Catania with Giarre and runs around the base of Etna. Bus services are frequent along the coast and from the main towns to the interior.

0 kilometres 12

0 miles 12

Sculpture of the shepherd Acis with the nymph Galatea

For additional keys to symbols *see back flap*

❶ Catania

Situated between the Ionian Sea and the slopes of Mount Etna, Sicily's second city (a UNESCO World Heritage site) has always had a close relationship with the volcano, and most of its buildings are made from black lava. According to the ancient historian Thucydides, the city was founded in 729 BC by Greek colonists from Chalcis *(see p160)*. Since then it has been flooded with lava and shaken by earthquakes, most radically in 1693, when it was razed to the ground. Catania today is the result of 18th-century rebuilding: broad, straight streets and large, unevenly shaped squares, a precaution against earthquakes.

Catania Town Centre

① Palazzo Biscari
② Piazza Duomo
③ Cathedral
④ Badia di Sant'Agata
⑤ Museo Civico Belliniano
⑥ Teatro Bellini
⑦ Pescheria
⑧ Via Cruciferi
⑨ Roman Theatre
⑩ Castello Ursino
⑪ Museo Verga
⑫ San Nicolò all'Arena
⑬ Via Etnea

🏛 Palazzo Biscari

Via Museo Biscari, Via Dusmet.
Tel 095-715 2508 or 321 818. **Open** by appt. 🔳 **palazzobiscari.com**

This is the largest private palazzo in 18th-century Catania. Construction was begun by Prince Paternò Castello on an embankment of the 16th-century city walls. Work continued for nearly a century and involved some of the leading architects of the time. The most interesting side of the building faces Via Dusmet, with a large terrace decorated with putti, telamons and garlands sculpted by Antonino Amato. The building is partly private and partly used as city administrative offices.

🏛 Piazza Duomo

The heart of city life lies at the crossing of Via Etnea and Via Vittorio Emanuele. The square boasts many fine Baroque buildings: **Palazzo del Municipio** (the Town Hall), the former **Chierici Seminary**, the **Cathedral** and **Porta Uzeda**, the city gate built in 1696 to connect Via Etnea with the port area. In the middle is the **Fontana dell'Elefante**, a well-known fountain sculpted in 1736 by Giovanni Battista Vaccarini. On a pedestal in the basin is an elephant made of lava, on the back of which is an Egyptian obelisk with a

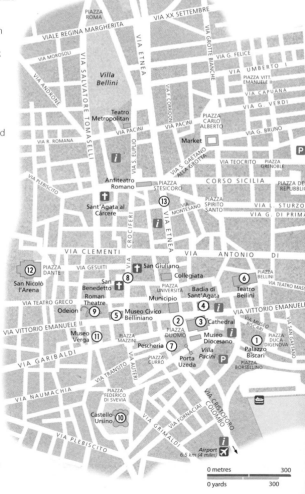

VISITORS' CHECKLIST

Practical Information
Road map E3. 🚗 300,000.
ℹ️ Town Hall, Piazza Duomo
(800-841 042); Porto di Catania,
Vecchio Dogana, Via Dusmet 2.
🚆 Mon–Sat, Piazza Carlo Alberto.
🎭 Feb: Festa di Sant'Agata, Jul–
Sep: Catania Musica Estate; Aug–
Sep: International Jazz Festival;
Oct: symphony and chamber
music concerts.
🌐 turismo.provincia.ct.it

Transport
✈️ Aeroporto V. Bellini (095-340
505). 🚉 Piazza Giovanni XXIII
(892021). 🚌 AST, Via Luigi Shirzo
230–232 (095-723 0535/511).

Entrance to the lovely 18th-century
Palazzo Biscari

globe on top. The latter, a late
Roman sculpture, has become
the city's symbol.

🏛️ Cathedral
Piazza Duomo. **Tel** 095-320 044.
Open 8am–1pm, 3–6pm daily.
🕐 8, 10, 11:30am & 6pm.
The principal church in
Catania is dedicated to
the city's patron saint,
Sant'Agata. It still has its
three original Norman
apses and transept. The
façade, with two tiers
of columns, is fully
Baroque thanks to
the design of GB
Vaccarini, who also
designed the left-
hand side of the
Cathedral. The
majestic interior has a cupola, a
tall transept and three apses. On
the second pilaster to the right
is the **Tomb of Vincenzo Bellini**;

on the first one to the left, a
15th-century stoup. A door in
the right-hand transept leads to
the Norman Cappella della
Madonna, with the remains of
various Aragonese rulers.

🏛️ Badia di Sant'Agata
Via Vittorio Emanuele II. **Open** 7:30am
–noon daily.
This masterpiece of Catanian
Baroque architecture was built
in 1735–67 and designed by
Giovanni Battista Vaccarini. The
façade is a play of convex and
concave surfaces. The
octagonal interior, a triumph
of Rococo decoration, is
equally impressive.

🏛️ Museo Civico Belliniano
Piazza San Francesco 9. **Tel** 095-715 05
35. **Open** 9am–7pm Mon–Sat,
9am–1pm Sun. **Closed** 1 Jan, 1 May,
25 Dec. 📷
Vincenzo Bellini's birthplace
(see p39) is now a museum
with mementos, signed
scores, musical instruments
and models of scenes from
some of his operas.

🎭 Teatro Bellini
Via Perrotta 12.
Tel 095-730 61 11.
📷 9am–noon
Tue–Sat. 📷
Named
after the
Catania-born
composer Vincenzo Bellini, this
theatre attracts praise from
both critics and the public for
its high-quality performances.

Detail of the façade of Teatro Bellini

The Baroque façade of Catania Cathedral, dedicated to Sant'Agata

For keys to map symbols see back flap

The lively Mercato della Pescheria (fish market) in Catania

🐟 Pescheria

Situated at the beginning of Via Garibaldi, the **Fontana dell' Amenano** fountain is fed by the waters of the underground Amenano river, which also forms a pool in the Roman theatre. Sculpted in 1867, the fountain is the focal point of a colourful fish market, the **Mercato della Pescheria**, which occupies the nearby streets and small squares every morning. The smells and atmosphere of the market are reminiscent of North Africa and the Middle East. At the end of Via Garibaldi is the monumental **Porta Garibaldi** city gate, built of limestone and lava in 1768 to celebrate the wedding of Ferdinand IV of Sicily.

🏛 Via Cruciferi

This street is lined with lavishly decorated Baroque palazzi and churches. The road begins at **Piazza San Francesco**, with the Baroque **San Francesco d'Assisi**. In the interior are the so-called *candelore*, carved and gilded wooden constructions which symbolize the various artisans' guilds in the city. Every February the *candelore* are carried in procession as part of the impressive celebrations honouring Sant'Agata, the city's patron saint. Outside the church is the **Arco di San Benedetto**, an arch connecting the fine **Badia Grande** abbey, designed by Francesco Battaglia, and the **Badia Piccola**, attributed to Giovanni Battista Vaccarini. To the left is **San Benedetto**, where the wooden portal carries scenes of the life of St Benedict, and **San Francesco Borgia**, at the top of a double flight of steps flanked by the former **Jesuit College**. Opposite stands **San Giuliano**, a masterpiece of Catanian Baroque architecture designed by Vaccarini.

🏛 Roman Theatre

Via Vittorio Emanuele 226. **Tel** 095-715 05 08. **Open** 9am–7pm daily. 🎫

Built of limestone and lava on the southern slope of the acropolis, the theatre had a diameter of 87 m (285 ft) and could seat 7,000 people. Although there was probably a Greek theatre on this site once, the present ruins are all Roman. The theatre was badly damaged in the 11th century, when Roger I authorized the removal of the marble facing and limestone blocks for use as building material for the Cathedral. What remains of the theatre today are the cavea, the edge of the orchestra and part of the backstage area of the theatre. Next to the theatre is the small semicircular **Odeion**, made of lava and used mainly for competitions in music and rhetoric. It had a seating capacity of 1,500. The entrance to the Odeion is near the top tiers of seats in the Roman theatre.

🏰 Castello Ursino

Piazza Federico di Svevia. **Tel** 095-345 830. **Open** 9am–7pm Mon–Sat, 9am–1:30pm Sun.

This castle was built in 1239–50 by Riccardo da Lentini for Frederick II and is one of the few vestiges of medieval Catania. The Castello Ursino originally stood on a promontory

The Roman theatre in Catania, now completely surrounded by buildings

Castello Ursino, one of the rare medieval buildings in Catania

overlooking the sea and was part of a massive defence system that once included the Motta, Anastasia, Paternò and Adrano castles. Castello Ursino is square, with four corner towers, and was rebuilt in the mid-1500s. On the eastern side of its exterior, above a large window, a five-pointed star with a cabalistic meaning is visible. In a niche on the façade, the Swabian eagle seizing a lamb with its claws is the symbol of Hohenstaufen imperial power. In the inner courtyard, where the kings of Aragon administered justice, there is a display of sarcophagi, columns and other pieces.

The upper rooms house the interesting **Museo Civico**, which has a fine art gallery with important works such as *The Last Judgement* by Beato Angelico, *The Last Supper* by the Spanish painter Luis de Morales, *St John the Baptist* by Pietro Novelli *(see p27)* and a dismantled polyptych by Antonello Saliba of the *Madonna and Child* taken from Santa Maria del Gesù.

🏛 Museo Verga
Via Sant'Anna 8. **Tel** 095-715 05 98. **Open** 9am–1pm, 2–7pm Mon–Sat. 🖼

The apartment where the great Sicilian author Giovanni Verga lived for many years and died in 1922 is on the second floor of a 19th-century building. The house contains period furniture and personal mementos. At the entrance are displayed reproductions of manuscripts, the originals of which are at the Biblioteca

Universitaria Regionale di Catania. The library in Verga's house boasts over 2,500 books from the author's collection, ranging from works by the Italian Futurist Marinetti to the Russian author Dostoevsky. The bedroom is quite simple, with a bed, a dressing table, a wardrobe and portraits of Verga painted by his grandson Michele Grita.

San Nicolò, intended to be the largest church in Sicily

🏛 San Nicolò l'Arena
Piazza Dante. **Tel** 095-715 99 12. **Open** 9am–1pm daily.
San Nicolò was built on the site of a Benedictine monastery damaged in the 1669 eruption.

After collapsing in the 1693 earthquake, the church was rebuilt in the 1700s. It now houses the faculty of letters of the University of Catania.

The nave has two aisles, separated from the central section by huge piers. In the transept is one of the largest sundials in Europe, restored in 1996. It was built in the mid-1800s by the German baron Wolfgang Sartorius von Waltershausen and is extremely precise. Twenty-four slabs of inlaid marble show the signs of the zodiac, days of the year and the seasons. At noon, sunlight falls on the spot from an opening in the roof, marking the day and month.

🏛 Via Etnea
Catania's main street goes up a slight incline and connects the most important parts of the city. Partly closed to traffic, Via Etnea has the most elegant shops and cafés in town. Halfway along it lies **Piazza Stesicoro**, with the ruins of the Roman amphitheatre, built in the 2nd century AD. Nearby is the vast **Piazza Carlo Alberto**, occupied from Monday to Saturday by Catania's huge central market. Back on Via Etnea is the **Collegiata**, a chapel built in the early 1700s and one of the most important late Baroque works in the city. The concave façade, designed by Stefano Ittar, is enlivened by columns, statues and niches. Near the end of Via Etnea is the **Villa Bellini**, a public garden with subtropical plants and busts of famous Sicilians.

The University building on Via Etnea, the most elegant street in Catania

Motta Sant'Anastasia, with its medieval tower dwarfed by Mount Etna

❷ Motta Sant'Anastasia

Road map E3. 7,600. Ferrovia Circumetnea (095-541 250). Pro Loco, Piazza Umberto 42 (095-308 161).

Mount Etna forms a constant backdrop to Motta. From the top of the village, with the massive tower of the 12th-century **Norman castle**, the snow-capped volcano gleams through the winter, gradually darkening in spring and summer. Not far away is the **Chiesa Madre** (Cathedral), also built in Norman times. At the foot of the old town is the heart of Motta Sant'Anastasia with its *pasticcerie* (pastry shops), Baroque churches and bustling atmosphere, placed as it is on a major route through the Catania region.

❸ Paternò

Road map E3. 46,000. Ferrovia Circumetnea (095-541 250). 095-797 04 20. Carnival (before Lent).

Surrounded by orchards of citrus fruit, this town lies at the foot of a **castle**, which has a stunning view of Mount Etna and the Simeto Valley. The massive square castle was built by Roger I in 1073, totally rebuilt in the 14th century and then restored twice in the 1900s. It lies up Via Matrice, which will also take you to the **Chiesa Madre**, the Cathedral dedicated to Santa Maria dell'Alto. The church was originally Norman, but it was rebuilt in 1342.

❹ Centuripe

Road map E3. 6,600. from Catania or Enna, Romano (0935-731 14). 0935-74755/380-790 43 93. Mon.

Known as "the balcony of Sicily" because of the wide views, Centuripe is especially pretty in February and March, when snow-capped Mount Etna forms a striking contrast with the blossom of orange and almond trees. An important Greek-

The 12th-century Norman castle dominating Paternò from above, with its wide-ranging views taking in the Simeto valley and Etna

The Circumetnea Railway

The picturesque carriages of the Ferrovia Circumetnea climb up the slopes of Mount Etna, passing through barren stretches of black lava alternating with luxuriant vegetation. This delightful route will take you back to the dawn of tourism, when the pace of travel was much slower than today. It takes about five hours to cover the 90 km (56 miles) or so between Catania and Giarre Riposto, the two termini, plus another hour to get back to Catania from Riposto via state rail. However, the rewards are magnificent views of terraced vineyards and almond and hazelnut groves, as well as the volcano itself.

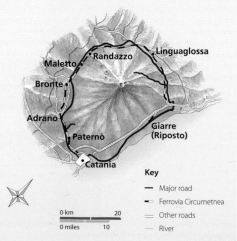

🚆 Ferrovia Circumetnea
Via Ceronda 352, Catania.
Tel 095-541 250. 🔳 circumetnea.it

Key

— Major road
•— Ferrovia Circumetnea
═ Other roads
— River

0 km   20
0 miles   10

Agira, perched on a sloping hillside, has preserved its fascinating Arab town plan

Roman town, it was destroyed by Frederick II and rebuilt in the 16th century. A long tree-lined avenue leads to a viewing terrace called **Castello di Corradino**, with ruins of an Imperial Roman mausoleum.

❺ Regalbuto

Road map E3. 🏔 8,200. 🚍 from Catania. 🚹 Pro Loco (0935-910 514).

This town was destroyed in 1261 by the inhabitants of Centuripe and rebuilt by Manfredi. The heart of Regalbuto is **Piazza della Repubblica**, with its multicoloured paving and **San Rocco**. **San Basilio** and **Santa Maria del Carmine** are also worth a look. Nearby is the **Lake Pozzillo dam**, the largest artificial basin in Sicily, and a **Canadian military cemetery** with the graves of 490 soldiers who were killed in 1943.

❻ Agira

Road map D3. 🏔 9,200. 🚍 from Catania. 🚹 Pro Loco, Piazza F. Crispi 1, (0935-961 239).

Because of its elevated position, Agira is clearly visible from a distance, with Mount Etna rising behind it. The ancient Siculan town of Agyron was colonized by the Greeks in 339 BC, and the ancient historian Diodorus Siculus was born here *(see p26)*. The most interesting aspect of Agyron's modern-day counterpart is its Arab layout, with Norman churches and patrician residences with Arab-style portals. Centrally located **Piazza Garibaldi** boasts **Sant'Antonio**, with a 16th-century wooden statue of San Silvestro and a painting on marble of *The Adoration of the Magi*. In the vicinity is **Santa Maria del Gesù**, with a crucifix by Fra' Umile da Petralia. In Piazza Roma is the lovely 16th-century façade of **San Salvatore**, with its bell tower covered with majolica tiles.

❼ Adrano

Road map E3. 🏔 35,500. 🚇 Ferrovia Circumetnea (095-541 250). 🚹 Pro Loco, Via Roma 56 (095-760 61 02). 🎭 Easter: the "Diavolata".

A sanctuary dedicated to the local deity Adranos stood on a lava plateau facing the Valle del Simeto, where Sicilian hounds *(cirnecos)* were trained as hunting dogs *(see p174)*. The city was founded in the Greek period by Dionysius the Elder, who chose this natural balcony to build a military stronghold.

The centre of town is Piazza Umberto I, site of the **Norman castle**, a massive, quadrilateral 11th-century construction. It houses the **Museo Archeologico**, with a collection of Neolithic pottery, Greek amphoras and millstones. A narrow stair, cut out of the Hohenstaufen wall in the Middle Ages, leads to the upper floors. Two have displays of archaeological items while the third houses the **Art Gallery**. The **Chiesa Madre**, built by the Normans and reconstructed in the 1600s, also stands in the same square.

Environs
A byroad below the town leads to a dirt road that passes through citrus orchards for 1 km (half a mile) to the **Ponte dei Saraceni**, a 14th-century bridge on the Simeto river, with an **archaeological zone** nearby.

The Saracen bridge on the Simeto river, near Adrano

❽ Mascalucia

Road map E3. 24,500. AST from Catania (095-7461 096). Pro Loco, Via Calvario 5 (095-727 77 90).

On the eastern slopes of the volcano, just above Catania, to which it is connected by an uninterrupted series of villages and hamlets, is Mascalucia, a town of largish houses and villas. It is worth stopping here to visit the **Giardino Lavico** at the Azienda Trinità farmstead, a small "oasis" surrounded by modern building development on the slopes of Etna. The "lava garden" consists of an organically cultivated citrus grove, a 17th-century house and a garden filled with prickly pears, yuccas and other plants that thrive in the lava soil. The orchard's irrigation canals were inspired by Arab gardens. For helicopter trips over Mount Etna, make inquiries at the Azienda.

Giardino Lavico
Azienda Agricola Trinità, Via Trinità 34. **Tel** 095-727 21 56. by appt.

❾ Aci Castello

Road map F3. 18,000. Corso Italia 302 (095-711 67 15). AST (095-746 10 96 or 840-000 323). Festa di San Mauro (15 Jan).

The name of this fishermen's village, a few kilometres from Catania, derives from the **Norman castle** built on the top

The castle at Aci Castello, destroyed by Frederick II of Aragon

of a basalt rock jutting into the sea. It was built in 1076 from black lava and in 1299 was the base for the rebel Roger of Luria. The castle was subsequently destroyed by Frederick II of Aragón (see p33) after a long siege. Some rooms in the surviving parts are occupied by the **Museo Civico**, with archaeological and natural history collections relating to the Etna region (temporarily closed). There is also a small **Botanical Garden**. The town, with straight streets and low-rise houses, marks the beginning of the **Riviera dei Ciclopi**: according to Greek mythology, Polyphemus and his friends lived on Etna.

❿ Aci Trezza

Road map F3. 24 Jun: San Giovanni Battista.

This picturesque fishing village, part of Aci Castello, was the setting for Giovanni Verga's novel I Malavoglia and for Luchino Visconti's film adaptation, La Terra Trema (see p26 and p28). The small harbour faces a pile of basalt rocks, the **Isole dei Ciclopi**, now a nature reserve. On the largest island there is a biology and oceanography station. According to Homer, Polyphemus hurled the rocks at the sea in an attempt to strike the fleeing Ulysses, who had blinded him.

The Aci Trezza stacks, hurled by Polyphemus at Ulysses, according to Greek myth

⓫ Acireale

Road map F3. 🏙 53,000. **FS** Catania Stazione, Centrale Piazza San Giovanni XXIII. 🚌 Messina–Catania. **i** Via Scionti 15 (095-895 249). 🎭 San Sebastiano (Jan); Carnival, traditionally costumed procession (Good Friday & Aug); Santa Venere (Jul).

Acireale stands on a lava terrace overlooking the Ionian Sea in the midst of citrus orchards. Since Roman times it has been famous as a spa town with sulphur baths. The present name of the town refers to the myth, sung by Virgil and Ovid, of the cyclops Polifemo, the shepherd Aci and the nymph Galatea. It is the largest town on the eastern side of Mount Etna and has been destroyed time and again by eruptions and earthquakes. It was finally rebuilt after the 1693 earthquake, emerging as a jewel of Sicilian Baroque architecture. The heart of town is **Piazza Duomo**, with its cafés and ice-cream parlours. Acireale is dominated by its **Cathedral**, built in the late 1500s. The façade has two cusped bell towers covered with multicoloured majolica tiles. The Baroque portal leads to the vast interior with its frescoed vaults. In the right-hand transept is the Cappella di Santa Venera, the patron saint of the town. On the transept floor is a meridian marked out in 1843 by a Danish astronomer. Piazza Duomo also boasts the **Palazzo Comunale**, with a Gothic door and a fine wrought-iron balcony, and **Santi Pietro e Paolo**, built in the 17th century. Close by is the **Teatro dei Pupi**, known for its puppet shows, and the **Pinacoteca dell'Accademia Zelantea**, with works by local painter Pietro Vasta, whose paintings also appear in the town's churches. The main street, **Corso Vittorio Emanuele**, crosses squares such as Piazza Vigo, with **Palazzo Pennisi di Floristella** and **San Sebastiano**.

Baroque detail, Acireale

The Chiesa Madre at Zafferana Etnea, on the eastern slopes of Etna

⓬ Zafferana Etnea

Road map E3. 🏙 8,000. 🚌 AST bus from Catania (095-746 10 96). **i** Pro Loco, Piazza L Sturzo 1 (095-708 28 25).

Famous for its honey, Zafferana Etnea lies on the eastern slopes of Etna and is one of the towns most often affected by recent lava flows. The most destructive eruptions occurred in 1852, when the lava reached the edge of town, and in 1992. The heart of Zafferana is its large tree-lined main square, dominated by the Baroque **Chiesa Madre**. The square is also the home of a permanent agricultural fair which, besides selling local wine and produce, has old farm implements on display.

Environs
Down the road towards Linguaglossa is **Sant'Alfio**, a town surrounded by vineyards and known for the huge 2,000-year-old tree called "Castagno dei cento cavalli" (Chestnut tree of 100 horses). According to legend, the leaves of this famous tree once protected Queen Jeanne d'Anjou and her retinue of 100 knights.

I Malavoglia

Published in 1881 in Milan, *I Malavoglia* (The House by the Medlar Tree) is a masterpiece by novelist Giovanni Verga (*see p26*) and of Italian *verismo*. Set on the Riviera dei Ciclopi at Aci Trezza, it describes the harsh life of fishermen and their constant struggle with the sea. The Toscano family, "I Malavoglia", are "all good seafaring people, just the opposite of their nickname" (*malavoglia* means ill-will). In 1947 Luchino Visconti made a film inspired by the book, *La Terra Trema*.

The beach at Aci Trezza, the setting for *I Malavoglia* (1881)

⓭ Mount Etna

Mount Etna is fundamental to Sicily's nature and landscape. The Italian writer Leonardo Sciascia *(see p27)* called it "a huge house cat, that purrs quietly and awakens every so often". Etna is Europe's largest active volcano and dominates the whole of eastern Sicily. Feared and loved, Etna is both snow and fire, lush vegetation and black lava. Around the crater you can still see the remnants of numbers of ancient vents. Further down is the eerie, barren landscape of the Valle del Bove.

Valle del Bove
Many recent lava flows have ended here. The craters Calanna and Trifoglietto I are of very ancient origin. This is one of the most fascinating places in the Etna area.

The Sicilian Hound
The Sicilian hound or *cirneco* is a breed of dog native to the Etna area. In ancient times it was a hunting dog.

KEY

① **Acireale**

② **Catania**

③ **Paternò**

④ **Ragalna**

⑤ **Nicolosi**

⑥ **The 1983** eruption was the first diverted by human effort.

⑦ **Rifugio Sapienza**

⑧ **2001 and 2002 eruptions**

⑨ **Zafferana Etnea**

⑩ **Calanna volcano**

⑪ **Valle del Bove**

⑫ **The principal craters**: Trifoglietto I and II, Mongibello.

⑬ **Secondary eruptive vents**

⑭ **1978 eruption**

⑮ **Secondary lava streams**

⑯ **The domes,** the upthrust of the Earth's crust, are formed when there is not enough pressure for the magma to overflow.

⑰ **1981 eruption**

⑱ **Taormina**

⑲ **1986, 1987, 1989, 1991 and 1999 eruptions**

⑳ **Riposto**

The Largest Volcano in Europe

Etna, or Mongibello (from the Italian monte *and the Arab* gebel, *both meaning "mountain"), is a relatively "recent" volcano that emerged two million years ago. It has erupted frequently in known history. Some of the most devastating eruptions were in 1381 and 1669, when the lava reached Catania. The most recent ones took place in 2001 and 2002. On these occasions the lava flow caused extensive damage to Rifugio Sapienza, destroyed the ski facilities and the cable-car apparatus and came within 4 km (2.5 miles) of the village of Nicolosi. Eruptions that have occurred in the last 20 years are shown here.*

Lowland Landscape
The breakdown of volcanic material in the valley below Mount Etna has resulted in very fertile land which supports almonds, olives, grapes, citrus fruit and vegetables below 1,000 m (3,280 ft).

Geologists and Vulcanologists
Mount Etna, without equal in Europe, has always attracted visitors. Since the late 1800s it has been the subject of systematic study by experts.

Geological History of the Volcano

Even in recent centuries the appearance of Mount Etna has altered. In 1865 the summit was at 3,313 m (10,867 ft); in 1932 it was 3,263 m (10,703 ft); and today it is 3,320 m (10,892 ft) high. Eruptions in the central crater are rare, but they are frequent in the side vents, and here they create smaller secondary cones.

On the eastern slope of Mount Etna is a huge chasm known as the Valle del Bove, the result of an immense explosion.

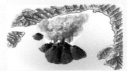
First stage, 200,000–100,000 years ago (Monte Calanna)

Second stage, 80,000 years ago (Vulcano Trifoglietto)

Third stage, 64,000 years ago (the cone collapses)

Fourth, current stage (the Mongibello cone)

Exploring Mount Etna

A protected area 58,000 ha (143,260 acres) in size, Mount Etna offers many opportunities for excursions, and attracts thousands of visitors every year. A popular excursion is from Zafferana to the Valle del Bove, the spectacular hollow whose shape was changed by the 1992 eruptions. The hike up to the large craters at the summit is not to be missed. Start off at the Rifugio Sapienza and Rifugio Citelli hostels and Piano Provenzana (after suffering eruption damage, these hiker centres are now being rebuilt). A trip around the mountain is also thrilling: from the Sapienza to the Monte Scavo camp, Piano Provenzana and the former Menza camp. There are also several lava grottoes.

The Effects of an Eruption
This chapel was one of many buildings destroyed in the massive lava flows caused by the 1983 eruptions.

Randaz

• **Maletto**

Grotta del Burò

Monte Sp 1,547 m,

SS284

• **Bronte**

Rifugio Monte Scavo

Monte Ruvolo 1,410 m, (4,624 ft)

Monte Nun 1,803 m, (5

Grotta della Neve

Skiing on Etna
Although there are few chair lifts, skiing on Mount Etna is a unique experience. Besides the regular ski runs you can do cross-country skiing or mountain climbing in the snow.

SS284

Monte Turchio 1,295 m, (4,248 ft)

Nature on Mount Etna

Despite the many eruptions and the bitter cold that freezes the terrain in winter, many species of plants have succeeded in colonizing the lava soil. At high altitudes you can see small lichens, camomile and soapwort on the slopes. Poplars thrive in the more humid areas. Further down are woods of beech, birch, larch and Corsican pine. Centuries of hunting have reduced the animal population, though there are still rabbits, weasels, wildcats and foxes, while the main bird species are the Sicilian partridge and the *Dendrocopus* woodpecker.

Pine forest on the slopes of Etna

Torrente Milia

• **Adrano**

• **Biancavilla**

| 0 kilometres | 3 |
| 0 miles | 3 |

Rifugio Sapienza
At over 1,800 m (5,904 ft), the Sapienza hostel is a base for hikers in the summer and for skiers in winter.

VISITORS' CHECKLIST

Practical Information
Road Map E2, E3, F3.
Parco dell'Etna: **Tel** 095-821 111.
Italian Alpine Club (CAI): **Tel** 095-715 35 15. Etna Alpine Guides: **Tel** 095-791 47 55. Rifugio Sapienza: (hostel): **Tel** 095-915 321. **W** parcoetna.ct.it

Transport
Catania V. Bellini 095-723 91 11. AST (095-746 10 96); SAIS (095-536 168). **FS** Catania (892021). Ferrovia Circumetnea (095-541 111).

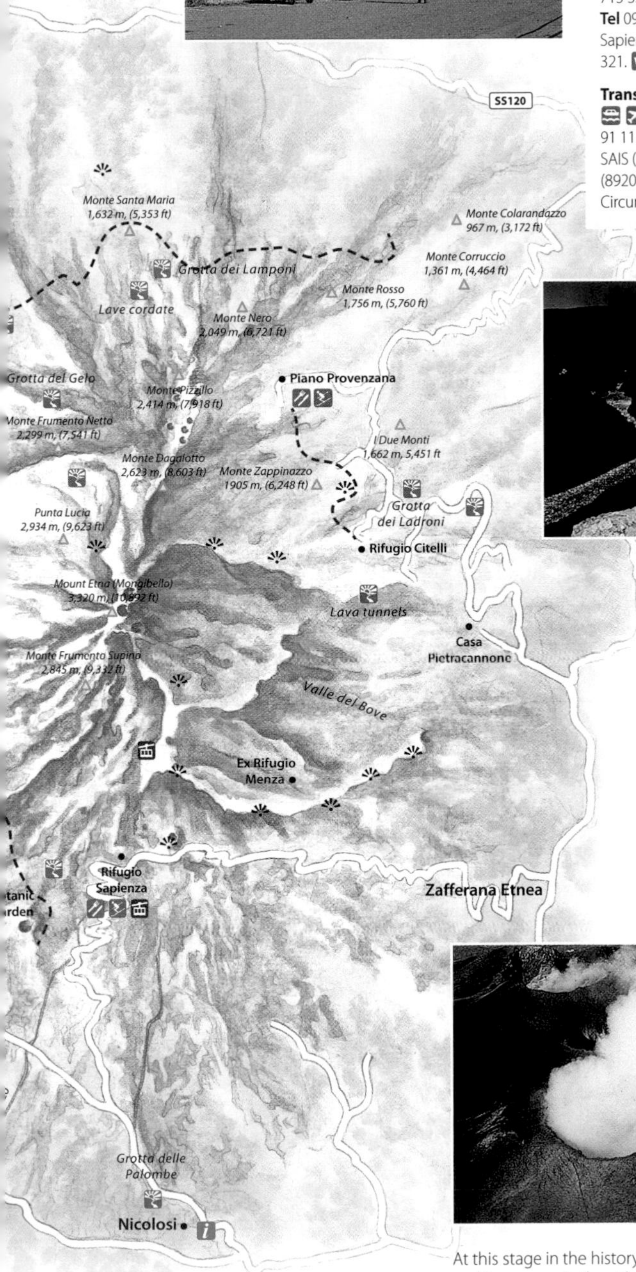

Monte Santa Maria
1,632 m, (5,353 ft)

Monte Colarandazzo
967 m, (3,172 ft)

Grotta dei Lamponi

Monte Corruccio
1,361 m, (4,464 ft)

Lave cordate

Monte Rosso
1,756 m, (5,760 ft)

Monte Nero
2,049 m, (6,721 ft)

Grotta del Gelo

Monte Pizzillo
2,414 m, (7,918 ft)

● *Piano Provenzana*

Monte Frumento Netto
2,299 m, (7,541 ft)

I Due Monti
1,662 m, 5,451 ft

Monte Dagolotto
2,623 m, (8,603 ft)

Monte Zappinazzo
1905 m, (6,248 ft)

Grotta dei Ladroni

Punta Lucia
2,934 m, (9,623 ft)

● *Rifugio Citelli*

Mount Etna (Mongibello)
3,320 m, (10,892 ft)

Lava tunnels

Casa Pietracannone

Monte Frumento Supino
2,845 m, (9,331 ft)

Valle del Bove

Ex Rifugio Menza

Eruptions and Lava Flows
The volcano can be visited even when it is active, provided you scrupulously follow instructions. Above, the 1991 eruption.

Key

 ═══ Major road
 ● ● Footpath (Trail)

Rifugio Sapienza

Zafferana Etnea

Grotta delle Palombe

● **Nicolosi**

Craters and Eruptions
At this stage in the history of Mount Etna, most of the eruptions occur in the side vents, while on the summit craters the occasional explosive eruption may take place.

⑭ Bronte

Road map E3. 🚗 18,500. 🚉 Ferrovia Circumetnea (095-895 249). 🛈 Pro Loco, Via D'Annunzio 8 (095-774 72 44 or 360-444 950). 🎉 Oct: Pistachio festival.

Situated on a terraced lava slope, Bronte was founded by Charles V. In 1799 Ferdinand IV of Bourbon gave the town and its estates to Admiral Horatio Nelson, who had helped him suppress the revolts in Naples in 1799. In 1860, after the success of Garibaldi's Red Shirts in Sicily, the peasants of Bronte rebelled, demanding that Nelson's land be split up among them, but their revolt was put down by Garibaldi's men. The episode was immortalized in a short story by Verga *(see pp26–7)*. The eruptions of 1651, 1832 and 1843 struck the centre of Bronte, which has however managed to retain its original character, with stone houses and steeply rising alleyways. The 16th-century **Annunziata** has a sandstone portal and, inside, an *Annunciation* (1541) attributed to Antonello Gagini *(see p57)* as well as some 17th-century canvases. In the village of Piana Cuntarati, the **Masseria Lombardo** farm has been converted into an Ethnographic Museum which, among many interesting objects, has an Arab paper mill dating from the year 1000. Today Bronte is famous for the production of pistachios.

Environs

Around 12 km (7 miles) from Bronte is **Castello di Maniace**, a Benedictine monastery founded by Margaret of Navarre in 1174, on the spot where the Byzantine general Maniakes had defeated the Arabs. Destroyed by the 1693 earthquake, the site became the property of Horatio Nelson. Today it looks like a fortified farm, with a garden of exotic plants. Nearby is the medieval **Santa Maria**, with scenes from the Book of Genesis sculpted on the capitals of the columns.

🏰 **Castello di Maniace**
Tel 095-690 018. **Open** 9am–1pm, 2:30–7pm (2:30–5pm Nov–Mar).

⑮ Randazzo

Road map E3. 🚗 11,500. 🚉 Ferrovia Circumetnea. 🛈 Pro Loco, Piazza Municipio 17 (095-923 955). 🎉 Easter Week, 15 Aug: Processione della "Vara", Jul–Aug: medieval festival. 🛒 Sun.
🌐 prolocorandazzo.it

Built of lava stone and set 765 m (2,509 ft) above sea level, Randazzo is the town closest to the craters of Mount Etna, but it has never been inundated with lava. In the Middle Ages it was surrounded by a 3-km (2-mile) city wall, some parts of which have survived, such as the **Porta Aragonese** gate on the old road to Messina. The major monument and symbol of the town is **Santa Maria**, a basilica built in 1217–39: the towered apses with the characteristic

Medieval window in central Randazzo

ribbing are all that is left of the original Norman construction, while the double lancet windows and portals are Catalan. The nave with its black lava columns has multicoloured marble altars and a marble basin sculpted by the Gagini School. **Corso Umberto**, the main street in Randazzo, leads to **Piazza San Francesco d'Assisi**, dominated by the **Palazzo Comunale**, once the monastery of the Minor Order, which has an elegant cloister with a cistern.

The narrow side streets have many examples of medieval architecture. The most characteristic of these is **Via degli Archi**, which has a lovely pointed arch and black lava cobblestone paving. In **Piazza San Nicolò** is the church of the same name, with a late Renaissance façade made of lava stone. In the interior there is a fine statue of San Nicola of Bari sculpted in 1523 by Antonello Gagini. The bell tower was damaged by an earthquake in 1783. Its reconstruction replaced the original cusp with a wrought-iron balcony. After a turn to the left, Corso Umberto crosses a square where **San Martino** stands. It has a beautiful bell tower with single lancet windows with two-coloured borders, and a polygonal spire.

The restored Via degli Archi Randazzo, with its cobbled lava paving

The Castello di Maniace, near Bronte, the property of Lord Nelson's heirs until 1981

The Randazzo skyline, dominated by the bell tower of San Martino

Opposite is the **Castle**, which was a prison in the 1500s, and is now the home of the **Museo Archeologico Vagliasindi**, with interesting Greek finds from Tissa, such as the famous vase depicting the punishment of the Harpies.

⑯ Linguaglossa

Road map F3. ⏁ 6,000. ☒ Ferrovia Circumetnea. ℹ Pro Loco, Piazza Annunziata 5 (095-643 094). ☒ Mount Etna festival (Last Sun in Aug). ⓦ prolocolinguaglossa.it

Linguaglossa is the largest village on the northeastern slopes of Etna as well as the starting point for excursions to the volcano summit and for the ski runs. Its name derives from a 17th-century lava flow that was called *lingua glossa* (big tongue). The town's streets are paved with black lava and the houses have wrought-iron balconies. The **Chiesa Madre**, dedicated to Santa Maria delle Grazie, is worth a visit for its Baroque decoration and fine coffered ceiling. Linguaglossa also boasts the **Museo Etnografico**, a museum with geological and natural history exhibits as well as everyday objects and craftsmen's tools.

🏛 **Museo Etnografico**
Piazza Annunziata. **Tel** 095-643 094. **Open** 9am–1pm Mon–Sat, 10am–1pm Sun. ☒

⑰ Giarre

Road map F3. ⏁ 27,200. ☒ Ferrovia Circumetnea. 🚌 from Catania. ℹ Town Hall (095-963 273/501); Proloco, Piazza Monsignor Alessi (095-970 42 57). ⓦ prolocogiarre.it

Lying amid citrus groves extending down to the sea, Giarre is famous for its handmade wrought-iron products. The heart of town is **Piazza Duomo**, dominated by the impressive Neo-Classical **Duomo**, built in 1794 and dedicated to Sant'Isidoro Agricola. There are many delightful patrician residences made of lava stone in the old town.

In the nearby village of Macchia is the **Museo degli Usi e dei Costumi delle Genti dell'Etna**, an ethnographic museum. One interesting exhibit here is a reproduction of a typical Etna farmhouse, with its old kitchen

and bread oven, well and washtub. Also on display are farm implements, looms, and period photographs and daguerreotypes.

🏛 **Museo degli Usi e dei Costumi delle Genti dell'Etna**
Lungotorrente Emanuele Filiberto, Macchia di Giarre. **Open** 3.30–5.30pm Mon–Thu; other times by appt only. ⓦ museogentietna.it

The rusticated façade of the late 18th-century Neo-Classical Duomo in Giarre

⑱ Street-by-Street: Taormina

On a bluff above the Ionian Sea, at the foot of Monte Tauro, Taormina is Sicily's most famous tourist resort. Immersed in luxuriant subtropical vegetation, it was a favourite stop for those on the Grand Tour and the preferred summer residence of aristocrats and bankers, from Wilhelm II of Germany to the Rothschilds. In its time the town has been Siculan, Greek and Roman, but its medieval layout gave it today's look.

Piazza IX Aprile
The second largest square in Taormina is home to the churches of San Giorgio and San Giuseppe, the Torre dell'Orologio and the Wünderbar Café.

★ **Piazza del Duomo**
This is the heart of town, at the western end of Corso Umberto I. In the middle of the square is a Baroque fountain, facing the Cathedral of San Nicolò and the Palazzo Comunale (Town Hall).

Villa Comunale
Located on a cliff with a stunning view, this lovely garden was donated to the town by a rich Englishwoman, an aristocrat who had fallen in love with Taormina.

For hotels and restaurants see pp202–205 and pp210–217

★ **Palazzo Corvaja**
The Norman structure, with a castellated façade with double lancet windows, was built over an Arab tower. It houses the Museo di Arte e Tradizione Popolari.

| 0 metres | 100 |
| 0 yards | 100 |

KEY

① **San Giorgio**

② **Convento di San Domenico**

③ **Palazzo dei Duchi di Santo Stefano** was built in the Norman period with Arab motifs.

④ **Porta Catania**

⑤ **Chiesa del Carmine**

⑥ **Badia Vecchia**

⑦ **Chiesa della Visitazione**

⑧ **Naumachie**

⑨ **Roman Odeion**

⑩ **Santa Caterina** was constructed in the mid-17th century over the ruins of the Odeion.

⑪ **Chiesa dei Cappuccini**

⑫ **San Pancrazio**

★ **Greek Theatre**
This is the second largest ancient theatre in Sicily, after the one in Syracuse. It was originally built in the Hellenistic age (3rd century BC) and was almost entirely rebuilt by the Romans in the 2nd century AD. The theatre has a magnificent view of the sea and Mount Etna.

Exploring Taormina

From Easter to October and during Christmas, Taormina is inundated with visitors, so if you prefer peace and quiet it is a good idea to go out of season. The climate is mild here even in the winter. The town is especially delightful in the spring, when the air is filled with the scent of orange and lemon blossom, the gardens are in bloom and Mount Etna is still snow-capped. A regular shuttle bus links the car park to the centre of town, or you can park at Mazzarò and take the cable car to town.

Corso Umberto I, running the length of the town

🚊 Corso Umberto I

The main street in Taormina begins at **Porta Messina** and ends at **Porta Catania**, a gate crowned by a building showing the municipal coat of arms. The street is lined with shops, *pasticcerie* and cafés famous for their glamorous clientele, like the **Wünderbar**, where you can try the cocktails that Liz Taylor and Richard Burton were so fond of. Halfway down the Corso is **Piazza IX Aprile**, a panoramic terrace with **Sant'Agostino** (now the Municipal Library) and **San**

The Wünderbar has always been a favourite with visiting film stars

Giuseppe. A short distance away is the **Porta di Mezzo** gate with the 17th-century Torre dell' Orologio, or clock tower. Above and below Corso Umberto I there are stepped alleyways and lanes passing through quiet, characterful areas. One such alley leads to the **Naumachie**, a massive Roman brick wall dating back to the Imperial age, with 18 arched niches that once supported a huge cistern.

🚊 Palazzo Corvaja

Piazza Vittorio Emanuele. **Tel** 0942-23243. **Open** 9am–1pm, 4–6pm Tue–Sun. 📞 0942-620 198. 📷

Taormina's grandest building dates from the 15th century, although it was originally an Arab tower. The austere façade topped by crenellation is made elegant by the three-mullioned windows and the limestone and black lava decorative motifs. The courtyard stairway decorated with reliefs of the *Birth of Eve* and *The Original Sin* takes you to the *piano nobile*, where the Sicilian parliament met in 1411 and where Queen Blanche of Navarre and her retinue lived for a short period. Some of the rooms are open to visitors. On the ground floor is

the local tourist information bureau. Next to the palazzo are the Baroque **Santa Caterina** and the ruins of the **Odeion**, a small Roman theatre.

🏛 Greek Theatre

Via Teatro Greco. **Tel** 0942-23220. **Open** 9am–1 hr before sunset daily. 📷 ✅

Set in a spectacular position, this theatre is one of the most famous Sicilian monuments in the world. It was built in the Hellenistic age and then almost completely rebuilt in the Roman period, when it became an arena for gladiatorial combat.

From the cavea, carved from the side of a hill, the view takes in Giardini-Naxos *(see p184)* and Mount Etna. The upper part of the nine-section theatre is surrounded by a double portico. The theatre originally had a diameter of 109 m (358 ft) and a seating capacity of 5,000. Behind the stage area stood a wall with niches and a colonnade. Some of the Corinthian columns are still standing.

The Greek Theatre in Taormina, once capable of seating 5,000 spectators

🚊 Villa Comunale

Via Bagnoli Croci. **Open** 9am–1 hr before sunset in summer; 8am–sunset in winter.

Dedicated to Duke Colonna di Cesarò, this public garden was bequeathed to Taormina by an English aristocrat, Florence Trevelyan, who fell in love with the town. Situated on a cliff with a magnificent view of Etna and the coast, the garden is filled with Mediterranean and tropical plants. A characteristic part of the garden is the arabesque-decorated tower, similar to a Chinese pagoda, that the owner used for bird-watching.

A view of Piazza del Duomo: in the foreground, the Baroque fountain, which faces the Cathedral

⛪ Cathedral

Piazza Duomo. **Tel** 0942-23123.
Open 9am–8pm. ⛪ Check website.
🌐 **arcipreturataormina.org**

The Cathedral (San Nicolò) was
built in the 13th century and
has been altered over the
centuries. The austere façade is
crowned by crenellation. The
17th-century portal is decorated
with a medallion pattern, and
over this are a small rose
window and two windows with
pointed arches. The nave has
two side aisles and a wooden
ceiling, as well as some
interesting works of art: *The
Visitation* by Antonio Giuffrè
(15th century), a polyptych by
Antonello Saliba of the *Virgin
Mary and Child*, and an alabaster
statue of the Virgin Mary by the
Gagini School. In Piazza Duomo,
in the middle of which is a
lovely Baroque fountain, is the
Town Hall, **Palazzo del
Municipio**, with a storey lined
with Baroque windows.

🏛 Palazzo dei Duchi di Santo Stefano

Via De Spuches. **Open** 8:30am–
12:30pm, 4:30–7:30pm (3:30–6:30pm
in winter), Tue–Sun. **Closed** Mon.

This 13th-century building near
Porta Catania was the residence
of the De Spuches, the Spanish
dukes of Santo Stefano di Brifa
and princes of Galati, two towns

on the Ionian coast near Messina.
In this masterpiece of Sicilian
Gothic architecture the influence
of Arab masons is clearly seen in
the wide black lava frieze
alternating with rhomboidal
white Syracusan stone inlay. Note
the trilobated arches and double
lancet windows on the façade.
The interior has a permanent
exhibition of the works of
sculptor Giuseppe Marzullo.

🏛 Castelmola

A winding road of 5 km (3 miles)
leads to this pretty village
perched on a rock. Today you
only see the ruins of a medieval
castle, but in antiquity this
may have been the site of
the ancient acropolis of
Tauromenion. From Castelmola
you can enjoy one of the most
famous panoramic views in the
world, especially fine at sunset.

Palazzo dei Duchi di Santo Stefano, influenced by Arab masons

View of Isola Bella from the steps that lead from Taormina to the beach at Mazzarò

🌊 Mazzarò

This small town is virtually Taormina's beach. It can be reached easily by cable car from Taormina or via the road leading to the Catania–Messina state road N114. An alternative is the steps which descend from the centre of Taormina passing through gardens of bougainvillea in bloom. From the **Bay of Mazzarò**, with its crystal-clear water, you can go on excursions to other sights along the coast: **Capo Sant'Andrea**, with the **Grotta Azzurra**, a spectacular marine grotto, can be visited by boat; to the south are the stacks of **Capo Taormina** and the beach at **Villagonia**; and to the north are **Isola Bella**, one of the most exclusive places in the area,

partly because of its clear waters, and the beaches at the **Baia delle Sirene** and the **Lido di Spisone**. Further on is the beach at **Mazzeo**, a long stretch of sand that leads as far as Letojanni and continues up to **Lido Silemi**.

Letojanni

This small seaside resort is 5 km (3 miles) from Taormina. Busy and bustling in the summer, it is perhaps best seen in the spring or autumn. Locals and visitors alike come here to dine out in one of the many good fish restaurants by the water.

🔟 Giardini-Naxos

Road map F3. 👥 9,000. ✈ Catania Fontanarossa 66 km (41 miles). 🚉 892 021. 🚌 Autolinee SAIS (0942-625 179). ℹ STR, Lungomare Tysandros 54 (0942-510 10).

Ancient Silenic mask

Between Capo Taormina and Capo Schisò, Giardini-Naxos is a seaside resort near what was once the first Greek colony in Sicily. Thucydides relates that Naxos was founded in 735 BC by Chalcidians led by the Athenian Thucles, and Naxos became the base for all further colonization of the island. Naxos was destroyed by Dionysius of Syracuse in 403 BC. On the headland of Capo Schisò, amid lemon trees and prickly pears, is the **Museo Archaeologico**.

Of the two phases in the life of the city, the one which yielded the most important (if scarce) archaeological finds dates from the 6th and 5th centuries BC, with remains of the city walls and houses as well as stones from a temple possibly dedicated to Aphrodite. In the village of **Giardini**, by the beach, there are still some fine mansions on the oldest streets.

🏛 Museo Archaeologico
Tel 0942-51001. **Open** 9am–1 hr before sunset daily. 🖼

The sea at Giardini-Naxos, the first Greek colony in Sicily

⓴ Castiglione di Sicilia

Road map E3. 🔺 4,000. 🚃 Ferrovia Circumetnea. 🚌 Giardini di Naxos (0942-625 301/550 929). 🅸 Town Hall (0942-980 348 or 800-010 552).

This village, voted one of Italy's most beautiful, lies on a crag dominating the **Alcantara Valley**. Founded by the Greeks, many years later it became a royal city under the Normans and the Hohenstaufens, and the fief of Roger of Lauria at the end of the 13th century.

Castiglione still retains its medieval layout, the narrow streets converging in central **Piazza Lauria**. From this point, moving up the hill, there are many churches. The first is the **Chiesa Madre**, or San Pietro, which still has a Norman apse; then there are the 17th-century **Chiesa delle Benedettine** and the Baroque **Sant'Antonio** and **Chiesa Della Catena**. At the top of the village is the **Castel Leone**, built by the Normans over Arab fortifications, where you have a view of the **medieval bridge** on the Alcantara river.

Environs

The **Alcantara ravine**, 20 m (66 ft) deep, cut out of black

The Alcantara river flowing between basalt cliffs

basalt by the rushing waters of the Alcantara river, is a marvellously compelling sight. If the weather is good, it is worth following the gorge for about 150 m (500 ft), but only if you can manage without raincoats and weatherproof gear. There is also a lift (elevator) that you can take to avoid the long flight of steps that leads from the parking area to the entrance of the ravine.

Forza d'Agrò, a medieval village with a 16th-century castle at the summit

The Peloritani Mountains

The Monti Peloritani form a ridge between two seas peaking in **Monte Poverello** (1,279 m/4,195 ft) and the **Pizzo di Vernà** (1,286 m/4,218 ft). It is a marvellous area for excursions, often with stunning views of the sea and Mount Etna, in a landscape of knife-edge ridges and woods. On 4 August a major pilgrimage is made to the **Antennamare Sanctuary**, while 7 September is the day for festivities at the **Sanctuary of the Madonna del Crispino**, above the village of **Monforte San Giorgio**. Many of the mountain villages are interesting from a historical and artistic point of view. **Forza d'Agrò**, dominated by a 16th-century castle; **Casalvecchio I Siculo**, with the Arab-Norman Basilica dei Santi Pietro e Paolo; **Savoca**, with Capuchin catacombs and embalmed bodies; **Ali**, which has a strong Arab flavour; **Itala**, overlooking the Ionian Sea, with San Pietro e Paolo, built by Roger I as a thanks offering for a victory over the Arabs; and lastly **Mili San Pietro** *(see p189)*, with the basilica-monastery of Santa Maria, which was founded in 1082 by Roger I.

㉑ Messina

The position of this ancient city, founded by the Sicels, who named it Zancle, has long been the key to its importance. Situated between the eastern and western Mediterranean, and between the two viceroyalties of Naples and Sicily, Messina has always been influenced by its role as a meeting point. Over the centuries it has been populated by Greek Armenians, Arabs, Jews and other communities from the large maritime cities of Europe, becoming increasingly important up until the anti-Spanish revolt of 1674–8, after which the city fell into decline. Already damaged by the 1783 earthquake, Messina was almost totally razed in 1908.

The votive column at the entrance to the port of Messina

Exploring Messina

The city developed around the harbour and its layout is quite easy to understand if you arrive by sea. The defences of the **Forte San Salvatore** and the **Lanterna di Raineri**, on the peninsula of the same name that protects the harbour to the east, are your introduction to Messina, which lies on the gently sloping sides of the Peloritani Mountains. The main streets are **Via Garibaldi** (which skirts the seafront by the harbour) and **Via I Settembre**, which leads from the sea to the centre of town around **Piazza Duomo**. Interesting attractions such as the **Botanic Garden** and the **Montalto Sanctuary** are located on the hillside above the city.

🏛 Santissima Annunziata dei Catalani

Piazza dei Catalani. **Tel** 090-675 175 or 668-42 11. **Open** by appt only.

Paradoxically, the devastating 1908 earthquake helped to "restore" the original 12th–13th-century structure of this Norman period church, as it destroyed almost all the later additions and alterations. The nave has two side aisles and leads to the apse with its austere brick cupola.

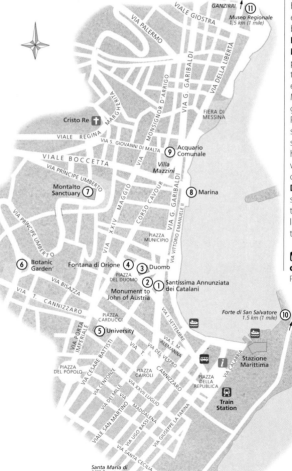

0 metres 600
0 yards 600

The Centre of Messina

① Santissima Annunziata dei Catalani
② Monument to John of Austria
③ Duomo
④ Fontana di Orione
⑤ University
⑥ Botanic Garden
⑦ Montalto Sanctuary
⑧ Marina
⑨ Acquario Comunale
⑩ Forte di San Salvatore
⑪ Museo Regionale

For keys to map symbols see back flap

The Orion Fountain, with the Duomo and the Torre dell'Orologio in the background

🏛 Monument to John of Austria

In the square in front of the Annunziata church is a statue of John of Austria, the admiral who won the famous Battle of Lepanto (1571), with his foot on the head of the defeated Ottoman commander Alì Pasha. The work was sculpted in 1572 by Andrea Calamech.

The pedestal celebrates the formation of the Holy League and the defeat of the Turks in this historic naval battle. One of the sailors taking part was the great Miguel de Cervantes, author of *Don Quixote*, who recovered from his wounds in a Messina hospital.

🏛 Duomo

The Cathedral is in Piazza Duomo, in the heart of town. Although it was reconstructed after the 1908 earthquake and the 1943 bombings, it has preserved its medieval aspect. It was built by Henry VI Hohenstaufen in 1197. The façade was totally rebuilt but you can still see the original central portal built in the early Middle Ages, decorated with two lions and a statue of the Virgin Mary and Infant Jesus. The side doors are decorated with statues of the Apostles and lovely inlay and reliefs. On the left-hand side of the façade is the large campanile, almost 60 m (197 ft) high, built to house a unique

object – the largest astronomical clock in the world, built by a Strasbourg firm in 1933. Noon is the signal for a number of mechanical figures to move in elaborate patterns, geared by huge cogwheels. Almost all of the impressive interior is the result of fine post-war reconstruction. Some sculptures on the trusses in the central section of the two-aisle nave, a 15th-century basin and the 1525 statue of St John the Baptist by Gagini are part of the original decoration. The doorways in the right-hand vestibule leading to the Treasury are of note, as is the tomb of Archbishop Palmieri, sculpted in 1195. In the transept is an organ, built after World War II, with five keyboards and 170 stops. The side aisles house many works of art, especially Gothic funerary monuments, most of which have been reconstructed.

🏛 Fontana di Orione

This lovely 15th-century fountain stands next to the Duomo. It

One of the two lions on the portal of the Duomo

incorporates statues representing four rivers: the Tiber, Nile, Ebro and Camaro (the last of which was channelled into Messina via the first aqueduct in the city specifically to supply the fountain with water).

🏛 University

The University is near **Piazza Carducci**. It was founded in 1548, closed by the Spanish in 1679 and reconstructed at last in 1927. Besides the university faculties, the complex also includes the small **Museo Zoologico Cambria** (tel: 090-394 447), with its fine collections of vertebrates, shells and insects. Follow Viale Principe Umberto, and you come to the **Botanic Garden** and the **Montalto Sanctuary**, with the *Madonna of Victory*, built after the Battle of Lepanto, standing out against the sky.

The 1908 Earthquake

At 5:20am on 28 December 1908, it seemed that nature was intent upon destroying Messina: an earthquake and a tidal wave struck at the same time, bringing over 91 per cent of the buildings to the ground and killing 60,000 people. Reggio Calabria, on the other side of the Straits of Messina, was also destroyed. Reconstruction began immediately. Some of the remains of the old town were salvaged by being incorporated into a new urban plan, designed by Luigi Borzi. His scheme gives Messina its present-day appearance.

Messina the day after the earthquake

🏛 Marina

After walking along the marina in 1789, the author Frances Elliot wrote: "There is nothing in the world like the Messina seafront. It is longer and more elegant than Via Chiaia in Naples, more vigorous and picturesque than the Promenade in Nice…". Not far away is another focal point in Messina, **Piazza dell'Unità d'Italia**. The buildings that lined the marina before the earthquake were part of the "Palazzata" complex, also known as the **Teatro Marittimo**. The Teatro was a series of buildings that extended for more than a kilometre in the heart of the port area – the centre of commercial transactions – which also included the homes of the most powerful families in Messina.

🏛 Acquario Comunale

The garden of the **Villa Mazzini** is decorated with busts and statues, and is also home to the Municipal Aquarium. Next door is the **Palazzo della Prefettura**, in front of which is the **Fountain of Neptune**, sculpted in the mid-1500s by Giovanni Angelo Montorsoli. The statues are 19th-century copies and the originals are on display in the Museo Regionale.

🏛 Forte San Salvatore

Beyond the busy harbour area, at the very tip of the curved peninsula that protects the harbour, is Forte San Salvatore, built in the 17th century to block access to the Messina marina. On top of one of the tall towers in this impressive fort is a statue of the *Madonna della Lettera*: according to tradition, the Virgin Mary sent a letter of benediction to the inhabitants of Messina in AD 42.

On **Via Garibaldi** is the bustling **Stazione Marittima**, the boarding point for the ferry boats that connect Messina to Calabria on the mainland of Italy.

One of the five panels of Antonello da Messina's *St Gregory Polyptych* (1473)

🏛 Museo Regionale

Viale della Libertà 465. **Tel** 090-361292. **Open** 9am–7pm Tue–Sat (last entrance 6:30pm), 9am–1pm Sun & hols (last entrance 12:30pm). **Closed** Mon.

This fascinating museum is close to Piazza dell'Unità d'Italia. It boasts a major collection of art works salvaged after the catastrophic 1908 earthquake. In fact, most of the works come from the Civico Museo Peloritano, which was in the now destroyed Monastery of St Gregory. The

Madonna and Child, Francesco Laurana

museum has 12 rooms that present an overview of the artistic splendour of old Messina and include a number of famous paintings. At the entrance there are 12 18th-century bronze panels depicting the *Legend of the Sacred Letter*. Some of the most important works include paintings from the Byzantine period and fragments from the Duomo ceiling (room 1); the Gothic art in room 2; the examples of Renaissance Messina in room 3; the *Polyptych* that Antonello da Messina (*see p27*) painted for the Monastery of St Gregory (room 4) and, in the

Bridging the Straits of Messina

Communications with the mainland have always been a fundamental issue for Sicily, and for over 30 years the question of building a bridge over the Straits of Messina has been debated. There has even been a proposal to build a tunnel anchored to the sea bed. This idea now seems to have been discarded, and work on the design of a bridge is under way. In 1981 the Società Stretto di Messina was established with the aim of designing a single-span suspension bridge over the straits to connect Torre Faro and Punta Pezzo – a distance of 3 km (2 miles). A multitude of problems still needs to be tackled, however, one of which is the constant danger of earthquakes.

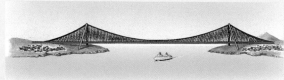

A 1997 design for the planned bridge over the Straits of Messina

same room, a *Madonna and Child* sculpture attributed to Francesco Laurana and a 15th-century oil on panel by an unknown Flemish artist.

Room 10 has two of the "pearls" of the museum, two masterpieces by Caravaggio, executed in 1608–1609: *The Raising of Lazarus* and *The Nativity*. This great artist's sojourn in Messina exerted an influence on other artists, giving rise to a local Caravaggesque school, as can be seen in the canvases by Alonso Rodriguez, *St Peter and St Paul* and *Doubting Thomas*, on view in room 7.

Environs

Proceeding northwards along the coastline of the Straits, past the Museo Regionale, you will come to **Grotta** and then, about 7 km (4 miles) from Messina, the turn-off to **Ganzirri**. A short drive along the coastal road takes you to the **Pantano Grande** (or Lago Grande), a lagoon that measures 30 ha (74 acres) and is at most 7 m (23 ft) deep. One side of the lagoon consists of a long sandbar and it is connected to the sea by an artificial canal. The Pantano Grande is supplied with fresh water from underground streams and it is used for shellfish farming on a large scale. This point is quite close to the easternmost tip of Sicily: 3 km (2 miles) away is **Torre Faro**, a fishing village known for its excellent swordfish, facing the coast of Calabria. The panorama here is dominated by the pylon

The Pantano Grande lake at Ganzirri, used for shellfish farming

and electric power cable that crosses the Straits of Messina for 3,646 m (11,959 ft) in a single span, from the power stations in Calabria. **Capo Peloro**, a short distance from Torre Faro, is crowned by a 16th-century tower that has been used for centuries as a lighthouse. Further along the coastal road you will come to the second, smaller lagoon of Ganzirri, known as the **Pantano Piccolo**. The lake is a stone's throw away from the Tyrrhenian Sea and is linked to the Pantano Grande.

⌂ Santa Maria di Mili

If you head southwards from Messina for about 12 km (7 miles), you will reach the villages of **Mili San Marco** and, higher up in the Peloritani Mountains, **Mili San Pietro**. Not far from the latter, in an area of wild landscape characterized by the deep **Forra di Mili** ravine, is the **Santa Maria di Mili Sanctuary**. The church is in a convent. It has been rebuilt several times and now has a 17th-century appearance. It was founded in 1090 by Roger I as proof of his recovered religious faith after taking Sicily from the Arabs. The Norman king later chose it as the burial site for his son.

The splendid 16th-century marble portal is crowned by a sculpture of the Madonna and Child. Above the two-aisle nave is a finely wrought wooden ceiling that dates from 1411. Once past the three arches marking off the apse area, this ceiling becomes a series of small domes, a characteristic feature of religious architecture of the Norman period.

The church of San Pietro e Paolo in Itala *(see p185)*

㉒ Tyndaris

Road map E2. 🚌 from Messina (090-892 021). 🛈 STR, Piazza Guglielmo Marconi (0941 241 136). **Open** 9am–1hr before sunset daily. 🚻 🛈 Pilgrimage of the Madonna Nera (8 Sep).

Ancient Tyndaris was one of the last Greek colonies in Sicily, founded by the Syracusans in 396 BC, when the Romans were beginning to expand their territory in the Mediterranean. The town also prospered under Roman rule and became a diocese during the early Christian period, after which time it was destroyed by the Arabs. A visit to the archaeological site is fascinating, partly because of the monuments but also because of the many details that give you an idea of everyday life in the ancient city. The town is laid out in a Classical grid plan consisting of two straight and parallel streets (*decumani*) intersected by other streets (*cardines*).

Past the walls through the main city gate, not far from the **Madonna di Tindari Sanctuary** (which houses the famous Byzantine *Madonna Nera* or Black Madonna, honoured in a pilgrimage held every September) is the **Greek Theatre**, situated on the slope of a rise and facing the sea; it has a

The Nebrodi Mountains

The Arabs occupied the Nebrodi Mountains for centuries and referred to them as "an island on an island". The name comes from the Greek word *nebros*, or "roe deer", because of the rich wildlife found in this mountain range, which separates the Madonie Mountains to the west from the Peloritani Mountains to the east. The Parco Regionale dei Monti Nebrodi is a nature reserve with extensive forests and some pastureland, which is covered with snow in the winter. In the middle of the park is the Biviere di Cesarò lake, a stopover point for migratory birds and an ideal habitat for the *Testudo hermanni* marsh turtle. The tallest peak is Monte Soro (1,850 m/6,068 ft). Higher up, the maquis is replaced by oak and beech woods.

❌ Parco Regionale dei Monti Nebrodi
Tel 0941-702 524.
ⓦ parcodeinebrodi.it

Horses grazing in the Parco Regionale dei Monti Nebrodi

diameter of more than 60 m (197 ft). Nearby is the **Agora**, which has, unhappily, been obscured by modern buildings.

In the theatre area are the remains of a **Roman villa** and **baths**. If you stroll through the streets of the ancient city you will see storehouses for food and the Greek-era drainage system. Next to the theatre is the **Museo Archeologico**, which has a large model of the Greek theatre stage, as well as Greek statues

and vases, a colossal head of the Emperor Augustus and prehistoric finds. One unmissable sight is the view below the **Promontory** of Tyndaris: the **Laguna di Oliveri**, celebrated by the poet and Nobel Prize winner Quasimodo (*see p27*).

🏛 Madonna di Tindari Sanctuary
Piazza Quasimodo. **Tel** 0941-369 003.
Open 6:45am–12.45pm, 2:30–7pm (to 8pm Jul–Aug) daily.
ⓦ santuariotindari.it

The unusual natural scenery at the Laguna di Oliveri, seen from the Promontory of Tyndaris

The sarcophagus of Roger I's wife Adelaide in Patti Cathedral

㉓ Patti

Road map: E2. 13,100. from Messina and Palermo (0941-892 021). STR Tyndaris (0941-241 136). comune.patti.me.it

On one of the stretches where the coastal scenery is most fascinating, just past the rocky promontory of **Capo Calavà** on the slopes overlooking the sea, is the town of Patti. Initially a fief of the Norman ruler Roger I, it was later destroyed during the wars with the Angevins and then frequently pillaged by pirates from North Africa.

Patti boasts an 18th-century **Cathedral** built over the foundations of the former Norman church. Inside is a sarcophagus with the remains of Queen Adelaide, Roger I's wife, who died here in 1118.

Along the road down to **Marina di Patti** are the ruins of a **Roman villa** which were brought to light during the construction of the Messina–Palermo motorway. This Imperial age building measures 20,000 sq m (215,200 sq ft) and comprises a peristyle, an apse-like room, thermal baths and many well-preserved mosaics. The villa was destroyed by an earthquake; on the basis of various archaeological finds, historians have been able to date this event to the second half of the 4th century AD.

Roman Villa
Via Papa Giovanni XXIII, Marina di Patti. **Tel** 0941-361 593. **Open** hours vary; call ahead. combined with Tyndaris.

㉔ Capo d'Orlando

Road map: E2. 11,300. STR Unità Operativa 1 (0941-912 784).

Forming part of a region known for the intensive cultivation of citrus fruits, the Nebrodi Mountains jut out into the sea at intervals. The coastal town of Capo d'Orlando lies at the foot of the **Rupe del Semaforo** cliff and the rocky hill after which the town was named.

A climb of about 100 m (328 ft) will take you to the top of the cliff. There, in a large open space, stand the remains of a 14th-century fortress and **Maria Santissima**, a church built in the late 1500s and now home to a number of interesting paintings. However, the main reward for climbing up the hill is the panoramic view of the sea and of the fishing boats moving about in the pretty harbour below.

㉕ Milazzo

Road map F2. 30,000. from Messina & Palermo (091-616 18 06). STR Unità Operativa 3 (090-922 28 65 or 922 27 90).

Milazzo began to take its place in written history when *Mylai* was colonized by the Greeks in 716 BC. The Normans later chose this peninsula as their main coastal stronghold. Frederick II personally designed the castle built here in 1239. The town was divided into three distinct zones in the Middle Ages – the **walled town**, the **Borgo** and the **lower town** – and it was expanded in the 1700s. The **Salita Castello** leads up to the **ancient rock**, which affords access to the walled town via a covered passageway. A doorway opens into **Frederick II's Castle**, surrounded by a wall with five round towers and the great hall of the **Sala del Parlamento** (Parliament Hall). On the same rise is the old **Duomo**, the original 17th-century cathedral, which is used as a congress hall.

Do not miss the chance of an excursion to **Capo Milazzo**, where you will be rewarded with towers, villas and, at the foot of the 18th-century lighthouse, a marvellous view of the Aeolian Islands, with Calabria beyond. This was the site of the 260 BC naval battle in which the Romans routed the Carthaginian fleet. Steps lead to the place where St Anthony is said to have taken refuge from a storm in 1221.

The castle at Milazzo, strengthened structurally by Alfonso de Aragón

㉖ The Aeolian Islands

Consisting of strikingly beautiful volcanic cliffs separated by inlets, sometimes quite deep, the Aeolian Islands (in Italian, Isole Eolie) are unique for their extraordinary rock formations and volcanoes, and for their history. The islands attract hordes of visitors every summer who come to bathe and dive, yet despite the crowds, each island somehow manages to preserve its own individual character. Dominating the islands, especially in the winter, is the sea, with migratory birds nesting on the cliffs and frequent storms, which can reinforce a sense of isolation, even in this age of rapid communications.

Filicudi
There are three villages on this island: Val di Chiesa, Pecorini and Filicudi Porto. On the Capo Graziano promontory are the ruins of a prehistoric village.

Alicudi
The 5 sq km (2 sq miles) of Alicudi do not leave room for many inhabitants. The highest peak is the Filo dell'Arpa – 675 m (2,214 ft).

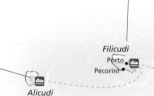

M a

Filicudi
Porto
Pecorini

Alicudi

Lipari
The main island in the archipelago, Lipari has many hot springs and fumaroles, evidence of its volcanic origin. The old town, with a castle and cathedral, is built within walls. There is an important Museo Archeologico Eoliano here, with an excellent collection.

Stromboli
The main attraction on this island is the climb up the volcano and the fine view from the "Sciara del Fuoco".

VISITORS' CHECKLIST

Practical Information
i Corso Vittorio Emanuele, Lipari town (090-988 00 95).

Transport
FS Milazzo. 🚌 from Catania airport, SAIS (090-673 782); from Messina to Milazzo Giunta (090-675 749). 🚢 Siremar, all year from Milazzo, summer only from Naples, **W** siremar.it; Ustica Lines, all year from Milazzo and Naples, **W** usticalines.it. In summer: connections from Messina, Palermo and Milazzo.

↑ *Naples*

Stromboli
Ginostra • ● Scari

Milazzo

Tirreno

Panarea
S. Pietro •

Panarea
This is the smallest Aeolian island, surrounded by rocks and small islands. It was inhabited in prehistoric times.

lina
Malfa
ella • S. Marina Salina

Acquacalda
Canneto
Lipari
Lipari

Porto
Levante
Vulcano

Milazzo,
Messina

0 kilometres   12

0 miles   12

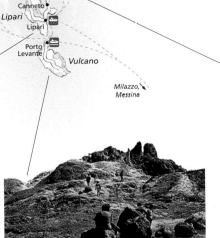

Vulcano
According to ancient mythology, the fabulous island of Vulcano was the workplace of the god of fire and blacksmiths, Hephaestus.

Salina
The island, consisting of two volcanic cones, is the second largest in the group and was named after the ancient salt mine *(salina)* at Lingua, now closed.

For keys to map symbols *see back flap*

Exploring the Aeolian Islands

The best starting point for a visit to the varied Aeolian Islands is Lipari, because it is the largest of the islands and the boat service is good. Here you can decide what type of holiday you want – natural history excursions, including Vulcano and Stromboli, the exclusive tourist resort at Panarea among villas and yachts, or the timeless tranquillity of Alicudi.

The summit of the Vulcano crater, an hour's climb from the base

Lipari

Road map E1. 11,000 (the municipality of Lipari includes all the other islands, except for Salina).

The main Aeolian island is not large – a little less than 10 km (6 miles) long and barely 5 km (3 miles) wide, culminating in **Monte Chirica**, 602 m (1,974 ft) high. The volcanic activity of the past can be noted here and there in the hot springs and fumaroles. The town of Lipari has two landing places: **Sotto-monastero** for ferry boats and **Marina Corta** for hydrofoils. Inevitably, this is the busiest stretch of the seafront.

The old **Cathedral** is worth a visit. Built by the Normans in the 11th century, it was rebuilt after a barbarous pirate raid completely destroyed the town in 1544. Next door to the Cathedral is the **Museo Archeologico Eoliano**, which takes up part of the **old castle**, built by the Spanish (who incorporated the ancient towers and walls) in order to put an end to the constant pirate raids. The first rooms in

the museum are devoted to prehistoric finds in Lipari. The adjoining rooms have objects from the same period, but from the other islands. Then there is a large section featuring Classical archaeological finds, some discovered under water. Part of the museum has volcano-related exhibits, with interesting detailed descriptions of the geological configuration of each island. Three further sights are the **Belvedere Quattrocchi** viewpoint, the ancient **San Calogero thermal baths** and **Acquacalda beach**, which was once used as a harbour for the ships that came to load the local pumice stone. The best way to get about is by scooter or bicycle, both of which can be rented in the town of Lipari.

Ancient theatre mask, Museo Archeologico Eoliano

🏛 **Museo Archeologico Eoliano**
Via Castello 2. **Tel** 090-988 01 74.
Open 9am–1pm, 3–6pm Mon–Sat, 9am–1pm Sun & hols. 🅿 🚾 regione.sicilia.it/beniculturali/museolipari

The archaeological zone at Lipari, home to many different cultures

Vulcano

Road map E1.

Close to Lipari is the aptly named island of Vulcano. Dedicated to Vulcan, the Roman god of fire and metalworking, Homer described the island as the workshop of Hephaestus, the Greek god of fire. The only landing place is the **Porto di Levante**, from which a paved road leads to the **Faro Nuovo** (new lighthouse). Vulcano consists of three old craters. The first, in the south between **Monte Aria** and **Monte Saraceno**, has been extinct for centuries; the **Gran Cratere**, on the other hand, is still active, the last eruption occurring in 1890. **Vulcanello**, the third crater, is a promontory on the northeastern tip of the island created almost 2,000 years ago by an eruption. The climb up to the middle crater is particularly interesting, and you can reach the top in less than an hour. Once there, it is worthwhile going down the crater to the Piano delle Fumarole. Bathing and mud baths are available all year round at the spas near Porto di Levante, while hot springs heat the sea around the stack *(faraglione)*.

Salina

Road map E1. 800.

The second-largest Aeolian island is 7 km (4 miles) long, 5.5 km (3 miles) wide, and 962 m (3,155 ft) high at its highest point, **Monte Fossa delle Felci**. There are three villages: **Santa Maria di Salina, Leni** and **Malfa**. Santa Maria overlooks the sea and is not far from a beach; it is connected to the other villages by an efficient minibus service which runs until late in the evening in the summer. Salina is also the site of a nature reserve, created to protect the two ancient volcanoes of **Monte dei Porri** and **Fossa delle Felci**. The dominant vegetation here is maquis, as the inhabitants have almost exterminated the forests that grew here in antiquity. The starting point for a visit to the reserve is the **Madonna del Terzito Sanctuary**, the object of colourful pilgrimages. Salina, and, in particular, the steep walls of the Pizzo di Corvo, is also a regular nesting ground for colonies of the rare Eleonora's falcon, which migrate to this spot every year from Madagascar.

Among the best-known local products is a highly prized sweet Malvasia wine.

Santa Maria di Salina, one of the three villages on the island

Panarea

Road map E1.

The smallest Aeolian island is surrounded by cliffs and stacks. Visitors land at the small harbour of **San Pietro** (the other villages are **Drauto** and **Ditella**). At **Capo Milazzese**, in one of the most fascinating spots in the Aeolian Islands, archaeologists have uncovered the ruins of a Neolithic village, founded at **Cala Junco**. Interesting finds such as Mycenaean pottery, tools and other items are on display in the local museum. A half-hour walk will take you to the village, starting off from **San Pietro** and passing through **Drauto** and the **Spiaggia degli Zimmari** beach. This island now has luxury tourist facilities.

Stromboli

Road map F1.

The still-active crater of the northeasternmost island in the archipelago has been described by travellers for more than 2,000 years. Italian volcanoes have always been both famous and feared. The ancient Greeks believed that Hephaestus, the god of fire (known as Vulcan to the Romans), lived in the depths of Mount Etna. Boats call either at **Scari** or **Ginostra**, but the island has other villages: **San Vincenzo, Ficogrande** and **Piscità**. The characteristic features of Stromboli are its stunning craggy coast (the deep waters are a favourite with swimmers and divers) and its famous volcano. For an excursion to the crater, start off from **Piscità**; you first come to the old **Vulcanological Observatory** and then the top of the **crater**. The best time to go is around evening, as the

The Stromboli volcano, active for 2,000 years

eruptions are best seen in the dark. The climb is not always accessible, and the volcano can be dangerous. It is best to go with a guide and to wear heavy shoes (or hiking boots) and suitable clothing. There are also boats offering evening excursions to take visitors close to the **Sciara del Fuoco** lava field for the unforgettable spectacle of lava flowing into the sea.

Filicudi

Road map E1.

Halfway between Salina and Alicudi, this extremely quiet island has three villages: **Porto, Pecorini a Mare** and **Val di Chiesa**. You can make excursions into the interior or, even better, take a boat trip around the island and visit the **Faraglione della Canna** basalt stack, **Punta del Perciato**, **Grotta del Bue Marino** and **Capo Graziano**.

Alicudi

Road map D1.

This island was abandoned for the entire Middle Ages and was colonized again only in the Spanish period. Tourism is a relatively recent arrival, and there are no vehicles. The steps and paths are covered on foot, and accommodation can be found in private homes. There is no nightlife, making this an ideal spot for those in search of a peaceful, relaxing break.

Typical Aeolian landscape at Cala Junco, on Panarea

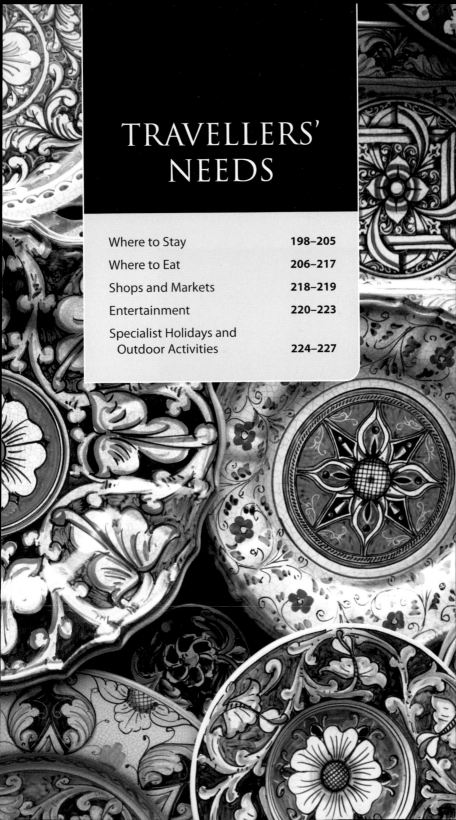

TRAVELLERS' NEEDS

WHERE TO STAY

Sicily has a huge range of places to stay, from simple family-run B&Bs and self-catering apartments to stylish boutique hotels and gorgeous historic *palazzi* and country villas. Although the coastline of Sicily has its share of bland, modern three- and four-star hotels and apartment complexes, with obligatory pool or private beach, if you know where to look there are also more interesting and original choices. A vibrant bed-and-breakfast scene has brought people from all walks of life – from aristocrats to artists – into the hospitality trade, making it ever easier for visitors to avoid the impersonality of service found in some hotels. The *agriturismo* (rural tourism) scheme has allowed the owners of country estates, vineyards and farms to convert palaces, villas and barns into rooms, suites and apartments. Use this section and the listings on pp202–5 to guide your choice.

Spa facilities can be found at most luxurious Sicilian hotels

Hotel Grading and Facilities

Sicilian hotels are classified by a star rating system, based on an easily quantifiable checklist of facilities and services, such as the number of rooms with en suite bathroom; whether there is a restaurant on site; and if there is 24-hour room service. However, the star rating is no guide to the subtler, more subjective charms of hotels, such as the style of decor or the helpfulness of the staff.

With the rise of the B&B guesthouse and *agriturismo* movements (Sicily has more B&Bs than anywhere else in Italy) and the increasing number of boutique hotels, in which the emphasis is on ambience and a more personalised style and service rather than conventional facilities, the star system has become increasingly irrelevant. Indeed, many hotels no longer advertise their star rating at all.

Prices too have been liberated by the rise of Internet brokering sites – and with rooms being increasingly priced according to demand, rather than season, it is often possible to secure a room in a luxury hotel for less than a third of the official rate.

Facilities for the disabled and access for people in wheelchairs are required by law in hotels and *agriturismi*, and many B&Bs have disabled access as well.

Prices

By law, every conventional hotel room (as opposed to B&B) in Italy must display the **Ente del Turismo** (Tourist Board) price for the room with the maximum charges during the year; these prices may not be exceeded. The prices displayed or quoted online usually include taxes and service, but it is always wise to check. A continental breakfast is often included as well, but again, check if booking online, either via the hotel's website or an accommodation broker site. In high season (August and sometimes July as well) you may be expected to take half- or full board in some hotels.

Tourist Season

Hotels in towns and cities are usually open all year round. On the minor islands and in seaside

The Art Nouveau façade of Grand Hotel Villa Igiea in Palermo *(see p202)*

The reception desk for Federico Secondo in Catania *(see p204)*

resorts, hotels are often open only from Easter to October, and in the high season (August and sometimes July as well) half-board is often obligatory. However, if travelling out of season to destinations like these, websites such as Airbnb *(see p200)* will help you find privately owned apartments and rooms (the lack of restaurants open off-season makes self-catering the best option).

Booking

Should you decide to go to Sicily in July or August you must book well in advance, especially if you want to stay on the coast, as the island gets very busy in peak season. The best deals are usually available via brokerage sites such as kayak.com, expedia.com and booking.com.

Tourist Villages

Resort villages allow you to enjoy a seaside holiday in a less formal atmosphere than in a hotel, and are good for families. Most are sited on the Sicilian coast, and many offer inclusive package deals. Accommodation may vary according to requirements, from rooms in a residence to small apartments with an outside terrace.

Each village offers a range of recreation and sports facilities. Besides one or more swimming pools, villages usually offer tennis courts and windsurfing, diving or sailing lessons. Some even pro-vide baby-sitting. Some villages offer all-inclusive holidays where the price even includes drinks at the bar. Charges in tourist villages are always calculated on a weekly basis.Alternatively, you may choose to book accomodation, then select and pay for any further recreation and sports facilities as you go along. This enables you to be independent, and at the same time provides a range of possible facilities. For full details make enquiries at a travel agency, or contact the major tour operators who manage these villages*(see p201)*.

Camping

Spending your holiday on a camping site is a good way of keeping costs down. Almost all the sites in Sicily are on the coast, with direct access to a beach. In the interior there are only a few sites on the slopes of Mount Etna, well situated for excursions. Camping outside official sites is prohibited, with camping on beaches especially frowned upon. If you want to stay on private property you must ask the owner's permission.

In general, campsites are clean and well-managed. Besides an area for tents and/or caravans (trailers), most sites also provide bungalows with private bathrooms and a kitchen area. Facilities often include grocery shops, pizzerias (occasionally, restaurants), laundries and organized sports facilities.

For longer stays, book well ahead of time, and in high season, phone in advance even for a one- or two-night stop. If you are touring, start to look for a site by early afternoon. Most campsites are open from Easter to October. The main ones are listed on page 201.

Hostels and Refuges

There are no official Italian Youth Hostel Federation youth hostels in Sicily, but there are a few privately run backpacker hostels (charging roughly €18 per night for a dormitory bed). However you will often find that a private apartment or B&B is just as cheap, if not cheaper. Websites such as couchsurfing. com are the best source of budget sleeps.

There are also several mountain refuges; most are found on Mount Etna, but the **Club Alpino Italiano** has two on the Madonie and Nebrodi mountains.

A pleasant place to sit in the evening at Scicli Albergo Diffuso in Trapani *(see p203)*

An airy hotel room that leads out to a garden at Scicli Albergo Diffuso in Trapani *(see p203)*

Bed and Breakfast

Ever since a law was passed to allow ordinary people to offer bed and breakfast in their homes, hundreds of B&Bs have opened in Sicily. The best offer excellent value for money, as well as the opportunity to experience Italian hospitality at its best, whether in a Palermo apartment, an Aeolian island village house or a stylish room in a Baroque palace. Although the rule is that B&Bs can have no more than three rooms, and that the owners live on the premises, this is often ignored. If you are looking for a B&B on spec, be sure to ask if there are any staff on the premises, and if not, how to contact the owner should the need arise; ask as well if breakfast is actually served in the B&B, or whether they have an arrangement with a local café. Occasionally use of the kitchen may be allowed.

If you are looking for B&Bs before you leave, it is well worth checking out online reviews by other travellers at sites such as www.tripadvisor.com.

Boutique Hotels

Sicily has some outstanding boutique hotels: in cities, in the countryside and by the sea. Placing an emphasis on smart design, they generally offer the same facilities and services as larger hotels, but in a more intimate setting. Some are run by hospitality-trade professionals, others by passionate newcomers, often from the worlds of architecture and design.

Agriturismi

The rural tourism or *agriturismo* scheme began in the 1980s, to enable farmers and landowners to boost falling revenues by renting out converted farm buildings to tourists. They can range from cool, state-of-the-art country hotels to simple, down-to-earth self-catering apartments. Some serve food made from home-grown produce, others have restaurants. Many offer activities such as horse-riding, and some have developed into little country resorts with swimming pools, tennis courts and bikes to rent.

Villas and Apartments

Sicily has a fantastic range of self-catering accommodation, ranging from unpretentious seaside apartments and city flats to palatial villas with pools and exquisitely restored ancient country houses. Companies such as **Vacation Rentals By Owner**, which operates

worldwide, the UK-based **Think Sicily** and **Travel Sicilia**, a Sicilian company, all have extensive portfolios of country and town houses, seaside villas and other privately owned holiday accommodation.

Airbnb is a worldwide web-based initiative allowing private owners to advertise rooms, apartments and villas. Both owners and clients are protected as payments are held by Airbnb until both parties confirm that they are satisfied.

DK Choice

The accommodation options featured on the following pages – listed by area and then by price – have all been carefully selected. Those singled out as DK Choices, however, stand out from the crowd in some way. They could offer 5-star luxury with impeccable service, or be set in a historically significant building such as a former monastery or a palazzo. They may offer exceptional value for money, or a welcome that makes you want to start planning your next visit straight away. They might offer rooms with views that will stay with you for a lifetime – of the Valle dei Templi in Agrigento, the erupting volcano of Stromboli in the Aeolian Islands, the bougainvillea-clad cliffs below Taormina, or the exuberant Baroque architecture of Syracuse or Ragusa. Whatever the reason, a DK Choice will provide an especially memorable stay.

An inviting bath and cosy dressing gowns at BB22 in Palermo *(see p202)*

DIRECTORY

Tourist Information

Assessorato Regionale del Turismo, Sport e Spettacolo
Via Notarbartolo 9,
Palermo.
Tel 091-707 82 30
🔳 regione.sicilia.it/
turismo/web_turismo

Hotel Chains

Framon Hotels
Via Oratorio San
Francesco 306,
Messina.
Tel 090-228 22 66
🔳 framon-hotels.com

Tourist Villages

Kastalia
Contrada Piombo,
Ragusa.
Tel 0932-82 6095.
🔳 kastalia.it

Serenusa Village
SS 115, km 240,
Licata.
Tel 085-836 97 77.
🔳 www.bluserena.it

Valtur
Via Milano 46,
Rome.
Tel 06-482 10 00.
🔳 www.valtur.it

Camping

Al Yag
Via Altarellazzo, Pozzillo,
Acireale (Catania).
Tel 095-764 17 63.
🔳 campingalyag.it/en/

Baia dei Coralli
Località Punta Braccetto,
Santa Croce Camerina
(Ragusa).
Tel 0932-918 192.
🔳 baiadeicoralli.it

Baia di Guidaloca
Scopello, Castellammare
del Golfo (Trapani).
Tel 0924-541 262.
🔳 campinguidaloca.it

Baia Makauda
Contrada Tranchina,
Sciacca (Agrigento).
Tel 0925-997 001
🔳 makaudabeach.it

Baia Unci
Località Canneto,
Lipari (Aeolian Islands).
Tel 090-981 19 09
🔳 campingbaiaunci.it/
en

Bazia
Contrada Bazia,
Furnari (Messina).
Tel 0941-800 130.
🔳 bazia.it/en/

Calanovella
Contrada Calanovella,
SS 113, km 90
(Messina).
Tel 0941-585 258.
🔳 calanovella.it

Capo Passero
Contrada Vigne Vecchie,
Portopalo di Capopassero
(Syracuse).
Tel 0931-842 030.
🔳 campingresidence
capopassero.it/

Costa Ponente
Contrada Ogliastrillo,
Cefalù (Palermo).
Tel 0921-420 085.
🔳 camping-
costaponente.com/en/

El Bahira
Contrada MaKari, San Vito
Lo Capo (Trapani).
Tel 0923-972 577
🔳 elbahira.it

Eurocamping Due Rocche
Contrada Faino, SS 115,
km 241, Butera
(Caltanissetta).
Tel 0934-349 006.
🔳 duerocche.it

Paradiso del Mare
Località Fontane Bianche
(Siracusa).
Tel 0931-790 333.
🔳 paradisodelmare.it

La Roccia
Località Cala Greca,
Lampedusa island.
Tel 0922-970 964.
🔳 laroccia.net

Mareneve
Contrada Piano Grande,
Milo (Catania).
Tel 095-708 21 63.

Miramare
Contrada Costicella,
Favignana (Trapani).
Tel 0923-921
🔳 web.tiscalinet.it/
campingmareneve/uk/
mainuk.htm

Rais Gerbi
Contrada Rais Gerbi,
Pollina Finale
(Palermo).
Tel 0921-426 570.
🔳 ralsgerbl.lt

Mountain Refuges

Club Alpino Italiano
🔳 cai.it

Rifugio Ragabo (Etna)
🔳 ragabo.it

Rifugio Sapienza (Etna)
🔳 rifugiosapienza.com

Bed & Breakfast

Bed & Breakfast Italia
🔳 bbitalia.it

BB Planet
🔳 bbplanet.it

Venere
🔳 venere.it

Agriturismo Associations

Terranostra
🔳 terranostra.it

Agriturismo.com
🔳 agriturismo.com

Self Catering

Think Sicily
🔳 thinksicily.com

Travel Sicilia
🔳 travelsicilia.com

AirBnB
🔳 airbnb.com
🔳 airbnb.it
🔳 airbnb.co.uk

Vacation Rentals By Owner
🔳 vrbo.com

Where to Stay

Palermo

Al Giardino Dell'alloro €
B&B Map E3
Vicolo San Carlo 8, 90133
Tel 338 -224 35 41
W giardinodellalloro.it
Charming, homely B&B in the heart of La Kalsa with many works by Sicilian artists gracing the walls. There's a courtyard where breakfast is served.

Alla Kala €
B&B Map E3
Via Vittorio Emanuele 71, 90133
Tel 091 743 4763
W allakala.it
Chic, shipshape accommodation with stylish designer rooms and a suite, all with magnificent views of the sailing marina. Very popular, so book in advance.

DK Choice

BB22 €
Historic Map C3
Largo Cavalieri di Malta 22, 90133
Tel 091-326 214
W bb22.it
Set in a 15th-century palazzo, BB22 is tucked away in a quiet little piazza behind the splendid church of San Domenico, a few steps from the exuberant Vucciria market. Designer decor in shades of stone contrasts with Rococo mirrors, inspired vintage pieces and lustrous textiles. Two rooms have a furnished balcony or terrace and breakfast is served in a small roof garden. The owners organize food and wine tours, in Palermo and further afield, and can arrange boat trips.

Modern decor set within a 15th-century palazzo at BB22, Palermo

La Dimora Del Genio €
B&B Map D4
Via Garibaldi 58, 90133
Tel 091-616 69 81
W ladimoradelgenio.it
Three cosy rooms in a centrally heated 17th-century *palazzetto*, furnished with a tasteful mix of antique family heirlooms, modern pieces and contemporary art. The owner lives on the premises, and offers cooking courses for guests.

Palazzo Pantaleo €
Historic Map B1
Via Ruggero Settimo 74/H, 90121
Tel 091 325 471
W palazzopantaleo.it
Spacious, light, airy rooms in an 18th-century palazzo, on a quiet little square just behind Piazza Politeama. On the upper floor is an apartment, and there's also a small kitchen where you can make drinks or snacks.

Quattro Quarti €
B&B Map C4
Via Vittorio Emanuele 376, 90134
Tel 091-583 687
W quattroquarti.it
Sophisticated B&B in part of a huge aristocratic palazzo owned by the Arone di Valentino family. In the main part of the palace, former guests have included the Duchess of Cornwall.

Grand Hotel Et Des Palmes €€€
Historic Map B1
Via Roma 398, 90139
Tel 091 602 811
W grandhotel-et-des-palmes.com
Founded in 1874, this hotel may not be quite as magnificent as it was in the days when Wagner stayed here (and penned *Parsifal*) but it remains a very comfortable chain hotel, well positioned at the more upscale end of Via Roma.

Grand Hotel Villa Igieia €€€
Luxury
Via Belmonte 43, 90142
Tel 091 631 2111
W hotel-villa-igiea.com
Art Nouveau villa designed for the Florio family by Ernesto Basile in 1900, beautifully located above the Acquasanta marina. It has a swimming pool, shady gardens, sumptuous rooms, a tennis court and elegant terraces perfect for an evening drink or romantic dinner.

Price Guide

Prices are based on one night's stay in high season for a standard double room, linclusive of service charges and taxes.

€	up to €80
€€	€80 to 180
€€€	over €180

Northwestern Sicily

CASTEL DI TUSA: Atelier Sul Mare €€€
Boutique Road Map D2
Via Cesare Battisti 4, 98070
Tel 0921 334295
W ateliersulmare.it
Set just metres from the sea, this innovative hotel showcases works by contemporary artists, in public areas and in the rooms.

CASTELLAMMARE DEL GOLFO: Case D'anna €
B&B Road Map B2
Corso Garibaldi 120, 91014
Tel 0924 31 101
W casedanna.it
Lovely, large, individually themed suites (Victorian, Sicilian, Art Deco and Neo-Romantic) in a centrally located, family-run place. The owners are extremely helpful and breakfast includes home-made pastries.

CEFALÙ: Baia Del Capitano €€
Resort Road Map D2
Contrada Mazzaforno, 90015
Tel 0921 420003
W baiadelcapitano.it
Pleasant, modern Mediterranean-style hotel set right on the beach. Facilites include a pool, tennis courts and restaurant, and there are lots of activities on offer.

ERICE: San Domenico €€
Traditional Road Map A2
Via Tommaso Guerrasi 26, 91016
Tel 0923 860 128
W hotel-sandomenico.it
Appealing family-run hotel in a medieval house in the heart of Erice, with comfortable rooms and rustic antiques. Breakfast is served in a tiny courtyard.

FAVIGNANA: Cas'almare €€
Boutique Road Map A2
Strada Comunale Frascia, 90123
Tel 0923 921085
W casalmarefavignana.com
Chic boutique hotel created from traditional fishermen's cottages, set on a rocky promontory and with a private lido – swimming from rocks – and ocean-facing terrace. Lovely breakfasts, too.

LEVANZO: Lisola Residence €
Villas and Apartments **Road Map** A1
Contrada Case, 90123
Tel *0923 194 1530*
w lisola.eu
Simple 19th-century workers' cottages, sleeping between two and four people. There's a large pool with parasols and sun-loungers, and free transport to the port (which is also an easy walk away).

MARETTIMO: La Terrazza €
B&B **Road Map** A1
Via G. Pepe 24, 90123
Tel *368-768 15 71*
w bedandbreakfastmarettimo.it
Simple but tastefully decorated rooms and – best of all – a big, partly shaded terrace with terrific views over the castle and sea, where breakfast is served.

**MARINELLA DI SELINUNTE:
Sicilia Cuore Mio** €
B&B **Road Map** A3
Via della Cittadella 44, 91022
Tel *0924 46 077*
w siciliacuoremio.it
Lovely B&B in a typical early 20th-century country house right across from the archaeological site, with a gorgeous roof terrace overlooking the sea. Lots of shady outdoor space.

DK Choice

**PETRALIA SOPRANA: La
Locanda di Cadì** €
Agriturismo **Road Map** D3
Borgo Cipampini, 90026
Tel *338 2890100*
w lalocandadicadi.it
An authentic family-run country inn, located in a tiny borgo outside the medieval mountain village of Petralia Soprana, complete with chickens running free and a friendly dog. It is best known as a place to eat, but there are rooms as well – simple, with whitewashed walls and exposed beams – and for anyone seeking peace and great food, staying here is an unforgettable experience.

**TRAPANI: Nuovo Albergo
Russo** €
Traditional **Road Map** A2
Via Tintori 4, 90123
Tel *0923 22 163*
w nuovorusso.altervista.org
Founded in the 1950s and still in the same family; there are heirlooms in the public areas. The rooms are simple, but the location is delightful.

The luxurious pool at Grand Hotel Villa Igiea under an atmospheric sky *(see p202)*

**USTICA: Stella Marina
Residence** €€
Villas and Apartments **Road Map** B1
Via Cristoforo Colombo 35, 90010
Tel *091 844 8121*
w stellamarinaustica.it
Stylish, contemporary self-catering mini-apartments in a small complex above the port. There's a spa and a spacious terrace for sunbathing and breakfasting.

Southwestern Sicily

**AGRIGENTO:
Villa Pirandello** €
B&B **Road Map** C4
Via F. Crispi 34, 92100
Tel *0922 22 275*
A Sicilian-English family runs this B&B in a 19th-century villa where Luigi Pirandello's wife lived. Simple, bright rooms and a sunny terrace – and the Terra restaurant *(see p213)* is in its shady garden.

AGRIGENTO: Mandranova €€
Agriturismo **Road Map** C4
SS115, km217, Palma di Montechiaro 92020
Tel *393 986 2169*
w mandranova.it
A beautifully restored farmhouse on a working olive oil estate; in the rooms, suites and self-catering cottages, antiques and contemporary design mingle perfectly. The excellent restaurant uses home-grown produce.

**LAMPEDUSA: I Dammusi Di
Borgo Cala Creta** €
Resort **Road Map** B5
C. da Cala Creta, 92010
Tel *0922 970883*
w calacreta.com
Accommodation in traditionally styled *dammusi*, with drystone walls, domed roofs and shaded

terraces, on one of the island's most magnificent little bays. There's a lovely restaurant as well.

DK Choice

**PANTELLERIA:
Pantelleria Dream** €€€
Resort **Road Map** A5
Località Tracino 91017
Tel *0923-915 670*
w pantelleriaexclusive.it
Individual lava stone and whitewashed *dammusi* with domed roofs and bamboo-shaded terraces spill down a hillside above the island's dramatic rocky coast. The interiors are simply furnished, with white walls and North African-style textiles. An infinity pool, cool jazz sounds in the bar, and lots of fresh local produce in the restaurant.

**PIAZZA ARMERINA: Suite
D'autore** €€
Bouique **Road Map** D4
Via Monte 1, 94015
Tel *0935 688 553*
w suitedautore.it
Quirky hotel in an old palazzo across from the Duomo. Rooms mix contemporary design, stylish artefacts, retro objects, original art and photography. The top-floor bar has fabulous town and country views, and there's free parking right outside.

**PIAZZA ARMERINA: Torre
Di Renda** €€
Agriturismo **Road Map** D4
Contrada Torre di Renda, 94015
Tel *0935 686937*
w torrerenda.it
Charming rooms in a country house surrounded by woods. Lovely gardens, a children's play area, a swimming pool and restaurant make it perfect for families in summer.

Southern Sicily

DK Choice

MARINA DI RAGUSA: La Moresca   €€€
Boutique **Road Map** E5
Via Dandolo, 97010
Tel *0932 239495*
W lamorescahotel.it
Within this smart little resort is a Moorish-style Art Nouveau villa that has been transformed into a *maison de charme*. Original tiled floors, jasmine-scented courtyards and carved doors are enhanced by contemporary touches such as steel walkways, a glass-walled breakfast room and billowing white linens. It is a short stroll to the nearby beach.

MODICA: L'orangerie   €€
B&B **Road Map** E5
Vico de Naro 5, 97015
Tel *347-067 46 98*
W lorangerie.it
Peaceful and elegant B&B with three huge suites (with kitchens) and four spacious rooms in a palazzo with frescoed ceilings and private flower-filled terraces.

NOTO: Montandon   €€
B&B **Road Map** E5
Via Antonio Sofia 50, 96017
Tel *339 524 4607*
W b-bmontandon.it.
Family-run with a walled garden and use of a barbecue. There's a communal terrace for breakfast, where you can also prepare yourself a snack or *aperitivo*. Each room is big and airy, with its own private terrace.

NOTO: Terre Di Vendicari   €€€
Boutique **Road Map** E5
Contrada Vaddeddi, 96017
Tel *346 359 3845*
W terredivendicari.it
Minimalist chic in a country hotel at the heart of the Vendicari nature reserve, with views out to sea over olive and lemon groves. Rooms are cool and stylish, with free-standing Philippe Starck baths. Fabulous swimming pool, beautiful grounds, and lovely walks to the beaches.

RAGUSA: Locanda Don Serafino   €€€
BOUTIQUE **Road Map** E5
Via 11 Febbraio, 15, 97100
Tel *0932 220065*
W locandadonserafino.it

Ten rooms occupying a row of carefully restored Baroque cottages, with the lounge tucked under exposed limestone vaults. No outdoor space, but mouth-watering dinners.

SCICLI: Albergo Diffuso   €
Villas and Apartments **Road Map** E5
Via Mormino Penna 15, 97018
Tel *0932 185555*
W sciclialbergodiffuso.it
An innovative concept – bed and breakfast or self-catering accommodation offered in 11 different houses around the historic centre. Reception (and breakfast) is at Bar Millenium on Scicli's loveliest street.

DK Choice

SYRACUSE: Hotel Gutkowski   €€
Boutique **Road Map** F4
Lungomare Vittorini 26, Ortygia, 96100
Tel *0931 465861*
W guthotel.it
Inspired Mediterranean minimalism and breathtaking sea views mark out this hotel on the eastern edge of Ortygia. White walls and linens and translucent curtains let the sea and sky remain the real stars. The furniture is spare but chic – Eames chairs, modern four-posters, and reclaimed wood. The best rooms have private terraces; for these, you may need to book in advance.

SYRACUSE: Palazzo Del Sale   €€
B&B **Road Map** F4
Via Santa Teresa 25, Ortygia, 96100
Tel *0931 65958*
W palazzodelsale.it
Stylish but relaxed boutique B&B in a 19th-century salt merchant's palazzo in Ortigia. The spacious rooms' decorative touches feature natural materials. The sea is two or three minutes' walk.

SYRACUSE: Residenza Dei Baroni   €
Villas and Apartments **Road Map** F4
Via Largo della Gancia 30–32, Ortygia, 96100
Tel *0931 67363*
W residencedeibaroni.it
One- and two- room apartments with cooking facilities in a neat sandstone palazzo in a corner of Ortygia's Lungomare Levante. All apartments have tiled floors, ochre walls and wrought-iron bedsteads. The place is well-run, and prices are excellent.

Picturesque view from a balcony suite at Albergo Diffuso, Scicli

Northeastern Sicily

CATANIA: Casa Barbero   €€
B&B **Road Map** E3
Via Caronda 209, 95128
Tel *095 580 514*
W casabarbero.com
Bold colours and contemporary design in a Liberty-era palazzo with six quiet rooms set around a courtyard. There are also two self-catering apartments, one by the sea in Acitrezza.

CATANIA: Frederico Secondo   €€
Historic **Road Map** E3
Via Maggiore Baracca, 2, 95012
Tel *0942 980 368*
W hotelfedericosecondo.com/
This understated hotel is set in an immaculately restored 13th-century palazzo in the centre of the hill village of Castiglione. Rooms are spacious with tasteful furnishings. An excellent base for exploring Etna, and the Alcantara valley.

DK Choice

FILICUDI: La Sirena   €€
Villas and Apartments **Road Map** E1
Loc. Pecorini Mare, 98050
Tel *090 988 9997*
W pensionelasirena.it
There's nowhere better for a relaxed island experience than this chilled-out restaurant with rooms overlooking the beach at Pecorini Mare, with fishing boats drawn up alongside. Choose between rooms above the restaurant with tiny water-front balconies, or apartments with cooking facilities in houses scattered around the village. Either way be sure to eat at the restaurant *(see pp216-7)*.

GIARDINI NAXOS: Hotel Palladio
Boutique €€€
Road Map F3
Corso Umberto I 470, 98035
Tel *0942 52267*
🇼 hotelpalladiogiardini.com
Friendly, genuinely family-run hotel in a 19th-century palazzo in a fabulous location on the seafront. Breakfasts are superb, with produce sourced from farms supporting the Slow Food and anti-Mafia movements.

LINGUAGLOSSA: Rifugio Ragabó
Hostels and Refuges €
Road Map F3
Pineta Bosco Ragabo, 95015
Tel *095 647 841*
🇼 ragabo.it
Simple, cosy wooden hotel and restaurant (with an open fire) high on Etna: a perfect base for an active mountain holiday in winter or summer. The two four-bed rooms are ideal for families.

LIPARI: Diana Brown
B&B €€
Road Map E1
Vico Himera 3, 98055
Tel *090-981 25 84*
🇼 dianabrown.it
Friendly and well-organized B&B located in a tiny lane parallel to the main Corso. Rooms are spic and span, with fridges and kettles; some have kitchenettes. There's a great roof terrace too.

LIPARI: Hotel Tritone
Luxury €€€
Road Map E1
Via Mendolita, 98055
Tel *090 9811595*
🇼 hoteltritonelipari.it
Luxurious, small resort-style hotel set away from the town bustle amid quiet gardens. There's a good pool, a lovely spa, a superb restaurant, and rooms all have a balcony or terrace.

MESSINA: Town House Messina
B&B €
Road Map F2
Via Giordano Bruno 66, 98123
Tel *090 2936097*
🇼 townhousemessina.it
Bijou B&B just off Piazza Cairoli, with minimalist decor in soft neutral tones and fabulous designer bathrooms. Breakfast is at a nearby café, Billé.

MILAZZO: Locanda Del Bagatto
Boutique €€
Road Map F2
Via Massimiliano Regis 7, 98057
Tel *090 9224212*
🇼 locandadelbagatto.com
Chic, minimalist designer rooms just a few minutes' walk from the port, adjoining a fabulous wine bar/restaurant.

PANAREA: Raya
Boutique €€€
Road Map E1
Loc. San Pietro, Panarea 98050
Tel *090 983013*
🇼 hotelraya.it
The most exclusive, expensive hotel in Sicily. The rooms, entirely furnished in natural materials, are built into the hill above the village, with sea views over groves of olives, hibiscus and bougainvillea.

PATTI: Casa Rubes
B&B €€
Road Map E2
Via Magretti 127
Tel *0941 21648*
🇼 casarubes.it
A relaxed, atmospheric B&B in a beautifully converted town house in the heart of the old town. The hosts are cordial and hospitable, and breakfast is served at a long table on the flower-filled terrace.

SALINA: La Salina Borgo Di Mare
Boutique €€
Road Map E1
Via Manzoni, Lingua 98050
Tel *090 9843441*
🇼 lasalinahotel.com
Lovely hotel occupying a cluster of restored buildings by Lingua's lagoon. Most rooms have sea views and a terrace, and there is also a small lido.

SALINA: Capo Faro
Boutique €€€
Road Map E1
Località Capo Faro, 98050
Tel *090 9844330*
🇼 capofaro.it
Stunning, contemporary rooms occuping Aeolian-style houses that look down to the sea across clifftop vineyards. Facilities are top-notch, from superb pool to classy restaurant. No under-12s.

STROMBOLI: Sirenetta Park Hotel
Resort €€€
Road Map F1
Località Ficogrande, 98050
Tel *090 986025*
🇼 lasirenetta.it

Whitewashed hotel right across the little road from Stromboli's largest sandy beach, with a flower-filled courtyard. There's a sea water pool and a restaurant, and a lido on the beach.

TAORMINA: Grand Hotel Timeo Et Villa Flora
Luxury €€€
Road Map F2
Via Teatro Greco 59, 98039
Tel *0942 23801*
🇼 belmond.com/luxury-hotels
Taormina's oldest hotel exudes old-world elegance: sumptuous reception rooms with huge windows, a "Literary Terrace" overlooking gardens and a beautiful pool. Most rooms have a terrace.

DK Choice

TAORMINA: Villa Carlotta
Boutique €€€
Road Map F2
Via Pirandello 81, 98039
Tel *0942 626058*
🇼 hotelvillacarlottataormina.com
Intimate hotel in a early 20th-century villa with a lush garden and fabulous views stretching from Etna across the Ionian sea to the coast of Calabria. Staff make guests feel special without being intrusive; rooms are very comfortable and individually designed and decorated. The gardens include a small, pretty pool overlooking a ruined chapel.

Zafferano Etnea Sotto I Pini
B&B €
Road Map G3
Via A. Diaz 208, 95019
Tel *095-956 696 or 340-673 89 26*
🇼 sottoipini.it
In the shadow of Etna, with terrific views of the volcano and the sea, this beautifully furnished villa is managed ecologically. Wherever possible, food is local, seasonal and organic.

The entrance to the Frederico Secondo, located in a 13th-century palazzo in Catania *(see p204)*

For more information on types of hotels *see pp198–201*

WHERE TO EAT AND DRINK

Sicilians have perfected the art of good food, best enjoyed when shared. Sicilian fruit, vegetables, fish and cheeses are highly regarded throughout Italy; Sicilians not only love their food but like nothing better than joining family and friends around a restaurant table, especially if the ingredients are fresh and local and the cooking genuine. Fish is one of the highlights of Sicilian cuisine, and the Sicilian talent for

making a tasty morsel of fish go a long way is to be seen in the plethora of inventive pasta sauces – a few sardines or anchovies, or a little tuna or swordfish cooked with combinations of chilli, capers, olives, pine nuts and tiny Sicilian cherry tomatoes. We list a selection of great places to eat on pp210–217, whether it's a piping hot street food snack, the perfect aubergine *parmigiano* or swordfish *involtini*.

Informal Eating

Sicily has great savoury snacks, sweet pastries and ice creams; its groceries, bakeries and, increasingly, gourmet delis can furnish all manner of goodies to eat on the go or for a picnic or self-catered meal.

Pizzerias abound and it's worth seeking out a good one. The best have a wood-burning oven *(forno a legno)* from which the pizzas emerge bubbling and blistered. For other hot takeaway food, look out for a *rosticceria*, where you'll typically find baked pasta dishes, roast chicken and the like. For a snack, a bar or *focacceria* can provide a range of *panini* (sandwiches), *arancini* (rice balls) and *impanate* (savoury pies). Adventurous travellers may want to explore the street food of the cities; favourite Palermo snacks are *pane ca meusa* (a hot offal sandwich) and *pane e panelle* (chickpea fritters in a bun).

Types of Restaurant

There are three main terms for a restaurant in Sicily, and until some years ago they were quite distinct. A *ristorante* was a "proper" restaurant, with table linen and waiters in uniform, somewhere a family would go for Sunday lunch or a treat. A *trattoria* was more basic and down-home, its menu chalked on a board or recited by the waiter, with paper to cover the tables and on which to write the bill. *Osterias* were simple hostelries where there would be cold cuts and cheese, and maybe a homely pasta dish or soup, to go with a glass or two of good wine.

One of the exquisitely presented dishes on offer at La Gazza Ladra, Modica *(see p215)*

That has all changed, and the choice of name for an establishment these days depends more on the tradition it identifies with than price, decor or ambience. *Ristorante* is now a neutral, generic term applied to anything from a Michelin-starred palace to a tourist spot. And while, of course, there are *trattorias* and *osterias* that have existed unchanged for decades, these days, *trattoria* often implies an interest in reviving and reinventing traditional

dishes; *osteria* – or *vineria* – signifies that there is an emphasis on sourcing the very best primary ingredients and wines, as promoted by the Slow Food movement, and, often, a more minimalist approach to cooking.

Reading the Menu

In the traditional pattern for an Italian meal, a pasta dish is not the main event but a separate course, sandwiched between an appetizer and a main course or entrée. *Antipasti* ("before pasta"), are hors-d'oeuvre-style dishes; then there are *primi*, or first courses: pasta dishes, risottos and, in Sicily, couscous. This is followed by a protein-based main course, often simply grilled fish or meat (vegetarians may find it easier to return to the *primi* menu for a second course). Vegetables are almost always ordered as side dishes *(contorni)*. However, in the cities and in tourist spots, where a less stately approach to a meal may be preferred, this pattern has become less rigidly adhered to.

Pasticceria di Pasquale in Ragusa: a typical gourmet deli *(see p215)*

Live music entertains dinners at vegan restaurant Moon, Syracuse *(see p216)*

Although printed menus are the norm, it is still common for the waiter to recite the day's list of specials at your table. In Sicily, good antipasti are vegetables in oil, seafood and fish salads and seafood soups.

Pasta dishes *(see p208)* may be light and very simply dressed, or hearty and filling, such as the mighty *pasta n'casciata*, macaroni pie with meat sauce, sausage, cheese and hard-boiled eggs. For main courses, chicken and veal escalopes are ubiquitous: inland, ring the changes with rabbit or pork; on the coast, there will be fish (typically tuna or swordfish), freshly cooked and sold by weight (ask for a rough price).

Sicilians love their desserts, but you will usually find fresh fruit on the menu if you haven't room for cannoli, cassata *(see p209)* or ice cream.

Many Sicilian restaurants offer fixed-price menus, aimed at either tourists or workers.

Wine

As you might expect, the very simplest, cheapest places – usually in the countryside – may offer only locally produced wine, served by the glass or litre. Elsewhere you will find Sicilian vintages from all over the island and perhaps wines from the mainland too. Only upscale places and specialist *enotecas* (wine shops) see the need to seek out wines from outside Italy.

Paying the Bill

Your bill may be a simple total, not itemized by individual dishes and drinks. If you do have an itemized bill, the total will include a cover charge (€1–€3) and a service charge. Tipping is not obligatory, but if you decide to leave a tip, calculate 10 per cent. Italian law requires all eating establishments to issue a bona fide printed receipt *(ricevuta fiscale)* to clients when they pay. Make sure you get a receipt as you may receive a hefty fine if you cannot produce a *ricevuta fiscale* if requested by a *finanziere* (the fiscal police).

Most restaurants and trattorias accept a range of cards, including MasterCard and Visa. Bars, cafés and small, family-run establishments may only accept cash.

Opening Hours

Restaurant hours are typical of the southern Mediterranean: in general, 1–3:30pm for lunch and 9pm–midnight for dinner. Many restaurants are closed on one day during the week, with the possible exception of the high season, in July and August. Closing times are shown in the listings on pages 210–17. Restaurants and trattorias may also close for up to a month for annual holidays. In large cities like Palermo this is usually in August, whereas on the coast and on the islands almost all restaurants close in the winter.

Making Reservations

In the evening, especially in popular holiday places in the summer, restaurants often get very crowded; it is a good idea to book, or arrive early, about 8pm, to avoid standing in line.

Phoning ahead is also advisable if you want to make sure that a restaurant's specialities will be available.

Children

Children are always welcome in all but the most sophisticated restaurants, particularly family-run places which may be willing to prepare special dishes or half-portions for youngsters (although some places will charge you the full price for it).

Smoking

Smoking in restaurants is no longer allowed. Smoking at tables outside is *de rigueur*.

DK Choice

The restaurants singled out as DK Choices represent the best of Sicilian cooking. Whether deeply traditional, with generations of experience informing the menu, or exciting and contemporary, inventing new takes on superb local ingredients, these are places singled out for their authentic, passionate preparation and presentation of food that will be a truly memorable experience.

Enjoy good wine and antipasto at *vineria* (wine bar) La Putia in Syracuse *(see p216)*

The Flavours of Sicily

Sicilian cuisine is Italy's most varied and exotic, influenced by the different settlers who have grown flavourful ingredients in the lava-enriched soil and hot sunshine. Homer's *Odyssey* describes the island's bounty of apples, pomegranates and grapes. The Normans brought their way of curing fish with salt and the Spanish imported tomatoes and peppers. But it was the Arabs' introduction of almonds, aubergines (eggplant), saffron and sugar cane that defines much of Sicilian cooking. Arabic traditions of stuffing vegetables, making sweet pastries and using rice, couscous and sweet-sour combinations are still used today.

Fresh herbs

Local farmer with a basket of freshly made ricotta

Northwestern Sicily

Cooking in Northwestern Sicily is often highly spiced, revealing a strong eastern influence, not least in the capital, Palermo, where the food markets have the feel of Arabian souks.

Blossom and fruits from the orange and lemon groves of La Conca d'Oro near Palermo perfume the air and feature in many dishes, while the vineyards around Marsala produce wines that are used in both savoury dishes and desserts. *Insalata d'arance* – orange salad – refreshingly combines oranges, mint and Marsala.

Historically, villages along the northwest coast thrived on tuna fishing, and Mazara del Vallo has one of the Mediterranean's largest deep-sea fishing fleets.

Southwestern Sicily

Inland the traditional fare is poultry, meat, offal and game. Liver is often cooked in a sweet-and-sour sauce while rabbit or goat is simmered with vegetables, herbs and spices. Fruits are made into preserves and pastes, almonds into marzipan treats. The speciality in Agrigento, where there is an almond festival each spring, is a

Tuna Lobster Squid Sardines

Mussels Clams

Selection of seafood from the clear waters of Sicily's coastline

Sicilian Dishes and Specialities

Antipasti include carpaccio of tuna or swordfish; *caponata* – aubergines (eggplant) in a rich sweet-and-sour tomato sauce with capers, olives, pine nuts and basil; and *frittedda* of artichokes, peas and broad (fava) beans. *Arancini* are small stuffed, fried balls of golden risotto rice, named for the little oranges they resemble. Fresh ricotta melds with aubergine and tomato as a sauce for *pasta alla Norma*. Seafood and shellfish are also added to pasta, such as *pasta al nero di seppia* (with cuttlefish ink) and *pasta con aragosta* (with lobster). Sardines, squid and mullet are cooked in myriad ways, like *calamari in umido* (squid and anchovies in tomato sauce) and *triglie allo scoglio* (red mullet in a sweet-sour onion sauce).

Local figs

Maccheroncini con le sarde is Sicilian macaroni with sardines, fennel, pine nuts, raisins, breadcrumbs and saffron.

Farmer selling fruit from the back of his truck in Taormina, Sicily

sweet *cuscus* with chocolate, pistachios and almonds. A savoury *cuscus*, cooked with fish or chicken stock, cloves and nutmeg in a terracotta pot, is found on Pantelleria, the closest point to the North African coast.

Northeastern Sicily

Dominated by Mount Etna and its fertile slopes, the east has fields, orchards, citrus groves and vines. Local dishes use herbs rather than spices.

On the coast, Messina is known for swordfish, often served simply grilled with herbs and lemon, and Catania for *risotto nero* using dark cuttlefish ink (sometimes topped with tomato sauce to resemble an Etna eruption).

Mountain snow, mixed with sugar and flower essence or juice, began the Sicilian tradition of sorbets and ice creams.

Southern Sicily

In Ragusa province, vast greenhouses dot the landscape, enabling the year-round production and export of fruit and vegetables. Yellow peppers, plump aubergines (eggplant), courgettes

Freshly harvested olives ready to be pressed into rich oil

(zucchini) and tomatoes are the basis for pasta sauces like *vermicelli alla Siracusana* (of Syracuse), which also uses black olives, capers and anchovies.

Pork from the pigs farmed inland has the distinctive taste of the prickly pears on which they feed, and the local sausages are often flavoured with wild herbs.

Milk from cows, sheep and goats is made into cheeses such as pecorino, which are sometimes studded with peppercorns or olives. Ricotta is crumbled onto stews, pasta and rice dishes and is an essential ingredient in many desserts.

WHAT TO DRINK

High-quality wines include Faro and Cerasuolo di Vittoria (both reds), Contea di Sclafari, Erice, Nero d'Avola and Etna wines from the slopes of the volcano (dry reds and whites).

Marsala, a fortified wine created by 18th-century English merchants, may be dry *(secco)* or sweet *(dolce)*.

Sweet *moscato* (muscat) comes from Noto, Syracuse and Pantelleria. Rare Malvasia from Lipari is known as "drinkable gold".

There are liqueurs made from almonds, lemon, prickly pears, and herbs and roots.

Pesce spada, swordfish steak, may be cooked in an orange sauce, or pan-fried or grilled with lemon and herbs.

Pollo alla Marsala is pan-fried chicken (veal may also be used) with Marsala, lemon juice, capers and parsley.

Cassata is Sicily's famous sponge cake, with ricotta, nuts, Marsala, chocolate, candied fruit and marzipan.

Where to Eat and Drink

Palermo

DK Choice

**Antica Focacceria
San Francesco** €
Street Food/Gourmet **Map** D3
Via A. Paternostro 58, 90133
Tel *091-320 264*
A bustling, exuberant
Palermitano institution, with a
glorious tiled interior. Traditional
street snacks are served
downstairs, such as *focaccia
schietta* (focaccia with offal and
caciocavallo cheese) and
sfincione (pizza with onion,
tomato, caciocavallo and
breadcrumbs). Full meals are
served upstairs, with several
good-value set menus.

Caffè al Riso €
Café **Map** C4
Via Vittorio Emanuele 365, 90134
Tel *091-588 515*
Minimalist bar with a shady
courtyard belonging to Palermo's
contemporary art museum,
serving hazelnut- and chocolate-
flavoured coffees, light lunches
and *aperitivos*. Free WiFi.

DK Choice

I Cuochini €
Street Food **Map** B1
Via Ruggero Settimo 68, 90121
Tel *091-581 158* **Closed** *Sun*
Founded in 1826, microscopic,
sparklingly tiled I Cuochini sells
deftly deep-fried Palermitani
street food, such as *panzerotti*
(savoury stuffed pastries),
arancini (small, stuffed fried
balls of golden risotto rice),
pasticcino (pastry with a sweet
filling of custard or candied
fruit), and *besciamelle fritte*
(breadcrumbed and deep-fried
bechamel) – all at less than a
euro, and all crisp and light as
a cloud.

Franco u Vastiddaru €
Street Food **Map** D3
Piazza Marina, 90133
Tel *091-325 987*
Hugely popular with Palermitani,
and famous for its savoury
snacks: chickpea pancakes, fried
croquettes and rice balls, and
offal-stuffed *pane con la milza*
(*pane ca meusa* in Sicilian). Order
at the counter and eat with gusto
at plastic tables on plastic plates
with plastic knives and forks.

Friggitoria Chiluzzo €
Street Food **Map** E3
Piazza Kalsa, 90133
Palermitani argue about who
makes the best *pane e panelle*
(chickpea pancakes in a bun) in
the city; this tiny kiosk is always a
contender. Order your sandwich
and a bottle of beer, and join the
crowd sheltering from the sun
under a large canopy.

Risto Cibus €
Deli **Map** C1
Via E. Amari 79, 90139
Tel *091-323 062*
Gourmet grocery store close to
the port with a great deli counter,
and a wood-fired oven. Delicious
pizzas and other hot and cold
dishes to eat in or take away.

Rosciglione €
Street Food **Map** B5
Via Gian Luca Barbieri 5, 90134
Tel *091-651 29 59* **Closed** *Sun*
This is the most famous cannolo
bakery in Palermo, where you
can watch the crisp shells being
made as you eat one filled with
cool, sweet ricotta.

Spinnato €
Café **Map** B1
*Via Principe di Belmonte 107–115,
90121*
Tel *091-749 51 04*
With its terrace on a pedestrianized
street famed for its shopping
outlets, this is a perfect place for
breakfast, afternoon tea or an
aperitivo served with roast almonds
and pistachios.

Trattoria Torrenuzza €
Seafood **Map** E3
Via Torrenuzza 17, 90133
Tel *091-252 55 32*

Antica Focacceria San Francesco serving
Palermian street food and gourmet meals

No-frills trattoria where fish is
grilled on an outside brazier. Eat
at streetside tables in summer,
or inside in winter; either way
you can feast on a seafood menu
including mussel soup, pasta
with mussels and clams as well
as mixed fried or grilled fish.

Ai Cascinari €€
Trattoria **Map** A4
*Via d'Ossuna 43–45,
90138*
Tel *091-651 98 04* **Closed** *Mon;
Tue & Sun lunch*
One brother serves tables and
the other cooks, using produce
from the nearby Capo market.
Lovely mixed antipasti including
red mullet fried in breadcrumbs
and *pane e panelle (see p73)*, and
a huge variety of inventive
Palermo-style pasta dishes.

Il Mirto e la Rosa €€
Seafood **Map** C1
*Via Principe di Granitello 30,
90139*
Tel *091-324 353* **Closed** *Sun*
A great option for vegetarians as
well as seafood lovers, with lots
of choices including *caponata*
with pistachio-spiked couscous,
home-made tagliolini with an
intense tomato sauce and grilled
aubergine and cheese from the
Nebrodi mountains. Leave room
for the voluptuous home-made
desserts and their home-made
cinnamon liqueur.

Primavera €€
Trattoria **Map** C4
Piazza Bologni 4, 90134
Tel *091-329 408* **Closed** *Mon*
Evocative setting on a pretty
piazza with a delightful garden,
and home-style cooking such as
pasta con le sarde (with sardines)
and bucatini with broccoli.
Good, inexpensive local wine
by the bottle.

Pizzeria Italia €€
Pizzeria **Map** B2
Via Orologio 54, 90133
Tel *091-589 885* **Closed** *lunch; Tue*
A great place for light pizzas
that arrive crunchy and blistered
from a wood-fired oven. There
are tables for sitting outside in
good weather.

Obika €€
Café **Map** C3
4th floor, Rinascente department
store, Via Roma 289, 90133
Tel *091-601 78 61*
Palermo branch of an exclusive
chain specializing in meticulously
sourced *mozzarella di bufala*,
which appears in exquisitely
presented salads and other light
dishes. Perfect for lunch or an
aperitif with nibbles.

Osteria Lo Bianco €€
Seafood **Map** C1
Via E. Amari 104, 90139
Tel *091-251 49 06* **Closed** *Sun*
dinner
Quintessential Palermo trattoria
decorated with religious
souvenirs and Juventus banners.
It serves traditional dishes
including finger-licking *ricciola*
(amberjack) in a spicy tomato
sauce and sardine croquettes.

Sant'Andrea €€
Trattoria **Map** C3
Piazza Sant'Andrea 4, 90133
Tel *328-131 45 95* **Closed** *lunch; Sun*
This chic little place, near the
busy Vuccıria market, features
prominently in Peter Robb's
cultural history *Midnight in Sicily*.
Seasonal and creative, with
the focus on carefully sourced
local ingredients.

Trattoria Il Vecchio Mafone €€
Seafood **Map** 3B
Via Judıca 4, 90134
Tel *091-507 96 21* **Closed** *Mon in*
winter, Sun in summer
Prides itself on spanking fresh
fish – on display for all to see.
Choose the fish you fancy, take
advice from the waiter about
how to have it cooked, then eat
an antipasto of raw prawns or a
plate of pasta with squid ink
while you wait.

Bye Bye Blues €€€
Gourmet **Road Map** C2
Via del Garofalo 23, 90100
Tel *091-684 14 15* **Closed** *Mon*
Situated out of town in Mondello
(see p72), but worth the trip. This
elegant, nationally renowned
restaurant serves sophisticated
dishes such as spaghetti with
puréed beans topped with sea
urchin, potato *tortelli* with a *ragù*
of Nebrodi pork, and an amazing
toffee apple cheesecake made
with Ragusan cheese.

Osteria dei Vespri €€€
Modern Sicilian **Map** D4
Piazza Croce dei Vespri 6, 90133
Tel *091-617 16 31* **Closed** *Sun*
Sophisticated dishes making
inspired use of local Sicilian

The rustic yet sophisticated dinning room at Nangalarruni in Castelbuono

ingredients. Dishes might include
black tagliolini served with red
mullet, ginger, red onion and
fresh broad (fava) beans, or
quail stuffed with prunes served
on a purée of cannellini beans
and celeriac.

MONDELLO: Charleston €€€
Gourmet **Road Map** C2
Via Regina Elena, 90149
Tel *091-321 14 43* **Closed** *Mon*
Incredible location north of the
city in Mondello *(see p72)*, in a
splendid Moorish-style Liberty
palace situated on the water's
edge, approached across a
bridge. Try king prawns in
crunchy filo pastry, artisan *fusıloni*
(giant pasta spirals) with scorpion
fish and datterini tomatos, or
melanzane Charleston – oven-
roasted aubergine stuffed with
fresh pasta, tomato, mozzarella
and basil.

Northwestern Sicily

CASTELBUONO: Fiasconaro €
Café **Road Map** D2
Piazza Margherita 10, 90013
Tel *0921-671 231* **Closed** *from 1pm*
Castelbuono is the only place in
Europe where manna, famous for
the sustenance it gave Moses
and the Israelites, is cultivated.
Fiasconaro is famous for its
gourmet panettone and other
goodies made with manna. Buy
a couple of cakes to take home,
but take time too to sit on the
café terrace and sample the
home-produced ice creams.

CASTELBUONO:
Nangalarruni €€
Trattoria **Road Map** D2
Via delle Confraternite 5,
90013
Tel *0921-671 228* **Closed** *Wed in*
Oct–Mar

The place to come for wild
mushrooms (and wild vegetables
too), in soups and pasta sauces,
and accompanying local pork –
best sampled on one of the
great-value set menus. Arrive
hungry, as portions are generous.

CEFALÚ: FoodSicily €
Gelateria **Road Map** D2
Via Bagno Cicerone 3, 90015
Tel *0921-422 654* **Closed** *Nov–Mar*
Wonderful gelateria by the beach
at the edge of the historic centre
where ice-cream flavours include
mango, raspberry, prickly pear,
and chocolate with chilli.

CEFALÚ: La Brace €€
European **Road Map** D2
Via XXV Novembre 10, 90015
Tel *0921-423 570* **Closed** *Mon, Tue*
lunch & mid-Dec–mid-Jan.
Intimate little place in which
beautifully executed European
classics such as steak
tournedos join Sicilian dishes
like swordfish *involtini*. Lots of
vegetarian options. Booking
ahead is essential.

CEFALÚ: Le Chat Noir €€
Traditional Sicilian **Road Map** D2
Via XXV Novembre 17, 90015
Tel *0921-420 697* **Closed** *Wed and*
Nov–Easter
Charming restaurant serving
delicious Sicilian dishes –such as
aubergine *parmigiana* with salty
ricotta and swordfish *involtini* – in
a whitewashed courtyard of a
16th-century building.

ENNA: Gtotta Azzura €
Trattoria **Road Map** D3
Via Colaianni 1, 94100
Tel *0935-243 28* **Closed** *One week in*
Sep (for the vintage)
Minuscule basement trattoria run
by the same couple for over 50
years. Simple food such as baked
pasta and grilled meat, and some
of the cheapest prices in Sicily.

ERICE: Pasticceria di Maria Grammatico
Café   €
Via Vittorio Emanuele 14, 91016
Tel *0923-869 390*   **Closed** *Wed in Nov–Easter*
Road Map A2
Cake shop and café renowned for its traditional marzipan fruits and pastries, all of them using recipes Maria Grammatico learned as a girl in a convent. Best sampled in the garden café.

ERICE: Monte San Giuliano
Traditional Sicilian   **Road Map** A2   €€
Vicolo San Rocco 7, 91016
Tel *0923-869 595*   **Closed** *Mon*
Magical entrance – up a flight of ancient steps and through a medieval arch. In summer you can sit outside among abundant greenery and look out to sea as you dine on Sicilian classics such as smoked fish, marinated anchovies and fish couscous.

ERICE: La Pentolaccia
Traditional Sicilian   **Road Map** A2   €€
Via G.F. Guarnotti 17, 91016
Tel *0923-869 099*   **Closed** *Tue*
Genial service in a former monastery. Wonderful home-made pasta; try ravioli stuffed with *cernia* (grouper) dressed with cherry tomato, swordfish, mint and prawns, or pasta Nostromo with John Dory roe, prawns, tomatoes and garlic.

FAVIGNANA: Paneficio Costanza
Street Food   **Road Map** A2   €
Via Roma, 91023
Tel *0923-921 773*
A contender for baking the best loaf in Sicily, with a crunchy fennel, anise and sesame seed crust and a toothsome crumb. Great biscuits and slices of pizza as well.

FAVIGNANA: La Bettola
Trattoria   **Road Map** A2   €€
Via Nicotera 47, 91023
Tel *0923-921 988*   **Closed** *Mon in Nov–Mar*
Pleasant, informal restaurant: sit on the terrace and eat local dishes such as fish couscous, *busiati* pasta with a pesto of tuna, anchovies, tomato and basil, or fish grilled on lava stone.

FAVIGNANA: Il Giardino delle Aloe
Trattoria   **Road Map** A2   €€€
Contrada Grotta Perciata, 91023
Tel *0923-187 068*   **Closed** *Nov–Mar*
Fresh fish from the island's fleet served in a garden of aloes near the tremendous bay of Cala Rossa. The menu depends on the catch – local *busiate* pasta with

mussels, for example, or a slice of the famous Favignana tuna, with sun-ripened fruit to follow. While it is a pleasant cycle ride to reach the restaurant, there is a free mini-bus for guests coming from town.

LÉVANZO: Paradiso
Seafood   **Road Map** A2   €€
Via Lungomare 6, 91023
Tel *0923-924 080* **Closed** *Nov–Easter*
Lovely sea views, a relaxed atmosphere and simple fish, seafood and pasta at this tiny island's only restaurant. Try tuna *polpette*, spaghetti with *pesto trapanese* (with basil, tomatoes and almonds) or catch of the day.

MARETTIMO: Caffè Tramontana
Café   **Road Map** A2   €
Via Scalo Vecchio, 91010   **Closed** *Nov–Easter*
A lovely place to while away the hours in Marettimo. Breakfast on almond, mulberry or watermelon granita, or come for an *aperitivo* accompanied by a plate of raw fish and watch the sun set over the fishing harbour and castle. Lovely tabletops by ceramic artist Nino Perrucca.

MARETTIMO: Il Veliero
Seafood   **Road Map** A2   €€
Corso Umberto, 91010
Tel *0923-923 274* **Closed** *Nov–Easter*
Atmospheric cane-covered Robinson Crusoe-esque terrace right on the water. Traditional pasta dishes, and fish caught by the owner. Arrive early for a good table and call in advance to reserve lobster.

MARSALA: Il Gallo e L'Innamorata
Osteria   **Road Map** A3   €€
Via S. Bilardello 18, 91025
Tel *0923-195 44 46*   **Closed** *Tue*
Friendly *osteria* loyal to the Slow Food movement, using fresh local ingredients to great effect and with a light touch in dishes such as fresh pasta with prawns and pistachio pesto, or *busiate* with cherry tomatoes, almonds, basil and shavings of bottarga.

MARSALA: Le Lumie
Seafood   **Road Map** A3   €€
Contrada Fontanelle 178B, 91025
Tel *0923-995 197*   **Closed** *Wed; Nov*
Located above Marsala, with fantastic views over the Mediterranean to the Egadi Islands – especially at sunset. The focus is on seasonal fish, including the kinds Sicilians eat at home like *capone* (gurnard) and *spatola* (scabbard fish) as well as more familiar species.

The warm interior of Monte San Giuliano in Erice

MAZARA DEL VALLO: Eyem Zemen
Tunisian   **Road Map** A3   €
Via Porta Palermo 36, 91026
Tel *3473-869 921*   **Closed** *Tue*
Genuine Tunisian food in a tiny no-frills place with a few tables outside. Try *brik* (deep-fried pastry parcels), unctuous aubergine salads, taboulleh, and spicy fish or meat couscous. Hot mint tea and Tunisian pastries for dessert.

SAN VITO LO CAPO: Al Ritrovo
Seafood   **Road Map** B2   €€
Viale Cristofero Colombo 314, 91010
Tel *0923-975 656*   **Closed** *Tue in Oct–May*
Dishes using traditional ingredients, such as smoked *lampuga* (mahi mahi) with broad beans purée, and *caponata* (aubergine dish) scented with chocolate and almonds. The *frittura del Golfo* (fried seafood) is excellent.

SAN VITO LO CAPO: Syrah
Seafood   **Road Map** B2   €€
Via Savoia 5, 91010
Tel *0923-972 028*   **Closed** *Tue*
Amiable restaurant near the beach, run by a young chef, his wife and his sister. The focus, naturally, is on fish, with creative but never over-elaborate dishes such as *polpettine* of squid in squid ink, basil-scented lasagne with lobster, a salad of the local fish *vope* (a sea bream) and sardines, and an incredibly ample mixed antipasto.

SAN VITO LO CAPO: Pocho
Seafood   **Road Map** B2   €€€
Località Isulidda, Contrada Macari, 91010
Tel *0923-972 525*   **Closed** *Tue in Oct–May*
Stylish, welcoming, and in a gorgeous location overlooking

the rocky coast. Sit on the panoramic terrace and indulge in the great value six-course set menu, which changes daily. The owner, Marilù, occasionally ends the evening with Sicilian songs. Sunday special is a couscous lunch.

TRAPANI: Calvino €
Street Food **Road Map** A2
Via N. Nasi 72, 91023
Tel *0923-214 64* **Closed** *Tue*
A Trapanese institution, with slices of crisp, delicious pizza served on greaseproof paper to take away. Anchovies and pecorino is a local speciality topping – or opt for a plate of sausages and potatoes roasted with onions in the pizza oven.

TRAPANI: I Grilli €€
Vineria **Road Map** A2
Corso Vittorio Emanuele 69, 91023
Tel *0923-206 63* **Closed** *Sun lunch in Apr–Oct; Wed in Nov–Mar*
Unusually for Sicily, the focus here is on carefully sourced grilled meats, along with French and Italian cheeses, salami and cured hams. Good terrace for people-watching on the main Corso. Extensive wine list.

TRAPANI: Ai Lumi €€
Traditional Sicilian **Road Map** A2
Corso Vittorio Emanuele 71–77, 91023
Tel *0923-872 418* **Closed** *Tue*
Romantic setting in the brick-vaulted rooms of a Baroque palace with a pretty terrace for summer. Good home-made pasta – try it with shrimp, asparagus tips and sea urchin, or linguine with crab – and fine braised rabbit among the mains.

Southwestern Sicily

AGRIGENTO: Caffetteria Grancafé Nobel €
Café/Bar **Road Map** C4
Viale della Victoria 11, 92100
Tel *0922-245 62*
With tables in the shade of the trees lining the avenue, this is a fine spot for breakfast (generously filled sweet *cornetti* and other pastries) an ice cream or an evening beer or *aperitivo*.

AGRIGENTO: Le Cuspidi €
Street Food **Road Map** C4
Viale della Vittoria, 92100
Tel *0922-595 914* **Closed** *Tue in winter*
The best ice cream in the province is here, halfway along a tree-shaded avenue where Agrigento folk come for their

ritual evening stroll. Flavours range from the traditional pistachio, hazelnut and chocolate to Mars® bar, mango, sachertorte and, most startlingly, pecorino (sheeps' cheese) ice cream, which tastes better than it sounds.

AGRIGENTO: La Posata di Federico Secondo €€
Modern Sicilian **Road Map** C4
Piazza Cavour 19 (off Viale della Vittoria), 92100
Tel *0922-282 89* **Closed** *Sun*
Elegant restaurant serving superb, strictly seasonal food, with the menu arranged according to the main ingredient (for example, artichoke). Perfect for a light lunch of antipasti, or a full four-course dinner. The signature dish is beef fillet served with Gorgonzola and honey.

AGRIGENTO: La Terra €€
Modern Sicilian **Road Map** C4
Via Francesco Crispi 34, 92100
Tel *0922-297 42* **Closed** *Mon; lunchtime Jun–Sep.*
A lovely setting in the garden of the playwright Luigi Pirandello's family villa, with a menu and wine list inspired by the Slow Food ethos. Seasonal Sicilian produce – for example, linguine with mussels, cherry tomatoes and *tenerumi* (courgette plant leaf fronds). Desserts include a Modica chocolate mousse.

LAMPEDUSA: Al Gallo d'Oro €€
Trattoria **Road Map** B5
Via Vittorio Emanuele 45, 92010
Tel *0922-970 249* **Closed** *Oct–May*
Cheery trattoria specializing in fish. Try pasta with fresh tuna, cherry tomatoes and parsley, or *trofie* pasta with swordfish, aubergine and salted ricotta. The oven-roasted fish is recommended too.

LAMPEDUSA: I Gemelli €€
North African **Road Map** B5
Via Cala Pisana 2, 92010
Tel *0922-970 699* **Closed** *lunch*
Delicous Tunisian dishes such as *brik* (stuffed savoury flaky pastries), merguez sausage and couscous. Fish is reckoned to be some of the best on the island.

LAMPEDUSA: Lampegusto €€
Traditional Sicilian **Road Map** B5
Via Vittorio Emanuele 19, 92010
Tel *388-628 43 56*
Simple modern restaurant and takeaway with a great choice of antipasti (try the octopus) and delicious pasta (try spaghetti with red mullet and wild fennel).

LAMPEDUSA: U Calacciuni €€
Seafood **Road Map** B5
Spiaggia della Guitgia, 92010
Tel *339-435 03 00* **Closed** *Nov–Apr*
Beach shack trattoria where what's on offer depends on what has been caught. Expect pasta with clams and mussels, or with sardines and wild fennel, followed by the day's catch.

> ### DK Choice
>
> ### LICATA: La Madia €€€
> **Gourmet** **Road Map** B5
> *Corso Re Capriata 22, 92027*
> **Tel** *0922-771 443* **Closed** *Tue; Jul–Aug: Sun lunch; Sep–Jun: Sun dinner*
> Unassuming-looking restaurant which many consider to be the best in Sicily. La Madia has a passionate following for the virtuoso wit and ceaseless inventions of chef Pino Cuttaia, who wreaks twists, turns and somersaults with meticulously sourced Sicilian produce, such as the *arancini* served with red mullet and wild fennel, or *spatola* (scabbard fish) stuffed with a crunchy caponata.

Alfresco dinning is a common sight outside the restaurants on Via Roma, Lampedusa

For more information on types of restaurants *see pp206–7*

PANTELLERIA: La Nicchia €€€
Traditional Sicilian **Road Map** A5
Contrada Scauri Basso, 91017
Tel *0923-916 342* **Closed** *lunch; Wed in Sep–May*
Dine in the garden of this renowned restaurant beneath the shade of an old orange tree, on dishes like shrimps in a sauce made from the local Zibbibo wine, or mint and *tumma* (fresh pecorino) ravioli in sage butter.

PETRALIA SOTTANA:
Petrae Lejum
Trattoria **Road Map** D3
Corso Paolo Agliata 113, 90027
Tel *0921-641 908* **Closed** *Thu in Aug; Tue–Thu dinner in winter*
Family-run trattoria where local produce is used to great effect in traditional mountain dishes such as gnocchi with wild boar sauce, or handmade tagliatelle with parsley, garlic, pecorino and pistachios from Bronte. Roasted or grilled meat to follow.

PIAZZA ARMERINA:
Il Fogher €€€
Trattoria **Road Map** D4
Contrada Bellia, SS 117 (towards Aidone), 94015
Tel *0935-684 123* **Closed** *Sun dinner, Mon*
Rustic elegance and fine cooking. Try bavette of farro flour with a *ragù* of goat kid and wild chard sprinkled with *primosale* cheese, or boned quail stuffed with dandelion greens, sun-dried tomatoes and olives roasted over eucalyptus and pine, with greens and broad bean purée.

POLIZZI GENEROSO: Giardino
Donna Lavia €€
Trattoria **Road Map** D3
Contrada Donna Laura, 90028
Tel *0921-551 104*
Restaurant in a former Jesuit monastery (that also has rooms) serving local meats, wild greens and herbs, and home-grown vegetables and pulses. Tagliatelle with borage, wild fennel and *fagioli badda* (a violet and white bean unique to the area) and roast suckling pig are typical.

POLIZZI GENEROSO: Itria €€
Trattoria **Road Map** D3
Via Beato Gnoffi 8, 90028
Tel *0921-688 790* **Closed** *Wed in winter*
Homely, family-run trattoria where you can watch the father cooking while the mother and son wait on tables. Abundant mixed antipasto (frittata of asparagus and ricotta, salami and hams from black Nebrodi pork, Madonie cheeses, olives and

other seasonal delicacies). In spring, go for a *pasta con la fritella* (with broad/fava beans, peas, artichokes and wild fennel), and in autumn look out for wild mushroom dishes.

SCIACCA: Il Grappolo €€
Osteria **Road Map** B3
Via Conzo 9A, 92019
Tel *0925-852 94* **Closed** *Tue*
Simple, rather spartan osteria serving locally caught fish with home-grown vegetables. Try fresh pasta with a sauce of red mullet and *bottarga* (cured fish roe), or spaghetti with squid ink, then follow with the fish of the day. Fish couscous is available on Wednesdays. In winter, phone ahead to request pork shank with orange blossom honey.

Southern Sicily

CALTAGIRONE: Il Locandiere €€
Seafood **Road Map** D4
Via Luigi Sturgo 55, 95041
Tel *0933-582 92*
Excellent fish, with lots of little twists on traditional Sicilian dishes. Try the marinated swordfish with orange and pistachio, or thin slices of cured tuna "bresaola" with ricotta and rocket, and follow with the fabulously tasty "swordfish sausage".

CALTAGIRONE: Coria €€€
Gourmet **Road Map** D4
Via Infermeria 24, 95041
Tel *0933-265 96* **Closed** *Mon; Sun in Jul–Sep; Sun dinner in Oct–Jun*
Excellent Sicilian gourmet fare, created by a talented young chef. Expect to find dishes such as spaghetti with scampi and wild asparagus, pork shank with

An elegant setting for fine dining at La Gazza Ladra in Modica *(see p215)*

Nero d'Avola *mosto* (wine must) and a purée of apples from Mount Etna, and for dessert, an incredible hemisphere of chocolate filled with ricotta, couscous and pistacchio ice cream.

CHIARAMONTE GULFI:
Majore €€
Traditional Sicilian **Road Map** E4/5
Via Martiri Ungheresi, 12, 97012
Tel *0932-928 019* **Closed** *Mon*
Founded in 1896, this venerable restaurant is dedicated to pork, which appears as salami and ham, as pasta sauce, in risotto as well as rolled, roasted and stuffed with sausage, cheese and whole hard-boiled eggs as a *falsomagro* – a Sicilian speciality.

MARINA DI RAGUSA:
Da Serafino €€
Seafood **Road Map** E5
Lungomare Doria, 97010
Tel *0932-239 522* **Closed** *Oct–Easter*
Founded in 1953, this elegant beach restaurant – owned by Don Serafino in Ragusa – is a summer tradition in Marina. It has its own private beach facilities. Come for simple, but expertly prepared, spanking fresh fish.

MODICA: Caffè Dell'Arte €
Café **Road Map** E5
Corso Umberto 1 114, 97015
Tel *0932-943 257* **Closed** *Tue*
The best pastries in Modica (including fabulous *impanata*, with minced meat, spices and cinnamon), along with their own chocolate, served in a little café on the Corso with seats inside and out. Children can have miniature cups of hot chocolate, sprinkled with cinnamon.

MODICA: La Locanda del
Colonello €€
Trattoria **Road Map** E5
Vico Biscari 6, 97015
Tel *0932-752 423* **Closed** *Wed*
Simple but slick little place run by the Palazzo Failla hotel. The mixed antipasto is a good way of sampling local specialities such as a crisp *scacce* (savoury pastry), while legumes dominate the primi in dishes such as *maccu*, a traditional broad (fava) bean soup, or pasta with chickpeas.

MODICA: Osteria dei
Sapori Perduti €€
Trattoria **Road Map** E5
Corso Umberto 1 228–30, 97015
Tel *0932-944 247* **Closed** *Tue in winter*
Traditional home cooking with a strong emphasis on beans and pulses, and lots of dishes you

won't find in most trattorias. Try
lolli con le fave (handmade pasta
with broad bean purée) or pasta
with broth and meatballs. The
menu is in Sicilian, but trans-
lations are available.

MODICA: Taverna Nicastra €€
Trattoria **Road Map** E5
Via Sant'Antonino 30, 97015
Tel *0932-945 884* **Closed** *lunch; Sun
and Mon (except by arrangement)*
Old-fashioned, with tables
outside on a flight of steps in the
upper part of the old town.
Specialities include home-made
sausages and salamis made on
the premises, and ravioli in a
sauce of tomato, pancetta, pork
and sausage. For dessert, choose
between a cannolo or a lemon,
cinnamon or almond-milk jelly.

MODICA: La Gazza Ladra €€€
Modern Sicilian **Road Map** E5
Via Blandini 5, 97105
Tel *0932-755 655* **Closed** *Mon; lunch
Tue–Fri*
Located in Palazzo Failla hotel,
this smart restaurant features
creative twists on traditional
Sicilian cuisine such as spaghetti
with anchovies, candied orange,
wild fennel flowers, chilli and wild
onion greens, and a fillet of
Nebrodi mountain pork with
cream of pine nuts and asparagus.

NOTO: Caffè Sicilia €
Gelateria **Road Map** E5
Corso Vittorio Emanuele 125, 96017
Tel *0931-835 013* **Closed** *Mon*
The Assenza brothers, Carlo
and Corrado, create innovative
as well as classic ice creams –
ranging from local almonds
blended with cinnamon to
lemon and saffron and even
basil, all according to season.

NOTO: Corrado Costanzo €
Gelateria **Road Map** E5
Via Spaventa 7, 96017
Tel *0931-835 243* **Closed** *Wed*
This is one of the best-known
gelaterias in Italy. Flavours
change according to the season
– try rose petal, jasmine or wild
strawberry in spring, or dark
chocolate spiked with mandarin
in winter.

**NOTO: Ristorante Crocifisso di
Marco Baglieri** €€
Modern Sicilian **Road Map** E5
Via Principe Umberto 46, 96017
Tel *0931-571 151* **Closed** *Wed*
Carefully sourced ingredients are
used in palate-zinging dishes
such as spaghetti with prawns
and wild asparagus, and rabbit
with orange blossom honey, wild
greens, celery, carrot and peppers.

The refined furnishings and warm coloured decor of Ristorante Il Duomo, Ragusa

NOTO: Trattoria del Carmine €€
Trattoria **Road Map** E5
Via Ducezio 1, 96017
Tel *0931-838 705* **Closed** *Mon in
Sep–Jun*
Cheap and cheerful trattoria
popular with budget-minded
locals and tourists. Bustling
atmosphere; a good option for a
tasty, inexpensive plate of pasta
and a glass of good house wine.

**PALAZZOLO ACREIDE:
Lo Scrigno dei Sapori** €€
Trattoria **Road Map** E4
*Via Maddalena 50,
96010*
Tel *0931-882 941* **Closed** *Mon;
2 weeks in Nov*
Delicious, inventive hearty
dishes for meat lovers such as
fetuccine with a rich hare and
hazelnut sauce, or pistachio-
crusted pork. In the evenings
pizza is served as well.

RAGUSA: La Bettola €
Trattoria **Road Map** E5
*Largo Kamarina, Ragusa Ibla
97100*
Tel *0932-653 377* **Closed** *Mon*
Simple, inexpensive family-run
place with traditional red-
checked tablecloths that has
been cheerfully serving its classic
Sicilian menu for over 30 years.
Look out for the tagliatelle with
cream and saffron, and *maiale
ubriaco* – literally, "drunken pork",
braised in wine and local herbs.

**RAGUSA: Pasticceria di
Pasquale** €
Café **Road Map** E5
*Corso Vittorio Veneto, Ragusa
Superiore 104, 97100*
Tel *0932-624 635* **Closed** *Mon*
A wonderful pasticceria that
alone makes a visit to the newer
(19th-century) part of Ragusa
worthwhile. It serves the best ice
cream in Ragusa, along with
some decadent pastries.

DK Choice

RAGUSA: Il Duomo €€€
Gourmet **Road Map** E5
*Viia Capitano Bocchieri 31,
Ragusa Ibla 97100*
Tel *0932-651 265* **Closed** *Mon
lunch & Sun in Apr–Oct; Sun lunch
& Mon in Nov–Mar.*
Meticulously sourced Sicilian
ingredients reworked to
stunning effect in one of Sicily's
greatest restaurants – it has two
Michelin stars. Expect the
unexpected – black truffle ice
cream, or a savoury cannolo
with a dab of caviar. Evening
tasting menus are elaborate;
there's a simpler, more accessibly
priced three-course lunch.

SCICLI: Satra €€€
Modern Sicilian **Road Map** E5
Via Duca degli Abruzzi 1, 97018
Tel *0932-842 148* **Closed** *Tue; Sun
lunch*
In the vaulted cellars of a former
convent, this restaurant has great
credentials (the cook came from
Michelin-starred Il Duomo in
Ragusa) and a seasonal menu
featuring innovative versions of
traditional dishes. Try handmade
spaghetti flavoured with chilli,
saffron and wild fennel, served
with sardines and pine nuts.

**SYRACUSE
Caseificio Borderi** €
Café **Road Map** F4
Via De Benedictis 6, Ortygia, 96100
Tel *329-985 25 00* **Closed** *Sun,
evenings.*
Busy café open from 4am: join
the queue as the ebullient
Andrea hands out nibbles and
good cheer while preparing
divine sandwiches and plates of
focaccia piled with Sicilian meats,
cheeses and preserves. Crates are
set up outside as seats, and wine
is served in plastic cups.

For more information on types of restaurants *see pp206–7*

SYRACUSE: Fratelli Burgio €
Deli   **Road Map** F4
Piazza Cesare Battisti 4, 96100
Tel *0931-600 69*   **Closed** *Sun; evenings*
Deli in the heart of Ortygia's market, with artisan, DOP and Slow Food Presidio cheeses and cured meats from all over Italy. Eat in with a fine glass of wine and nibbles, or take away for a gourmet picnic.

DK CHOICE

SYRACUSE: Moon   €
Vegan   **Road Map** F4
Via Roma 112, 96100
Tel *0931-522 54 80*
Something quite different for Sicily: vegetarians will thrive in this contemporary cultural centre and restaurant, in a vaulted Liberty-era palazzo with a pretty courtyard. Live jazz and world music or dance performances enliven many an evening, while the light, inventive menu might include couscous with pine nuts, capers, mint and basil or "spaghetti" of julienned courgette with a range of pestos. Everything is home-made.

SYRACUSE: Piano B   €
Trattoria   **Road Map** F4
Via Cairoli 18, 96100
Tel *0931-668 51* **Closed** *lunch; Mon*
Beautifully light pizza, fine quality meats cooked over charcoal and traditional Roman dishes (a homage to the owner's mother) such as *carciofi alla giudia* (deep-fried artichokes), *fiori di zucca fritti* (deep-fried courgette flowers) and *baccala in pastella* (battered salt cod).

SYRACUSE: La Putia   €
Vineria   **Road Map** F4
Via Roma 8, 96100
Tel *339-888 80 78*
Tiny place on one of the main streets of Ortygia, serving outstanding wines at affordable prices and a daily changing menu of simple home-cooked bruschette, pasta and soups.

SYRACUSE: Zsa   €
Trattoria   **Road Map** F4
Via Roma 73, 96100
Tel *0931-464 280*   **Closed** *Mon*
Excellent pizza, with light, crisp dough and good quality ingredients in the toppings. The pasta alla Norma, with unctuous roast aubergine and grated *ricotta salata*, is fantastic. Alternatively try a warming *stufata*, with fennel and chilli-scented sausage and potato.

SYRACUSE: Apollonion   €€
Seafood   **Road Map** F4
Via Campisi 18, 96100
Tel *0931-483 362*   **Closed** *Tue*
Intimate fish restaurant in which there is just one choice of a set meal every day at the fixed price of €35. Expect four antipasti, pasta with shellfish or seafood, roast fish, and a home-made dessert. Bottled wine, water, coffee and liqueurs included.

SYRACUSE: Il Blu   €€
Vineria   **Road Map** F4
Via Nizza 50, 96100
Tel *0931-445 052* **Closed** *lunch in Nov–Mar*
The welcoming owners serve wonderful fresh-fruit proseccos and daiquiris on a terrace looking out to sea. There is food too – including Sicilian sashimi and *pane cunzato* (giant bruschetta).

SYRACUSE: Sicilia in Tavola €€
Trattoria   **Road Map** F4
Via Cavour 28, 96100
Tel *392-461 08 89*   **Closed** *Mon*
Cosy, bustling place that serves hearty dishes of handmade pasta along with simple fish antipasti and a dessert of the day. Try spaghetti with clams, prawns and crushed pistachio or ravioli with sea urchin.

SYRACUSE: La Tavernetta €€
Trattoria   **Road Map** F4
Via Cavour 44, 96100
Tel *0931-663 85*   **Closed** *Thu*
Quintessential trattoria, family-run with passion. Opt for the catch of the day, first in *spaghetto matallotta* (cooked with cherry tomatos, capers, olives and oregano), then filleted with a wine and seafood or zingy lemon sauce.

SYRACUSE: Vineria Café Eno'ntelodico   €€
Modern Sicilian   **Road Map** F4
Via Cavour 9, 96100
Tel *0931-185 60 49*
A stylish but relaxed fusion of café, wine bar and restaurant, using carefully sourced ingredients in interesting ways. Recommended are the ravioli with Puglian *burrata* cheese, prawn carpaccio with ginger, and the Sicilian pork marinaded in Hyblaean honey and peppercorns.

SYRACUSE: Don Camillo   €€€
Gourmet   **Road Map** F4
Via Maestranza 96, 96100
Tel *0931-671 33* **Closed** *Sun & hols; 2 weeks in Jan and Jul*
Refined, formal restaurant in the vaulted 15th-century rooms of a former convent. Gourmet

The well-stocked bar at Japanese restaurant Oxidiana in Catania

versions of Sicilian specialities like pasta with tuna, mint and cherry tomatos, or the splendid fish baked in a crust of bread.

Northeastern Sicily

CATANIA: Osteria Antica Marina   €€
Seafood   **Road Map** E3
Via Pardo 29, 95100
Tel *095-348 197*   **Closed** *Wed*
No-frills trattoria in the heart of the fish market, with set menus and paper-laid tables. Quality can vary, but the atmosphere is great, especially at lunchtime.

CATANIA: Mè Cumpari Turiddu   €€
Gourmet   **Road Map** E3
Via M. Ventimiglia 15, 95100
Tel *095-715 01 42* **Closed** *Sun; Aug*
Rigorously sourced, quality ingredients are treated well in *sformato* of spiny artichokes (a local delicacy); local paddlefish rolls with vegetables; home-made pasta with a sauce of Nebrodi black pork; or winter soup of lentils from Ustica or *fagioli bedda* from Polizzi.

CATANIA: Oxidiana   €€
Japanese   **Road Map** E3
Via Conte Ruggero 4A, 95129
Tel *095-532 585*   **Closed** *lunch*
Sushi and California rolls, along with tataki, tempuras, stir-fries and a marvellous sesame-crusted tuna (try it in May and June, the height of the tuna season). Vegetarian and gluten-free options too.

FILICUDI: La Sirena   €€
Seafood   **Road Map** E1
Pecorini Mare, 98050
Tel *090-988 99 97* **Closed** *Oct–Easter*

Located on the seafront, with fishing boats docked alongside. Sit on the shaded terrace and tuck into orange-scented *involtini* of swordfish or an unforgettable tuna, fennel seeds, raisins and almonds burger.

LIPARI: Da Filippino   €€
Gourmet   **Road Map** E1
Piazza Municipio, 98055
Tel *090-981 10 02*   **Closed** *Mon; Oct–Mar*
Highly regarded restaurant, founded in 1908. Look out for *bresaola di tonno* (sweet and luscious home-cured tuna) and the robust soup of beans, wild fennel and sardines. For dessert, don't miss the exotic *mousse di gelsomino*, flavoured with jasmine flowers.

LIPARI: Kasbah Café   €€
Modern Sicilian   **Road Map** E1
Vico Selinunte 45, 98055
Tel *090-981 10 75*   **Closed** *lunch; Nov–Feb*
Chic but unpretentious, with a beautiful garden and spanking fresh fish. Try *treccine* with local shrimps, aubergine and cherry tomatoes, or *tagliolini* with clams, courgette (zucchini) flowers, basil and black pepper. There are good pizzas, too.

MESSINA: Al Gattopardo   €€
Traditional Sicilian   **Road Map** F2
Via Santa Cecilia 184, 98123
Tel *090-673 076*
Tables outside on a lovely tree-lined avenue, excellent pizzas (try the Messinese, with escarole, mozzarella, anchovies and black pepper) along with a fine *zuppa di cozze* (mussel soup) and a delicious lemon risotto with prawns and *cernia* (grouper).

DK Choice

MILAZZO: Locande del Bagatto   €€
Vineria   **Road Map** F2
Via M. Regis 11, 98057
Tel *090-922 42 12*   **Closed** *Sun*
British food critic Matthew Fort reckoned that Milazzo was the only place in Sicily where it was impossible to eat well. He was wrong. This welcoming, feel-good wine bar and restaurant, close to the port, serves consistently well-executed dishes made from ingredients sourced with true passion. Try the heavenly beef carpaccio, with or without shavings of artichoke. Great Sicilian wines – and a knowledgeable owner, Rafaelle, to advise you.

PANAREA: Da Adelina   €€
Seafood   **Road Map** E1
Via Comunale, San Pietro 98050
Tel *090-983 246*   **Closed** *Nov–Feb*
Intimate candlelit restaurant with a roof terrace overlooking the harbour and a menu of seasonal dishes such as *moscardini* – tiny octopus, cooked with tomato, capers, wild fennel and chilli – followed by the mixed fish of the day, fried or grilled.

SALINA: Bar Alfredo   €
Café   **Road Map** E1
Via Alfieri, Lingua, 98050
Tel *090-984 33 07*   **Closed** *Nov–Easter*
The granitas of Bar Alfredo are famous throughout Italy. All are made on the tiny premises by Alfredo and his sons, and in season you'll find black fig, prickly pear and *gelsi* (mulberry) on the menu. Almost equally famous is the gargantuan *pane cunzato*, grilled bread piled high with combinations of local tomatoes, capers, roast aubergine, tuna, olives and ricotta.

SALINA: Porto Bello   €€
Seafood   **Road Map** E1
Via Lungomare 2, 98050
Tel *090-984 31 25*   **Closed** *Nov–Easter*
Set right above the harbour, this restaurant is famous for inventing *pasta al fuoco* – pasta with chopped raw cherry tomatos, chilli and grated *ricotta infornata* (oven-baked ricotta) – and for serving raw prawns with a yogurt salsa. Main courses depend on the catch of the day.

STROMBOLI: Lapillagelato   €
Gelateria   **Road Map** E1
Via Roma, 98050
Tel *333-320 89 66* **Closed** *Oct–Easter*
Home-made ice cream with natural ingredients, and no hydrogenated fats, added

colours or preservatives. Fig, dark chocolate with cinnamon and the vanilla with caramel are divine.

STROMBOLI: La Lampara   €€
Trattoria   **Road Map** E1
Via Vittorio Emanuele, 98050
Tel *090-986 009*   **Closed** *lunch; Nov–Easter*
Atmospheric place where you dine under a pergola of climbing vines among huge pots of basil and rosemary. Pizza, pasta and grilled meat and fish.

TAORMINA: Vecchia Taormina   €
Pizzeria   **Road Map** F2/3
Vico Ebrei 3, 98039
Tel *0942-625 589*
Labyrinthine, bustling pizzeria, with a few tables outside as well. Pizzas come light, blisteringly hot and bubbling, straight from the wood-fired oven.

TAORMINA: Al Duomo   €€
Traditional Sicilian   **Road Map** F2/3
Vico Ebrei 11, 98038
Tel *0942-625 656*   **Closed** *Mon in winter*
Charming little restaurant where the focus is on serving carefully sourced local ingredients in traditional rustic dishes such as *maccu* (a soup of dried broad beans), and a hearty lamb stew.

TAORMINA: Maffei's   €€€
Seafood   **Road Map** F2/3
Via San Domenico di Guzman 1, 98038
Tel *0942-240 55*   **Closed** *Jan–Feb*
Small, rather formal restaurant, with a lovely bougainvillea-shaded terrace, where the specials (based on the catch of the day) are written on a chalkboard, and courteous, knowledgeable staff take time to guide your choices.

Live music adds to the ambience at Moon, Syracuse *(see p216)*

SHOPS AND MARKETS

All the most well-known fashion designer shops can be found in the larger Sicilian cities (such as Palermo, Catania and Syracuse), together with smart chain stores stocking household articles and furniture. In tourist resorts it is possible to find shops specializing in Sicilian handicrafts, in particular ceramics, although the best items are sold in the places where they are made. Sicilian pastry shops sell delicious cakes, *cannoli* pastries, *cassata* cakes and *torroncini* (almond nougat). Keep an eye out for the delicatessens selling local specialities, such as spiced capers, *ventresca* (tuna in oil), tuna *(tonno)*, salted mullet roe *(bottarga)* and aubergine *caponata*. You can also buy excellent produce such as organic fruit, olive oil, honey and fruit jam at farmhouses offering accommodation for visitors. Another good and typically Sicilian purchase is salt.

A shop specializing in wrought-iron products

Opening Hours

Generally, shops, boutiques and department stores are open from 8 or 9am to 1pm, and in the afternoon opening hours are 4–8pm. In the summer these hours may be extended, particularly in tourist resorts. In the cities, most shops close for two or three weeks in August. Seaside resort towns, on the other hand, usually operate on a seasonal basis, opening only from June to September.

How to Pay

In the larger cities, the leading shops and department stores accept major credit cards, especially Visa and MasterCard, whereas in the towns and villages many shops still prefer cash payment. In Palermo, Catania and Syracuse, some top hotels have deals with shops and restaurants for discounts of up to 40 per cent. The concierge will be able to tell you if your hotel takes part in this scheme.

Handicrafts

Sicilian ceramics are probably the most highly appreciated handicrafts product of all. Light blue, yellow and green are the dominant colours in the lovely ceramics made in Caltagirone; they are richly decorated with volutes, flowers and geometric motifs. Tiles also come in a variety of styles. The multicoloured majolica tiles bear 9th-century motifs and can be used as decorative objects.

In Caltagirone, Sciacca, Santo Stefano di Camastra and Burgio, the main production centres for striking Sicilian ceramics, there are shops and workshops selling plates, jugs, tiles, vases, mugs and statuettes. The **Laboratorio Branciforti** in Caltagirone makes jugs, vases and dishes with traditional motifs.

At Sciacca, Salvatore Sabella translates folk designs onto plates, bottles and lamps to make original works of art at **Ceramiche Artistiche Sabella**. The **Artigianato del Sole** also has a good range: as well as dinner services, jugs and ornamental plates, they make furniture, such as tables made of lava stone, and majolica tiles. Many artisans work in wrought iron. Among the good workshops near Giarre and Giardini Naxos is the **Laboratorio Patanè** and in Cefalù, **A Lumera**.

Two traditional puppet-makers still active are **Opera dei Pupi Vaccaro** in Syracuse and **Vincenzo Argento** in Palermo, whose studios are open to the public. Another typical gift is the *coppola*, the traditional Sicilian cap.

Open-Air Markets

If you want to experience the atmosphere of the old quarters of Sicilian towns and buy local produce, you have to go to the outdoor markets. In Palermo, the **Vucciria** market, immortalized by artist Renato Guttuso, is at its most atmospheric when the fishermen are setting up their stalls. In Via Argenteria pause at the stall of **Antonino Giannusa**, who offers an amazing range of preserves as well as an excellent Palermo-style pesto sauce. Another market worth visiting is the **Ballarò**, between Piazza del Carmine and Piazza Ballarò, which is busiest around noon. In Catania, by Piazza Duomo,

Renato Guttuso's *La Vucciria* (1974), a depiction of Palermo's marketplace

there is a colourful **fish market** every morning, and produce markets at Piazza Carlo Alberto and Porta Uzeda. On Sundays the Porto di Catania area fills with an **antiques market**, offering everything from vintage household items to rare pieces of Sicilian workmanship. While out towards the airport, at the **flea market** held at the old fruit market of San Giuseppe La Rena on Viale Amerigo Vespucci, craft stalls and second-hand dealers lay out their wares.

Ice-Cream Parlours and Pastry Shops

Popular pastry shops include **Alba** and **Bar Massaro** in Palermo, **Castorina** in Acireale and **Colicchia** in Trapani, where you can enjoy coffee or an aperitif. Sicilian pastry shops are a delight for the eye and tastebuds with their *cannoli, cassata* and almond paste

Marzipan figure, an Erice speciality

cookies. Some cake shops offer their own specialities. These include the marzipan sweets with citron filling at the **Antica Pasticceria del Convento** in Erice; ricotta puff pastries at **Scivoli** in Caltagirone; vanilla- or cinnamon-flavoured chocolate at the **Antica Dolceria Bonaiuto** in Modica; ricotta and pistachio *cannoli* at **Savia** in Catania; chestnuts filled with citrus fruit jam and topped with dark chocolate at the **Caffè Sicilia** in Noto; and nougat at **Geraci**, in Caltanissetta.

Sicily is a paradise for ice-cream buffs. **Gran Caffè Eldorado**, in Acireale, serves a fantastic almond and coffee granita, and the speciality at **Stancampiano** is frozen yoghurt with blackberries or Nutella with whipped cream. In Taormina **Niny Bar** is the place to go, and in Catania it is **Saint Moritz**.

A stall with a variety of Sicilian cheese in a Catanian market

Regional Specialities

Delicatessens and *agriturismo* are ideal places for regional specialities. Smoked swordfish and tuna in oil can be found at the **Casa del Pesce** in Syracuse; salted mullet roe at **Quartana** in Erice. **Azienda Agricola Trinità** has tangerines, olive oil, honey and wine. In Ortigia, **Caseificio Borderi** offers cheeses made by dairyman Andrea Borderi and his family in accordance with old Sicilian traditions. **Fiasconaro** produces a green-golden ice cream made with Bronte pistachios and at Christmas they serve a variety of deliciously flavoured *panettoni*.

DIRECTORY

Ceramics

Artigianato del Sole
Via Santa Margherita 72, Misterbianco (Catania).
Tel 095-398 472.

Ceramiche Artistiche Sabella
Corso Vittorio Emanuele 3, Sciacca (Agrigento).
Tel 0925-847 49.
🔳 ceramiche artistiche.it

Laboratorio Branciforti
Scala S. Maria del Monte 5, Caltagirone (Catania).
Tel 0933-244 27.
🔳 www.impronta barre.it

Wrought Iron

A Lumera
Corso Re Ruggero 180, Cefalù. **Tel** 0921-921 801.
🔳 alumeracefalu.it

Laboratorio Patanè
Via Regina Margherita 111, Giardini-Naxos (Messina).
Tel 0942-511 49.

Puppets

Opera dei Pupi Vaccaro
Via Giudecca 5, Syracuse.
Tel 0931-465 540.

Vincenzo Argento
Corso Vittorio Emanuele 445, Palermo.
Tel 091-611 36 80.

Pastry Shops

Alba
Piazza Don Giovanni Bosco 7d, Palermo.

Antica Dolceria Bonaiuto
Corso Umberto I 159, Modica. **Tel** 0932-941 225.

Antica Pasticceria del Convento
Via Guarnotta Gian Filippo 1, Erice. **Tel** 0923-869 777.

Bar Massaro
Via Ernesto Basile 26, Palermo. **Tel** 091-489 922.

Caffè Sicilia
Corso Vittorio Emanuele 125, Noto (Syracuse).

Castorina
Corso Savoia 109, Acireale. **Tel** 095-601 547.

Colicchia
Via delle Arti 6, Trapani.
Tel 0923-547 612.

Geraci
Via Canonico Pulci 10, Caltanissetta.
Tel 0934-581 570.

Savia
Via Etnea 302, Catania.
Tel 095-322 335.

Scivoli
Via Milazzo 123, Caltagirone (Catania).
Tel 0933-231 08.

Ice-Cream Parlours

Gran Caffè Eldorado
Corso Umberto 3–5, Acireale. **Tel** 095-601 464.

Niny Bar
Via Vittorio Emanuele 216, Letojanni-Taormina (Messina). **Tel** 0942-361 04.

Saint Moritz
Viale Raffaello Sanzio 10, Catania. **Tel** 095-437282.

Stancampiano
Via Notarbartolo 51–56, Palermo. **Tel** 091-681 7244.

Regional Specialities

Azienda Agricola Trinità
Via Trinità 34, Mascalucia.
Tel 095-727 21 56.
🔳 aziendatrinita.it

Casa del Pesce
Via Emmanuele de Benedictis, Syracusa.
Tel 0931-691 20.

Caseificio Borderi
Via De Benedictis 6, Ortigia. **Tel** 329-985 25 00.

Fiasconaro
Piazza Margherita10, Castel-buono.
Tel 0921-677 231.

Quartana
Via Manzoni 112, Erice.
Tel 0923-539 200.

ENTERTAINMENT IN SICILY

The entertainment on offer in Sicily is wide-ranging and varied, and the programmes for cultural, musical and theatrical events are particularly imaginative. In the cities, the theatres put on a long and eclectic winter season, while in the spring and summer the ancient sites become the venues for top-level classical Greek theatre and symphony concerts. There are also many cultural events connected with artists and personalities who have contributed to Sicily's colourful history. Added to this, there are numerous folk festivals and vibrant carnival celebrations. Far from being performed for the benefit of tourists, these are genuine expressions of the spirit of Sicily. The nightlife is lively in the main towns and the seaside resorts also stay active until the small hours.

Practical Information

Information in English about what is on in Sicily is difficult to find, but there are several excellent Italian-language websites that offer up to date details on events. The most informative for the island as a whole is www.lasicilia.com/eventi_sicilia.cfm, which lists events in all nine provinces for any particular day. For Palermo, www.palermoweb.com provides a comprehensive guide to entertainment in Sicily's largest city.

The site www.sicilycinema.it offers a complete guide to what is playing in all of the island's cinemas.

Booking Tickets

There are several nationwide booking agencies operating in Sicily, including **Box Office** and **Feltrinelli**. Each of these has offices in the main Sicilian centres. The more prominent theatres and music venues also have their own websites where you can book online.

Opera, Theatre and Classical Music

Palermo's **Teatro Massimo** stages a year-long opera programme that includes favourites such as Verdi and Puccini alongside more contemporary composers, like Samuel Barber. The theatre's orchestra readily embraces an eclectic mix of music, including tribute bands to The Beatles. The **Teatro Politeama Garibaldi**, home to the Sicilian Symphony Orchestra, hosts classical music concerts throughout the year, as well as artists such as Paolo Conte.

Palermo's main playhouse is the **Teatro Biondo**, the repertoire of which ranges from Greek tragedies and Tennessee Williams to August Strindberg and Eduardo De Filippo. With its great acoustics, Catania's **Teatro Massimo Bellini** is a favourite with performers. The opera season lasts all year, while the Bellini Orchestra's concert season runs from October to June. The 477-seat **Teatro**

Programme for a performance at the Teatro Greco in Syracuse

Sangiorgi, owned by Teatro Bellini, stages contemporary music, chamber music, operetta and experimental theatre. Catania's chief theatre is the **Teatro Stabile**, which presents mainstream drama by the likes of Shakespeare, Molière and Pirandello.

Sicily's ancient Greek and Roman outdoor theatres come into their own in the warmer months, providing spectacular settings for traditional and modern drama. One of the best known is the **Teatro Greco** in Syracuse, a large and well-preserved monument dating back to the 5th century BC. A classical theatre season is held here every year in May and June (see p42).

Every year, Segesta's temple is the atmospheric backdrop for both traditional and modern plays (see p42), while Taormina's ancient Greek theatre plays host to music and drama during **Taormina Arte** (see p43), a series of events running from June to

Live performances are always popular in the summer months

September. In early June, the theatre stages La Kore, the fashion world's equivalent of the Academy Awards.

Each year Agrigento pays tribute to Luigi Pirandello, the great Sicilian novelist and playwright. In December, the Convegno di Studi Pirandelliani *(see p45)*, held at the **Centro Nazionale Studi Pirandelliani**, provides an opportunity for students to visit the places that inspired him. The event includes lectures and performances of his plays.

You don't need to understand Italian to appreciate a good puppet show. Puppet theatre reached the height of its popularity in the mid-1800s, but there has been renewed interest in this traditional art. Based on local folklore and comedy and usually involving one of Charlemagne's knights, Orlando, fighting the Saracens, puppet theatre is performed throughout Sicily.

In Palermo the **Museo Internazionale delle Marionette** puts on interesting tourist performances and also stages an annual international puppet festival

The scenic setting of a classical production at the Teatro Greco in Syracuse

(see p45), but for a more authentic experience, visit the delightful **Cuticchio Puppet Theatre**. Puppet shows can also be enjoyed in Acireale and Syracuse.

Cinema

At Taormina's annual **FilmFest**, movies are screened in the ancient Greek theatre, against the dramatic backdrop of Mount Etna. At over 50 years old, this is the longest lasting film festival in Italy after Venice.

Today its focus is predominantly on new directors and films emerging from developing countries.

Lipari, in the Aeolian Islands, hosts its own film festival, **Un Mare di Cinema**, in the first week of August. Since 1990, directors and actors have vied for the festival's prestigious Etesto d'Oro prize.

Sicily is also a popular film location *(see p28)*. Sicilian director Giuseppe Tornatore filmed his Academy Award-winning *Cinema Paradiso* (1989) in Palazzo Adriano near Palermo, and his wartime film *Malena* (2000) was also shot in various locations on the island, including Messina, Siracusa, Noto and Taormina. His film *Baaria* (2009), showcased at the Venice Film Festival, was about his hometown of Bagheria and its post-war history. Filmed almost

completely on the Aeolian island of Salina, Michael Radford's poignant *Il Postino* (1994) features some splendid scenes shot around the village of Pollara.

Carnivals and Folk Festivals

February is carnival time in Italy, and this period is also celebrated with enthusiasm in many Sicilian towns. One of the most spectacular events is the **Carnevale di Acireale** *(see p45)*, blending poetry, games, music, dance and a procession of colourful floats through the town centre. The carnival continues for a number of days and on the last night it ends with a brilliant fireworks display. The famous **Carnevale di Sciacca** *(see p45)* is symbolized by a huge puppet and a procession of floats through the town's streets. In the same month, the people of Catania worship the memory of **Sant'Agata** *(see p45)*, whose relics, including a veil that the faithful believe once shielded Catania from lava erupting out of nearby Mount Etna, are carried through the town.

In Agrigento, the imminent arrival of spring is celebrated each February with the **Festa del Mandorlo in Fiore** *(see p45)*. As the fragrant smell of almond blossom fills the air, a procession makes its way to the lovely Valle dei Templi. Coinciding with this is the **Folklore Festival** *(see p45)*,

A traditional Sicilian puppet in full armoured suit

Carnival time in Sicily spells a week of crowds and colour

featuring dance, traditional costumes and music.

Noto also welcomes spring, but not until the third week in May, with **L'Infiorata** *(see p42)*, which sees the laying down of a carpet of flowers arranged to depict religious or mythological themes.

Easter is an important time for religious festivals. In Caltanissetta, a week is given over to processions, including the Good Friday carrying of a crucifix made of black wood, which was found in a cave in 1625 *(see p42)*. A week-long festival held in Enna culminates on Easter Sunday, when images of Christ and the Madonna are brought together in the Piazza Duomo *(see p42)*. Trapani's **Mystery Procession** *(see p42)* is almost 400 years old. Winding its way through the town, it showcases 20 wooden and fabric sculptures embellished with silver, and each one is carried on the shoulders of at least ten men.

Caltigirone produces a dazzling spectacle for the feast of its patron saint, the **Festa di San Giacomo** *(see p43)*, with 4,000 candles illuminating the 142 steps of the Scala di Santa Maria del Monte.

In July, the feast day of the patron saint of Palermo, **Santa Rosalia** *(see p43)*, involves actors and musicians recreating the arrival of the Flemish painter Antony van Dyck, who visited Palermo in 1624 and painted Saint Rosalia interceding to rescue the town from the plague. In August, Piazza Armerina celebrates its French heritage with the **Palio dei Normanni** *(see p43)*. The three days of festivities begin with a re-enactment of Roger I's entrance into the town and culminate in a medieval tournament.

Christmas is the occasion for a number of festivals. The town of Agira, near Enna, is the setting of the only **Presepe Vivente** (Nativity play) in Italy to take place on Christmas night. More than 100 players in period costume take part in the festival, which also features ancient crafts such as spinning, carpentry and pasta-making.

Another fascinating Presepe Vivente is played out in the northwestern town of Custonaci, in a cave called Grotta Mangiapane, named after the family that lived in it from the 1800s until 1945.

Traditional and Popular Music

Traditional Sicilian folk music has a loyal following. Among the best-known exponents are Carmelo Salemi and Giancarlo Parisi, players of the *zampogna* (bagpipes), *friscalettu* and other Sicilian wind instruments. They are regular performers at festivals such as Agrigento's **Folklore Festival** *(see p45)*, Taormina's **Womad**, Palermo's **World Festival on the Beach** and the **Ortygia Festival**.

Jazz also finds a dedicated audience. The Palermo-based Brass Group, an association that promotes this genre of music, has its headquarters in a historic building called **Lo Spasimo**, which is also home to the Sicilian Jazz Orchestra. In Catania the best place for live music is **La Chiave**, where they play blues on Thursdays and jazz on Sundays.

Nightlife

Sicily's lively nightlife centres on the cities in winter and the tourist resorts in summer. Discos often charge a cover fee that can be as high as €20.

Palermo has its share of pubs, including **Mikalsa**, **Agricantus** and **Cambio Cavalli**. New musical talent is showcased at the **Biergarten**, **I Candelai** and **Malox**. Popular discos in the inner city are **Tonnara Florio**, in the ancient district of Arenella, the **Anticlea Pub** and the **Country Club**, whose large dance floors become open-air in summer. Outside central Palermo are well-known discos like **Il Moro** and **Kandinsky Florio**.

Located just out of Catania is **Banacher**, an outdoor club that attracts a mix of locals and tourists; here you can dance amid a maze of plants.

Buzzing Taormina caters for all tastes, from casual cafés to late-night discos. **La Giara** is a popular apéritif and after-dinner drink spot that does not get crowded until after 10pm. **Bar Morgana** is for the young and fashionable and is open till late. In the seaside town of Giardini Naxos is **Marabù**, a beautiful open-air disco where you can dance until the early hours.

Catania boasts one of the most vivacious nightlife scenes in Sicily

DIRECTORY

Bookings

Box Office
Via Cavour 133, Palermo.
Map 1 C2. **Tel** 091-335 566. Via G Leopardi 95, Catania. **Tel** 095-722 53 40.

Feltrinelli Palermo
Via Camillo 133, Palermo.
Map C2. **Tel** 091-588 581/781 291.
w lafeltrinelli.it

Ticket One
w ticketone.it

Opera, Theatre and Classical Music

Centro Nazionale Studi Pirandelliani
Vicolo Santa Lucia 1, Agrigento. **Tel** 0922-290 52.
w cnsp.it

Cuticchio Puppet Theatre
Via Bara all'Olivella 95, Palermo. **Map** 1 B2.
Tel 091-323 400.
w figlidarte cuticchio.com

Museo Internazionale delle Marionette
Piazzetta A. Pasqualino 5. **Map** 2 E3. **Tel** 091-328 060.
w museomarionette palermo.it

Teatro Politeama Garibaldi
Piazza Ruggero Settimo, Palermo. **Map** 1 A/B1.
Tel 091-607 25 11/32.

Taormina Arte
Tel 0942-211 42.
w taormina-arte.com

Teatro Biondo Stabile
Via Teatro Biondo 11, Palermo. **Map** 1 C3.
Tel 091-743 43 00.

Teatro delle Marionette
Via Nazionale per Catania 195, Acireale.
Tel 095-764 80 35 or 347-806 14 14.
w operadeipupi.com

Teatro delle Marionette
Via Giudecca 5, Syracuse. **Tel** 093-146 55 40.
w pupari.com

Antica Compagnia Opera dei Pupi Famiglia Puglisi
Via Catullo 2, Sortino, Syracuse. **Tel** 0931-965 496.

Teatro Greco
Corso Gelone 103, Syracuse. **Tel** 0931-487 248/200.
w indafondazione.org

Teatro Massimo
Piazza Giuseppe Verdi, Palermo. **Map** 1 B2.
Tel 091-605 32 67.
w teatromassimo.it

Teatro Massimo Bellini
Via Perrota 12, Catania.
Tel 095-730 61 11.
w teatromassimo bellini.it

Teatro Sangiorgi
Via A di Sangiuliano 233, Catania. **Tel** 095-730 61 11.
w teatromassimo bellini.it/sangiorgi.asp

Teatro Stabile
Via Fava 39, Catania.
Tel 095-731 08 11/88.
w teatrostabile catania.it

Cinema

Taormina FilmFest
Tel 094-223 243.
w taorminafilmfest.it

Un Mare di Cinema
Lipari. **Tel** 090-981 29 87.
w centrostudieolie.it

Carnivals and Folk Festivals

Carnevale di Acireale
Acireale. **w** carnevale acireale.com

Carnevale di Sciacca
Sciacca.
w carnevaledisciacca.it

Feste del Mandorlo in Fiore
Agrigento. **Tel** 0922-250 19. **w** sagradel mandorlo.net

Festa di San Giacomo
Caltagirone.
Tel 093-353 809.

Festa di Sant'Agata
Catania. **Tel** 800 841 042.
w comune.catania.it/ la_citta/santagata

Festa di Santa Rosalia
Palermo. **Tel** 091-540 326.
w santuariosanta rosalia.it

Folklore Festival
Agrigento.
w sagradelmand orlo.net

L'Infiorata
Noto.
w infioratadinoto.it

Mystery Procession
Trapani. **Tel** 092-354 55 11.
w processione misteritp.it

Palio dei Normanni
Piazza Armerina. **Tel** 0935-681 641.
w paliodeinormanni.it

Presepe Vivente
Agira.
w agira.org/Presepe-Vivente/

Presepe Vivente
Custonaci. **Tel** 340-143 22 91. **w** presepevivente dicustonaci.it

Traditional and Popular Music

La Chiave
Via Landolina 64, Catania.
Tel 347-948 09 10.

Lo Spasimo
Via Dello Spasimo 15, Palermo. **Tel** 091-616 64 80.
w thebrassgroup.it

Womad
Taormina. **w** womad.org

World Festival on the Beach
Palermo. **w** wwfestival. com

Nightlife

Agricantus
Via XX Settembre 82, Palermo. **Tel** 091-309 636.

Anticlea Pub
Viale Galatea 6, Palermo.
Tel 091-346 762.

Banacher
Via Vampolieri 2, Aci Castello. **Tel** 095-271 024 or 347-372 39 01.

Bar Morgana
Scesa Morgana 4, Taormina.
Tel 094-262 00 56.

Biergarten
Viale Regione Siciliana 6469, Palermo.
Tel 347-304 68 46 or 340-615 74 56.

Cambio Cavalli
Via Patania 54, Palermo.
Map 1 C2.
Tel 091-581 418.

I Candelai
Via dei Candelai 65, Palermo. **Map** 1 B3.
Tel 091-327 151.

Country Club
Via dell'Olimpo 5, Palermo. **Tel** 091-982 16 50 or 331-251 59 98.

La Giara
Vico La Floresta 1, Taormina.
Tel 094-223 360.

Kandinsky Florio
Via Discesa Tonnara, Palermo.

Malox
Piazzetta della Canna 8–9, Palermo. **Map** 1 B3.
Tel 392-499 68 94.

Marabù
Via Iannuzzo, Giardini Naxos, Taormina.
Tel 392-077 23 58.

Mikalsa Pub
Via Torremuzza 27, Palermo.
Tel 339-314 64 66.

Il Moro
Via M. Pottino 3, Palermo.
Tel 091-546 213.

Tonnara Florio
Piazza Tonnara 4, Palermo.
Tel 091-637 56 11.
w tonnara florio.com

SPECIALIST HOLIDAYS AND OUTDOOR ACTIVITIES

For most visitors to Sicily, sporting activities tend to be water-based: swimming, fishing, windsurfing and diving in the crystal-clear waters off the extensive coast and the many islands that dot the Tyrrhenian and Mediterranean seas. Sailing enthusiasts have a vast choice of enticing routes on a variety of charter craft. There are plenty of other outdoor activities to enjoy too, such as hiking along old pathways in the Madonie and Nebrodi mountains or on Mount Etna. In the winter, the snowy slopes of the imposing volcano provide good conditions for downhill as well as cross-country skiing. Horse riding, including organized programmes of long-distance trekking, is also becoming increasingly popular in Sicily. Visitors can embark on many of these activities under their own steam, though an ever-growing number of local and overseas agencies offer a good choice of all-inclusive outdoor and sporting holidays.

Sailing has become an increasingly popular activity in Sicily

Sailing

The coastline and inlets of Sicily and the region's wonderful islands are a paradise for sailing aficionados, and the sport is especially popular along the island's northern coast. True to their name – derived from the Greek god of wind – the Aeolian Islands (see pp192–5) guarantee a constant stiff breeze, as does the distant Pelagie archipelago (see pp128–9) off the south-western coast.

In 2005, the international races held in the waters off the coast of Trapani as part of the prestigious America's Cup trials represented a landmark event for Sicily. This, along with the coming and going of yachts from all over Europe, has had a very positive influence of late, triggering a series of improvements in nautical tourism facilities in the many port towns along the coast.

Yachts of varying sizes and degrees of comfort are available for charter at ports all around the island through companies such as **Onda Eoliana**. Many nautical centres hold sailing courses for the uninitiated, including **Centro Vela** in Lampedusa, though qualified multilingual crews can always be requested to transport passengers who desire a thoroughly relaxing sailing experience. **Syracuse Sailing Team** offers a number of trips around Sicily's islands and **EtnaSail** can arrange an unusual trip in a traditional Turkish-style *caicco* boat.

The **Velalinks** website (www.velalinks.it) is helpful in locating charter companies and instructors. There are also several UK-based companies that organize all-inclusive sailing holidays.

Windsurfing

This energetic sport can be practised at most Sicilian seaside resorts thanks to conditions that guarantee constant winds. Virtually every beach in Sicily offers rental facilities. Mondello beach (see p76), just outside Palermo, is well-served by **Albaria Windsurfing Club**. However, expert windsurfers claim that the best places for the sport are the Aeolian Islands and the Capo Passero area (see p152) in the south where the Ionian and Mediterranean seas merge. This same area is also favoured by kitesurfers. The popular beach location of Pozzallo has rental facilities, and expert instruction for different abilities is also available. The **Kitesicilia** website (www.kitesicilia.it) offers suggestions on the island's hot spots and a list of local contacts.

Windsurfers can often be spotted in the waters around Sicily

Diving

The sea beds around Sicily are the delight and joy of scuba- and free-divers, who head for the offshore islands – especially the Aeolians (see pp192–5), which are of volcanic origin. The island of Ustica (see p113) has a marvellous marine reserve, making it an ideal spot for underwater sports. Agencies here include **Alta Marea**, which offers diving courses for all levels of experience, and **Barracuda**.

Almost in Tunisian waters, the Pelagie islands of Pantelleria (see p128) and Lampedusa (see p129) offer superb diving in brilliantly clear waters. As well as fish, you may spot some historical artifacts such as Roman amphorae from an ancient shipwreck on the sea bed. **Divex Centro Subacqueo** has a particularly good range of diving trips from Pantelleria. Generally speaking, most seaside resorts offer at least basic diving facilities, including refills of your oxygen cylinder. The resort of Terrasini, on the coast west of Palermo, offers both instructors and facilities.

If you are planning to dive independently, always make sure that someone knows of your whereabouts and plans. The Italian website **Dive Italy** has useful information and a number of operators, such as **The Sicilian Experience**, can organize diving holidays.

The crystal-clear waters that surround the Aeolian Islands favour snorkelling and diving

Walking and Trekking

There is an impressive range of rewarding walking itineraries all over Sicily. The choice includes hills, mountains, coastal districts and fantastic limestone gorges such as the ones at Pantalica

The rugged coastline in the Riserva dello Zingaro, ideal for hiking

(see p161) and Cava d'Ispica (see p153) in the Monti Iblei (Hyblaei Hills). The protected park area around Mount Etna (see pp174–7) offers marvellous opportunities for high-altitude trips among the lava fields and grottoes. Qualified leaders from **Etna Guides** escort thrilling climbs to the smoking summit craters. To the east is the Alcantara river valley (see p185), which offers easy routes through old settlements and a fascinating basalt ravine gouged out by the impetuous watercourse.

The rugged Madonie mountains and park feature spectacular panoramas, marked paths and rare vegetation in the Vallone Madonna degli Angeli, near Piano Battaglia (see p98) and the Pizzo Carbonara summit.

Highlights of the vast, rolling Nebrodi mountain chain (see p190), another protected area, include the Biviere di Cesarò, a pretty lake and important staging point for migratory birds. **Parco Regionale dei Monti Nebrodi** provides extensive and helpful information about the area. Close by, and towering over the village of Alcara Li Fusi, is the dramatic Rocche di Crasto, home to the griffon vulture.

These impressive rock formations are accessible on clear paths. Other interesting areas for walkers include Piana degli Albanesi (see p100) and the divine coastline of the **Riserva dello Zingaro** (see p101).

Several islands have unusual walking opportunities, such as the Aeolians (see pp192–5), with ascents of volcanoes, both extinct and active, on Stromboli (where a guide is essential), Vulcano, Salina and Lipari. **Magma Trek's** tour leaders are particularly knowledgeable about the science and history of Stromboli's active volcano.

In both the interior and main cities of Sicily, visitors can find a number of sports associations and guesthouses offering trekking holidays and excursions. **Club Alpino Italiano** also organizes excursions on a regular basis, as does **Explore Worldwide**.

The awesome ravine gouged out of the basalt rock by the course of the Alcantara river

Horse riding on a Sicilian beach

Horse Riding

This popular activity is gathering an increasingly loyal following, especially among local inhabitants. Sicily's rugged, mountainous interior is perfectly suited to horse riding, featuring numerous routes that are easily accessible from village centres.

One particularly interesting multi-day itinerary is the one that stretches for 70 km (43.5 miles) and runs east to west along the central ridge of the Nebrodi mountain range (see p190), following age-old droving routes. This region is home to 5,000 native horses, a pretty, dark variety known as San Fratellino. Believed to descend from an ancient breed known to the Greeks and Romans, the horses are left to graze freely.

Many *agriturismo* farms and some of the larger holiday villages have riding schools that cater to varying levels of ability. Tucked away in the divine Anapo Valley (see p161) near a wild gorge, **Pantalica Ranch** arranges horse riding trips. **Centro Ippico Amico del Cavallo** is an equestrian centre based in Misterbianco, close to Catania, which offers one-day trips as well as longer treks on horseback. There are also many establishments dotted around the slopes of Mount Etna offering various horse riding excursions.

For further information on the most important horse riding centres in Sicily, contact the **Associazione Nazionale Turismo Equestre** (ANTE) in Rome.

Making the most of the brief skiing season on Mount Etna

Skiing

If the weather is good, the panorama from the slopes of Mount Etna (see pp174–7) is simply awe-inspiring, with the sea at Taormina mirroring the sunlight and the volcano's fumes rising lazily above you.

However, do not expect to find state-of-the-art skiing facilities here. There is no artificial snow (the perennial drought in Sicily precludes anything of the kind), and the heat of the volcano tends to melt the snow in a hurry, so the skiing season is limited to a few

months, from late December until March. Thanks to a cable-car and four ski lifts, you can ski up to 3,000 m (9,850 ft) above sea level on the runs around **Rifugio Sapienza** and the old Montagnola crater.

On the northern flank of the mountain, reconstruction of both facilities and runs continues in the wake of destructive 2002 eruptions that all but wiped out the small-scale resort of Piano Provenzana (see p176).

Perfect for all age groups, the thrill of tobogganing is another good, fun activity. Mount Etna is not only for downhill-skiing enthusiasts, though their numbers continue to grow with each year. There is also a beaten track near the Grande Albergo, just below Rifugio Sapienza, which is ideal for cross-country skiing.

The volcano also attracts lovers of alpine techniques, telemarking and even the increasingly popular pursuit of snowshoeing; real off-the-beaten-track activities.

The wonderfully wild Nebrodi range (see p190) also gets a decent snow cover and offers many opportunities for exploration with cross-country skis and snowshoes. Piano Battaglia (see p98), in the Madonie mountains, attracts weekenders from Palermo for its lovely, if limited, pistes and lifts.

Finally, thrill-seekers will enjoy the uniquely Sicilian sport of travelling down the black volcanoes of the Aeolian Islands (see pp192–5) on a snowboard. But be warned, the dry lava surface is much harder than snow.

Snowboarding on a lava field on Vulcano, one of the Aeolian Islands

DIRECTORY

Sailing

Centro Nautica
(charter & rental) Baia
Levante, Vulcano. **Tel** 393-
915 19 01 or 339-337 27
95. W baialevante.it

Centro Vela
(courses) Lampedusa.
Tel 333-540 13 60.
W centrovela
lampedusa.com

Coastguard
Emergencies at sea:
Tel 1530.
W guardiacostiera.it

Etnasail
Catania **Tel** 095-712 69
52. W etnasail.com

Gulliver
(rental & courses)
Favignana. **Tel** 0923-921
011 or 333 201 33 11.
W gullivervela.it

Harbour Office
Lipari. **Tel** 090-981 13 20.

Harbour Office
Ustica. **Tel** 091-844 96 52.

Nauta
(charter & rental) Lipari.
Tel 090-982 23 05.

Nautica Levante
(charter & rental) Salina.
Tel 368-675 795, 348-469
94 91 or 338-690 04 03.
W nauticalevante.it

Onda Eoliana
(rental) **Tel** 090-984 42 00
or 339-776 80 98.
W ondaeoliana.com

Orzare
(charter, rental & courses)
Catania. **Tel** 349-818 60
07. W orzare.it

Sailing Information
W windfinder.com/
forecast/lampedusa

Seacilia
(charter, rental & courses)
Pantelleria. **Tel** 338 299
45 35.
W seacilia.it

**Syracuse Sailing
Team**
(charter) **Tel** 0931-608 08.
W sailingteam.biz

Trinacria Sailing
Tel 348-409 61 61.
W trinacriasailing.com

Velalinks
W velalinks.it

Windsurfing

**Albaria Windsurfing
Club**
Tel 091-453 595.
W albaria.org

Kitesicilia
Tel 333-633 85 44.
W kitesicilia.it

Diving

Alta Marea
Ustica. **Tel** 347-175 72 55
or 338-185 02 89.
W altamareaustica.it

Barracuda
Ustica. **Tel** 370-718 16 21.
W barracudaustica.com

**Centro Immersioni Lo
Verde**
Lampedusa.
Tel 0922-971 986.
W lampedusadiving
loverde.it

Dive Italy
W diveitaly.com

**Divex Centro
Subacqueo**
Pantelleria. **Tel** 345 037
95 77.
W pantelleriadiving.it

**Diving Center
La Gorgonia**
Lipari. **Tel** 335-571 75 67
or 360-863 455.
W liparidivingcenter.it

Diving Cala Levante
Tel 0923-915 174.
W calalevante.it

Hospital
(hyperbaric chamber)
Tel 090-988 51

**La Sirenetta Diving
Center**
Stromboli. **Tel** 338-891 96
75 or 347-596 14 99.
W lasirenettadiving.it

Lipari Diving Centre
Tel 338-298 35 95.
W liparidivingcenter.it

Profondo Blu
Tel 091-844 96 09.
W ustica-diving.it

Ricarica ARA
Filicudi. **Tel** 090-988 99 84.

Ricarica ARA
Diving Center La
Gorgonia
Tel 090-981 26 16.
W lagorgoniadiving.it

**Ricarica ARA di
Rosalia Ailara**
Tel 091-844 96 05.
W ustica-ara.it

Salina Diving
Tel 338-495 90 80.
W salinadiving.com

Scubaland
Tel 335-844 33 53.

**The Sicilian
Experience**
6 Palace Street, London
SW1E 5HY. **Tel** 020-7828
9171. W thesicilian
experience.co.uk

**Sotto l'Acqua del
Vulcano**
Tel 090-986 390.

Walking and
Trekking

Club Alpino Italiano
Catania. **Tel** 095-715 35
15. W caicatania.it
Palermo. **Tel** 091-329 407.

Etna Guides
Tel 095-791 47 55 or 389-
349 60 86.
W etnaguide.com

Explore Worldwide
W explore.co.uk

Magma Trek
Stromboli. **Tel** 090-986 57
68. W magmatrek.it

Parco dell'Etna
Nicolosi. **Tel** 095-821 111.
W parcoetna.it

**Parco Fluviale
dell'Alcantara**
Francavilla di Sicilia.
Tel 0942-98 99.
W parcoalcantara.it

Parco delle Madonie
Petralia Sottana. **Tel** 0921-
684 011. W parcodelle
madonie.it

**Parco Regionale dei
Monti Nebrodi**
Caronia. **Tel** 0921-333 015
(cross-country ski info:
095-697 818).
W parcodeinebrodi.it

Riserva dello Zingaro
Tel 0924-351 08 or 800-
116 616.
W riservazingaro.it

Horse Riding

**Associazione
Nazionale Turismo
Equestre**
Rome. **Tel** 06-3265 0230.
W fitetrec-ante.it

**Centro Guide
Equestri Ambientali
Sanconese**
Tel 339-620 62 89.
W meinfo.it/gea

**Centro Ippico Amico
del Cavallo**
Misterbianco. **Tel** 095-461
882 or 329 950 98 49.
W amicodelcavallo.
com

Pantalica Ranch
Tel 0931-954 425.
W pantalicaranch.it

Rifugio Villa Miraglia
Portella Femmina Morta,
Nebrodi. **Tel** 095-697 397.

Skiing

Funivia dell'Etna
Tel 095-911 158 or 094-
191 41 41/2.
W funiviaetna.com

**Rifugio Ostello della
Gioventù**
Piano Battaglia. **Tel** 0921-
649 995.

Rifugio Sapienza
Tel 095-915 321.
W rifugiosapienza.com

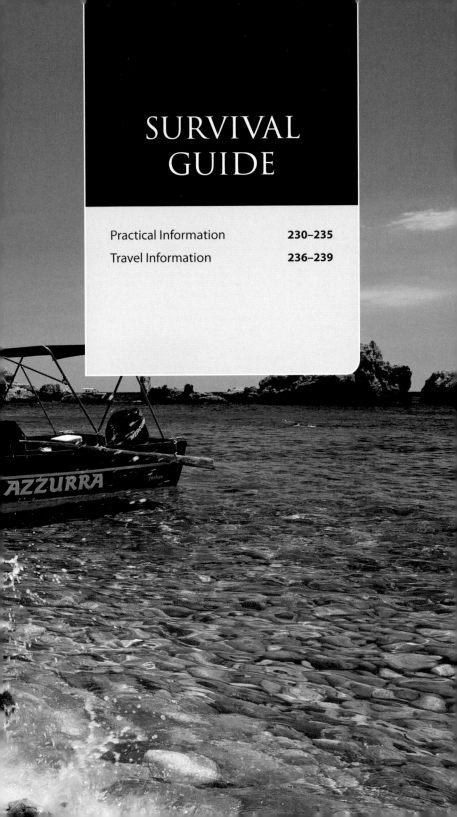

SURVIVAL
GUIDE

PRACTICAL INFORMATION

The Sicilian coastline, one of the most beautiful in Italy, attracts thousands of visitors every year. The island's unique history and artistic and cultural heritage, as well as its numerous spectacular monuments, are as much an attraction – if not a greater one – than its marvellous landscape. But whenever your reason for visiting the island known to the ancients as Trinacria, there is always something exciting to explore. Everyone comes expecting to enjoy the food and wine, the coastline and art treasures, as well as sports activities and spas.

When to Go

Sicily enjoys a Mediterranean climate, with hot, dry summers and mild to cold, rainy winters. From late March to June and from September to October, the pleasant weather allows for plenty of time outdoors. Those interested in Sicilian history and culture would do well to plan their visit for a time other than the crowded – and very hot – months of July and August. Spring and autumn are the best seasons to visit inland areas, including Mount Etna, the Madonie mountains and the Riserva dello Zingaro nature reserve.

Visas & Passports

European Union (EU) residents and visitors from the US, Canada, New Zealand and Australia need no visa for a stay of up to three months. Information concerning visas can be obtained in advance at your nearest Italian consulate. Non-EU citizens must carry a valid passport, while for EU citizens any ID will suffice. By law you must carry your ID with you at all times, as it may be needed during a road block (*see p232*).

Customs Information

Any customs formalities are completed at the first Italian arrival point (usually the mainland). Non-EU citizens can claim back sales tax (IVA) on purchases costing over €154.94. Consulates can generally provide up-to-date information on particular customs regulations.

Tourist Information

The provincial capitals of Sicily have an official tourist board, the Servizio Turistico Regionale (STR), which generally includes *Unità Operative* (Operating Units) or smaller bureaus located in towns within the provincial capital. Brochures and information on how to organize your trip are available at **STR** offices, **Town Halls**, Pro Locos (local tourist information points), or the **Assessorato al Turismo della Regione Sicilia** in Palermo.

Admission Prices

Entrance fees for museums and archaeological sites vary from €2 to €10. Young people and senior citizens are usually allowed in free of charge or pay a reduced fee. If reductions are available, a valid form of identification will be needed.

Opening Hours

Sicilian museums and archaeological sites are usually open every day in the morning except on Monday. Most churches in Sicily are open to the public for morning and evening mass. If a church is closed, you can always try asking the priest or sacristan to let you in for a brief visit.

Off season, most hotels, especially those along the coast, remain closed, so if you plan to travel during the winter months, it is advisable to book well in advance.

One of the special characteristics of Sicilian life is that people dine later than on the mainland, particularly in summer when the weather can be very hot. The midday meal may begin as late as 2pm, and evening meals may not be served until 10pm. Restaurants are closed one day a week and for annual holidays, usually in the winter.

Shops are open Monday to Saturday from 8 or 9am until 1pm and then from 4 to 8pm (in the winter), or 4:30/5pm to 8:30/9:00pm (in the summer). With the exception of shopping centres and DIY stores, most shops are closed on Sundays and Monday mornings.

Travellers with Special Needs

Sicily is not particularly well organized to cater for disabled visitors; however conditions for

Tourist information sign

Souvenir shop selling local craft items in Taormina

travellers with special needs are improving throughout the island. Ramps, lifts and modified WCs are available in an increasing number of places. Some restaurants have wheelchair access to the dining area, but not to the WC.

For those travelling without an escort to Sicily, it is best to consider a specially designed package tour, or contact an organization for disabled travellers before you set off.

Visitors travelling by train can request **RFI** (Italian Railway Network) assistance at the Sala Blu at Messina train station, by calling their National Telephone Number or by contacting **Trenitalia**'s call centre.

A street artist sketches a child's portrait in Piazza IX Aprile, Taormina

Travelling with Children

Sicily is great for travelling with children and Sicilians are very welcoming to families. Numerous castles can be found all across the island and exploring them is a fun-filled activity for curious youngsters and history enthusiasts. An excursion to spectacular Mount Etna (see pp174–7) is also a delightful and easily accessible family adventure.

Children will enjoy spending time at the many public beaches, which are located all around the Sicilian coastline. The temperature of the sea is warm from June to October, so swimming is pleasant.

Theme parks are becoming increasingly popular in Sicily. Take the kids and head for **Etnaland**, a theme park near

Catania, **Bioparco di Sicilia** or **Parco Avventura Madonie** near Palermo.

Most restaurants welcome children (see p207), and many offer Sicily's tastiest summer speciality, ice-cream.

For a family holiday with a difference, consider staying in a rural area of Sicily on a working farm (agriturismi), where children can watch products being made (see p200).

Travelling on a Budget

Accommodation can be the biggest expense when visiting Sicily, but if planned carefully there are ways to save money. Renting a self-catering holiday-house can be a good choice for either long or short stays and buying fresh local produce at the supermarkets can help reduce food costs. Other good budget options include B&Bs, which are found both in the towns and on the coast, or staying at a traditional farm-house (agriturismi) in the countryside (see p200). Hostels are rare, but campsites abound along the coastal regions and are considered the most basic and cheapest form of accommodation (see p199).

Eating at a trattoria or agriturismi is a cheaper alternative to the smarter or more touristy restaurants, and is also a great way to savour local and traditional specialities.

Responsible Tourism

Environmental awareness has been slowly gathering strength in Sicily and several initiatives have been put in place across the main towns. Recycling is gradually being introduced in some places. Supermarkets no longer use non-biodegradable plastic bags. Sicilians are also starting to understand the importance of reducing carbon emissions and, as a result, organic shops, restaurants and street markets are springing up across the island.

Staying at family-run guest-houses or on an agriturismi helps support local economies.

DIRECTORY

Tourist Information

Assessorato al Turismo della Regione Sicilia
Via Notarbartolo 9, Palermo.
Tel 091-7078 100/230/276.
🅦 regione.sicilia.it/turismo

STR Agrigento
Tel 0922-203 91.

STR Palermo
Tel 091-6398 011.
🅦 palermotourism.com

STR Syracuse
Tel 0931-464 255.
🅦 siracusaturismo.net

STR Taormina
Tel 0942-232 43 or 232.

STR Trapani
Tel 0923-565 412/872 652/543 427.

Town Hall Info Point
Tel 091-611 7887.

Travellers with Special Needs

RFI
Tel 199-30 30 60 (National Telephone Number).
🅦 rfi.it

Trenitalia
Tel 892 021 (Italian State Railways); 199-89 20 21 (Trenitalia's call centre).
🅦 trenitalia.com

Travelling with Children

Bioparco di Sicilia
Via A.Vespucci 420 - 90044, Carini, Palermo province.
Tel 091-867 6811/348-580 23 34.
🅦 bioparcodisicilia.it

Etnaland
C.da Agnelleria, 95032 Belpasso, Catania province.
Tel 095-7913334.
🅦 etnaland.eu

Parco Avventura Madonie
Località Gorgonero, 90027 Petralia Sottana.
Tel 0921-639 80 28/800 234 169.
🅦 parcoavventuramadonie.it

Personal Security and Health

On the whole, Sicily is a safe, unthreatening place for visitors. In the cities and at busy tourist spots, such as the ferry ports and main stations, it is wise to keep a close eye on your belongings. Do not carry more money than needed for the day. Also, avoid leaving valuables in your car, especially if the parking area is unattended. However, in the smaller towns, villages and rural areas, petty crime is rare.

A typical *vigili urbani* (municipal police) car

Police

There are several different police forces in Sicily. The state police, *polizia*, wear blue uniforms and deal with criminal offences or issue *permessi di soggiorno* (residence permits) to foreigners and passports to Italian citizens. The *vigili urbani*, or municipal police, wear blue uniforms in winter and white in summer, and issue heavy fines for traffic and parking offences. They can usually be spotted patrolling the streets and regulating traffic. The military police or *carabinieri* wear red-striped trousers and manage offences ranging from theft to speeding. The *guardia di finanza*, or the tax police, wear grey uniforms and deal with tax evasion and customs. Crimes should be reported to the police or at the *carabinieri* office,

where you can get a signed form that you will need when making an insurance claim. If your car has been towed away, request the help of the *vigili urbani* on the street.

What to Be Aware Of

When travelling it is best not to carry large sums of money. Visitors should be wary of bag snatchers who operate in quiet streets and especially in cities such as Palermo or Catania. Take proper care of your valuables in a crowded and busy market place or while using public transport. Also, beware of beggars and pickpockets.

Women travelling alone, or even in small groups, may need to take extra care when going out at night.

It is advisable to stay away from unauthorized minicab drivers, who are not insured and frequently overcharge. In particular, they operate at airports and train stations. Hotel touts and unofficial tour guides are also best avoided; instead stick to the official tourist agencies.

Generally, travelling on Sicilian roads poses few problems; however, you may be stopped at a *posto di blocco* (police or army roadblock), particularly around coastal resorts. Roadblocks are routine and should be no cause for alarm. Officers usually check your ID and the vehicle, and they may also search your car or test your blood alcohol level. It is strictly against the law to drink and drive and even a small amount of alcohol can result in the suspension of your driving licence. Parking is generally safe;

however, in the cities it is best to leave your car in a car park with an attendant.

In an Emergency

For immediate medical attention, contact the First Aid (*Pronto Soccorso*) department of a main hospital such as **Villa Sofia CTO** in Palermo or **Ospedale Vittorio Emanuele** in Catania. Alternatively, check the White Pages (*Pagine Bianche*) or Yellow Pages (*Pagine Gialle*) for a doctor (*medico*) or a dentist (*dentista*). Emergency care in public hospitals is free, even for foreigners.

Lost and Stolen Property

In major cities bus stations, airport terminals and train stations usually have their own lost property offices such as Prestia e Comandè at **Stazione Centrale** (Palermo's main train station). In small towns or villages, it is best to inquire at the ticket offices or at the nearest police station.

To report stolen or lost items, head to the nearest *questura* (police station) or *carabinieri* office. In the case of lost passports, contact your embassy or consulate; for lost credit cards or travellers' cheques, contact the bank or the issuing company's office.

Hospitals and Pharmacies

Sicily has a network of first aid stations. All tourist resorts operate seasonal emergency treatment centres (*guardia medica*). For access to paediatricians, visit the **Ospedale dei Bambini "G. Di Cristina"** in Palermo or the **Ospedale Garibaldi-Nesima** in Catania.

For minor problems, pharmacists can recommend over-the-counter medication. Pharmacies (*farmacia*) are open from Monday to Friday 8:30am–1pm and 4–7:30pm and on Saturday mornings. A list of night and public holiday timings is posted on or near the shop door.

State policeman   City policeman

A local pharmacy with a green cross sign

Minor Hazards

In summer, whether you are at the seaside or indoors, do not overdo sunbathing, as it may cause serious burns and sunstroke.

If you are out for a walk or hiking, keep your distance from sheepdogs as they are trained to chase away all intruders. While exploring the tumbled stones of the ancient cities of Magna Graecia, or during a hike in the mountains, be wary of snakes, which are a common sight in summer.

Sicilians are very hospitable but are also reserved, so when hiking always ask permission before crossing over private property or a fenced area. Remember to close the fence behind you so that any animals in the field cannot escape.

No inoculations are needed before travelling to Sicily, but do carry mosquito repellent. Water from taps and potable street fountains is piped from the hills, and is fresh and safe to drink.

Travel and Health Insurance

Visitors from the EU should obtain the European Health Insurance Card (EHIC) before travelling. This is available online (www.dh.gov.uk) or at a post office. The card comes with a booklet of advice and information on the procedure for claiming free medical treatment.

When booking air travel tickets, it is best to inquire whether there are waivers pertaining to any medical emergencies. It can be difficult to arrange travel insurance once you reach Sicily, so it is always advisable to purchase it before you travel.

Fire Hazards

The summer heat can leave the countryside susceptible to fires. Visitors and residents alike are requested to do all they can to prevent fires from breaking out. Sadly, fires are a scourge in Sicily as well as the rest of southern Italy. Some of them are due to natural occurrences, while others are genuine accidents, but most are cases of arson. Fire can spread rapidly, especially in the dry summer vegetation, and the wind may carry the fire for long distances in a very short time. Firefighting is usually entrusted to the local fire departments. Forest rangers, volunteers and specially equipped firefighting planes are located at strategic points around the island.

Fire Prevention Rules

1. Do not throw cigarettes out of your car.
2. Never light a fire, except in areas where this is explicitly permitted.
3. If you see a fire, call **1515** at once.
4. Do not stop or park your car to watch a fire; you may block the road and interfere with the firefighting operations.
5. Pay attention to the wind direction: it is extremely dangerous to be downwind of a fire, as it may spread rapidly and catch you unawares.

DIRECTORY

Police

Carabinieri
Tel 112.

In an Emergency

Ambulance/Medical Emergencies
Tel 118.

Catania
Ospedale Vittorio Emanuele
Via Plebiscito 628, 95122.
Tel 800-284 284 (Numero Verde).

General Emergencies
Tel 113.

Palermo
Villa Sofia CTO
Tel 091-7804031 (Pronto Soccorso).

Lost and Stolen Property

Stazione Centrale
Corso A. Amedeo 74, Palermo.
Tel 091 586351.
w prestiaecomande.it

Hospitals and Pharmacies

Catania
Ospedale Garibaldi-Nesima
Via Palermo 636, 95122.
Tel 095-7595123/7595121
(Pronto Soccorso Pediatrico).

Palermo
Ospedale dei Bambini "G. Di Cristina"
Tel 091-6066028 (Pronto Soccorso Pediatrico).

Pharmacy Maymone
Via Catania 122, Palermo.
Tel 091-584096.

Consulates

United Kingdom
Via N Coviello 27, Catania.
Tel 095-716 7336 (emergency 24-hr assistance: +44 (0) 207 008 1500). w embassypages.com

United States
Via Vaccarini 1, Palermo. Tel 091-305 857. w usembassy.it

Fire Hazards

Fire Department
Tel 115.

Forest Fires
Tel 1515.

Banking and Local Currency

Most hotels, restaurants, shops and petrol stations accept major credit cards. Those paying with a credit card may be asked to show identification, such as a passport. Foreign currency can be changed in banks, although these are often crowded. All banks will cash travellers' cheques. Bureaux de change and foreign exchange machines can only be found in airports and major towns. ATMs (*bancomat*) are widespread and accept most major cards with a PIN number.

A *bancomat* or automatic teller machine

Banks and Bureaux de Change

Banks are generally open from 8:30am to 1:30pm and 2:30/2:45 to 3:30/3:45pm from Monday to Friday. Banking hours are restrictive and can also be slightly erratic, so acquire a small amount of local currency before arriving in Sicily. The main bank is **Banco di Sicilia**, part of the Unicredit Group.

Bureaux de change tend to give poor exchange rates. The bureaux are often open all day, and in some places stay open until late at night.

ATMs

ATMs (automatic teller machines) can be found in major towns, as well as in some small villages. To avoid complications, check which cards the ATM accepts before inserting your card. Costs for cash withdrawals will be set by your bank. Bear in mind that ATMs may run out of notes during weekends or before a major holiday.

Before travelling, make sure you inform your bank that you are travelling to Italy, to prevent your card being blocked.

Credit and Debit Cards

Major credit cards are widely accepted throughout Sicily. VISA and MasterCard are the most popular, while American Express is often not accepted. Travelling with more than one debit (and credit) card is recommended in case one is not accepted.

Some restaurants, cafès and shops require a minimum expenditure to accept a credit card payment. Always make sure you have some cash in case your card is not accepted.

Currency

The euro (€) is the common currency of the European Union. It went into general circulation on 1 January 2002, initially for 12 participating countries. Italy was one of those 12 countries.

Euro Bank Notes

Euro bank notes have seven denominations. The €5 note (grey) is the smallest, followed by the €10 note (pink), €20 note (blue), €50 note (orange), €100 note (green), €200 note (yellow) and €500 note (purple). All notes show the stars of the European Union.

5 euros

10 euros

20 euros

50 euros

Euro Bank Coins

The euro has eight coin denominations: €1 and €2; 50 cents, 20 cents, 10 cents, 5 cents, 2 cents and 1 cent. The €2 and €1 coins are both silver and gold in colour.

5 cents

10 cents

20 cents

50 cents

1 euro

2 euros

Communications and Media

Communication in Sicily is generally efficient; however some parts of the island are still isolated, especially inland. Public telephones, operated by Telecom Italia, are widespread and Internet points are also available. The postal service is slow, but couriers provide a fast, reliable alternative. Foreign-language newspapers and magazines are on sale in towns. State-run and privately owned television stations exist, but only satellite television and radio stations broadcast foreign-language programmes.

A well-equipped Internet point in a Sicilian town

International and Local Telephone Calls

International calls can be made using an international phone card, which can be purchased at tobacconists and newsstands. These provide an economical way to call abroad from public phones. Rates are slightly higher when calling from a mobile phone. Check with your hotel before using a card from your room, as extra charges may be applied.

To make a local call, always include the preliminary 0, followed by the area code and then the number.

Public Telephones and Mobile Phones

To use a public telephone, a **Telecom Italia** phone card is needed, which are available from newsstands, post offices and *tabacchi* displaying the black-and-white T sign.

If you plan to use your mobile phone, either set up a roaming agreement with your provider, or purchase a local SIM card. **TIM** and **Vodafone** are the main providers in Sicily.

Internet

The Internet is widely available, particularly in urban areas. Telecom Italia provides Internet services in the country's major train stations and public phone centres. Privately operated Internet points can be found in most towns. **Internet Train**, with over 40 branches, is the most visible; simply buy a charged magnetic card, which can be used across the network. There are Wi-Fi hotspots across Sicily and many of them are free.

Postal Services

Post offices open from 8:25am to 1:50pm weekdays, and 8:25am–noon on Saturday. Letters can take between four days and two weeks to arrive. For a faster service it is best to use the *posta prioritaria* (express post). A more reliable option is *raccomandata* (recorded delivery). Anything of value should be sent by *assicurata* (insured post). For urgent communications, use **DHL** or **Fedex**, or try the state couriers, *Postacelere* and *Paccocelere*, which are based at all the main post offices.

Mobile phone users at Catania Fontanarossa international airport

Newspapers and Magazines

The leading local papers are *Il Giornale di Sicilia* and *L'Ora* in Palermo, *Gazzetta del Sud* and *L'Eco del Sud* in Messina, *Libertà* in Syracuse and *La Sicilia* in Catania. English-language papers and magazines are sold in major towns.

Television and Radio

Television channels include the state-owned RAI and Mediaset. There are also many local channels. Most foreign programmes are dubbed into Italian, although satellite channels, such as BBC World News, Sky and CNN, show news and sports programmes in English. There are three national radio stations.

DIRECTORY

Country Codes

00 44 (UK)
00 1 (US & Canada)
00 61 (Australia)

Public Telephones and Mobile Phones

Telecom Italia
W telecomitalia.com/ trovatelefonopubblico

TIM
Via della Libertà 37/D, Palermo.
Via Etnea 47, Catania. W tim.it

Vodafone
Via della Libertà 19-21-23, Palermo. Via Etnea 74, Catania.
W vodafone.it

Internet

Internet Train
W internettrain.it

Wi-Fi Hotspot Finders
W wifi.gratis.it/hotspot_ sicilia.html;
W openwifispots.com

Postal Services

DHL
Tel 199-199 345. W dhl.it

Fedex
Tel 199-151 119. W fedex.com

Poste Italiane
W poste.it

TRAVEL INFORMATION

The two main airports in Sicily are at opposite ends of the island, one at Palermo and the other at Catania. In the holiday season, charter flights may land directly at one of these, but the majority of travellers flying to Sicily will fly first to a mainland airport, usually Milan or Rome, before changing to a connecting flight. A good ferry service links Sicily with the mainland (connecting Reggio Calabria and Messina). The state railway, Ferrovie dello Stato (FS), runs regular trains using this ferry link. The smaller offshore islands are also easy to reach by ferry and some of them, for example Lampedusa, even have a small airport.

Ticket counters at Catania Fontanarossa airport

Airports

The island's main airports are **Palermo Punta Raisi** and **Catania Fontanarossa**, and both serve international flights (see below). The former also serves domestic flights to and from Rome, Naples, Bologna, Milan, Pisa, Genoa, Turin, Verona, Cagliari, and the Sicilian islands of Pantelleria and Lampedusa. Catania serves the eastern side, with flights to and from Rome, Milan, Turin, Naples, Verona, Genoa and Pisa. The smaller **Trapani Birgi** airport offers connections only to and from Palermo and the islands of **Pantelleria** and **Lampedusa** (the latter has a tiny airport linked to Rome, Milan and Verona). The airports on the islands connect to Trapani and Palermo airports, and to other mainland towns. A new airport in **Comiso** serves the Ragusa–Syracuse area.

Arriving by Air

There are regular flights from the Italian mainland to Palermo and Catania. Direct charter flights from European cities operate all year round, linking London Gatwick to Catania or Palermo. **British Airways** runs a London–Catania service, while **Ryanair** flies from Stansted to Palermo and Comiso. British Airways offers flights from Gatwick to Catania, while **easyJet** provides direct flights from Gatwick to Palermo. The Italian state airline, **Alitalia**, has no direct London–Sicily flights. **American**, **Delta** and **United Airlines** offer direct flights from the United States to Rome, where you can catch a connecting flight to Sicily.

Tickets and Fares

For those flying from Italy, affordable flight tickets to Sicily can be bought from **Meridiana fly**. Ryanair offers the cheapest fares for those travelling from London to Palermo. Generally, most airlines use their websites to promote sales and bargain tickets. Booking well in advance can also secure very competitively priced air tickets. The lowest prices are usually available in April, May, October and November, as well as during winter, except for public holidays.

Domestic Flights

Alitalia, Meridiana fly and **Air One** offer frequent services from the Italian mainland. The latter company also offers flights to Sicily's neighbouring islands, more frequently in the summer. Other minor companies such as **Blu-Express by Blu Panorama Airlines** offer cheaper flights in high season.

Arriving by Rail

The Italian State Railway (**FS**) operates services throughout Italy, with regular links to Sicily. Those planning to travel to Sicily by train should reserve a seat (the trains are crowded in high season) and be prepared for a long, and often uncomfortable, journey. By way of compensation, the coastline as you travel to the south of Rome is stunningly beautiful. If possible, book a berth or couchette (sleeping compartment) before you travel.

Stately façade of the train station in Palermo

A ferry boat connecting the island of Sicily with mainland Italy

Arriving by Car

Car ferries go regularly across the Straits of Messina, and taking a car to Sicily should not present any particular problems. A red warning triangle and fluorescent vests must be carried at all times, for use in the event of a breakdown.

Arriving by Ferry

Reggio Calabria is the principal mainland port with ferry services to Sicily such as **Caronte & Tourist**. **Tirrenia** offers ferries between Palermo, Genoa and Naples. In summer, car ferries also operate, between Messina and Naples.

Domestic Ferries

Ferry services to the Sicilian islands are well organized and operate regularly. Several ferry companies, such as **Siremar**, **Ustica Lines** and **SNAV** (Societa Navigazione Alta Velocita) operate on different routes (for more information visit www. ferries-online.com).

Ferries *(traghetti)* and hydrofoils *(aliscafi)* can get quite crowded in the summer, but services continue all year round. In the archipelagoes, such as the Aeolian Islands, local ferry companies operate services alongside the major ones. Information about these companies and their time-tables and schedules can be obtained from the local tourist information bureaux or the Pro Loco offices.

DIRECTORY

Airports

Aeroporto di Comiso
97013 Comiso
Tel 0932-961 467.
w aeroportodicomiso.
eu

Catania Fontanarossa
95121 Catania
Tel 095-3405 05/ 723 91 11.
w aeroporto.catania.it

Lampedusa
ENAC – DA, Cinisi,
Palermo. **Tel** 0922-971 548.
w lampedusa35.com

Palermo Punta Raisi
Aeroporto Falcone E
Borsellino, Cinisi, Palermo.
Tel 800-541 880/091-702
0 111. **w** gesap.it

Pantelleria
Via Venezia N. 32'
Pantelleria. **Tel** 0923-911
398. **w** aeroportodi
pantelleria.it

Trapani Birgi
91100 Trapani. **Tel** 0923-
842 502.
w aeroportotrapani.
com

Arriving by Air

Alitalia
Tel +39 06 65649 (overseas); 0871-424 14 24 (UK);
800-223 5730 (US).
w alitalia.co.uk;
w alitaliausa.com

American Airlines
Tel 800-433 73 00.
w aa.com

British Airways
Tel 0844-493 0787.
w britishairways.com

Delta Airlines
Tel 800-241 41 41.
w delta.com

easyJet
Tel 0843 104 5000 (UK);
199-201 840 (Italy).
w easyjet.com

Ryanair
Tel 0871-246 00 00.
w ryanair.com

United Airlines
Tel 800-538 29 29.
w united.com

Tickets and Fares

Meridiana fly
Tel 0871 423 3711 (UK);
89 29 28 (Italy); 1-866 387
6359 (US).
w meridiana.it

Domestic Flights

Air One (Italy)
Tel 199-207 080.
w flyairone.it

**Blu-Express by Blu
Panorama Airlines**
Tel 199-419 777 (Italy);
06-989 566 77 (overseas).
w blu-express.com

Arriving by Rail

**Ferrovie dello Stato
(FS)**
w fsitaliane.it

Arriving by Ferry

Caronte & Tourist
Tel 800-627 414
(Messina).
w carontetourist.it

Tirrenia
Calata Marinai d'Italia,
Palermo. **Tel** 081-892 123
(Italy); +39 02 26302803
(overseas). **w** tirrenia.it

Domestic Ferries

Siremar
Tel 081-497 29 99
(Naples); 091-749 33 15
(Palermo).

SNAV
Tel 081-428 55 55
(Naples);
091-587 404 (Palermo).
w snav.it

Ustica Lines
Via Orlandini 48, Trapani.
Tel 0923-873 813
(Trapani).
w usticalines.it

Getting Around Sicily

The heart of the largest island in the Mediterranean is rugged and mountainous and the roads become steep and winding. Visitors should note that what may look like a short journey on the map may in fact take quite a long time. The bus network connects most towns and villages. Sicily's rail network includes a full circuit of Mount Etna, a journey that takes around 5 hours. The trains are generally slow and unreliable (except those in the main provincial capitals). A car is usually needed to reach the more rural areas.

A fast, straight road crossing a valley in the interior of Sicily

Green Travel

Despite the fact that environmental awareness has gradually increased, pollution in Sicily still remains a problem. The fight against smog continues, as many Sicilians rely exclusively on their cars. However, in big cities such as Palermo or Catania there are car-sharing and bike-sharing schemes. Bike lanes, electric car charging stations and car-free Sundays are some of the initiatives that have been introduced. Video cameras prevent unauthorized cars from entering most historic town centres (*centro storico*), while many bus lines cover almost all major sights and attractions. Though often busy and chaotic, public transport is always a better option than driving in the towns and cities.

Getting Around by Train

Given the varied and often mountainous topography of Sicily, remote areas are not accessible by train, and even where there are lines, services can be slow.

The two major railway lines run south from Messina to Catania and Syracuse, and west in the direction of Palermo. A secondary route branches off from the Messina–Palermo line at Termini Imerese and goes – fairly slowly – to Agrigento. Another line connects Palermo with Trapani, Marsala,

Mazara, Castelvetrano and Ribera. North of Catania, the privately run Ferrovia Circumetnea railway line (*see p170*) offers a stunning scenic route around Mount Etna.

Getting Around by Bus

In Sicily, local investment in infrastructure has focused on developing the roads rather than the railway. An extensive network of local bus services connects even the smallest villages, and there are good long-distance bus links to the popular resorts.

Bus services in cities and large towns are reliable and easy to use. In Palermo the transport network is operated by **AMAT**, in Catania by the **AMT** and in Messina by the **ATM**. Tickets can be bought at tobacconists (*tabaccai*) and newsagents (*giornalai*), or from the AMAT kiosks, which also provide transport maps. These tickets are valid for 90 minutes. Validate your ticket in the yellow machine once on board.

Getting Around by Car

For those eager to discover the lesser-known parts of Sicily, travelling by car or motorcycle is the best way. The rules of the road are the same as for the rest of Italy, including driving on the right, speed limits (50 km/h, 30 mph in towns) and wearing compulsory seat belts in cars and helmets for motorcyclists. Parking is a problem, especially in Palermo and Catania and also in historic town centres. Petrol (*benzina*) is usually expensive.

The main roads and motor-ways linking the major towns are mostly in good condition. This includes the Messina–Palermo, Messina–Catania, Catania–Syracuse and Catania–Palermo roads.

Bear in mind that on some of these routes, including long stretches of the southern coast, the roads may be busy with traffic. It is advisable to buy an up-to-date road map, such as those published by the Touring Club Italiano.

The Ferrovia Circumetnea travels around Europe's largest volcano

Car Hire

Almost all the major car hire companies have branch offices throughout Sicily, including at the airports and seaports, and also in every provincial capital.

Car hire *(autonoleggio)* is expensive in Italy, and should be organized before you arrive. For those renting cars from a major firm such as **Avis**, **Europcar**, **Hertz** or **Rent a Car**, you must check the rental conditions to see what is included and whether additional insurance is needed. Several holiday companies offer inclusive fly-drive deals, enabling you to pick up your car on arrival at the airport. This is normally cheaper than renting a car separately. Some of the offshore islands have scooters and motorcycles, as well as cars, for hire.

Quiet road along the scenic Tyrrenian coast

Great Drives

In Catania you don't have to drive far to find a scenic route. A particularly great drive is from Zafferana Etnea up to Rifugio Sapienza, which is the highest point on Mount Etna and offers truly stunning views of the volcano. To continue the drive, head down through Nicolosi. Another spectacular drive is in the province of Trapani, along the road which leads from Valderice, near Trapani, to Erice, a medieval town located on top of a hill. The road up the headland to San Vito Lo Capo is also worth driving for its wildness, while the coastal road along the salt marshes from Trapani to Marsala is amazing, with its picturesque windmills and fantastic views of the Egadi Islands.

Bikes for rent, the best way to see the small islands

Join the road SS115 and enjoy the stretch between Noto and Modica, regarded as one of the prettiest, pastoral areas in the countrysidee. The province of Ragusa has many beautiful rural roads, characterized by a network of dry stone walls and open fields, like around Donnafugata Castle.

Getting Around by Bicycle

The roads in the interior are fairly quiet and are suitable for cycling. **Rent a Bike** provides bicycles for hire, while travel agencies such as **Ciclofree** offer bike excursions, with the added convenience of vans to carry your luggage. However, Sicilian drivers are not used to seeing cyclists on the road, so it is best to stay alert at all times.

Mountain biking is also becoming popular in Sicily, particularly in the Peloritani, Nebrodi and Madonie mountain areas.

Getting Around on Foot

The main sites in most Sicilian towns, cities and seaside villages are concentrated and can be covered on foot, but make sure you wear sturdy and comfortable shoes.

An enjoyable way to explore Palermo and Catania is on foot, since the major attractions are in easy walking distance of each other. There are also a number of cultural sightseeing walking tours available in both cities. The best way to get around in Trapani, Syracuse and Agrigento is also on foot.

In the countryside and at nature reserves expert guides offer walking tours to areas of natural beauty.

DIRECTORY

Getting Around by Bus

AMT (Catania)
Tel 800-018 696/095 7519 111.
W amt.ct.it

AMAT (Palermo)
Tel 091-350111/199-240 800.
W amat.pa.it

ATM (Messina)
Tel 090-228 5266/903 7169.
W atmmessina.it

Car Hire

Avis
Tel 091-591 684 (Palermo);
095-340 500/7231 715 (Catania).
W avisworld.com

Europcar
Tel 199-307 030; 091-591 688/
6525 325/6525 531 (Palermo);
095-349 150/7232 942 (Catania).
W europcar.com

Hertz
Tel 091-213 112 (Palermo);
095-341 595/345 279/7234 655
(Catania).
W hertz.com

Rent a Car (Maggiore)
Tel 199-151 120; 091-591 681
(Palermo); 095-340 594 (Catania);
0931-66548 (Syracuse).
W maggiore.it

Getting Around by Bicycle

Rent a Bike (Acireale, near Catania)
Tel 346-231 7451 (English);
328-342 6518 (Italian).
W rentbike.it W solebike.eu

Rent a Bike (Cefalù, near Palermo, Syracuse)
W sicily-bike.de

Ciclofree
Tel 0931-940 397/339 24 39 358.
W ciclofree.com

General Index

Acknowledgments

Dorling Kindersley would like to thank the following people, museums and organizations, whose contributions and assistance have made the preparation of this book possible. Dorling Kindersley would also like to thank all the people, organizations and businesses, too numerous to mention individually, for their kind permission to photograph their establishments.

Alessandra Arena; Ms Puleo, Assessorato al Turismo Regione Sicilia; AAPT Caltanissetta, Egidio Cacciola, AAST Acireale; Grazia Incorvaia, AAST Agrigento; AAST Caltagirone; AAST Capo D'Orlando; Ms Lidestri, AAST Catania and Acicastello; AAST Cefalù; Ms Petralia, AAST Enna; AAST Giardini Naxos; AAST Messina; AAST Milazzo; Salvatore Giuffrida, AAST Nicolosi; AAST Palermo and Monreale; AAST Patti; Ivana Taschetta, AAST Piazza Armerina; AAST Sciacca; AAST Syracuse; AAST Taormina; Mario Cavallaro, APT Syracuse; Ms Mocata, APT Trapani; Carlo Rigano, Associazione Culturale Sicilia '71 di Mascalucia, Paolo Mazzotta, Biblioteca "E Vittorietti", Palermo; Barbara Cacciani; Franco Conti, Carthera Aetna; Nicolò Longo; Prof Giorgio De Luca, Istituto Europeo di Scienze Antropologiche; Giorgia Conversi; EPT Agrigento; Nello Musumeci, EPT Catania; Dr Ragno, EPT Messina; Dr Majorca, EPT Palermo; Manilo Peri, Fondazione Culturale Mandralisca, Cefalù; Dr Rosano, Framon Hotels; Galleria Regionale di Sicilia – Palazzo Abatellis (Palermo); Domenico Calabrò, Gazzetta del Sud; Gisella Giarrusso; Ernesto Girardi; Salvo Amato, Giuliano Rotondi Freelance Studio, Acireale; Carmelo Guglielmino; Mr Altieri, Hotel Baglio della Luna; Hotel Baglio Santa Croce; Hotel La Tonnara di Bonagia; Col Girardi; Hotel Villa Paradiso dell'Etna; Luigi Lacagnina and his family; Maggiore Budget Autonoleggi; Prof Gaetano Maltese; Emma Marzullo; Meridiana; Museo Archeologico Regionale Paolo Orsi (Syracuse); Museo Etnostorico dei Nebrodi; Prof Iberia Medici, Museo-Laboratorio Village, Giarre; Ignazio Paternò Castello; Società Aerofotogrammetrica Siciliana (Palermo); Sandro Tranchina; Teatro Massimo (Palermo); Teatro Biondo (Palermo); Prof Amitrano Svarese, Faculty of Anthropological Sciences, University of Palermo; Mara Veneziani; Pia Vesin.

Revisions Team
Louise Abbott, Umesh Aggarwal, Emily Anderson, Jasneet Arora, Shruti Bahl, Claire Baranowski, Ros Belfold, Marta Bescos, Maria Carla Barra, Tessa Bindloss, Michelle Clark, Lucinda Cooke, Imogen Corke, Michelle Crane, Conrad van Dyk, Gadi Farfour, Emer FitzGerald, Rhiannon Furbear, Prerna Gupta, Katharina Hahn, Gerard Hutching, Claire Jones, Sumita Khatwani, Suresh Kumar, Cathia Licitra, George Ninno, Carly Madden, Hayley Maher, Alison McGill, Sonal Modha, Casper Morris, Vikki Nousiainen, Susie Peachey, Helen Peters, Maria Consuelo Petrolo, Arun Pottirayil, Lucy Richards, Ellen Root, Giuliano Rotondi, Sands Publishing Solutions, Beverly Smart, Ellie Smith, Mary Sutherland, Conchita Vecchio, Richa Verma, Ajay Verma, Stewart J Wild, Debra Wolter.

Picture Credits
a-above; b-below; c-centre; f-far; l-left; r-right; t-top

All the photographs reproduced in this book are from the Image Bank, Milan, except for the following:

4Corners: SIME / Alessandro Saffo 2-3. Aeroporto di Catania: 235bc, 236cl. Alamy Images: Caro 234tr; CuboImages srl/ Riccardo Lombardo 44bl; Jeff Gilbert 213br; Brenda Kean 10bc,

13tr; LOOK Die Bildagentur der Fotografen GmbH 210bc; Peter Forsberg 230c; Matthew Richardson 239cl; Neil Setchfield 74; Felix Shoughi 13br. Fabrizio Ardito: 20bl, 87br, 106bl, 114, 117tr, 119br, 120cl, 121cr, 122tr, 122bl, 123cr, 124tl, 124br, 125br, 126t, 126c, 127b, 130cl, 132bl, 135bl, 147tl, 147br, 148bl, 153tl, 153br, 157tl, 157cr, 160c, 160b, 161br, 170tl, 170cr. Archivio Apt Siracusa: 140tl, 141bl, 143br. Archivio APT Trapani: 90cl, 91b. Archivio EPT Palermo: 113cr. Archivio Framon Hotels: 194cl, 195tl, 195br. AWL Images: Peter Adams 84-85; Katja Kreder 46-47, 88, 228-229; Sabine Lubenow 162; Ken Scicluna 196-197. BB 22 Palermo: 200br, 202bl. The Bridgeman Art Library: © The FORBES Magazine Collection, New York 8-9. Cephas Picture Library: Lehmann 220bl. Corbis: Dave Bartruff 208cl; 209tl; Hal Beral 239tc; LANNINO-BUCCA 41cra; Owen Franken 209c; Robert Harding World Imagery / Ellen Rooney 11tc. Fabio De Angelis: 52cl, 52bl, 53cr, 54tl, 54bc, 57br, 59cr, 60tl, 64tr, 64bc, 65cr, 65br, 67tc, 69br, 70cr, 71tl, 72br, 73br, 77bl, 78tc, 94c, 208br, 232cr, 235cl, 236br. Il Dagherrotipo: 226br. DK Images: 33bl, 39tr, 39tl, 48cr, 61br, 64c, 76cr, 80–81c, 150br; Nigel Hicks 120tr; Ian O'Leary 208tr, 209bc, 209br; Consuelo Petrolo 232cla. Dreamstime.com: Diego Barucco 18; Sergio Bertino 10cl; Goran Bogicevic 43cl; Emicristea 14bl; Kcho 114; Stanisa Martinovic 12br; Martin Molcan 14tr; Zuzana Randlova 15tr; Jozef Sedmak 50; Vvoevale 151br, 231cl, 233tl. Hotel Federico Secondo II: 199tl, 205br. Cristina Gambaro–Gino Frongia: 73bl, 89b, 90bl, 94cl, 95b, 96b, 97tl, 98c, 99c, 101bc, 102cl, 102bl, 106tl, 108tr, 110tl, 110b, 111tl, 121bl, 137b, 150c, 181br, 208cr. Getty Images: DEA / G. Dagli Orti 145cra; Danita Delimont 12tc; Ingolf Pompe 230br. Grand Hotel Villa Igiea: 198cla, wbr, 203tr. La Putia: 207br. Leonardo media ltd: 195tl. Monte San Giuliano: 212tr. Moon: 207tl, 217br. Nangalarruni: 211tr. Nicolò Longo: 22crb, 23crb. Oxidiana: 216tr. Palazzo Failla Hotel: La Gazza Ladra 205c, 214bc. Pasticceria Di Pasquale: 206br. Pro Loco Canicattì: 127tl. Reculez: 208bl, 209bl. Ristorante Il Duomo: 215tr. Ristorante Cin Cin: 208br. Robert Harding Picture Library: Riccardo Lombardo 15bc. Ronald Grant Archive: 28tr, 28cla. Giuliano Rotondi: 3c, 21tr, 26tr, 26cl, 26bc, 27tr, 27cl, 27bc, 28bc, 29tl, 29tc, 29v, 30, 32tr, 32c, 32br, 33tl, 33tc, 33cl, 33br, 34cl, 34cb, 34br, 35tl, 35cla, 35bla, 35bl, 36ca, 36clb, 36bl, 36bc, 37cr, 37bc, 38cl, 38br, 39cr, 39bl, 40tr, 40cla, 40clb, 40bl, 40br, 41ca, 41bl, 41bc, 49cr, 55c, 55br, 58t, 70tr, 70cl, 71tc, 71c, 73t, 76bl, 79tl, 96tc, 96c, 98tl, 103tr, 103c, 106br, 107cr, 107br, 109tl, 110cl, 110cr, 132tr, 132br, 133tr, 133br, 138bc, 149bl, 154tr, 155cr, 156b, 158cl, 158br, 159tl, 160tl, 161cr, 164bl, 167tl, 168tl, 171t, 173bl, 173br, 176tr, 177tl, 179br, 180bl, 182cl, 187br, 189tr, 189bl, 208tr, 220cr, 221tr, 221bl, 222br, 224br, Sbriglio: 141tl, 142, 146c, 148cl, 148br, 149cr, 149bl, 150tl, 150tr, 151tr, 151cl, 152c, 152br, 164tr. Marka, Milan: Sante Malli 227br. Photo SCALA, Florence: 41crb; Cinecitta Luce 40cb. Marco Scapagnini: 146tr, 149tr, 151cr, 208tc, 222tl. Scicli Albergo Diffuso: 199br, 200tl, 204tr. TipsImages: Tommaso Di Girolamo 136; Guido Alberto Rossi 62. Front Endpapers: AWL Images: Katja Kreder Lclb, Sabine Lubenow Rtl; Dreamstime.com: Kcho Lbc, Jozef Sedmak Ltr; TipsImages: Tommaso Di Girolamo Lbr, Guido Alberto Rossi Ltl.

Sheet Map Cover: Axiom Photographic Agency: Francesco Tomasinelli / Tips.

Jacket
Front main and spine t - Axiom Photographic Agency: Francesco Tomasinelli / Tips.

Phrase Book

In Emergency

Help!	Aiuto!	eye-yoo-toh
Stop!	Fermati!	fair-mah-tee
Call a doctor.	Chiama un medico.	kee-ah-mah oon meh-dee-koh
Call an ambulance.	Chiama un' ambulanza.	kee-ah-mah oon am-boo-lan-tsa
Call the police.	Chiama la polizia.	kee-ah-mah lah pol-ee-tsee-ah
Call the fire department.	Chiama i pompieri.	kee-ah-mah ee pom-pee-air-ee
Where is the telephone?	Dov'è il telefono?	dov-eh eel teh-leh-foh-noh?
The nearest hospital?	L'ospedale più vicino?	loss-peh-dah-leh pee-oo vee-chee-noh?

Communication Essentials

Yes/No	Sì/No	see/noh
Please	Per favore	pair fah-vor-eh
Thank you	Grazie	grah-tsee-eh
Excuse me	Mi scusi	mee skoo-zee
Hello	Buon giorno	bwon jor-noh
Goodbye	Arrivederci	ah-ree-veh-dair-chee
Good evening	Buona sera	bwon-ah sair-ah
morning	la mattina	lah mah-tee-nah
afternoon	il pomeriggio	eel poh-meh-ree-joh
evening	la sera	lah sair-ah
yesterday	ieri	ee-air-ee
today	oggi	oh-jee
tomorrow	domani	doh-mah-nee
here	qui	kwee
there	la	lah
What?	Quale?	kwah-leh?
When?	Quando?	kwan-doh?
Why?	Perchè?	pair-keh?
Where?	Dove?	doh-veh?

Useful Phrases

How are you?	Come sta?	koh-meh stah?
Very well, thank you.	Molto bene, grazie.	moll-toh beh-neh grah-tsee-eh
Pleased to meet you.	Piacere di conoscerla.	pee-ah-chair-eh dee coh-noh-shair-lah
See you later.	A più tardi.	ah pee-oo tar-dee
That's fine.	Va bene.	va beh-neh
Where is/are ...?	Dov'è/Dove sono...?	dov-eh/doveh soh-noh?
How long does it take to get to ...?	Quanto tempo ci vuole per andare a ...?	kwan-toh tem-poh chee voo-oh-leh pair an-dar-eh ah ...?
How do I get to ...?	Come faccio per arrivare a ...?	koh-meh fah-choh pair arri-var-eh ah...?
Do you speak English?	Parla inglese?	par-lah een-gleh-zeh?
I don't understand.	Non capisco.	non ka-pee-skoh
Could you speak more slowly, please?	Può parlare più lentamente, per favore?	pwoh par-lah-reh pee-oo len-ta-men-teh pair fah-vor-eh?
I'm sorry.	Mi dispiace.	mee dee-spee-ah-cheh

Useful Words

big	grande	gran-deh
small	piccolo	pee-koh-loh
hot	caldo	kal-doh
cold	freddo	fred-doh
good	buono	bwoh-noh
bad	cattivo	kat-tee-voh
enough	basta	bas-tah
well	bene	beh-neh
open	aperto	ah-pair-toh
closed	chiuso	kee-oo-zoh
left	a sinistra	ah see-nee-strah
right	a destra	ah dess-trah
straight ahead	sempre dritto	sem-preh dree-toh
near	vicino	vee-chee-noh
far	lontano	lon-tah-noh
up	su	soo
down	giù	joo
early	presto	press-toh
late	tardi	tar-dee
entrance	entrata	en-trah-tah
exit	uscita	oo-shee-ta
toilet	il gabinetto	eel gah-bee-net-toh
free, unoccupied	libero	lee-bair-oh
free, no charge	gratuito	grah-too-ee-toh

Making a Telephone Call

I'd like to place a long-distance call.	Vorrei fare una interurbana.	vor-ray far-eh oona in-tair-oor-bah-nah
I'd like to make a reverse-charge call.	Vorrei fare una telefonata a carico del destinatario.	vor-ray far-eh oona teh-leh-fon-ah-tah ah kar-ee-koh dell desstee-nah-tar-ree-oh
Could I speak to... I'll try again later.	Potrei parlare con... Ritelefono più tardi	po-tray par-lah-reh con ree-teh-leh-foh-noh pee-oo tar-dee
May I leave a message?	Posso lasciare un messaggio?	poss-oh lash-ah-reh oon mess-sah-joh?
Hold on.	Un attimo, per favore.	oon ah-tee-moh, pair fah-vor-eh
Could you speak up a little, please?	Può parlare più forte?	pwoh par-lah-reh pee-oo for-teh?
local call	telefonata locale	te-leh-fon-ah-tah loh-cah-leh

Shopping

How much does this cost?	Quant'è, per favore?	kwan-teh pair fah-vor-eh?
I would like ...	Vorrei ...	vor-ray...
Do you have ...?	Avete ...?	ah-veh-teh...?
I'm just looking.	Sto soltanto guardando	stoh sol-tan-toh gwar-dan-doh
Do you take credit cards?	Accettate carte di credito?	ah-chet-tah-teh kar-teh dee creh-dee-toh?
What time do you open/close?	A che ora apre/ chiude?	ah keh or-ah ah-preh/kee-oo-deh?
this one	questo	kweh-stoh
that one	quello	kwell-oh
expensive	caro	kar-oh
cheap	a buon prezzo	ah bwon pret-soh
size, clothes	la taglia	lah tah-lee-ah
size, shoes	il numero	eel noo-mair-oh
white	bianco	bee-ang-koh
black	nero	neh-roh
red	rosso	ross-oh
yellow	giallo	jal-loh
green	verde	vair-deh
blue	blu	bloo

Types of Shop

antique dealer	l'antiquario	lan-tee-kwah-ree-oh
bakery	il forno/ il panificio	eel forn-oh/ eel pan-ee-fee-choh
bank	la banca	lah bang-kah
bookstore	la libreria	lah lee-breh-ree-ah
butcher	la macelleria	lah mah-chell-eh-ree-ah
cake shop	la pasticceria	lah pas-tee-chair-ee-ah
delicatessen	la salumeria	lah sah-loo-meh-ree-ah
department store	il grande magazzino	eel gran-deh mag-gad-zee-noh
pharmacy	la farmacia	lah far-mah-chee-ah
fishseller	il pescivendolo	eel pesh-ee-ven-doh-loh
florist	il fioraio	eel fee-or-eye-oh
greengrocer	il fruttivendolo	eel froo-tee-ven-doh-loh
grocery	alimentari	ah-lee-men-tah-ree
hairdresser	il parrucchiere	eel par-oo-kee-air-eh
ice-cream parlour	la gelateria	lah jel-lah-tair-ree-ah
market	il mercato	eel mair-kah-toh
newsstand	l'edicola	leh-dee-koh lah
post office	l'ufficio postale	loo-fee-choh pos-tah-leh
shoe shop	il negozio di scarpe	eel neh-goh-tsioh dee skar-peh
supermarket	il supermercato	eel su-pair-mair-kah-toh
tobacconist	il tabaccaio	eel tah-bak-eye-oh
travel agency	l'agenzia di viaggi	lah-jen-tsee-ah dee vee-ad-jee

Sightseeing

art gallery	la pinacoteca	lah peena-koh-teh-kah
bus stop	la fermata dell'autobus	lah fair-mah-tah dell ow-toh-booss
church	la chiesa/ la basilica	lah kee-eh-zah/ lah bah-seel-i-kah
closed for holidays	chiuso per le ferie	kee-oo-zoh pair leh fair-ee-eh
garden	il giardino	eel jar-dee-no
library	la biblioteca	lah beeb-lee-oh-teh-kah
museum	il museo	eel moo-zeh-oh
train station	la stazione	lah stah-tsee-oh-neh
tourist information	l'ufficio di turismo	loo-fee-choh dee too-ree-smoh

Staying in a Hotel

Do you have any vacant rooms?	**Avete camere libere?**	*ah-veh-teh kah-mair-eh lee-bair-eh?*
double room	**una camera doppia**	*oona kah-mair-ah doh-pee-ah*
with double bed	**con letto matrimoniale**	*kon let-toh mah-tree-moh-nee-ah-leh*
twin room	**una camera con due letti**	*oona kah-mair-ah kon doo-eh let-tee*
single room	**una camera singola**	*oona kah-mair-ah sing-goh-lah*
room with a *bath, shower*	**una camera con bagno, con doccia**	*oona kah-mair-ah kon ban-yoh, kon dot-chah*
porter	**il facchino**	*eel fah-kee-noh*
key	**la chiave**	*lah kee-ah-veh*
I have a *reservation.*	**Ho fatto una prenotazione.**	*oh fat-toh oona preh-noh-tah-tsee-oh-neh*

Eating Out

Do you have a table for …?	**Avete una tavola per … ?**	*ah-veh-teh oona tah-voh-lah pair … ?*
I'd like to *reserve a table*	**Vorrei riservare una tavola**	*vor-ray ree-sair-vah-reh oona tah-voh-lah*
breakfast	**colazione**	*koh-lah-tsee-oh-neh*
lunch	**pranzo**	*pran-tsoh*
dinner	**cena**	*cheh-nah*
The bill, *please*	**Il conto, per favore.**	*eel kon-toh pair fah-vor-eh*
I am a vegetarian.	**Sono vegetariano/a.**	*soh-noh veh-jeh-tar-ee-ah-noh/nah*
waitress	**cameriera**	*kah-mair-ee-air-ah*
waiter	**cameriere**	*kah-mair-ee-air-eh*
fixed-price *menu*	**il menù a prezzo fisso**	*eel meh-noo ah pret-soh fee-soh*
dish of the day	**piatto del giorno**	*pee-ah-toh dell jor-no*
appetizer	**antipasto**	*an-tee-pass-toh*
first course	**il primo**	*eel pree-moh*
main course	**il secondo**	*eel seh-kon-doh*
vegetables	**il contorno**	*eel kon-tor-noh*
dessert	**il dolce**	*eel doll-cheh*
cover charge	**il coperto**	*eel koh-pair-toh*
wine list	**la lista dei vini**	*lah lee-stah day-ee vee-nee*
rare	**al sangue**	*al sang-gweh*
medium	**al puntino**	*al poon-tee-noh*
well done	**ben cotto**	*ben kot-toh*
glass	**il bicchiere**	*eel bee-kee-air-eh*
bottle	**la bottiglia**	*lah bot-teel-yah*
knife	**il coltello**	*eel kol-tell-oh*
fork	**la forchetta**	*lah for-ket-tah*
spoon	**il cucchiaio**	*eel koo-kee-eye-oh*

Menu Decoder

l'acqua minerale gassata/naturale	*lah-kwah mee-nair-ah-leh gah-zah-tah/ nah-too-rah-leh*	mineral water fizzy/still
aceto	*ah-cheh-toh*	vinegar
aglio	*al-ee-oh*	garlic
l'agnello	*lah-niell-oh*	lamb
al forno	*al for-noh*	baked/roasted
alla griglia	*ah-lah greel-yah*	grilled
l'aragosta	*lah-rah-goss-tah*	lobster
arrosto	*ar-ross-toh*	roast
basilico	*bah-zee-lee-koh*	basil
la birra	*lah beer-rah*	beer
la bistecca	*lah bee-stek-kah*	steak
il brodo	*eel broh-doh*	broth
il burro	*eel boor-oh*	butter
il caffè	*eel kah-feh*	coffee
i calamari	*ee kah-lah-mah-ree*	squid
i carciofi	*ee kar-choff-ee*	artichokes
la carne	*la kar-neh*	meat
la cipolla	*la chip-oh-lah*	onion
i contorni	*ee kon-tor-nee*	vegetables
le cozze	*leh coh-tzeh*	mussels
i fagioli	*ee fah-joh-lee*	beans
il fegato	*eel fay-gah-toh*	liver
il finocchio	*eel fee-nok-ee-oh*	fennel
il formaggio	*eel for-mad-joh*	cheese
le fragole	*leh frah-goh-leh*	strawberries
il fritto misto	*eel free-toh mees-toh*	mixed fried dish
la frutta	*la froot-tah*	fruit
frutti di mare	*froo-tee dee mah-reh*	seafood
i funghi	*ee foon-ghee*	mushrooms
i gamberi	*ee gam-bair-eh*	shrimp
il gelato	*eel jeh-lah-toh*	ice cream
l'insalata	*leen-sah-lah-tah*	salad
il latte	*eel laht-teh*	milk
lesso	*less-oh*	boiled
la melanzana	*lah meh-lan-tsah-nah*	aubergine (eggplant)
la minestra	*lah mee-ness-trah*	soup
l'olio	*loh-lee-oh*	oil
il pane	*eel pah-neh*	bread
le patate	*leh pah-tah-teh*	potatoes
le patatine fritte	*leh pah-tah-teen-eh free-teh*	French fries
il pepe	*eel peh-peh*	pepper
la pesca	*lah pess-kah*	peach
il pesce	*eel pesh-eh*	fish
il polipo	*eel poh-lee-poh*	octopus
il pollo	*eel poll-oh*	chicken
il pomodoro	*eel poh-moh-dor-oh*	tomato
il prosciutto	*eel pro-shoo-toh*	ham
cotto/crudo	*kot-toh/kroo-doh*	cooked/cured
il riso	*eel ree-zoh*	rice
il sale	*eel sah-leh*	salt
la salsiccia	*lah sal-see-chah*	sausage
le seppie	*leh sep-pee-eh*	cuttlefish
secco	*sek-koh*	dry
la sogliola	*lah soll-yoh-lah*	sole
i spinaci	*ee spee-nah-chee*	spinach
succo d'arancia/ **di limone**	*soo-koh dah-ran-chah/ dee lee-moh-neh*	orange/lemon juice
il tè	*eel teh*	tea
la tisana	*lah tee-zah-nah*	herbal tea
il tonno	*eel ton-noh*	tuna
la torta	*lah tor-tah*	cake/tart
l'uovo	*loo-oh-voh*	egg
vino bianco	*vee-noh bee-ang-koh*	white wine
vino rosso	*vee-noh ross-oh*	red wine
il vitello	*eel vee-tell-oh*	veal
le vongole	*leh von-goh-leh*	clams
lo zucchero	*loh zoo-kair-oh*	sugar
gli zucchini	*lyee dzu-kee-nee*	zucchini
la zuppa	*lah tsoo-pah*	soup

Numbers

1	**uno**	*oo-noh*
2	**due**	*doo-eh*
3	**tre**	*treh*
4	**quattro**	*kwat-roh*
5	**cinque**	*ching-kweh*
6	**sei**	*say-ee*
7	**sette**	*set-teh*
8	**otto**	*ot-toh*
9	**nove**	*noh-veh*
10	**dieci**	*dee-eh-chee*
11	**undici**	*oon-dee-chee*
12	**dodici**	*doh-dee-chee*
13	**tredici**	*tray-dee-chee*
14	**quattordici**	*kwat-tor-dee-chee*
15	**quindici**	*kwin-dee-chee*
16	**sedici**	*say-dee-chee*
17	**diciassette**	*dee-chah-set-teh*
18	**diciotto**	*dee-chot-toh*
19	**diciannove**	*dee-chah-noh-veh*
20	**venti**	*ven-tee*
30	**trenta**	*tren-tah*
40	**quaranta**	*kwah-ran-tah*
50	**cinquanta**	*ching-kwan-tah*
60	**sessanta**	*sess-an-tah*
70	**settanta**	*set-tan-tah*
80	**ottanta**	*ot-tan-tah*
90	**novanta**	*noh-van-tah*
100	**cento**	*chen-toh*
1,000	**mille**	*mee-leh*
2,000	**duemila**	*doo-eh mee-lah*
5,000	**cinquemila**	*ching-kweh mee-lah*
1,000,000	**un milione**	*oon meel-yoh-neh*

Time

one minute	**un minuto**	*oon mee-noo-toh*
one hour	**un'ora**	*oon or-ah*
half an hour	**mezz'ora**	*medz-or-ah*
a day	**un giorno**	*oon jor-noh*
a week	**una settimana**	*oona set-tee-mah-nah*
Monday	**lunedì**	*loo-neh-dee*
Tuesday	**martedì**	*mar-teh-dee*
Wednesday	**mercoledì**	*mair-koh-leh-dee*
Thursday	**giovedì**	*joh-veh-dee*
Friday	**venerdì**	*ven-air-dee*
Saturday	**sabato**	*sah-bah-toh*
Sunday	**domenica**	*doh-meh-nee-kah*

Road Map of Sicily

Isola di Ustica

Egadi Islands

Trapani

Isola Marettimo

Marettimo

Isola di Levanzo
Levanzo

Favignana

Isola Favignana

Tunis, Cagliari

Capo San Vito

San Vito lo Capo

Riserva dello Zingaro

Isola delle Femmine

Capo Gallo

Mondello

Golfo di Palermo

Falcone-Borsellino

Terrasini

Carini

Capo Zafferano

Solunto

Castelluzzo

Scopello

Balestrate

Palermo

Monreale

Bagheria

Campofelice di Roccella

Erice

Castellammare del Golfo

Partinico

Misilmeri

Termini Imerese

Trapani

Paceco

Fulgatore

Alcamo

Piana degli Albanesi

Caccamo

Cerda

Trapani Birgi

Rilievo

Segesta

Calatafimi

San Cipirello

Marineo

Villafrati

Ciminna

Mozia

Camporeale

Montemaggiore Belsito

Isole dello Stagnone

Val di Màzara

Roccamena

Vicari

Caltavuturo

Alia

Tabaccaro

Salemi

Gibellina

Corleone

Prizzi

Lercara Friddi

SICI

Marsala

Motya

Santa Ninfa

Poggioreale

Bisacquino

Castronuovo di Sicilia

Vallelunga Pratameno

Strasatti

Partanna

S. Margherita di Belice

Palazzo Adriano

Mussomeli

Pizzolato

Castelvetrano

Sambuca di Sicilia

Burgio

Cammarata

Capo Feto

Mazara del Vallo

Campobello di Mazara

Menfi

Caltabellotta

Alessandria della Rocca

Casteltermini

Milena

Selinunte

Marinella di Selinunte

Porto Palo

Ribera

San Cat

Capo Granitola

Sciacca

Cattolica Eraclea

Aragona

Racalmuto

Capo San Marco

Seccagrande

Raffadali

Canicat

Capo Bianco Eraclea Minoa

Montallegro

Favara

Naro

Siculiana

Agrigento

Campobello di Licata

Porto Empedocle

San Leone

Palma di Montechiaro

Marina di Palma

Licata

Pelagie Islands

Key

- ✈ Airport
- ⛴ Ferry port
- ── Motorway (highway)
- ⋯⋯ Tunnel
- ── Main road
- ══ Minor road
- ── Railway line

Pelagie Islands

Porto Empedocle

Linosa

Isola di Linosa

Pantelleria

Trapani

Pantelleria

Punta Spadillo

Scàuri

Isola di Lampedusa

Lampedusa

Tyr

Mediter
Se